ACTIVE SPEECH

Active Speech

Critical Perspectives on Teresa Deevy

Edited by Úna Kealy and Kate McCarthy

https://www.openbookpublishers.com

©2025 Úna Kealy and Kate McCarthy (eds)
Copyright of individual chapters remains with the chapter's author(s)

This work is licensed under a Creative Commons Attribution-NonCommercial 4.0 International (CC BY-NC 4.0). This license allows you to share, copy, distribute and transmit the text; to adapt the text for non-commercial purposes of the text providing attribution is made to the authors (but not in any way that suggests that they endorse you or your use of the work). Attribution should include the following information:

Úna Kealy and Kate McCarthy (eds), *Active Speech: Critical Perspectives on Teresa Deevy*. Cambridge, UK: Open Book Publishers, 2025, https://doi.org/10.11647/OBP.0432

Further details about CC BY-NC licenses are available at http://creativecommons.org/licenses/by-nc/4.0/

Copyright and permissions for the reuse of many of the images included in this publication differ from the above. This information is provided in the captions and in the list of illustrations. Every effort has been made to identify and contact copyright holders and any omission or error will be corrected if notification is made to the publisher.

All external links were active at the time of publication unless otherwise stated and have been archived via the Internet Archive Wayback Machine at https://archive.org/web

Digital material and resources associated with this volume are available at https://doi.org/10.11647/OBP.0432#resources

Information about any revised edition of this work will be provided at https://doi.org/10.11647/OBP.0432

ISBN Paperback 978-1-80511-430-7
ISBN Hardback 978-1-80511-431-4
ISBN PDF 978-1-80511-432-1
ISBN HTML 978-1-80511-434-5
ISBN EPUB 978-1-80511-433-8
DOI: 10.11647/OBP.0432

Cover design: Jeevanjot Kaur Nagpal

Cover image: Photo by Jed Niezgoda (www.jedniezgoda.com). © All rights reserved. Suzanne Savage and Lianne Quigley performing in Teresa Deevy's *Possession* which was created and directed by Amanda Coogan in collaboration with Lianne Quigley, Alvean Jones, Linda Buckley, Dublin Theatre of the Deaf, and Cork Deaf Community Choir. Creative producer Lynette Moran produced *Possession* at the Project Arts Centre 21–24 February 2024, while Susan Holland produced the production at the Granary Theatre for the Cork Midsummer Festival performances, 21–23 June 2024. *Possession* was funded as part of ART:2023: A Decade of Centenaries Collaboration (the Arts Council and the Department of Tourism, Culture, Arts, Gaeltacht, Sport, and Media).

To our mothers, Jean Kealy and Marian McCarthy, ... as we planned
and
in memory of Teresa Deevy's nieces,
Clare Brazil (née Hearne) and Barbara Hearne
and of Waterfordians and Deevy scholars
Seán Dunne and Eibhear Walsh

Contents

Foreword
Teresa Deevy: A Journey of Discovery ix
Marjorie Brennan

Acknowledgements xiii

Notes on Contributors xv

List of Figures xxv

List of Abbreviations xxix

Teresa Deevy: Life, Scholarship, Practice 1
Úna Kealy and Kate McCarthy

ACCESS AND ARCHIVES 39

1. 'Why Would Anyone Be Interested in My Old Aunt Teresa?':
Illuminating Teresa Deevy's Legacy 41
Eileen Kearney

2. The Teresa Deevy Archive and the Development
of Collections and Curation in Maynooth University Library 57
Hugh Murphy

3. TSI: Teresa Deevy, or What Do We Know about [The] Reapers? 77
Shelley Troupe

4. Mysteries of the Teresa Deevy Archive:
Reconsidering the plays of D.V. Goode 91
Caoilfhionn Ní Bheacháin Mitchell

DEEVY'S IRELAND: A COUNTRY IN CONTEXT 115

5. 'Very Seldom Are Messages Properly Given':
Teresa Deevy's Dark Matter 117
Chris Morash

6. 'I Must Just Make an Opening Elsewhere':
Teresa Deevy's Involvement with Studio Theatre Practice,
1934–1958   131

Úna Kealy and Kate McCarthy

7. 'It Is Myself I Seen in Her':
Points of Departure in Teresa Deevy's *The King of Spain's Daughter*
(1935)   155

Willy Maley

DRAMATURGY, GENRE, AND THEORY   173

8. Finding Money in the Walls:
Uncovering the Feminist Power of Teresa Deevy's
Dramaturgy through an Embodied, Practice-Based Approach   175

Ann M. Shanahan

9. Becoming a Domesticated Irish Woman:
Teresa Deevy's Critique of Idealised Representations
of Womanhood in *Katie Roche*   201

Dayna Killen and Úna Kealy

10. The Liminal Space of Widowhood
in Teresa Deevy's *Wife to James Whelan* (1937)   227

Christa de Brún

PRODUCTIONS AND PRACTITIONERS   241

11. Teresa Deevy's *Katie Roche*:
Art, Culture, and Performance   243

Cathy Leeney

12. Teresa Deevy and Contemporary Performance Practice:
Edited Transcript of Teresa Deevy Practitioner Panel Discussion   263

Jonathan Bank, Caroline Byrne, Amanda Coogan, and Lianne Quigley

13. 'You Can Feel the Change in the Air':
Reflecting on *Talk Real Fine, Just Like a Lady*,
a Shapeshifting of Teresa Deevy's *The King of Spain's Daughter*   289

Amanda Coogan, Alvean Jones, and Lianne Quigley

Index   319

Foreword
Teresa Deevy: A Journey of Discovery

Marjorie Brennan

She was a very rare spirit, the sort of person one can never forget.

This striking description of Teresa Deevy by a fellow (unnamed) writer was recollected by the late Seán Dunne of the *Cork Examiner* in an article published in the newspaper in March 1984.[1] At that time, Deevy's ground-breaking work had, unfortunately, receded in the collective memory. In that year, I was a first-year student at Our Lady of Mercy secondary school in Waterford, Ireland, with many years of learning ahead. My favourite subjects were English and History, not an unusual combination for a would-be journalist, and I devoured every poem, book, short story, and play that we studied. It was only years later, as awareness grew of the great disservice done to women's creativity down the ages, that it dawned on me that most of the work I had studied at school was by men. It would be many years again before I would even learn about the existence of Deevy, once considered one of Ireland's leading playwrights and once a girl, like me, sitting at a desk in a school in Waterford wondering what the future held.

I came across Dunne's piece when I was researching a feature for the *Irish Examiner* about Deevy and her play *Katie Roche*, which was performed in a new production at the Abbey Theatre in the autumn of 2017.[2] Deevy had come to my attention the previous November, when her play *Wife to James Whelan* was staged at Garter Lane theatre

---

1 Seán Dunne, 'Rediscovering Teresa Deevy', *Cork Examiner,* 20 March 1984, p. 10.
2 *Katie Roche* by Teresa Deevy, directed by Caroline Byrne, and produced by the Abbey Theatre, Dublin, 28 August–23 September 2017.

in Waterford.³ The more I delved into her extraordinary life, the more astonished I became that she, and her work, had been forgotten to the point that not only were her plays no longer performed or mentioned, but I had no idea that she even existed. I had studied the life and work of W.B. Yeats and, later, Augusta Gregory, John Millington Synge, Seán O'Casey—all closely connected with the Abbey—without knowing that a Waterford woman had her plays performed on the same stage to great acclaim. How had that happened? While I had long felt aggrieved that generations of girls had been taught, unconsciously or otherwise, that the work of women didn't matter, Deevy's erasure smarted in a more personal way because we shared a native city and, I would imagine, a pride in that place where we were nurtured. I began to think that not only should Deevy's work have been taught in our school, she should have been held up as an example of what a woman could achieve in a society, at best, indifferent and, at worst, hostile to their creative efforts.

And what, too, could we have learned from her as an example of resilience and determination in the face of adversity? A deafened woman who went to London to learn lip-reading, lived independently with the help of her sister, Nell, for many years, had her plays performed at Ireland's National Theatre and broadcast on radio, visited Republican prisoners as a member of Cumann na mBan, and travelled alone on pilgrimages abroad at a time when most Irish people didn't even own a passport. This would have been an enthralling narrative for us schoolgirls, with the added piquancy of familiarity and pride in terms of place. Then there was the way she tackled contentious social issues with a bravery often lacking in her male contemporaries, interrogating the role religion played in Irish society and its effect on women, which surely would have been appreciated by pupils of a Catholic convent school, albeit a relatively enlightened one.

There were also many personal resonances for me in Deevy's life—she had attended University College Cork (UCC), where I had also studied and, later, made her life in Dublin, as I had in my twenties. In my research, I also came across the tantalising suggestion that Deevy might have embarked on the same career at one point. In an article presented

---

3   *Wife to James Whelan* by Teresa Deevy, directed by Jim Nolan and featuring a community cast. Produced by, and at, Garter Lane Arts Centre, supported by the Arts Council of Ireland Theatre Artist Residency bursary scheme, 11–19 November 2016.

to Kilkenny Literary Society on March 25th, 1966, Frank McEvoy said that 'The President of Cork University, taken by the satirical bent of her essays, suggested that she take up journalism'.[4]

The same echoes resounded in terms of Deevy's champion, Dunne, a fellow UCC student and Waterfordian who would go on to 'take up' journalism. A much-admired poet and writer, Dunne was also literary editor of the *Cork Examiner*, as it was called when he worked there.[5] I had heard a great deal about Dunne when I began working in the *Examiner* myself, going on to read his wonderful memoir *In My Father's House*, which was published in 1991 and became a bestseller.[6] However, until I began researching Deevy, I had never known about his efforts to revive interest in her work.

Dunne helped get her play, *Temporal Powers*, into print, and also conducted a search for a copy of *Wife to James Whelan* when it was considered lost during the 1980s. While his efforts proved unsuccessful at the time, later, in the 1990s, a copy of the script was found in an envelope in the family home. Dunne grew up in St John's Park, not far from where Deevy lived as a child. His was very much a working-class milieu, much like my own, though unlike the more genteel circumstances in which Deevy grew up.

The article quoted at the start of this foreword was a substantial one, the range of which is rarely seen in newspapers today. Dunne gave a comprehensive and valuable insight into Deevy's life and work, speaking to relatives and friends of hers, delivering a well-rounded portrait of a creative and quirky presence who was also a much-loved sister and aunt. As I discovered more about Dunne's role in reviving interest in her work, there was a pleasing circularity and a sense of connection with a man who had also plied his trade in the *Examiner* newsroom.

Like Dunne, I was compelled to bring Deevy's story to a wider audience and I pitched a documentary to RTÉ (Ireland's national television broadcaster), which, many twists and turns later, was commissioned in a revised format. In an inspired pairing, Amanda Coogan, a renowned artist and child of Deaf adults, presented the documentary.[7] It told the

---

4   Maynooth, Russell Library (RL), The Teresa Deevy Archive, Frank McEvoy, Teresa Deevy: Her Plays: Read to the Kilkenny Literary Society, 25 March, 1966, MS PP/6/III/176 16.
5   The *Cork Examiner* was renamed the *Irish Examiner* in 1996.
6   Seán Dunne, *In My Father's House* (Oldcastle: Gallery Press, 2018).
7   *Tribute: The Teresa Deevy Story* was produced by Bernadine Carraher for Mind the

story of Deevy's life and work in tandem with Coogan's plan to stage her ballet, *Possession*, based on the famous Irish saga, the *Táin Bó Cúailnge*.[8] While conducting research for the documentary, it was a privilege to discuss Deevy with some of her family and scholars who were and are intensely passionate about her work.

These academics, particularly Úna Kealy and Kate McCarthy of South East Technological University, are to be commended for the generosity with which they share their scholarship and the determination they have shown in seeking wider recognition for Deevy. The academic interest in Deevy and her work is greatly encouraging and vital in keeping the flame alive, as is the continuing exploration of her life and work by artists such as Coogan and members of Dublin Theatre of the Deaf. However, it would be wonderful to see the educational establishment as a whole row in behind such efforts, so that younger generations are not deprived of knowing more about this exceptional woman, as I was growing up in her native city. Society has, thankfully, moved in on in many ways since Deevy was alive, but the marginalisation which she experienced on the double—as a woman and a deafened person—still, unfortunately, exists. The manner in which she rose above this while refusing to let it constrain her creativity makes her a remarkable figure in our cultural history. A presence in our theatres and our educational spaces is surely the least she deserves.

M.B. Cork, 2024.

Bibliography

Dix, Claire, *Tribute: The Teresa Deevy Story*, online documentary, RTÉ Player, 10 November 2022, https://www.rte.ie/player/movie/tribute-the-teresa-deevy-story/326740520026

Dunne, Seán, *In My Father's House* (Oldcastle: Gallery Press, 2018)

Dunne, Seán, 'Rediscovering Teresa Deevy', *Cork Examiner*, 20 March 1984, p. 10

Gap Films for RTÉ, directed by Claire Dix, shot by Andrew Cummins, and edited by Cara Holmes. Claire Dix, *Tribute: The Teresa Deevy Story*, online documentary, RTÉ Player, 10 November 2022, https://www.rte.ie/player/movie/tribute-the-teresa-deevy-story/326740520026

8   Maynooth, Russell Library (RL), The Teresa Deevy Archive, *Possession or Cattle of the Gods*, PP/6/156.

Acknowledgements

This project has taken time, and many people have contributed in many ways. We acknowledge the excellent scholarship of the practitioners and researchers who prepared the ground for the Active Speech project over many decades. Thanks to our friends, families, students, and audiences who have attended the Deevy talks, workshops, readings, and performances that we have facilitated over the last decade. We thank the practitioners, presenters, and attendees of the Active Speech conference including Irish Sign Language interpreters Isabelle Murphy, Amanda Coogan, Michael Feeney, Vanessa O'Connell, and Caoimhe Coburn-Gray; Dublin Theatre of the Deaf; Charlotte Headrick and Hayden Wilcox; the Abbey Theatre; the Mint Theater; the Faculty of Arts and Humanities (formerly the School of Humanities), and the Centre for Technology-Enhanced Learning (CTEL), South East Technological University (formerly Waterford Institute of Technology) for their support as we convened that conference. The Active Speech conference was made possible with funding support from SETU Research Connexions, Waterford Libraries, and the Waterford Institute of Technology Teaching and Learning Excellence Award.

We thank those who have contributed chapters and their editorial expertise to this collection and the reviewers who offered excellent and constructive criticism. We thank the Open Book Publishers team for their advice, support, and encouragement, and photographers Patrick Brown, Ros Kavanagh, Richard Termine, Carol Rosegg Photography, Patrick Redmond, and Jed Niezgoda for permission to use their artwork.

We acknowledge and are grateful for the support of: the late Phyllis Doolin and the Deevy family, especially the late Clare Brazil, the late Barbara Hearne, Jacqui and Bill Deevy; South East Technological University faculty, in particular, Suzanne Denieffe, Susan Flynn, Erin McNamara Cullen, Jenny O'Connor, Fiona Ennis, Deirdre Grant, Helena

Walsh-Kiely, Christa de Brún, Rob O'Connor, Fionnuala Brennan, Helen Arthur, Ken McCarthy, Peter Windle, Susie Cullinane, Jo Holohan, Geraldine Canny, Hannah Butler, Dorothy Hearne, Dayna Killen, and Aaron Kent; Hugh Murphy, Helen Fallon, Roisín Berry, Maynooth University Libraries; Department of English faculty, Maynooth University; David Clare and Fiona McDonagh, Mary Immaculate College, University of Limerick; Aideen Wylde, University of Galway; Tracey McEneaney and Sinéad O'Higgins, Waterford Libraries; Barry Houlihan, University of Galway; Mairéad Delaney, Abbey Theatre; Barbara McCormack, Royal Irish Academy; Pat McEvoy, *Waterford News and Star*; Liam Murphy, *Munster Express*; Geoff Harris and Mary O'Neill, WLR FM; independent journalists Clodagh Finn and Marjorie Brennan; Irish Sign Language interpreter Ela Cichocka; Maria Ryan, National Library of Ireland; Sr June Fennelly and the Ursuline community in Waterford; Joan Dalton; Nicholas Kavanagh; Mick O'Meara; Wexford Libraries; library and archive staff in SETU, Maynooth University, Trinity College Dublin, University College Cork, University College Dublin, the Abbey Theatre, and the National Library of Ireland; Síle Penkert at Garter Lane Arts Centre; Caroline Senior; Jim Nolan; Mary Boland at Theatre Royal Waterford; and, Willy Maley and Dini Power.

We thank Hugh Murphy, Deputy University Librarian in Maynooth University, whose commitment to Deevy and open access informed, encouraged, and supported us throughout this project.

This publication received grant assistance from SETU Research Connexions and Maynooth University.

Notes on Contributors

Jonathan Bank has been the Artistic Director of the Mint Theater Company in New York City since 1995. Focused on lost and forgotten plays and playwrights, Bank has unearthed and produced over sixty plays, but he is most proud of Mint's *Teresa Deevy Project*, a committed effort to create new life for this exceptional writer's work. The project began in 2010 with a plan to produce two of Deevy's plays and, eventually, grew to include four full productions: *Wife to James Whelan* (2010), *Temporal Powers* (2011), *Katie Roche* (2013), and *The Suitcase under the Bed* (2017), which featured four of Deevy's one-act plays. In addition to the productions, the project also involved numerous readings of Deevy's one-act plays and the publication of two books: *Teresa Deevy Reclaimed: Volume One* (2011) and *Teresa Deevy Reclaimed: Volume Two* (2017). Fintan O'Toole praised the Mint in the *Irish Times* in 2013, writing: 'There has been no coherent exploration of Deevy's work as a whole by any Irish company. Instead, the Mint Theater in New York, which specialises in rediscovering lost work, has engaged in what it calls the Teresa Deevy Project […] There are good reasons, both social and artistic, why Irish theatre should pay attention to this project'. In 2017, the *Irish Times* wrote about the Mint under the headline: 'The New York theatre that's kept Teresa Deevy's flame alive'.

Marjorie Brennan is a journalist who has written extensively on arts and culture for the *Irish Examiner*. She was, formerly, a parliamentary reporter in Dáil Éireann. She holds a Master's degree in Digital Arts and Humanities from University College Cork, for which her main research topic was feminism and social media activism. She was a consultant and researcher on the RTÉ One documentary, *Tribute: The Teresa Deevy Story*. Based in Cork, she is originally from Waterford city.

Caroline Byrne is a theatre director. Previously, she was an Associate Director at the Gate Theatre, Notting Hill; she is an ongoing Education Associate at the Royal Shakespeare Company, and is, currently, Associate Director at the Abbey Theatre. Recent directing credits include: *Dancing at Lughnasa* (Gate Theatre); *Portia Coughlan* (Abbey Theatre); *Spring Awakening* (Young Vic Theatre); *Faustus: That Damned Woman* (Headlong, Lyric Hammersmith); *Woman and Scarecrow* (Royal Academy of Dramatic Art); *All's Well That Ends Well* (Sam Wanamaker Playhouse); *Katie Roche* (the Abbey Theatre, National Theatre of Ireland); *Oliver Twist* (Regent's Park Open Air Theatre); *The Wheel* (Milton Court Theatre); *The Taming of the Shrew* (Shakespeare's Globe); *Parallel Macbeth* (Clare Theatre, Young Vic); *Eclipsed* (Gate Theatre, London); and, *Shakespeare in a Suitcase* (co-directed with Tim Crouch for the Royal Shakespeare Company). She has also directed productions at the Bush Theatre, the Bristol Old Vic, and the Birmingham Rep.

Amanda Coogan has been described by the *Irish Times* as the leading practitioner of performance art in Ireland. Her extraordinary work is challenging, provocative, and always visually stimulating. Her artworks encompass a multitude of media—objects, text, moving and still images, all circulating around her live performances. Her expertise lies in her ability to condense an idea to its essence and communicate it through her body. Her 2015 live exhibition, *I'll Sing You a Song from around the Town*, was described by *Artforum* as 'performance art at its best'. Amanda has collaborated with Deaf artists to realise two of Deevy's works: *Talk Real Fine, Just Like a Lady*, an interpretation of *The King of Spain's Daughter*, which was staged in the Abbey Theatre (2017), and the premiere of *Possession*, staged in Project Arts Centre, Dublin, and in The Granary Theatre, Cork, both in 2024.

Christa de Brún lectures in English Literature at South East Technological University. She holds a BA in English and Philosophy and an MA in Contemporary European Philosophy from University College Dublin, an MPhil in Anglo-Irish Literature from Trinity College Dublin, and a PhD in Literature and Education from Maynooth University. An academic and a poet, Christa has published in the fields of literature, critical consciousness, and education, and has a number of creative publications.

José Francisco Fernández is Professor in English literature at the University of Almería, Spain. His most recent work focuses on the narrative of Samuel Beckett and Beckett's reception in Spain, including articles published in specialised journals such as *Journal of the Short Story in English, Journal of Beckett Studies, AUMLA, Studi Irlandesi*, and *Arcadia*, among others. He has also translated into Spanish four novels and four short stories by Samuel Beckett. He taught Anglo-Irish literature in the Master's degree in English Studies at the National Distance Education University (UNED) and has been general editor of the journal *Estudios Irlandeses*.

Shonagh Hill is a Research Fellow (AHRC) at Queen's University Belfast (QUB) working on a project entitled 'Feminist Temporalities in Contemporary Northern Irish Performance'. Prior to this, she was a Marie Skłodowska-Curie Fellow at QUB. Shonagh's monograph, *Women and Embodied Mythmaking in Irish Theatre*, published by Cambridge University Press in 2019, provides an historical overview of women's contributions to, and an alternative genealogy of, modern Irish theatre. In 2022, she co-edited an anthology of plays with Lisa Fitzpatrick, *Plays by Women in Ireland (1926–33): Feminist Theatres of Freedom and Resistance* (Methuen). Shonagh has also co-edited a special issue of *Feminist Encounters: A Journal of Critical Studies in Culture and Politics* entitled 'Repealing the 8th: Irish Reproductive Activism' (March 2022).

Alvean Jones is a member of the Irish Deaf community, serving on a multitude of committees, and is involved with adult and continuing education as an administrator, having worked for many years as a tutor. Alvean is secretary of the Deaf Heritage Centre Ireland, and has an abiding interest in history, and Irish Deaf history, specifically. In 2016, she co-edited a book on the history of St Mary's School for Deaf Girls entitled *Through the Arch* to celebrate the 170th anniversary of that school. She has worked with Dublin Theatre of the Deaf since 1994 as an actor, writer, and director. In 2015, Alvean performed in Amanda Coogan's RHA exhibition and in Coogan's 2016 Belfast International Arts Festival production *Run to the Rock*. In May 2017, Alvean performed with Kate Romano in Ailís Ní Ríain's play, *I Used to Feel*, which was staged for Cork Midsummer Festival and revived as part of the Dublin Fringe Festival in September 2018. Alvean collaborated with Coogan as a researcher, dramaturge, and performer contributing in multiple ways to *You Told Me to Wash and Clean My Ears* (2014) and to *Talk Real Fine, Just Like a Lady* (2017), both staged at the Peacock Theatre. Alvean performed in *Death of the Innocents* (2021) by the Belfast-based Deaf theatre company D'Sign Arts at the Lyric Theatre in Belfast. In 2024, she co-curated and performed in the premiere of Teresa Deevy's *Possession* (2024), which was staged in Project Arts Centre, Dublin and The Granary Theatre, Cork. Alvean has created several videos translating historical articles and Irish Deaf history into Irish Sign Language and is currently working on an anthology of Irish Deaf history.

Úna Kealy lectures in Theatre Studies and English in South East Technological University (SETU). Prior to her career in academia, Úna worked as a drama workshop facilitator and arts manager in Britain and Ireland in both state-funded and commercial theatre organisations. In 2022, she worked with Amanda Coogan, Alvean Jones, Lianne Quigley, Dublin Theatre of the Deaf, Cork Deaf Community Choir, and SETU staff and students on a research project entitled Lyrical Bodies, an investigation of Teresa Deevy's ballet *Possession*, which was performed in Project Arts Centre, Dublin and The Granary Theatre, Cork as part of the Cork Midsummer Festival in 2024. With Kate McCarthy, she has co-authored 'Writing from the Margins: Re-framing Teresa Deevy's Archive and Her Correspondence with James Cheasty c.1952–1962', *Irish University Review* 52.2 (2022); 'Shape Shifting the Silence: An Analysis of Talk Real Fine, Just like a Lady by Amanda Coogan in collaboration with Dublin Theatre of the Deaf: An Appropriation of Teresa Deevy's *The King of Spain's Daughter* (1935)', in *The Golden Thread: Irish Women Playwrights, Vol 1: 1716–1992* (Liverpool University Press, 2021); and 'Participatory Performances: Spaces of Creative Negotiation', in *The Palgrave Handbook of Contemporary Irish Theatre and Performance* (Palgrave, 2018). Other publications include 'Resisting Power and Direction: *The King of Spain's Daughter* by Teresa Deevy as a Feminist Call to Action', *Estudios Irlandeses*, 15 (2020) and 'Stasis, Rootlessness and Violence in *Lay Me Down Softly*', in *The Art of Billy Roche: Wexford as the World* (Peter Lang, 2012). With Richard Hayes, she co-authored 'Artistic Vision and Regional Resistance: *The Gods Are Angry, Miss Kerr* and the Red Kettle Theatre Company, a Case Study', in *The Palgrave Handbook of Contemporary Irish Theatre and Performance* (Palgrave, 2018).

Eileen Kearney is a leading Irish theatre scholar and director. In the 1980s, her re-discovering of playwright Teresa Deevy prompted her to devote many years of her career to bringing Irish women playwrights to critical notice. She has directed productions and taught university theatre all over the United States, including Pomona College, Santa Clara University, Gonzaga University, Webster University, University of Texas in Austin, Texas A&M University, and University of Colorado Denver. At the playwright Patricia Burke-Brogan's request, she directed the 2013 American premiere of *Stained Glass at Samhain*, which addresses the atrocities of the Magdalene Laundries. She acted in New York and Los Angeles before university teaching. She has published numerous articles in Irish and theatre journals, focusing on women's contributions to the field. Her book, *Irish Women Playwrights, 1908–2001* (co-edited with Charlotte Headrick), was published by Syracuse University Press in 2014, and is now in its second printing. She has been a member of American Conference for Irish Studies since 1985.

Dayna Killen graduated with a PhD from SETU, Waterford in 2024 having been awarded a WIT/SETU PhD Scholarship. Her doctoral thesis focuses on how four Irish women playwrights—Augusta Gregory, Eva Gore-Booth, Margaret O'Leary, and Teresa Deevy—found creative opportunities in navigating stereotypical representations depicting women as married mothers located inside domestic spaces. In that work, Dayna originated the term the 'domesticated Irish woman' to denote a gender representation popularised during the early decades of the twentieth century in Irish society, which the aforementioned playwrights interrogate in their creative work. Dayna, furthermore, investigates a developmental process whereby the behaviours, appearances, aspirations, and spaces occupied by Irish women playwrights and their contemporaries were shaped to fit idealised representations of women as domesticated Irish women. As a Fulbright awardee, Dayna studied at the Keough-Naughton Institute for Irish Studies at Notre Dame. Prior to undertaking her doctorate, Dayna completed an MSc in Global Financial Information Systems at SETU (then WIT) and obtained a first-class honours degree in Drama and Theatre Studies with English Literature from Liverpool Hope University.

Cathy Leeney is currently Adjunct Assistant Professor in Drama Studies in the University College Dublin (UCD) School of English, Drama, and Film where she taught and supervised research for over twenty years and where, with Finola Cronin, she co-founded UCD's MA in Theatre Practice. Cathy trained as a director with the British Theatre Association in London and has directed and assistant directed professional productions in Dublin (Project Arts Centre, Abbey Theatre, Tivoli Theatre, Peacock Theatre) and Belfast (Grand Opera House). Publications include *Seen and Heard: Six Plays by Irish Women* (ed., Carysfort Press, 2003); *The Theatre of Marina Carr* (co-edited with Anna McMullan, Carysfort Press, 2003); *Irish Women Playwrights 1900–1939* (Peter Lang, 2010); *Analysing Gender in Performance* (co-edited with Paul Halferty, Springer, 2023); *The Plays of Maura Laverty* (co-edited with Deirdre McFeely, Liverpool University Press, 2023). She has also published extensively on the subjects of performance analysis, theatre and nation, gender in performance, and women's playwriting and acting in Ireland. Cathy initiated, and was Chair of, the Prague Quadrennial Board (2005–2008) which, through the support of the Irish Theatre Institute, Culture Ireland, Arts Council of Ireland, and Dublin Corporation, enabled Ireland's first national entry to the Prague Quadrennial International Exhibition of Scenography and Architecture in 2008. She was founding Vice-chair of the Irish Society for Theatre Research (ISTR) (2007), and board member of Galloglass Theatre Company and of the Gaiety School of Acting. She works as a dramaturg and is currently developing an analysis for the first production of W.B. Yeats's *The Only Jealousy of Emer*.

Willy Maley taught at the University of Glasgow from 1994–2024. He has co-edited several essay collections on Irish literature and history, including *Representing Ireland: Literature and the Origins of Conflict, 1534–1660* (Cambridge University Press, 1993), *Celtic Connections: Irish-Scottish Relations and the Politics of Culture* (Peter Lang, 2013), *Romantic Ireland: From Tone to Gonne: Fresh Perspectives on Nineteenth-Century Ireland* (Cambridge Scholars Publishing, 2013), and *Scotland and the Easter Rising: Fresh Perspectives on 1916* (Luath Press, 2016). He has published essays on a range of Irish writers from major modern authors like Beckett, Joyce, O'Casey, Synge, and Yeats to contemporary figures including Marina Carr and Martin McDonagh. He has authored two previous essays on Teresa Deevy: '"She Done *Coriolanus* at the Convent": Empowerment and Entrapment in Teresa Deevy's *In Search of Valour*', *Irish University Review*, 49.2 (2019), and with Kirsty Lusk, 'Drama Out of a Crisis: James Connolly's *Under Which Flag* (1916) and Teresa Deevy's *The Wild Goose* (1936)', *Irish Studies Review*, 30.4 (2022).

Caoilfhionn Ní Bheacháin Mitchell is Associate Professor of Communications in the Kemmy Business School at the University of Limerick. Her current research focuses on intellectual and creative networks between 1880 and 1960, and she has a specific interest in cultural history focusing on publishing and book history, subscriptions, theatre management, and the creative industries in general. She works on the playwright Teresa Deevy, the Dun Emer Guild and Press, and the historian and activist Alice Stopford Green with recent articles appearing in the *Journal of Victorian Culture, Women's History Review, Irish University Review,* and the *Edinburgh Companion to Women in Publishing.*

Kate McCarthy is Lecturer in Drama at the Faculty of Arts and Humanities, South East Technological University (SETU). Her public engagement takes many forms, including: theatre practice, workshops, drama and theatre education projects, educational resources, public talks, and podcasts, as well as publications and conference contributions. Alongside co-authored publications on Teresa Deevy and contemporary regional theatre practice with Úna Kealy, she has co-authored book chapters and co-created educational resources about Waterford's Magdalene Laundry and Saint Dominick's Industrial School (with Jennifer O'Mahoney, SETU) and on drama education (with Marian McCarthy, UCC). As a practitioner, she facilitates and devises performances and drama education projects in Ireland and Britain. Kate is a co-researcher on the Lyrical Bodies Project and the Waterford Memories Project. She is the Policy and Advocacy Elected Member of the Irish Society for Theatre Research (ISTR) (2023–2026).

Chris Morash, FTCD, MRIA, is the Seamus Heaney Professor of Irish Writing in Trinity College, Dublin. Among his publications in the field of Irish studies are *Writing the Irish Famine* (Oxford University Press, 1996), *A History of the Irish Theatre: 1601–2000* (Cambridge University Press, 2002), *A History of the Media in Ireland* (Cambridge University

Press, 2009), *Mapping Irish Theatre* (with Shaun Richards) (Cambridge University Press, 2014), and *Yeats on Theatre* (Cambridge University Press, 2021). His 2023 book, *Dublin: A Writer's City* (2023), is the first in the Imagining Cities series he is editing for Cambridge University Press. He has co-edited *The Oxford Handbook of Modern Irish Theatre* with Nicholas Grene (Oxford University Press, 2016) and is currently editing *The Cambridge History of the Irish Novel*. In 2021, he curated the *Unseen Plays* series of audio dramas for the Abbey Theatre, which included a production of Teresa Deevy's *Light Falling*. He has been involved with the Mint Theater's Deevy Project since 2009, as part of which he co-edited (with Jonathan Bank and John Harrington) two volumes of Deevy's plays *Teresa Deevy Reclaimed* (2011 and 2017); these editions draw on manuscript and published sources. While previously working in Maynooth University (1990–2013), he was instrumental with Jonathan Bank, Hugh Murphy, and Jacqui Deevy in establishing the Teresa Deevy Archive in Maynooth University Library. He has served as Vice-Provost of Trinity College, Dublin (2016–2019), is on the Board of the Irish Theatre Institute, and has been a member of the Royal Irish Academy since 2008.

Ciara L. Murphy lectures in Drama at Technological University Dublin. She has recently published her monograph *Performing Social Change on the Island of Ireland: From Republic to Pandemic* (Routledge, 2023). She is lead researcher on the national Safe to Create project, which aims to impact change on the culture and practices of the arts and creative sectors in Ireland to provide safer working conditions for all workers. She has published widely on contemporary Irish performance practice.

Hugh Murphy is Deputy University Librarian in Maynooth University where he completed his doctorate in early nineteenth-century Irish history. Previously, he led the Collections and Content Department in the Library, and it was in this post that he was responsible, with Chris Morash, for bringing the Teresa Deevy Archive to Maynooth. He has worked previously in University College Dublin Library and in the National Library of Ireland as well as lecturing in Information and Library Studies in UCD and book history and archival studies in Maynooth University. He has published in the areas of collection development, collection management, and library strategy, and has spoken nationally and internationally on these topics. Hugh is currently a member of the editorial board of the *New Review of Academic Librarianship*.

Lianne Quigley is an Artistic Director of Dublin Theatre of the Deaf (DTD). She is a Deaf activist and co-led the campaign for the legal recognition of Irish Sign Language (ISL). Lianne is Chairperson of the Irish Deaf Society, a Deaf-led civil rights organisation. She performed in and co-directed the Coogan/DTD collaborative project *You Told Me to Wash and Clean My Ears* (2014), directing the forty-strong, Deaf community cast. She wrote and directed *I Have Spread My Dreams Under Your Feet: The Story of W.B. Yeats* (2015), performed at the Deaf Village Ireland, and led the choreographic research in the Coogan/DTD collaboration, *Talk Real Fine, Just Like a Lady* (2017). Lianne has written, directed, and performed in DTD productions *1916* (2016) and *Suffragette* (2018), both performed at the Deaf Village Ireland. In 2020, with Alvean Jones, Lianne co-wrote and performed *Letter 8*, which was commissioned by the Abbey Theatre as part of the *Dear Ireland* series. In 2022, she worked with Amanda Coogan, Alvean Jones, DTD, Cork Deaf Community Choir, and staff and students of South East Technological University to devise a production of Teresa Deevy's ballet *Possession*, which was performed in February in the Project Arts Centre, Dublin and in The Granary Theatre, Cork in June as part of the Cork Midsummer Festival, both in 2024.

Ann M. Shanahan is a scholar-artist specialising in feminist directing and pedagogy, gender and theatrical space, and theatre and social change. She has directed over sixty productions and writes about her own, and others', directing practice. She is a Professor and Chair in the Department of Theatre and Drama at the University of Wisconsin-Madison. Prior to this appointment, she served as Artistic Director, and was Chair of the Department of Theatre at Purdue University, and served in the faculty in Theatre and Women's Studies and Gender Studies at Loyola University Chicago for twenty years. Selected recent publications include: *Landscapes of Perception: Meredith Monk, Robert Wilson and Richard Foreman* (Methuen, 2023); 'Making Room(s): Staging Plays about Women and Houses', in *Performing the Family Dream House: Space, Ritual and Images of Home* (University of Iowa, 2019); 'Teaching Maria Irene Fornés's *Fefu and Her Friends*', in *How to Teach a Play:*

Exercises for the University Classroom (Bloomsbury Methuen, 2019); and 'Pirated Pedagogy: Re-purposing Brecht's Performance Techniques for Revolutions in Teaching', in *New Directions in Theatre Pedagogy* (Palgrave MacMillan, 2018). Ann is founding co-editor of the Peer-Reviewed Section of the *SDC Journal* (Stage Directors and Choreographers Society) and, from 2024–2030, is co-director of the Comparative Drama Conference (CDC), which will be convened in alternate years at the London Academy of Music and Dramatic Art (LAMDA) and the University of Wisconsin at Madison.

Shelley Troupe worked as an administrator for a diverse range of arts companies including the Irish Repertory Theatre and the National Asian American Theatre Company (both in New York City) as well as the Galway International Arts Festival and Youth Theatre Ireland. She completed her PhD at the University of Galway examining the ongoing partnership between two of Ireland's key artistic contributors, Galway's Druid Theatre (*The Leenane Trilogy, DruidMurphy, DruidO'Casey*) and playwright Tom Murphy (*A Whistle in the Dark, Baileangaire, The House*). Her research involves works that are off-canon and the ways in which life and historical events are reflected and refracted in theatrical production. Publications include essays/articles in *The Oxford Handbook of Modern Irish Theatre, The Palgrave Handbook of Contemporary Irish Theatre*, and *Irish Studies Review*.

List of Figures

Fig. 11.1	Ros Kavanagh, production image from *Katie Roche* (2017), directed by Caroline Byrne for the Abbey Theatre, Amharclann na Mainistreach, featuring Caoilfhionn Dunne as Katie Roche. © Ros Kavanagh. All rights reserved.	p. 243
Fig. 12.1	Richard Termine, production image from Teresa Deevy's *Temporal Powers* (2011), directed by Jonathan Bank, Mint Theater, featuring Rosie Benton as Min Donovan. © Richard Termine. All rights reserved.	p. 264
Fig. 12.2	Carol Rosegg, production image from Teresa Deevy's *Wife to James Whelan* (2010), directed by Jonathan Bank, Mint Theater, featuring Aidan Redmond as Tom Carey and Janie Brookshire as Nan Bowers. © Carol Rosegg Photography. All rights reserved.	p. 266
Fig. 12.3	Patrick Redmond, 'Talk real fine', production image from *Talk Real Fine, Just Like a Lady* (2017), created by Dublin Theatre of the Deaf in collaboration with Amanda Coogan, produced by Live Collision, Peacock Theatre, Amharclann na Mainistreach, featuring Ann O'Neill as Mrs Marks. © Patrick Redmond. All rights reserved.	p. 271
Fig. 12.4	Patrick Redmond, 'The men shade their eyes and look left and right', production image from *Talk Real Fine, Just Like a Lady* (2017), created by Dublin Theatre of the Deaf in collaboration with Amanda Coogan, produced by Live Collision, Peacock Theatre, Amharclann na Mainistreach. © Patrick Redmond. All rights reserved.	p. 272

Fig. 12.5	Patrick Redmond, 'The sign for Ireland', production image from *Talk Real Fine, Just Like a Lady* (2017), created by Dublin Theatre of the Deaf in collaboration with Amanda Coogan, produced by Live Collision, Peacock Theatre, Amharclann na Mainistreach. © Patrick Redmond. All rights reserved.	p. 273
Fig. 12.6	Ros Kavanagh, production image from *Katie Roche* (2017), directed by Caroline Byrne for the Abbey Theatre, Amharclann na Mainistreach, featuring Caoilfhionn Dunne as Katie Roche. © Ros Kavanagh. All rights reserved.	p. 274
Fig. 12.7	Ros Kavanagh, production image from *Katie Roche* (2017), directed by Caroline Byrne for the Abbey Theatre, Amharclann na Mainistreach, featuring Siobhán McSweeney as Amelia. © Ros Kavanagh. All rights reserved.	p. 275
Fig. 12.8	Patrick Redmond, production image from *Talk Real Fine, Just Like a Lady* (2017), created by Dublin Theatre of the Deaf in collaboration with Amanda Coogan, produced by Live Collision, Peacock Theatre, Amharclann na Mainistreach, featuring Paula Clarke as Annie. © Patrick Redmond. All rights reserved.	p. 277
Fig. 12.9	Richard Termine, production photo from *Strange Birth* as part of *The Suitcase under the Bed* (2017), directed by Jonathan Bank, Mint Theater, featuring Aidan Redmond as Bill and Ellen Adair as Sara Meade. © Richard Termine. All rights reserved.	p. 279
Fig. 12.10	Ros Kavanagh, production image from *Katie Roche* (2017), directed by Caroline Byrne for the Abbey Theatre, Amharclann na Mainistreach, featuring Caoilfhionn Dunne as Katie Roche, set and costume design by Joanna Scotcher, and lighting design by Paul Keogan. © Ros Kavanagh. All rights reserved.	p. 282
Fig. 12.11	Patrick Redmond, 'The women's sign for white', production image from *Talk Real Fine, Just Like a Lady* (2017), created by Dublin Theatre of the Deaf in collaboration with Amanda Coogan, produced by Live Collision, Peacock Theatre, Amharclann na Mainistreach. © Patrick Redmond. All rights reserved.	p. 286

Fig. 13.1	Photographer unknown. (L-R) Nell and Teresa Deevy. © Courtesy of Jacqui Deevy. All rights reserved.	p. 292
Fig. 13.2	Patrick Redmond, production image from *Talk Real Fine, Just Like a Lady* (2017), created by Dublin Theatre of the Deaf in collaboration with Amanda Coogan, produced by Live Collision, Peacock Theatre, Amharclann na Mainistreach. © Patrick Redmond. All rights reserved.	p. 298
Fig. 13.3	Patrick Redmond, production image from *Talk Real Fine, Just Like a Lady* (2017), created by Dublin Theatre of the Deaf in collaboration with Amanda Coogan, produced by Live Collision, Peacock Theatre, Amharclann na Mainistreach. © Patrick Redmond. All rights reserved.	p. 300
Fig. 13.4	Patrick Redmond, production image from *Talk Real Fine, Just Like a Lady* (2017), created by Dublin Theatre of the Deaf in collaboration with Amanda Coogan, produced by Live Collision, Peacock Theatre, Amharclann na Mainistreach, featuring Amanda Coogan as Annie. © Patrick Redmond. All rights reserved.	p. 301
Fig. 13.5	Michael O'Meara, front cover of programme for *Talk Real Fine, Just Like a Lady*, created by Dublin Theatre of the Deaf in collaboration with Amanda Coogan, produced by Live Collision, Peacock Theatre, Amharclann na Mainistreach, 2017. © Michael O'Meara. All rights reserved.	p. 302
Fig. 13.6	Patrick Redmond, production image from *Talk Real Fine, Just Like a Lady* (2017), created by Dublin Theatre of the Deaf in collaboration with Amanda Coogan, produced by Live Collision, Peacock Theatre, Amharclann na Mainistreach. © Patrick Redmond. All rights reserved.	p. 303
Fig. 13.7	Patrick Redmond, 'Talk real fine', production image from *Talk Real Fine, Just Like a Lady* (2017), created by Dublin Theatre of the Deaf in collaboration with Amanda Coogan, produced by Live Collision, Peacock Theatre, Amharclann na Mainistreach, featuring Ann O'Neill as Mrs Marks. © Patrick Redmond. All rights reserved.	p. 305
Fig. 13.8	Patrick Redmond, production image from *Talk Real Fine, Just Like a Lady* (2017), created by Dublin Theatre of the Deaf in collaboration with Amanda Coogan, produced by Live Collision, Peacock Theatre, Amharclann na Mainistreach. © Patrick Redmond. All rights reserved.	p. 307

List of Abbreviations

AET	Abbey Experimental Theatre
AHRC	Arts and Humanities Research Council
ATHE	Association for Theatre in Higher Education
BBC	British Broadcasting Corporation
CDC	Comparative Drama Conference
CODA	Child of Deaf Adult(s)
DRI	Digital Repository of Ireland
DTD	Dublin Theatre of the Deaf
EBL	Eavan Boland Library
IRA	Irish Republican Army
ISL	Irish Sign Language
ISTR	Irish Society for Theatre Research
LAMDA	London Academy of Music and Dramatic Art
LSF	Langues de Signes Français
MU	Maynooth University
MUL	Maynooth University Libraries
NAL	National Archives of Ireland
NLI	National Library of Ireland
NTC	National Theatre Conference
NTD	National Theater of the Deaf
OA	Open Access
QUB	Queen's University Belfast
RHA	Royal Hibernian Academy
RIA	Royal Irish Academy
RTÉ	Raidió Teilifís Éireann
SDC	Stage Directors and Choreographers Society
SETU	South East Technological University
UCC	University College Cork
UCD	University College Dublin
UL	University of Limerick
UNCRID	United Nations Conventions on the Rights of Persons with Disabilities

Teresa Deevy: Life, Scholarship, Practice

Úna Kealy and Kate McCarthy

Teresa Deevy was born on the 21 January 1894 in Waterford and spent the early years of her life at 3 Eldon Terrace, Waterford, before moving to a house the family named 'Landscape' on Passage Road, Waterford. The last child of thirteen children—two of whom died in infancy— her father, Edward Deevy, died when she was two; her mother, Mary Bridget Deevy (née Feehan), died in 1930 when Teresa was thirty-six.[1] One of Deevy's sisters, Mary, was a nun at the Ursuline Convent, also in Waterford, when Deevy was a boarder at the school, but Mary (Moll) endured poor health and died as a result of contracting the Spanish Flu in 1917. Two of Deevy's sisters became nuns, and one brother became a Jesuit priest; none of her other five sisters married. Members of the Deevy family were known for their nationalist sympathies and Deevy's uncle, Fr Thomas Feehan, who was a parish priest in the Diocese of Ossory, was silenced by his bishop for his views on the Land League.[2]

Deevy's mother, Mary Bridget Deevy, prioritised her daughters' education and, upon reaching secondary school age, Deevy, one of eighty-one students, boarded at Saint Mary's secondary school in the Ursuline Convent as many upper-middle-class girls did at that time.[3] 'Tessa'

---

1 Edward Deevy died on 12 March 1896. Teresa Deevy's siblings included Edward, Mary (Moll or Mollie), Anne (Nance), Agnes, Frances (Fan), Josephine (Jo), Margaret (Peg), John (Jack), William, and Ellen (Nell). Her sibling Henry Deevy died aged three days in August 1890 and another sister, also called Margaret, died aged twenty days in September 1877.

2 Martina Ann O' Doherty, 'Teresa Deevy and *Wife to James Whelan'*, *Irish University Review*, 25.1 (1995), 25–28. Public support for the Land League was regarded by the Catholic Church as provocative and unwelcome.

3 Deevy achieved Honours in English, and passed Irish, French, Botany, Arithmetic, and Algebra ('Results of Examinations Held in June, 1911 [sic]', *St Ursula's Annual*, 3 (1911), 49).

Deevy was a student in the senior grade of the senior division from 1911 to 1912, experiencing there a formal and informal curriculum of music (Deevy played piano and sang second soprano), sport, dramatic, critical and journalistic writing, and debating.[4] A debate in 1911, for example, invited audience and participants to consider whether women should have equal social and political rights with men, while a series of guest lecturers to the school that year lectured on: Sheridan Le Fanu, Saint Bridget, approaches to studying history, the development of Irish music, and the genre of the passion play. Regular school trips to musical recitals and concerts in Waterford city occurred and students were encouraged to write poetry, literary reviews, plays, and short stories for publication in the school magazine—*St Ursula's Annual*. Drama and performance were significant aspects of the student-led activities in Saint Mary's, and poetry readings and dramatic productions regularly occurred across all year groups. The girls' enthusiastic attendance and participation in these activities resonates in accounts written by them:

> The principal items of the day were 'Robert Emmet' acted by the Seniors and two French Plays in which the Juniors showed their dramatic powers. In the course of these celebrations we discovered that both Classes [sic] were fortunate in the possession of many brilliant actresses.[5]

The girls also performed Shakespeare's *As You Like It*, which was enhanced, rather than marred, by Josie Noonan's 'risibility in parts of the play' and the fact that Annie Tubridy 'in her excitement [at multi-role playing] once mistook her costume, and appeared for the part of William, while dressed as Sir Oliver Martext'.[6] While comic performances were appreciated by the students, so too were the more sombre. In a production of Dickens' *A Christmas Carol*, Preparatory Division student Ethel Stephenson's characterisation of Marley's ghost haunted those present long after the production finished:

> A shudder still passes through our frame as we think of her on that night of the play with a ghastly palor [sic] overspreading her countenance, in the form of large quantities of flour, and her hair in a pig-tail, standing out at an angle of 45°. The noise of the chains and the cash boxes still

---

4 Ibid.
5 'School Notes Kept by the Seniors', *St Ursula's Annual*, 3 (1911), 69–74 (p. 73).
6 '"As You Like It"', *St Ursula's Annual*, 4 (1911), 73.

rings in our ears.⁷

It seems that, at the end of performances, 'critics' (possibly other students, or perhaps teachers) were invited to the stage to adjudicate on what had been presented. Formative, perhaps, in Deevy's dramaturgical approach was criticism offered at the end of *A Christmas Carol*, which reads:

> On the stage we were natural, simple affecting,
> Tis only that when we were off we were acting.
> —(After Goldsmith.)⁸

Mary Deevy also supported Deevy's literary creativity and confidence by encouraging her to 'invent small stories about everyday things around the house'.⁹ Writers must start somewhere, and it was the Ursuline Convent magazine—*St. Ursula's Annual*—which provided Deevy with her first opportunity to test her authorial confidence and voice, writing, for example, about the books that she and her classmates read, and had read to them, as part of evening recreational activities. In 'Books We Have Read', Deevy's love of literature emanates from her reflections on that which she and her friends enjoyed that school year. She writes:

> One evening on coming up to class for recreation we found a strange 'blue' atmosphere. On examination, we discovered that the cause of this change was the presence of a hitherto unknown creature called 'The Blue Bird'. The room was so beautifully and suddenly transformed by this unexpected visitor that each on[e] was filled with curiosity for what was to come—Maeterlinck's 'Blue Bird' [sic].¹⁰

Short pieces such as these reveal Deevy as, what Cathy Leeney describes, 'optimistic, energetic and intellectually alive', while Martina Ann O'Doherty asserts that Deevy's writings from this time attest

---

7   'Preparatory Division Notes', *St Ursula's Annual*, 4 (1911), 78–79 (p. 78).
8   Ibid., p. 79. The paraphrasing of Oliver Goldsmith is from the poem 'Retaliation', a satirical combination of epitaphs, including one of eighteenth-century actor David Garrick. The original Goldsmith quotation reads as: 'On the stage he was natural, simple, affecting,/ 'Twas only that, when he was off, he was acting' (lines 101–102). Oliver Goldsmith, 'Retaliation', in *The Miscellaneous Works of Oliver Goldsmith, M.B. Containing All His Essays and Poems* (London: W. Griffin, 1775).
9   Seán Dunne, 'Rediscovering Teresa Deevy', *Cork Examiner*, 20 March 1984, p. 10.
10 Teresa Deevy, 'Books We Have Read', *St Ursula's Annual*, 3 (1911), 66–67.

to a student with 'a lively, cheerful personality and an infectious ebullience'.[11]

Deevy pursued a BA Arts at University College Dublin (UCD), but the onset of Ménière's disease occurred whilst she was a student there. It is likely that the symptoms of the disease (which affects the inner ear and can result in tinnitus and/or reduced audiological capability) as well as symptoms of vertigo (which can cause nausea, vomiting, and anxiety)—which O'Doherty records that Deevy experienced—impacted Deevy's ability to continue studying at UCD.[12] She returned to Waterford before moving to Cork to continue her studies at University College Cork (UCC).[13] O'Doherty records that the choice to relocate to UCC was so that Deevy could live relatively 'close to her family and [...] attend the Cork Eye, Ear, and Throat Hospital' in Cork city. However, 'growing deafness' caused Deevy to leave UCC 'in late 1914' without graduating.[14] Thereafter, she went to London to study lip-reading and, during this time, her interest in theatre grew—she would attend the theatre, often reading the script before she went.[15] The plays of Anton Chekhov and George Bernard Shaw appealed to her, particularly, and she had resolved on becoming a dramatist by the time she returned to Ireland. She became politically active upon returning home, joining Cumann na mBan and visiting prisoners in Ballybricken Jail, Waterford.[16] In 1918,

---

11   Cathy Leeney, *Irish Women Playwrights, 1900–1939: Gender and Violence on Stage* (New York: Peter Lang, 2010), p. 161; O'Doherty, 'Teresa Deevy and *Wife to James Whelan*', p. 25.

12   Martina Ann O'Doherty, 'Teresa Deevy Playwright (1894–1936)', *Decies—The Waterford Archaeological and Historical Society Journal*, 51 (1995), 108–113 (p. 112). We are grateful to Selina Collard of UCD Archives for confirmation that Teresa Deevy's name appears on the register at UCD in the Faculty of Arts. Teresa Deevy's name appears in the University Calendar list of students as attending the college and taking first year classes during the 1913–1914 session.

13   We are grateful to Timmy O'Connor, University Archives Collection, UCC, who confirmed that Deevy attended UCC as a student for the 1914–1915 academic year. Curiously, Deevy's name is not listed in the Register covering the years 1911–1918, but her signature does appear in the 1914–1915 Roll Book and her name is listed on the record of students for that year. It is possible that Deevy commenced at UCC after the Register closed, which might account for this anomaly. Deevy's name is not listed amongst students who passed examinations in 1915 or 1916, nor does her name appear on lists recording degree conferrings in the National University of Ireland calendars for 1916 and 1917.

14   O'Doherty, 'Teresa Deevy Playwright (1894–1936)', p. 110.

15   Ibid.

16   Cumann na mBan (the Irish Women's Council) held their first 'official' meeting on

she approached Nicholas Whittle, Director of Elections for the political party Sinn Féin, to offer her support and services to the campaign. Whittle reports that she worked, writing, in the election headquarters twelve hours a day, every day, for five weeks.[17]

It was Mary Deevy's ambition that her daughter should write a book and, as Leeney notes, though Mary died in 1930, Deevy dedicated *Katie Roche* 'To mother, as we planned'.[18] The dedication is a recognition of the importance of her mother's support and encouragement. From 1930–1958, Deevy wrote plays (seven of which were produced by the Abbey including *Light Falling* in 1948), short stories, children's stories, reviews, and an outline story for a ballet entitled *Possession* or *The Cattle of the Gods*.[19] What photographic images we have of Teresa Deevy are predominantly those of an established playwright; more difficult to find is the young, aspiring dramatist who smiles from the pages of the Abbey Theatre Festival programme published in 1938. This aberration exists even though, at the height of Deevy's career during the 1930s, the Abbey Theatre produced *Reapers* (1930), *A Disciple* (1931), *Temporal Powers* (1932), *The King of Spain's Daughter* (1935), *The Wild Goose* (1936), *Katie Roche* (1937), and toured to Cambridge (UK) and New York with *Katie Roche*. In 1939, *Holiday House* was under contract at the Abbey, but the directors 'agreed that the contract with Miss Deevy should be allowed to lapse', and it was never staged.[20]

---

2 April 2014 at Wynn's Hotel, Dublin. Their objectives included: '1. To advance the cause of Irish Liberty. 2. To organise Irishwomen in furtherance of this object [sic]. 3. To assist in arming and equipping a body of Irishmen for the defence of Ireland. 4. To form a Fund [sic] for these purposes, to be called "The Defence of Ireland Fund." [sic]'. See Digital Repository of Ireland (DRI), Devereux, Newth & Co., 'Cumann na mBan Membership Booklet', 1914, https://doi.org/10.7486/DRI.9593tv98p, and Dunne, 'Rediscovering Teresa Deevy'.

17 Nicholas Whittle, 'An Appreciation: Teresa Deevy, Playwright', *Waterford News and Star*, 1 Feb 1963, p. 6.

18 Leeney, *Irish Women Playwrights, 1900–1939*, p. 161. Deevy's dedication to her mother comes from *Famous Plays 1935–6* (London: Victor Gollancz, 1936). The plays in this anthology include: *St Helena* by R. C. Sherriff and Jeanne De Casalis; *Call it a Day* by Dodie Smith (C. L. Anthony); *After October* by Rodney Ackland; *Red Night* by James Lansdale Hodson; *Awake and Sing* by Clifford Odets; and, *Katie Roche* by Teresa Deevy.

19 A question mark exists over the exact number of plays that Deevy authored, as some of the scripts found in her archive after her death are either accredited to a pseudonym or are not credited to any author.

20 The minutes of an Abbey Board meeting held on 28 April 1939 record the following: 'The Board decided against the production of "Holiday House" and agreed that the

In 1940, Deevy was re-working a new play, *Wife to James Whelan*, but this work had come 'to a standstill'.[21] The Abbey rejected the play in 1942. Given that the Abbey directors allowed the contract for *Holiday House* to lapse in 1939, Deevy's assessment of that rejection in 1942 was that the Abbey had 'no further use' for her plays.[22] In a letter to her friend, Florence Hackett, Deevy writes about the loss of the Abbey as a production venue for her new work, but also shares with Hackett that she was 'trying to get [it] done elsewhere'.[23] The 'elsewhere' was within the studio and amateur drama and theatre network that was particularly active at this time. O'Doherty notes that Deevy also sent the play to the Gate, but Christine Longford 'refused to stage it because the theatre did not possess a suitable cast'.[24] A radio broadcast of *Wife to James Whelan* was produced in 1946. New work by Deevy returned to the Abbey in 1948, when Ria Mooney produced Deevy's one-act play, *Light Falling*, at the Peacock. On 3 May 1949, Josephine Albericci, W. O'Gorman, and P.J. O'Connor produced *In Search of Valour* for the Dublin School of Acting, which had been previously produced by the Abbey in 1931 under the title *A Disciple*.[25]

Scant research into Deevy's life in Dublin between 1930 and the late 1950s exists, but her correspondence illuminates aspects of her life at that time, including how she, with her sister Nell, navigated her life as a deafened artist.[26] Her correspondence suggests a woman whose insight

---

contract with Miss Deevy should be allowed to lapse'. See Barry Houlihan, 'Outside the Canon: Theatre, Social Change, and Archival Memory' (unpublished doctoral thesis, National University of Ireland, Galway, 2018), p. 105.
21 Dublin, Eavan Boland Library (EBL), Florence Hackett Collection, Teresa Deevy to Florence Hackett ('Landscape 1940'), MS 10722, item 28. The Berkeley Library was denamed in April 2023. In October 2024, the University Board at Trinity College Dublin renamed the library as the Eavan Boland Library. Citations in this publication reflect this change.
22 Dublin, Eavan Boland Library (EBL), Florence Hackett Collection, Teresa Deevy to Florence Hackett (undated), MS 10722, item 33.
23 EBL, MS 10722, item 33. In the 1940s and 1950s, the Abbey produced revivals of *Katie Roche* on the mainstage and at the Peacock (Dublin Repertory Company, 1948); the 1949 production on the mainstage (dir. Ria Mooney) ran for fifty-one performances.
24 O'Doherty, 'Teresa Deevy and *Wife to James Whelan*', p. 27.
25 *In Search of Valour* was produced at the Royal Irish Academy of Music Theatre, Dublin, alongside *The Green Branch* by T.C. Murray and *The Old People* by Seamus de Faoite (see 'Two New Plays', *Evening Herald*, 15 April 1949, p. 5).
26 Kate McCarthy and Úna Kealy, 'Writing from the Margins: Re-framing Teresa

into human experience, interactions, and body language had become well-honed. We conclude that this was the case in response to Deevy's own accounts of how she vicariously experienced and reacted to radio dramas through watching live recordings of them, and watching her friends and family's reactions whilst they listened to the radio. Describing her first visit to see St John Ervine's play *John Ferguson*, recorded for radio broadcast in the BBC's Belfast studio, Deevy described her fascination 'watching it'.[27] Recounting to her friend Florence Hackett her account of watching her family's reaction to a radio broadcast of Hackett's play, Deevy enthuses, 'It was splendid—at least if I can judge by the family reactions'.[28] In another letter, again describing her experience of watching family and friends listening to a radio drama at home in Landscape, Deevy writes, 'Nance, Nell and Phyllis listened last night— and I watched their amusement. Then Nell told me the story of it'.[29] Deevy typically writes 'we' when recalling social events suggesting that Nell was frequently, if not always, by her side. More than an interpreter, Nell also seems (consciously or otherwise) to have performed the role of selecting and summarising events or points of interest for her sister, Teresa, when recounting or recalling information or events. In a letter to Hackett commenting on an Irish PEN event, Deevy mentions 'As she remembers she [Nell] tells me parts of the speeches'.[30] A month later, in March 1936, an unnamed reporter for the *Irish Times* recorded his

---

Deevy's Archive and Her Correspondence with James Cheasty', *Irish University Review*, 52.2 (2022), 322–340, https://www.euppublishing.com/doi/pdf/10.3366/iur.2022.0570

27 Dublin, Eavan Boland Library (EBL), Florence Hackett Collection, Teresa Deevy to Florence Hackett (undated), MS 10722, item 23. St John G. Ervine, *John Ferguson: A Play in Four Acts* (New York: Macmillan, 1920).

28 Dublin, Eavan Boland Library (EBL), Florence Hackett Collection, Teresa Deevy to Florence Hackett (undated), MS 10722, item 23.

29 Dublin, Eavan Boland Library (EBL), Florence Hackett Collection, Teresa Deevy to Florence Hackett (2 February 1939(?)) [sic], MS 10722, item 24. While this evidence of Deevy's experience of radio broadcasts exists, we have not found an account of whether, or how, she experienced the BBC television broadcasts of *The King of Spain's Daughter* and *In Search of Valour*, both of which were directed by Denis Johnston in 1939.

30 Dublin, Eavan Boland Library (EBL), Florence Hackett Collection, Teresa Deevy to Florence Hackett, 9 February 1936, item 11. Irish PEN/PEN na hÉireann is a subsidiary to PEN International, which was founded in 1926, as a worldwide association of writers which argued that 'freedom of expression and literature are inseparable' (see PEN, https://irishpen.com/international-pen-centres/).

experience of interviewing Deevy:

> It was only possible to converse with the assistance of her sister. She reads what is said by her sister in labial signs as formed by uttered words, and, having grasped the meaning, turns with a smile to reply to the inquirer, who has addressed his question to her sister.[31]

The account of the interview, alongside details of Nell's role, suggests that, while Deevy could lip-read, her ability to do so was limited. However, regardless of her limitations as a lip-reader, Deevy had an active social life and, with Nell, found ways to recover and/or minimise the impact of missing what she did not hear. In some social situations, perhaps when Nell was chatting to others, Deevy asked conversationalists to write rather than speak—a fact evidenced in her mention of a 'writing tablet' (a note pad) that she had bought 'for all my friends to scribble on for me'.[32] Deevy's friends included Hugh Hunt, Shelah Richards, Lennox Robinson, Jack B. Yeats, and Denis Johnston, but Nell was an essential part of her interaction with the world. On a trip to London in December 1948, while staying with her sister, Josie, Deevy wrote to Hackett about the difficulty of securing permission to visit Britain in the aftermath of the war, writing: 'Great fun getting permits—My agent sent a most obliging letter—showing how badly she needed to see me—and <u>my interpreter</u>!'.[33] The underlining and exclamation mark in the letter suggesting the joy that Nell's companionship brought Deevy, and Nell's important place in her life. Deevy was 'a guest of honour' at the Christmas 1949 meeting of the Women Writers' Club, informing Hackett that Denis Johnston 'spoke beautifully (Nell tells me) of my work'.[34]

It seems that, anticipating that she would not catch all the dialogue when she attended theatre productions, Deevy read the relevant dramatic scripts prior to attending performances, choosing, when she could, seats in the front row of the dress circle or the stalls: '—good places for a

---

31 'A New Abbey Play: Miss T. Deevy's "Katie Roche": Interview with the Author', *Irish Times*, 14 March 1936, p. 10.
32 Dublin, Eavan Boland Library (EBL), Florence Hackett Collection, Teresa Deevy to Florence Hackett (undated), MS 10722, item 21.
33 Dublin, Eavan Boland Library (EBL), Florence Hackett Collection, Teresa Deevy to Florence Hackett, 17 December 1948, MS 10722, item 45.
34 Dublin, Eavan Boland Library (EBL), Florence Hackett Collection, Teresa Deevy to Florence Hackett, 'Christmas 1949', MS 10722, item 57.

deaf person to follow—(I have to secure that you know)'.³⁵ In a letter to James Cheasty, written at the beginning of their correspondence, Deevy writes that she is keen to see a play of his produced and asks: 'Perhaps before it comes on—if you had a spare script you'll let me see it—I would like to read the play before seeing it—' but, the following year, following last-minute changes to the script during rehearsal, reassures him that she will 'be able to follow by watching'.³⁶ In another letter, and in advance of their first in-person meeting, Deevy prepares Cheasty for their conversation, writing: 'You & I have a lot to say to one another yet—if you do not mind writing on scraps of paper for me. My friends often do that when I can't follow'.³⁷

Elected to the prestigious Irish Academy of Letters, 1954 was a year of mixed emotions for Deevy as, Nell, her beloved sister, died.³⁸ The actor and producer Phyllis Ryan recalls that Nell 'had been [Teresa's] ears and voice for many years', and describes Nell's death as Teresa Deevy's 'great tragedy'.³⁹ In a letter acknowledging condolences on her sister's death, Deevy wrote:

> I do not find it easy to write about her. We were so very close to one another I am desolate now. But that is to be faced,—and she would not have us sad. She always wished people to be gay and light hearted [sic]. She was,—and is, a gallant soul.⁴⁰

O'Doherty asserts that Nell's death in 1954 was the loss of not just a sister but of 'an indispensable lip-reading interpreter'.⁴¹ Recalling his friendship with Deevy during the 1950s, Cheasty also wrote of the important relationship between Teresa and Nell:

---

35 Maynooth, Russell Library (RL), James Cheasty Archive, Teresa Deevy to James Cheasty, 21 June 1962.
36 Maynooth, Russell Library (RL), James Cheasty Archive, Teresa Deevy to James Cheasty, 19 December 1952; Maynooth, Russell Library (RL), James Cheasty Archive, Teresa Deevy to James Cheasty, 20 September 1953.
37 Maynooth, Russell Library (RL), James Cheasty Archive, Teresa Deevy to James Cheasty (undated).
38 W.B. Yeats and George Bernard Shaw founded the Academy of Letters in 1932 'to reward publicly literary achievement and to organise writers to oppose literary censorship' (see 'UCD Irish Academy of Letters', https://www.ucd.ie/specialcollections/archives/irishacademy/).
39 Phyllis Ryan, *The Company I Kept* (Dublin: Town House, 1996), p. 108.
40 Maynooth, Russell Library (RL), James Cheasty Archive, Teresa Deevy to Ellen Cheasty, 10 March 1954.
41 O'Doherty, 'Teresa Deevy and *Wife to James Whelan*', p. 26.

> Although completely deaf [Teresa] was a great conversationalist. My replies were transmitted to her by Nell whom she was able to lip-read. Nell was really Teresa's ears and when Nell died a few months later it was the greatest blow dealt to Teresa in her life-time. But she bore it with characteristic heroism.[42]

In a letter to poet, literary critic, and academic John Jordan in 1955, Deevy wrote:

> It is easier for a person, when with me, to be the only one, for then one doesn't mind so much having to repeat or (better still for me) to write. You did not appear to mind—yet I was reluctant to hold up general conversation by asking lots of things that would have been good to discuss with you.[43]

Jordan was researching an article reviewing Deevy's dramatic work that year. Deevy continued to live in Waterloo Road before moving to a flat with a garden in Clyde Road. In a letter to Jordan that November, Deevy explains the change of her Dublin address as motivated by finding life in Waterloo Road 'too lonely'—presumably as a result of Nell's death.[44] When Jordan's article was published the following year, she wrote:

> I am moved more than I can tell you by the reading of this grand article of yours. Thank you—if you could know how warming, how stimulating I have found your deeply sympathetic [illegible possibly 'entry'] into my work I think you would feel repaid, at least in part for the labour you have given. You have laboured, you have dug, and have brought up once more many of my deepest thoughts and feelings that, from lying long too far down, were almost dead.[45]

Also in 1955, Deevy corresponded with Nathamal Sahal sending him her dramatic texts and supporting his analysis of her work.[46] In 1956, the Studio Theatre Club produced *Wife to James Whelan* to 'critical acclaim'

---

42 Maynooth, Russell Library (RL), James Cheasty Archive, '21: The Curtain Rises' 18–21, p. 18.
43 Dublin, National Library of Ireland (NLI), John Jordan Papers 1945–1988, Teresa Deevy to John Jordan (13 October 1955), MS 35,072.
44 Ibid.
45 Dublin, National Library of Ireland (NLI), John Jordan Papers 1945–1988, Teresa Deevy to John Jordan (30 June 1956), MS 35,072. See John Jordan, 'Teresa Deevy: An Introduction', *Irish University Review*, 1.8 (1956), 13–26.
46 Nathamal Sahal, *Sixty Years of Realistic Irish Drama* (Bombay: Macmillan, 1971).

and, the following year, produced *In the Cellar of My Friend*.⁴⁷ In 1958, *Supreme Dominion* was produced as part of the Luke Wadding Centenary celebrations. Deevy continued to divide her time between Waterford and Dublin, keeping up her apartment in Clyde Road until 1959.⁴⁸ She returned to the family home in Waterford at the end of the decade—travelling up and down to Dublin to see theatre productions when she could—but with three ageing sisters living in Landscape, there was caring work for Deevy to do. Deevy's sisters, Josephine and Margaret, died on 26 January 1960 and 6 January 1961, respectively. From brief comments made in a postcard to Cheasty, it seems that, after the deaths of Josephine and Margaret, Deevy assumed sole responsibility for the care of her older sister, Fan, necessitating her (Deevy's) full-time residence in Waterford.⁴⁹ Caring for Fan was, no doubt, challenging as O'Doherty, who interviewed Deevy's family and friends in the early 1990s, records that towards the end of her own life Deevy was increasingly affected by the impact of Ménière's disease and 'recurring vertigo [... and] seldom ventured out of doors'.⁵⁰ In Deevy's final illness, she was cared for in a nursing home in Ballygunner, Waterford where she died on 19 January 1963, two days before her sixty-ninth birthday.⁵¹

While Sahal published *Sixty Years of Realistic Irish Drama* in 1971, a 'reclamation' of Deevy's work began in earnest with Patience Ochu,

---

47 O'Doherty, 'Teresa Deevy and *Wife to James Whelan*', p. 27. A critic in the *Evening Herald* critiqued *Wife to James Whelan* as 'a fine production' (see 'Studio Theatre Club Success: Fine Production of New Play by Teresa Deevy', *Irish Independent*, 5 October 1956, p. 3), and a critic in the *Evening Herald* noted that 'The interest is in the dialogue, which is excellent' (see 'New Play', *Evening Herald*, 5 October 1956, p. 6). Evidence that the Studio Theatre Club produced *In the Cellar of My Friend* comes from a brief mention in a letter from Deevy to Cheasty dated 28 June 1957 (see McCarthy and Kealy, 'Writing from the Margins'). While Désirée Bannard Cogley (also known as Madame, Daisy, and Toto Cogley) established the Studio Theatre Club in the mid-1920s, it ceased operation for a time and was revived when Cogley returned from England after the Second World War when it was managed administratively and artistically by Cogley and her son, Fergus Cogley.

48 Maynooth, Russell Library (RL), Teresa Deevy to James Cheasty, 31 October 1957; Maynooth, Russell Library (RL), Teresa Deevy to James Cheasty, 3 June 1957. From the postmarks on her letters to her friend James Cheasty, a young playwright from Waterford whom she mentored during the 1950s, we know that Deevy kept the 'Garden Flat' in Dublin up to, at least, 1959, when she returned to Waterford.

49 Maynooth, Russell Library (RL), Teresa Deevy to James Cheasty, 28 June 1962.

50 O'Doherty, 'Teresa Deevy Playwright (1894–1936)', p. 112.

51 Teresa Deevy is buried in the Deevy family plot in Ballygunner graveyard, Waterford city.

Seán Dunne, and Eileen Kearney's research in the early 1980s. Ochu submitted an MA thesis on Deevy's work in 1981; Dunne published an introduction to Deevy in the *Cork Examiner* in 1984 and in *The Journal of Irish Literature* in 1985; and Kearney completed a doctoral thesis in 1986, publishing her scholarship on Deevy in articles throughout her career.[52] In 1987, Clodagh Walsh directed *The King of Spain's Daughter* for Red Kettle Theatre Company (Waterford), which played in Garter Lane Arts Centre in Waterford and in Watermans Arts Centre, London. O'Doherty completed a MA thesis on Deevy in 1992. In 1994, Judy Friel directed *Katie Roche* for the Abbey Theatre. In 1995, the silver jubilee issue of *Irish University Review* entitled *Teresa Deevy and Irish Women Playwrights*, which included the first publication of *Wife to James Whelan*, furthered the reclamation of Deevy's work, bolstering her reputation as a dramatist.[53] O'Doherty, Cathy Leeney, Shaun Richards, Christie Fox, and Fiona Becket's scholarship, and the inclusion of *The King of Spain's Daughter* within *The Field Day Anthology of Irish Writing: Irish Women's Writings and Traditions, Volume V* further substantiated Deevy's literary

---

52 Patience Ochu, 'Women in Three Plays by Teresa Deevy' (unpublished master's thesis, University of Ottawa, 1981); Dunne, 'Rediscovering Teresa Deevy'; Seán Dunne, 'Teresa Deevy, an Introduction', *The Journal of Irish Literature*, 14.2 (1985), 3–15; Eileen Kearney, 'Teresa Deevy (1894–1963): Ireland's Forgotten Second Lady of the Abbey Theatre' (unpublished doctoral thesis, University of Oregon, 1986); Eileen Kearney, 'Teresa Deevy (1894–1963)', in *Irish Playwrights, 1880–1995: A Research and Production Sourcebook*, ed. by Bernice Schrank and William W. Demastes (Westport, CT: Greenwood Press, 1997), pp. 80–92; Eileen Kearney, 'The Plays of Teresa Deevy: A Checklist', *The Journal of Irish Literature*, 14.2 (1985), 16–17; Eileen Kearney, 'Current Women's Voices in the Irish Theatre: New Dramatic Visions', *Colby Quarterly, Contemporary Irish Drama*, 27.4 (1991), 225–232; Eileen Kearney, 'Teresa Deevy: Ireland's Forgotten Second Lady of the Abbey Theatre', *The Theatre Annual*, 40 (1985), 77–90.

53 Martina Ann O'Doherty, 'The Representation of Women in the Plays of Teresa Deevy (1894–1963)' (unpublished MA thesis, National University of Ireland, 1992); *Irish University Review*, 25.1 (1995), Silver Jubilee Issue: Teresa Deevy and Irish Women Playwrights issue includes articles by: Christopher Murray, 'The Stifled Voice', 1–10; Maureen Waters, 'Lady Gregory's *Grania*: A Feminist Voice', 11–24; Martina Ann O'Doherty, 'Teresa Deevy and *Wife to James Whelan*', 25–28; Teresa Deevy, 'Wife to James Whelan: A Play in Three Acts', 29–87; Cathy Leeney, 'Themes of Ritual and Myth in Three Plays by Teresa Deevy', 88–116; Judy Friel, 'Rehearsing *Katie Roche*', 117–125; Stephan Murray, 'The One-Act Plays of Teresa Deevy', 126–132; Eibhear Walshe, 'Lost Dominions: European Catholicism and Irish Nationalism in the Plays of Teresa Deevy', 133–142; Anthony Roche, 'Woman on the Threshold: J. M. Synge's *The Shadow of the Glen*, Teresa Deevy's *Katie Roche* and Marina Carr's *The Mai*', *Irish University Review*, 25.1 (1995), 143–162; and, Martina Ann O'Doherty, 'Deevy: A Bibliography', 163–170.

reputation in the late 1990s.⁵⁴

In 2003, Eibhear Walshe published a selection of Deevy's plays; in 2004, Leeney published a further critical essay on Deevy and, in 2010 and 2011 respectively, Leeney and Gerardine Meaney separately analysed Deevy's work within extended studies of Irish women writers.⁵⁵ Caoilfhionn Ní Bheacháin Mitchell contextualised and interpreted Deevy's work as a commentary on Irish social and political life of the 1930s in two essays in 2011 and 2012 during which time the Mint Theater editing-publishing team—Jonathan Bank, Christopher Morash, and John P. Harrington— began work on two anthologies of Deevy's collected work published in 2011 and 2017.⁵⁶ The publication of these volumes coincided with a resurgence of interest in producing Deevy's work with the Mint Theater (New York), under the directorship of Jonathan Bank, premiering *Wife to James Whelan* (2010) and producing *Temporal Powers* (2011) and *Katie Roche* (2013).⁵⁷ Also in 2013, Charlotte Headrick premiered *The King of*

---

54 O'Doherty, 'Deevy: A Bibliography'; O' Doherty, 'Teresa Deevy and *Wife to James Whelan*'; O'Doherty, 'Teresa Deevy Playwright (1894–1936)'; Shaun Richards, '"Suffocated in the Green Flag": The Drama of Teresa Deevy and 1930s Ireland', *Literature & History*, 4.1 (1995), 65–80; Cathy Leeney, 'Deevy's Leap: Teresa Deevy Re-Membered in the 1990s', in *The State of Play: Irish Theatre in the 'Nineties*, ed. by Eberhard Bord (Germany: Wissenschaftlicher Verlag Trier, 1996), pp. 39–49; Fiona Becket, 'A Theatrical Matrilineage? Problems of the Familial in the Drama of Teresa Deevy and Marina Carr', in *Ireland in Proximity: History, Gender, Space*, ed. by Scott Brewster, Virginia Crossman, Fiona Becket, and David Alderson (London: Routledge, 1999), pp. 80–108.

55 Teresa Deevy, *The Selected Plays of Teresa Deevy*, ed. by Eibhear Walshe (Cork: Cork University Press, 2003); Cathy Leeney, 'Ireland's "Exiled" Women Playwrights: Teresa Deevy and Marina Carr', in *The Cambridge Companion to Twentieth-Century Irish Drama*, ed. by Shaun Richards (Cambridge: Cambridge University Press, 2004), pp. 150–163; Leeney, *Irish Women Playwrights, 1900–1939*; Gerardine Meaney, *Gender, Ireland and Cultural Change: Race, Sex and Nation* (London: Routledge, 2011); Cathy Leeney, 'Women's Traditions in Theatre, 1920–2015', in *A History of Modern Irish Women's Literature*, ed. by Heather Ingman and Clíona Ó Gallchoir (Cambridge: Cambridge University Press, 2018), pp. 312–33.

56 Caoilfhionn Ní Bheacháin, 'Sexuality, Marriage and Women's Life Narratives in Teresa Deevy's *A Disciple* (1931), *The King of Spain's Daughter* (1935) and *Katie Roche* (1936)', *Estudios Irlandeses*, 7 (2012), 79–91; Caoilfhionn Ní Bheacháin, '"The Seeds beneath the Snow": Resignation and Resistance in Teresa Deevy's *Wife to James Whelan*', in *Irish Women Writers: New Critical Perspectives*, ed. by Elke D'hoker, Raphaël Ingelbien, and Hedwig Schwall (New York: Peter Lang, 2011), pp. 91– 110; *Teresa Deevy Reclaimed*, 2 vols, ed. by Jonathan Bank, John P. Harrington, and Christopher Morash (New York: Mint Theater, 2011 and 2017). Christopher Morash was instrumental in the initial conservation of Deevy's archive in Maynooth University.

57 *Wife to James Whelan* by Teresa Deevy, directed by Jonathan Bank, produced by and

Spain's Daughter in America in Oregon State University, Corvallis. In 2015, Kearney and Headrick anthologised *The King of Spain's Daughter* within *Irish Women Dramatists 1908–2001*, and *Wife to James Whelan* was staged by Garter Lane Arts Centre, Waterford.[58] Also in 2015, Anthony Roche considered Deevy within his analysis of the Irish dramatic revival; *White Ships*, a devised production responding to *The King of Spain's Daughter* was performed in the Vintage Tea Rooms in Waterford; and a rehearsed reading of *The King of Spain's Daughter* was presented at the Medieval Museum, Waterford.[59] In 2016, Fintan O'Toole included *Katie Roche* in *Modern Ireland in 100 Artworks*, writing that the play is 'so strange and so compelling' in its characterisation of an Irish woman who does not conform to the role of woman as prescribed by the new State.[60]

In 2017, *The King of Spain's Daughter* was staged as a rehearsed reading in Limerick and, the following year, a multi-lingual rehearsed reading of *The King of Spain's Daughter* was performed at Garter Lane Arts Centre.[61] As part of *The Suitcase under the Bed* programme in 2017, the Mint Theater produced the global premieres of *Holiday House* and *Strange Birth*—a rehearsed reading of the latter was staged for Culture Night Waterford

---

at the Mint Theater, New York, 29 July–3 October 2010; *Katie Roche* by Teresa Deevy, directed by Jonathan Bank, produced by and at the Mint Theater, New York, 26 January–31 March 2013.

58 *Irish Women Dramatists 1908–2001*, ed. by Eileen Kearney and Charlotte Headrick (New York: Syracuse University Press, 2014), pp. 41–58; *Wife to James Whelan* by Teresa Deevy, directed by Jim Nolan and featuring a community cast, was produced by and at Garter Lane Arts Centre and was supported by the Arts Council of Ireland Theatre Artist Residency bursary scheme, 11–19 November 2016.

59 Anthony Roche, *The Irish Dramatic Revival 1899–1939* (Bloomsbury: London, 2015); *White Ships* was performed by Waterford Institute of Technology (WIT) Theatre Studies students, directed by Úna Kealy, and staged in The Vintage Tea Rooms, Waterford, 1 May 2015; Teresa Deevy's *The King of Spain's Daughter* was performed as a rehearsed reading by WIT staff and students in Waterford Medieval Museum as part of Culture Night, 18 September 2015.

60 Fintan O'Toole, '1936: *Katie Roche*', in *Modern Ireland in 100 Artworks*, ed. by Fintan O'Toole, Catherine Marshall, and Eibhear Walshe (Dublin: Royal Irish Academy and Irish Times, 2017), pp. 61–63 (p. 63).

61 *The King of Spain's Daughter* by Teresa Deevy (directed by Úna Kealy and Kate McCarthy and read by BA in Contemporary and Applied Theatre students of Mary Immaculate College, University of Limerick) formed part of the programme of the Irish Women Playwrights and Theatremakers Conference convened by David Clare, Aideen Wylde, and Fiona McDonagh hosted by Mary Immaculate College, University of Limerick 8–10 June 2017; *The King of Spain's Daughter* by Teresa Deevy (a tri-lingual reading in English, Italian, and Spanish) read in Garter Lane Arts Centre for Culture Night, 21 September 2018.

in the same month.⁶² The Mint also produced *In the Cellar of My Friend* and *The King of Spain's Daughter* as part of that programme that year.⁶³ Also, in 2017, Caroline Byrne directed *Katie Roche* for the Abbey Theatre, and the Peacock Theatre simultaneously staged an appropriation of *The King of Spain's Daughter* by Amanda Coogan and Dublin Theatre of the Deaf entitled *Talk Real Fine, Just Like a Lady*.⁶⁴ Marie Kelly created an educational research pack associated with these Abbey productions.⁶⁵

In 2019 and 2020, Willy Maley, Kealy, and Ní Bheacháin published three critical essays on Deevy's dramatic work, focusing on *A Disciple*, *The King of Spain's Daughter*, and *Temporal Powers*, respectively.⁶⁶ Andrés Romera translated the text into Spanish in 2020 as *La Hija del Rey de España* in 2020.⁶⁷ 2021 saw two scholarly events designed to investigate and develop Deevy scholarship: Emily Bloom in Columbia University and Lauren Arrington in Maynooth University co-hosted a seminar entitled 'Disability and the Archive: Teresa Deevy in Context', while Kealy and McCarthy of Waterford Institute of Technology (now renamed South East Technological University (SETU)) in partnership

---

62 *Strange Birth* and *Holiday House* by Teresa Deevy, directed by Jonathan Bank, and produced by the Mint Theater, New York, 21 July–30 September 2017; *Strange Birth* by Teresa Deevy, directed by Rebecca Phelan, and produced at Garter Lane Arts Centre, 15 September 2017.

63 *In the Cellar of My Friend* and *The King of Spain's Daughter* by Teresa Deevy, directed by Jonathan Bank, and produced by the Mint Theater, New York, 21 July–30 September 2017.

64 *Katie Roche* by Teresa Deevy, directed by Caroline Byrne, and produced by the Abbey Theatre, Dublin, 28 August–23 September 2017; *Talk Real Fine, Just Like a Lady* created by Dublin Theatre of the Deaf in collaboration with Amanda Coogan, produced by Live Collision, Peacock Theatre, Amharclann na Mainistreach, 19–23 September 2017.

65 *Abbey Theatre Research Pack: Teresa Deevy: Katie Roche*, researched and compiled by Marie Kelly, School of Music and Theatre, University College Cork (Dublin: Abbey Theatre, 2017).

66 Willy Maley, '"She Done *Coriolanus* at the Convent": Empowerment and Entrapment in Teresa Deevy's *In Search of Valour*', *Irish University Review*, 49.2 (2019), 356–369; Úna Kealy, 'Resisting Power and Direction: *The King of Spain's Daughter* by Teresa Deevy as a Feminist Call to Action', *Estudios Irlandeses*, 15 (2020), 178–192; Caoilfhionn Ní Bheacháin, '"It Was Then I Knew Life': Political Critique and Moral Debate in Teresa Deevy's *Temporal Powers* (1932)', *Irish University Review*, 50.2 (2020), 337–355.

67 Andrés Romera, 'Translation of *The King of Spain's Daughter* (1935), by Teresa Deevy', *Estudios Irlandeses*, 15 (2020), 193–221. Romera's is the third translation of *The King of Spain's Daughter*: the first two translations, both into Irish and both entitled *Iníon Rí na Spáinne*, were translated, first, by the poet Máirtín Ó Direáin (which was broadcast by Radio Éireann in 1952) and, second, by Séamus Ó Néill (published in 1972).

with Hugh Murphy of Maynooth University, and Waterford Libraries, collaborated to convene Active Speech: Sharing Scholarship on Teresa Deevy, the first conference devoted to Deevy's work.[68] In 2021, Kealy and McCarthy published an analysis of *Talk Real Fine, Just Like a Lady*, which discussed how the production revealed systemic institutional trauma, the marginalisation of the Deaf community in Ireland, and 'celebrate[d] the expressive potential of ISL [Irish Sign Language]'.[69] Recent productions of 'rarely-performed' Deevy plays include a reading of *Light Falling* (dir. Caroline Byrne) featured as part of the limited podcast series *Unseen Plays* (2021),[70] and a rehearsed reading of *Within a Marble City*, as part of the Waterford Imagine Arts Festival (2022).[71] In 2022, Morash published a short essay on *Katie Roche* in *Fifty Key Irish Plays*, outlining some of the interlinking reasons for Deevy's career trajectory from 'prolific playwright' to 'virtually unknown'.[72] Also in 2022, three studies focusing on Deevy were published: Kirsty Lusk and Maley considered *The Wild Goose* alongside James Connolly's *Under Which Flag?*; Mária Kurdi analysed *Katie Roche* and *The King of Spain's Daughter* in conjunction with J.M. Synge's work to explore patriarchal authority; and McCarthy and Kealy analysed documents sent by Deevy to Cheasty

---

68 The Active Speech: Sharing Scholarship on Teresa Deevy conference website is archived by the National Library of Ireland. Captured on 10 June 2021, and part of the Irish Literature: Festival and Awards Collection, it is available at: https://wayback.archive-it.org/12996/20210610101303/https:/activespeech2021.org. Active Speech: Sharing Scholarship on Teresa Deevy was accessible to Deaf, deafened, and hard of hearing participants as papers were audio recorded and audio captioned, and some were signed in Irish Sign Language. We acknowledge the support of Hugh Murphy and Maria Ryan of the National Library of Ireland in supporting the digital archiving of the conference website.

69 Úna Kealy and Kate McCarthy, 'Shape Shifting the Silence: An Analysis of *Talk Real Fine, Just Like a Lady* (2017) by Amanda Coogan in Collaboration with Dublin Theatre of the Deaf, an Appropriation of Teresa Deevy's *The King of Spain's Daughter* (1935)', in *The Golden Thread: Irish Women Playwrights, 1716–2016*, 2 vols, ed. by David Clare, Fiona McDonagh, and Justine Nakase (Liverpool: Liverpool University Press, 2021), I, 197–210 (p. 210).

70 Curated by Morash, this series featured readings of 'rarely performed Irish plays', classified as readings, rather than radio drama, because there was 'no intention to create the full auditory world of the play'. See Trinity College Dublin, 'Bringing Unseen Irish Drama to the Digital Airwaves—Prof Chris Morash Curates New Abbey podcast', 2 November 2021.

71 *Within a Marble City* by Teresa Deevy, directed by Kate McCarthy, and produced by Waterford Imagine Arts Festival, 27 October 2017.

72 Chris Morash, '*Katie Roche* (1936) by Teresa Deevy', in *Fifty Key Irish Plays*, ed. by Shaun Richards (Oxon: Routledge, 2023), pp. 56–60 (p. 56 and p. 57).

that challenge prevailing narratives concerning her involvement—or lack thereof—in theatre post 1942.[73] From February to June 2022, performance artist Amanda Coogan, Dublin Theatre of the Deaf, and SETU Theatre Studies faculty and students collaborated to create *The Possession Project*—'a living installation' inspired by Deevy's *Possession or The Cattle of the Gods*.[74] *The Possession Project* was also performed as a durational, site-responsive, and immersive performance in October 2022 in the Choristers' Hall (Waterford Museum of Treasures) as part of the Imagine Arts Festival.[75] In November 2022, RTÉ aired a documentary entitled *Tribute: The Teresa Deevy Story*, which captured the exploration of Deevy's *Possession* in the context of Coogan's collaboration with Dublin Theatre of the Deaf and SETU.[76]

In 2023, a group called The Elders (facilitated by Michelle Read in collaboration with Andrea Scott of Floating World Productions) presented a rehearsed reading entitled *I am Teresa Deevy*, which staged a dinner party where Deevy meets some of the characters from her plays.[77] In 2025, The Elders produced *The Somewhat Imagined, Partly Historical, True Story of the Forgotten Irish Playwright Teresa Deevy* in the Maureen

---

73 Kirsty Lusk and Willy Maley, 'Drama Out of a Crisis: James Connolly's *Under Which Flag* (1916) and Teresa Deevy's *The Wild Goose* (1936)', *Irish Studies Review*, 30.4 (2022), 453–475; Mária Kurdi, 'Taking the "Black Stick": Ageing Husbands and Fathers in the Plays of J.M. Synge and Teresa Deevy', in *Ageing Masculinities in Irish Literature and Visual Culture*, ed. by Michaela Schrage-Früh and Tony Tracy (New York: Routledge, 2022), pp. 17–32; McCarthy and Kealy, 'Writing from the Margins'.

74 The installation took place as part of Amanda Coogan's residency at Hugh Lane Gallery 14–18 June 2022 during which Coogan invited members of Dublin Theatre of the Deaf (DTD) and students and faculty of SETU to perform with her. For more, see Hugh Lane Gallery, 'Possession', https://hughlane.ie/explore_learn/seamus-nolan-traveller-collection-2/. Filmed versions of Coogan's performance in collaboration with DTD and SETU are available at https://www.youtube.com/watch?v=KXrFOjv-lyA and https://www.youtube.com/watch?v=HnGxl1Uf2rw.

75 *The Possession Project* was staged in the Choristers' Hall, Waterford Medieval Museum on 27 October 2022 as part of the Imagine Arts Festival. For more details, see Clodagh Finn, 'Amanda Coogan: "When I Was Growing Up, We Didn't Sign in Public because It Outed Our family as Different, or Disabled"', *Irish Examiner*, 15 October 2022.

76 Funded by RTÉ, *Tribute: The Teresa Deevy Story* was produced by Bernadine Carraher for Mind the Gap Films for RTÉ, directed by Claire Dix, shot by Andrew Cummins, and edited by Cara Holmes. Claire Dix, *Tribute: The Teresa Deevy Story*, online documentary, RTÉ Player, 10 November 2022.

77 *I am Teresa Deevy* by The Elders, directed by Michelle Read, and produced by Floating World Productions at the Maureen O'Hara Studio, dlr Mill Theatre, Dundrum, Dublin, 2023.

O'Hara Studio, dlr Mill Theatre, Dundrum, Dublin.[78] Recent scholarship, such as Katherine M. Huber's 2024 analysis of *One Look and What It Led To*, argues for reclamation of 'the airwaves as a feminist environment'.[79] Analysing sound elements, sound directions, and silence in *Dignity, Within a Marble City, Going Beyond Alma's Glory*, and *One Look and What It Led To* through feminist, eco-feminist, and media studies lenses, Huber argues that Deevy's use of realism and naturalism exposes the gender hierarchies that limited opportunities for women in Ireland and globally. Also published in 2024, Moonyoung Hong's analysis offers this global connection through a 'transnational feminist reassessment' of women writers including Deevy, Maura Laverty, Kim Ja-rim, and Jeon Ok-joo, all of whose texts expose the patriarchal, capitalist, and post-colonial narratives of modernity and, in Deevy's case, 'the violence [that such narratives] enact on women who are left out of these hegemonic narratives or are positioned to legitimise State and Church ideologies'.[80] Building on *The Possession Project*, Coogan, composer Linda Buckley, Jones, Quigley, and members of Dublin Theatre of the Deaf, and Cork Deaf Community Choir collaborated to create a new opera, *Possession*, intertwining live art, Irish Sign Language, musical composition, and performance in the staging of Deevy's ballet in Cork and Dublin.[81] Dayna Killen's doctoral dissertation of 2024 included analysis of Deevy's life and work, while S.J. De Matteo chose Deevy's later dramatic work as the focus of an M.Litt. thesis also completed that year.[82]

---

78 *The Somewhat Imagined, Partly Historical, True Story of the Forgotten Irish Playwright Teresa Deevy*, directed by Michelle Read, and produced by Floating World Productions at the Maureen O'Hara Studio, dlr Mill Theatre, Dundrum, Dublin, 21 January–1 February 2025.
79 Katherine M. Huber, 'Aural Interruptions: The Politics of Sound in Teresa Deevy's Radio Plays', *Review of Irish Studies in Europe*, 7.1 (2024), 7–23 (p. 21).
80 Moonyoung Hong, 'Women Playwrights at the Crossroads: A Comparative Study of Ireland and Korea in the Mid-Twentieth Century', *Review of Irish Studies in Europe (RISE)*, 7.1 (2024), 77–98 (p. 86).
81 Teresa Deevy's *Possession* was created and directed by Amanda Coogan in collaboration with Lianne Quigley, Alvean Jones, Linda Buckley, Dublin Theatre of the Deaf, and Cork Deaf Community Choir. Creative producer Lynette Moran produced *Possession* at the Project Arts Centre 21–24 February 2024, while Susan Holland produced it at the Granary Theatre for the Cork Midsummer Festival, 21–23 June 2024. *Possession* was funded as part of ART:2023: A Decade of Centenaries Collaboration (the Arts Council and the Department of Tourism, Culture, Arts, Gaeltacht, Sport, and Media).
82 Dayna Killen, '"I Took Up the Inkpot and Flung It at Her": Women Playwrights

Public lectures, talks, workshops, and podcasts over the last decade have considered Deevy's work for, and with, a wider audience, and suggest new directions in Deevy scholarship, some of which are explored in this collection. In 2016, for example, Úna Kealy, Barbara McCormack, and Dayna Killen curated and delivered *A Quiet Subversive*, an exhibition and four-part public lecture series at SETU Waterford Library; it was during this series that new archival material, in the form of Deevy's correspondence with Cheasty, came to light. The Mint Theater has digitally archived much of its production and supporting interpretive work, and Kealy and McCarthy have, since 2015, hosted, curated, and presented public lectures, workshops, and rehearsed readings focusing on Deevy's work.[83] In 2020, Bloom presented a lecture on 'Teresa Deevy and RTÉ: Accessibility on the Airwaves' as part of The Irish Women's Writing Network Lecture Series. In 2022, Kealy, McCarthy, and Jenny O'Connor participated in a d/Deaf-accessible podcast about Deevy, the Lyrical Bodies Project, and their work with Coogan and Dublin Theatre of the Deaf.[84] Also, in 2022, Coogan participated in a podcast

---

and the Domesticated Irish Woman at the Abbey Theatre, 1902–1937' (unpublished doctoral thesis, South East Technological University, 2024); S.J. De Matteo, 'The Theology of Teresa Deevy: Exhuming the Playwright's Life and Later Works' (unpublished M.Litt. thesis, Trinity College Dublin, The University of Dublin, 2024).

83 The Mint Theater's production archive is found at https://minttheater.org/production-archives; for details of dissemination events on Deevy's life and work see Kealy and McCarthy's research profiles at https://research.setu.ie/en/persons/una-kealy and https://research.setu.ie/en/persons/kate-mccarthy, respectively.

84 Rob O'Connor, *9Plus Podcast—Teresa Deevy & Lyrical Bodies project*, Season 2, Episode 3, online video recording, YouTube, 14 November 2022, https://www.youtube.com/watch?v=5G2C4G_rsXo. This podcast provides a captioned video, a video with Irish Sign Language translation, and full text transcript. Fiona Murphy explains that: 'Identity is a fluid concept and a personal choice. Lowercase deaf refers to deafness as a medical condition. It does not indicate the degree of hearing loss an individual may have. Some people with hearing loss may prefer to use the term "hard of hearing". Uppercase Deaf refers to people who identify as culturally Deaf and may use sign language. Given the ongoing suppression of sign-language education, not all Deaf people are fluent signers or even have access to the Deaf community. Again, this word does not indicate the degree of hearing loss an individual may have'. See Fiona Murphy, *The Shape of Sound* (Melbourne: Text Publishing Company, 2021), n.p. Thus, our capitalising of the word 'Deaf' in this chapter recognises Deafness as a social category and Deaf people as a group who share a particular history and culture. In line with Dublin Theatre of the Deaf, the Irish Deaf Society, the Irish Deaf Youth Association, the Centre for Deaf Studies, Trinity College Dublin, and researchers in the field, we capitalise the letter D in the word Deaf, when appropriate, to signal accord with the positive values within

entitled 'Teresa Deevy: The Life and Legacy of an Extraordinary Irish Playwright', discussing her recent work on Deevy's unpublished text, *Possession*.[85]

O'Toole comments that, by Deevy's death in 1963, 'she had fallen into obscurity, and it would be many decades before she would be written back into the story of Irish theatre'.[86] Arguably, the productions, events, media transmissions, and scholarship recounted here suggest that Deevy's work has found a place in that story, and her legacy is finding consistency with expectations for her dramatic legacy as it was predicted by Augusta Gregory and Lennox Robinson in 1931.[87] However, rather than writing Deevy 'back into the story of Irish theatre' through reclaiming her legacy, we must, through practice and scholarship, change 'how the story of Irish theatre has been told', acknowledging that the accepted story, and its accompanying canon, is gendered, exclusionary, and 'dominated by major institutions and figures'.[88] Accepting the rejection of Deevy's new work by the Abbey,

---

the Deaf community and Deaf culture. We use a lowercase d when referring to audiological status. When we determine that the reference is to both audiological status and Deaf culture, we use the term d/Deaf. For more on d/Deaf, see the entry on 'Deaf, deaf', in the Centre for Integration and Improvement of Journalism, *The Diversity Style Guide* (2024).

85 The Women's Podcast, *Teresa Deevy: The Life and Legacy of an Extraordinary Playwright*, podcast, 10 November 2022, https://www.irishtimes.com/podcasts/the-womens-podcast/teresa-deevy-the-life-and-legacy-of-an-extraordinary-irish-playwright/; Deevy's text exists in two copies in the Teresa Deevy Archive, MS PP6158 and PP6156. The title of MS PP6158 (for which there is no title page) reads: 'Ballet. 'Cattle of the Gods' (from 'Cattle Raid of Cooley' as told by Eleanor Hull.)'. In a handwritten note, Deevy has added underneath '("Possession—desire for it causes all trouble)' [sic]. MSPP6156 (which includes a title page) reads as follows: 'Ballet. "Possession" or "Cattle of the Gods." (from "Cattle Raid of Cooley" as told by Eleanor Hull.)'.

86 O'Toole, '1936: *Katie Roche*', p. 63.

87 Augusta Gregory, noting Lennox Robinson's report of the popularity of Deevy's *Reapers*, in language laden with intersecting discriminations, anticipates Deevy's continued success, writing: 'She [Deevy] is entirely deaf & writes the most naturalistic dialogue in the world. Strange if our two most popular playwrights should prove to be a deaf woman & a cripple in County Antrim!'. See Augusta Gregory, *Lady Gregory's Journals, vol. II, Books Thirty to Forty-four: 21 February 1925–9 May*, ed. by Daniel Murphy (New York: Oxford University Press, 1987) [Gerrard's Cross: Colin Smythe].

88 O'Toole, '1936: *Katie Roche*', p. 63; Cathy Leeney, 'Women and Irish Theatre before 1960', in *The Oxford Handbook of Modern Irish Theatre*, ed. by Nicholas Grene and Chris Morash (Oxford: Oxford University Press, 2016), pp. 269–285 (p. 269); Barry Houlihan, 'Introduction: The Potential of the Archive', in *Navigating Ireland's Theatre*

or the Gate, for example, as reasons which quashed or diminished her ambition for theatrical production of her own work belies Deevy's active pursuit of multiple creative opportunities. Acts of recovery will continue as practice and scholarship engage with Deevy and her work in different contexts as outlined above and, hopefully, new archival material will come to light. However, as Leeney argues, the 'integration of this recovery into canonical judgement' proves 'more problematic', requiring 'disruption [...] and reassessment', not only of the canon but, 'of how Irish theatre has operated, has energized or stultified the fluid thing that is the nation'.[89]

Analysing Deevy's work through scholarship and production histories is important and ongoing work, but to fully acknowledge her creative oeuvre we must 'recalibrate' the canon and, as Sihra argues, 'tilt the very angles of theatre history itself in order to reveal new spectrums of meaning-making in which women's creative power is fundamental'.[90] In offering counter-narratives, which recover and 'reveal[ing] the lost contributions', scholarship and practice can disrupt the story by making this creative power tangible.[91] In tilting the canon and, by extension, practice, the industry, and scholarship, we disrupt, reassess, and create, as Deevy once suggested, 'an opening elsewhere'.[92] For Deevy, such openings allowed her work to 'span[s] media (theatre, radio, and television) and a range of theatrical styles' from the 1920s onwards, thus evidencing her tenacity in seeking out diverse production opportunities

---

Archive: Theory, Practice, and Performance, ed. by Barry Houlihan (Bristol: Peter Lang, 2019), pp. 9–27 (p. 12 and p. 17).

89   Leeney, 'Women and Irish Theatre', p. 269.
90   Melissa Sihra, 'Coda—Spinning Gold: Threads of Augusta Gregory and Marina Carr', in *The Golden Thread: Irish Women Playwrights, 1716–2016*, 2 vols, ed. by David Clare, Fiona McDonagh, and Justine Nakase (Liverpool: Liverpool University Press, 2021), II, 221–240 (p. 221).
91   Drawing on performance, scholarship, and archive materials, Elizabeth Brewer Redwine applies an intersectional analysis of gender and class to 'reveal[ing] the lost contributions of female performers', thus countering 'the story of authoritative texts at the Abbey'. See Elizabeth Brewer Redwine, 'Introduction', in *Gender, Performance, and Authorship at the Abbey Theatre* (Oxford: Oxford University Press, 2021), pp. xiii–xxvii (p. xvi and p. xxi).
92   The quotation is taken from an undated letter fragment sent by Deevy to Florence Hackett catalogued within the Hackett Archive alongside two other pages of a separate and complete letter itemised as number '33' within the Florence Hackett Archive, Trinity College Dublin, MS 10722.

as creative people are wont to do.[93]

Active Speech: Critical Perspectives on Teresa Deevy brings production histories, practice, scholarship, and the archive into dialogue, offering a more nuanced and three-dimensional understanding of Deevy's creative legacy at this moment in time.[94] This collection is the result of the Active Speech: Sharing Scholarship on Teresa Deevy conference convened in Waterford in 2020. Participants were invited to contribute papers considering: Deevy's work in its historical context; how her work has been translated from dramatic to theatrical texts or radio productions; the nuances of her dramatic vision; her dramaturgical style; her work in other literary genres; and incomplete works. Participants were also invited to consider Deevy's work using a variety of theoretical lenses, to analyse the ways that Deevy's work is shared through public and private archival holdings, and to challenge the ways that Deevy's work is interpreted, taught, translated, or adapted. The response to the invitation posed by the Active Speech conference, and this subsequent edited collection, was richly varied and this resulting collection contributes to the developing narrative of how Irish women playwrights interrogate and expose inequities and challenges presented by dominant and/ or prevailing social, cultural, political, and canonical hierarchies and ideological norms. Inevitably, however, gaps in scholarship remain and we acknowledge that important additional work remains outstanding, most particularly in the domain of reading Deevy's work through the lens of disability studies; a greater diversity of voices and approaches to disability presents a particularly rich and valuable focus for future Deevy scholarship. Additionally, the activity of amateur dramatic companies in relation to Deevy's work merits analysis. The scope for future research into Deevy's work remains richly diverse.

This volume contributes to the efforts of practitioners and scholars previously mentioned to recalibrate the canon by including essays and transcribed interviews that: reflect on the importance of considering

---

93 Leeney, 'Women and Irish Theatre', p. 282. In 1939, the BBC transmitted two live studio productions—*The King of Spain's Daughter* (Saturday, 25 February) and *In Search of Valour* (Wednesday, 28 June), both were produced by Denis Johnston; unfortunately, 'no archival copy is known to exist'.

94 The collection is the result of the Active Speech: Sharing Scholarship on Teresa Deevy project, which espoused an education-focused, collaborative, and inclusive ethos from the initial call for conference papers in 2020 to this open access publication.

how archival documents and special collections inform and challenge traditional theatre scholarship and previously-held conceptions about Deevy and her work; analyse how Irish society and, thus, the nation was (and is) shaped and directed by prevailing beliefs, mores, and ideologies within the first half of the twentieth century; broaden the field's understanding of Deevy's dramaturgy, theatrical aesthetic, and productions of her work; and interrogate and critique the work of d/Deaf, deafened, hard-of-hearing, and hearing theatremakers. As an open access publication, the collection challenges how knowledge in the field is, predominantly, communicated. Democratising knowledge in sharing it more openly, in a diversity of ways, is an essential activity in canon recalibration. *Active Speech: Critical Perspectives on Teresa Deevy* provides an accessible collection of critical analysis of Deevy's work to encourage further scholarship, practical interpretation, and critical engagement with her work, and supports educators, theatremakers, and researchers in recognising the significance of Deevy's work as 'intrinsic' to Irish drama, theatre, and performance.[95]

Authors and Chapters

This volume is structured along four thematic strands: Access and Archives; Deevy's Ireland: A Country in Context; Dramaturgy, Genre, and Theory; and Productions and Practitioners. We gratefully acknowledge the work undertaken by the section editors for their work in supporting the editorial process across these sections: Úna Kealy, Ciara L. Murphy, Shonagh Hill, and José Francisco Fernández.

Access and Archives

The chapters contained within the section 'Access and Archives' analyse the ways that Deevy's work is shared through public and private archival holdings and challenge the ways that Deevy's private and public

---

95 Sihra, 'Coda', p. 221. We are ever grateful to our collaborator, Hugh Murphy, Deputy University Librarian, Maynooth University, who encouraged us to publish with an open access publishing company. The open access nature of the publication aligns with the generosity of Maynooth University Library in making a wide range of archival materials in the *Teresa Deevy Archive* accessible to the public.

writings are accessed, interpreted, taught, or adapted. Eileen Kearney's chronicle of, and reflection on, her research into Deevy's life and work during the early 1980s opens the collection and exemplifies how tenacity can create a trail that leads to the important discovery and recovery of neglected work. The testament that Kearney eloquently pays to the friendship, generosity, and collegiality of Seán Dunne and his family brings to the fore the value of research collaboration and conveys the energy, dynamism, and undaunted persistence that is also characteristic of Deevy's attitude towards her work and her friendships. The result is an essay that negotiates the liminal space between academic formality, intellectual rigour, and accessibility.

Hugh Murphy's chapter contextualises the Teresa Deevy Archive within the curatorial holding and special collections of Maynooth University Library (MUL) analysing how Deevy's archive is positioned within a collections management policy that has evolved, since the 1970s, to focus on figures who considered themselves, or were considered by others, as outside the parameters of the powerful or the popular. Documenting how MUL's collections reflect curatorial biases over the institution's history, Murphy considers the practical and ethical challenges and benefits of devising a collections management policy that is driven by an institutional commitment towards increasing social justice. Contextualising the Teresa Deevy Archive alongside those of Irish poet, translator, and broadcaster Pearse Hutchinson (1927–2012), and writer and activist Ken Saro-Wiwa (1941–1995), the chapter considers how the role of the curator, the act of curatorship, and the power of representation impacts the ways in which a collection is framed and accessed. Murphy's analysis of MUL's commitment to destabilising and deconstructing the boundary walls that restrict access to archival collections through open access is both instructive and inspirational.

Shelley Troupe opens a Theatre Studies Investigation assembling pieces of the incomplete picture of the surviving textual and production evidence of Deevy's [*The*] *Reapers*—which premiered at the Abbey on 18 March 1930, providing insight into the challenges and imagined possibilities of text recovery. In the absence of a script to analyse, Troupe draws on theatre reviews, scholarship, production images located in newspaper archives, W.B. Yeats' feedback to Deevy, and the original Abbey Theatre production programme to: highlight inconsistencies with the play's title; support her conjectures on the plot and thematic concerns of the play; identify influences in Deevy's work; and question the production practices at the Abbey at that time. At its conclusion, the essay reveals how new archival material—or considering material anew—can bring the pieces of the jigsaw a little closer together.

Caoilfhionn Ní Bheacháin Mitchell's focus is the provenance and dating of the plays *Practice and Precept, Let Us Live,* and *The Firstborn,* currently conserved within the Teresa Deevy Archive in Maynooth University and listed as documents possibly authored by Deevy between 1914 and 1919. The essay also considers the contents of the Teresa Deevy Archive as a means to reflect, more generally, on women's literary archives. The essay creates a compelling argument that the named plays are incorrectly dated within the Teresa Deevy Archive. The plays are briefly introduced and compared to works known to have been authored by Deevy. Analysis of possible authorship forms the core of the essay and the voyage of discovery into a suite of plays that have never before received any critical attention and this, in tandem with Ní Bheacháin Mitchell's dogged determination to shed light on this literary mystery, makes for excellent reading. The meticulous nature of the analysis in relation to the plays' provenance provides an exemplar of analysis. The revelation of documents found towards the end of the research journey makes for an exciting plot twist and demonstrates the unpredictable nature of archival research.

Deevy's Ireland: A Country in Context

The chapters in this section consider the social and cultural context of Deevy's life and writing and include chapters considering censorship and/or resistance to censorship by Irish artists; comparative analysis of Deevy's work with other playwrights and theatremakers; and the position of Deevy's work within the canon of Irish dramatic literature that emerged during the twentieth century. Chris Morash explores Deevy's theatrical aesthetic, arguing that it is founded on the interplay of atmosphere and light and splintered syntax and silences all of which suggest that 'some other meaning' is at work. The analysis of moments of exultation in *In the Cellar of My Friend, The King of Spain's Daughter, Katie Roche, Wife to James Whelan,* and *Port of Refuge* explores how, at critical moments, Deevy's characters renounce possession of their material wants and their desires, which allows them to immerse themselves in the phenomenological world. This analysis leads Morash to explore how Deevy opposes dogmatic Catholicism with Catholic mysticism in her work. He also identifies a tendency by scholars to foreground Deevy as a deafened writer, playwright, and woman, but not focus on her religious identity. Morash explores how Deevy's Catholic mysticism informs her theatrical aesthetic arguing that *Supreme Dominion, In the Cellar of My Friend, One Look and What It Led To*, and *Light Falling* pivot on 'incommunicable' and 'private' moments and that analysis of these moments, informed by an appreciation of the 'dark matter' of Deevy's dramaturgy, offers a rich avenue for further research.

Úna Kealy and Kate McCarthy argue that, before the Abbey's rejection of *Wife to James Whelan*, Deevy was interested in radio as a medium for her work and sought out production opportunities outside the Abbey and internationally. The essay contextualises the evolution and dynamism of studio theatre practice in Dublin the 1940s and 1950s, drawing on Deevy's correspondence with Florence Hackett and James Cheasty, evidencing these decades as a period of creative opportunity for, and endeavour by, Deevy within a vibrant network of studio and amateur drama and theatre practice. Analysis considers Deevy's ambition for her theatre work outside the Abbey Theatre and expands scholarship outwards from select institutions and literary texts which are, in the main, the focus of Irish theatre scholarship of that period. Kealy and McCarthy's analysis of Deevy's correspondence reveals her interaction with theatre practice and the industry at that time as complex and varied, and evidences an entrepreneurial playwright intent on creating opportunities for her work regionally, nationally, and internationally.

Willy Maley considers whether in Annie Kinsella, in *The King of Spain's Daughter*, Deevy creates a character who talks back against patriarchal values, or whether Annie is 'another victim of male violence wishing fatalistically for more'.[96] Maley considers the play's ending as a point of departure, comparing Annie with James Joyce's Eveline and Synge's Pegeen Mike who remain stranded and in anguish as

---

96 See Chapter 7 (p. 155) in this volume.

their stories come to a close. In developing the argument of 'talking back', Maley explores how Deevy challenges the limited choices, i.e., domestic service, emigration, and cultural isolation, available to young Irish women in the 1930s, leaving the audience to question Annie's choice at the end of *The King of Spain's Daughter*.[97] The interpretation of Annie's challenge to Jim, at the discovery of his plans for Molly and Dot; the focus on how Deevy's characters acknowledge sisterhood; and the comparisons to Joyce's 'Eveline' contribute an original and nuanced reading of Deevy's text.

Dramaturgy, Genre, and Theory

Chapters within this section interrogate the nuances of Deevy's dramatic vision and how she experimented with naturalism, realism, symbolism, and expressionism. Ann M. Shanahan's chapter offers an exploration and analysis of some of Deevy's texts with, through, and in relation to the body. Shanahan interprets Deevy's texts through her own lived experience and the materiality of her own body, arguing that the material world is a key aspect of Deevy's dramaturgy. Shanahan argues that Deevy's dramaturgy is a connective dramaturgy, which uses material aspects of theatre production, i.e., actors' bodies, theatre space, and stage properties that simultaneously model and mirror humankind's struggle to communicate, express the inexpressible, and connect. Shanahan contends that Deevy's dramaturgy evokes and invokes physical and emotional experiences and that, at key moments, Deevy uses certain characters as a meta-audience as a means of underlining what has taken place. In analysing Deevy's use of liminal spaces and material objects, Shanahan argues that Deevy's dramaturgy is designed to move characters towards communication and epiphany.

In their chapter focusing on *Katie Roche*, Dayna Killen and Úna Kealy read that play as Teresa Deevy's critique of idealised representations of Irish womanhood, in particular, the hegemonic, ideologically inflected representation that they define as the 'domesticated Irish woman'.[98] Defining the domesticated Irish woman as an idealised representation,

---

97 bell hooks, 'Talking Back', *Discourse: Journal for Theoretical Studies in Media and Culture*, 8 (1986–1987), 123–128 (p. 123).
98 See Chapter 9 (p. 201) in this volume.

which formed, and into which Irish women were pressed, during the first half of the twentieth century, Killen and Kealy consider the influences and ideologies that underpinned and shaped representations of Irish women during the early decades of the twentieth century. Synthesising the work of gender constructivist theorists, Simone de Beauvoir and Judith Butler, with Michel Foucault's discussion of how individuals are shaped into docile bodies, Killen and Kealy argue that, in *Katie Roche*, Deevy deploys space, characters' physicality, and language (within her dialogue and stage directions) to deconstruct and interrogate a developmental process whereby young women and girls in Ireland, during the early decades of twentieth century, were shaped into idealised representations of Irish womanhood.

Christa de Brún's chapter draws on the concept of the widow as a liminal figure and considers *Wife to James Whelan* as a commentary that makes visible the ideological apparatus and institutional oppression of women in 1930s Ireland. In arguing that the cultural history of widowhood in Ireland has been 'largely hidden from public knowledge', and using *Wife to James Whelan* to explore the widow as a liminal figure, de Brún presents a stimulating discussion that connects with major themes within Deevy's oeuvre.[99] Arguing that the association of women's activities, roles, and identities within domestic spaces was central within ideological narratives in mid-twentieth century Ireland, and drawing on the idea of widowhood as a social death and Victor Turner's concept of threshold people, de Brún reads Nan McClinsey, in her widowhood, as a threshold figure suspended within a liminal state of economic precarity, but also argues that Nan's liminal state offers her opportunities to renegotiate her identity and engage with the world in spaces other than the domestic. De Brún argues that widow characters, such as Deevy's Nan, expose a patriarchal status quo that is materially and ideologically flawed.

Productions and Practitioners

This final section analyses how examples of Irish and international productions of Deevy's dramatic work have been translated from

---

99 See Chapter 10 (p. 227) in this volume.

dramatic to theatrical and performance texts. Chapters in this section also include edited and transcribed interviews, which offer practitioner reflections on producing, performing, and adapting Deevy's work. Cathy Leeney's essay provides an overview of the historical context of *Katie Roche*, followed by analysis of two productions of the play staged in 1994 and 2017. Arguing for *Katie Roche* as a text worthy of contemporary revival and for the continuing relevance and imaginative revival of plays located within a specific historical context, Leeney analyses *Katie Roche* as a complex and layered text in terms of theatre genres, as well as a text containing a valuable record of the conditions experienced by some Irish women in the 1930s. Leeney argues for, what she describes as, Deevy's layered and 'kaleidoscopic'[100] dramaturgy with its dissonances of genre and stylistic complexity before analysing how these dissonances were realised in productions directed by Judy Friel in 1994 and Caroline Byrne in 2017, both produced by the Abbey Theatre. Leeney develops existing scholarly work to analyse: Deevy's complex dramaturgical style; productions of Deevy's work; and the value of interpreting and reinterpreting plays to enhance 'the liveliness, flexibility, and renewal of the Irish theatrical canon', reminding us that challenging moments of maturation, as they are experienced by Deevy's girls and young women, continue to resonate with contemporary women and girls.[101]

The final contributions within *Active Speech: Critical Perspectives on Teresa Deevy* are transcripts of two conference panels, which took place online, via Zoom, in December 2020 as part of Active Speech: Sharing Scholarship on Teresa Deevy conference. In recasting a live, online conversation as prose, some parts of the discussions are edited and adapted from the original transcriptions; square brackets denote editor insertions to support ease of reading. Captioned and Irish Sign Language (ISL) translated recordings of the original panel discussions are available.[102] In Chapter 12's transcript, Jonathan Bank, Caroline Byrne, Amanda Coogan, and Lianne Quigley discuss how they first encountered Deevy's work and share their unique approaches to working

---

100 See Chapter 11 (p. 243) in this volume.
101 See Chapter 11 (p. 243) in this volume.
102 *Practitioners' Panel*, online video recording, YouTube, 10 December 2020, https://youtu.be/fSX7FqOVFXk and *Practitioners' Panel: Talk Real Fine, Just Like a Lady*, online video recording, YouTube, 12 February 2021, https://www.youtube.com/watch?v=EIRLkX_95R8&t=35s

with her texts from their perspectives as directors, performance artists, and performers. Having worked with several of Deevy's texts and co-edited *Teresa Deevy Reclaimed*, volumes one and two, Bank discusses his directorial choices, which allowed the Mint Theater team (New York) to explore the contradictions within Deevy's characters. With reference to *Talk Real Fine, Just Like a Lady* (2017), Quigley and Coogan consider the Dublin Theatre of the Deaf's (DTD) embodied response to *The King of Spain's Daughter*. Incorporating women's sign—a distinctive version of Irish Sign Language (ISL)—DTD, with Coogan, aligned the lived experiences of Deaf women in Ireland with the system of oppression that Deevy explores in the text. This production also celebrated ISL and contributed to the successful campaign for its recognition as one of Ireland's official languages. Also informed by Deevy's visual language, Byrne discusses her approach to *Katie Roche*, one which illuminated the expressionist qualities of that text. In so doing, Byrne's production foregrounded Katie as an artist who is, ultimately, confined by her gender and class.

In Chapter 13's transcript, Amanda Coogan, Alvean Jones, and Lianne Quigley discuss the importance of Deevy as a deafened artist. In articulating their process and its inclusive performance design for d/Deaf, hard-of-hearing, and hearing audiences, they explain how Deevy inspires them to create new work that foregrounds the lived experience of d/Deaf people. The discussion contextualises the system of education for deaf children in Ireland in the twentieth century, focusing on the injustices and trauma experienced by deaf children who were segregated and then categorised into different groups depending on their level of vocal acquisition. Coogan, Jones, and Quigley explore the rationale for, and process of, creating an immersive performance with members of DTD, a performance which responded to these injustices in embodying and celebrating women's sign. In casting the audience as the outsider in a theatre environment where Deaf experience and women's sign were dominant, *Talk Real Fine, Just Like a Lady* made the hidden histories of the Deaf community visible. As Ireland's national theatre, Coogan, Jones, and Quigley acknowledge the Abbey Theatre's support for ISL work, demonstrating the importance of inclusive, funded theatre spaces to communities. The production and discussion serve as reminders of the importance of bearing witness to human rights injustices and celebrates the joy in working collectively, through the arts, towards a more inclusive and hopeful future.

As we planned the Active Speech conference and imagined this collection, we were reading Deevy's personal copy of St John Ervine's *How to Write a Play*.[103] Inscribed with Teresa's name and glossed in her hand—reading it was like finding a window into her thoughts on playwrighting. Noting passages of interest, marking sections in the margins, and creating a list of notable paragraphs on the title page for ease of reference, Deevy was an engaged and opinionated reader who did not always agree with Ervine. For example, after he criticised J.M. Synge's dialogue in *Riders to the Sea* as 'contrived stuff [...] after a time, tiresome and tedious', Deevy expostulates: 'Rot! This is all wrong'.[104] A little later, in response to Ervine's assertion that Synge's 'highly contrived language' was 'entirely unrepresentative of the speech that Maurya was likely to use', she writes simply 'I dont [sic] agree'.[105] As with any archival research, the process of reading Deevy's comments in Ervine's text was intriguing, instructive, and demanding of measured, critical reflection. Deevy's comments, lists, and glossing in Ervine's text added to what we knew from reading, directing, and performing her work, from experiencing productions and reading the work of critics and scholars who have interpreted her work. Deevy's dramaturgy invites an intensity of linguistic expression, movement, gesture, sound, and setting, which combine to create dramatic action that is, to paraphrase Ervine, unclogged by words. Ervine's advice that 'It is better to be spare than to be tedious' could be taken as Deevy's playwrighting maxim.[106] However, it was these four sentences below, marked by Deevy with vertical and horizontal lines, that caught our attention:

> Action is of several sorts. It may consist of what the people do: it may consist of what they say; it may consist of what they think. There are active words and inactive words, and active thoughts and inactive thoughts, <u>and the activity lies in their power to carry the play forward from one state of being to another</u>. [...] This activity, this movement, this

---

103 St John Ervine, *How to Write a Play* (London: George Allen & Unwin, 1928). We gratefully acknowledge David Clarke for loaning us this copy, which exists within his private collection.
104 Ibid., pp. 20–21.
105 Ibid. p. 22.
106 Ibid. p. 44.

growth is a matter not only of words, but of repeated words. It is the *growing* [...] [italicised emphasis in the original, underlining added by Deevy].[107]

Ervine's emphasis on action and activity caught Deevy's attention and inspired us. From the phrase 'active words' we created 'active speech' which, for us, expresses Deevy's ambition for her dramaturgy. Ervine's assertion that action is contained in a character's thought, speech, and deed spoke to our experience of the careful and nuanced work undertaken by so many theatre practitioners, artists, and researchers who have interpreted the concentrated dynamics of Deevy's work. Our adoption of the word 'speech' is not to prioritise spoken language but an attempt to suggest Deevy's dramaturgy as multi-linguistic, composed of the languages of gesture, scenography, dialogue, and subtext in complex interplay. The phrase 'active speech' felt right as a call to herald our conference and, in the intervening years, as this collection has taken shape, the phrase has come to encapsulate an ambition of our own. It has come to express our contribution to carrying forward, through a variety of actions, the work of those who have already interpreted, produced, animated, and critiqued Deevy' work. Our ambition is that *Active Speech* will support further recognition of the contribution that women have made and continue to make to Irish theatre practice and that this sharing of scholarship will contribute to a growing awareness and appreciation of how diverse people contribute to, enrich, and expand Irish theatre practice and scholarship.

Bibliography

'A New Abbey Play: Miss T. Deevy's "Katie Roche": Interview with the Author', *Irish Times*, 14 March 1936, p. 10, https://repository.dri.ie/catalog/5999vb49s#dri_iiif_view

Bank, Jonathan, John P. Harrington, and Christopher Morash (eds), *Teresa Deevy Reclaimed*, 2 vols (New York: Mint Theater, 2011 and 2017)

---

107 Ibid. p. 98.

Becket, Fiona, 'A Theatrical Matrilineage? Problems of the Familial in the Drama of Teresa Deevy and Marina Carr', in *Ireland in Proximity: History, Gender, Space*, ed. by Scott Brewster, Virginia Crossman, Fiona Becket, and David Alderson (London: Routledge, 1999), pp. 80–108

Brewer Redwine, Elizabeth, *Gender, Performance, and Authorship at the Abbey Theatre* (Oxford: Oxford University Press, 2021), https://doi.org/10.1093/oso/9780192896346.001.0001

Centre for Integration and Improvement of Journalism, *The Diversity Style Guide* (2024), https://www.diversitystyleguide.com/glossary/deaf-deaf/

De Matteo, S.J., 'The Theology of Teresa Deevy: Exhuming the Playwright's Life and Later Works' (unpublished M.Litt. thesis, Trinity College Dublin, The University of Dublin, 2024)

Deevy, Teresa, *The Selected Plays of Teresa Deevy*, ed. by Eibhear Walshe (Cork: Cork University Press, 2003)

Deevy, Teresa, 'Wife to James Whelan: A Play in Three Acts', *Irish University Review*, 25.1 (1995), 29–87

Dix, Claire, *Tribute: The Teresa Deevy Story*, online documentary, RTÉ Player, 10 November 2022, https://www.rte.ie/player/movie/tribute-the-teresa-deevy-story/326740520026

Dunne, Seán, 'Rediscovering Teresa Deevy', *Cork Examiner*, 20 March 1984, p. 10

Dunne, Seán, 'Teresa Deevy, an Introduction', *The Journal of Irish Literature*, 14.2 (1985), 3–15

Ervine, St John G., *John Ferguson: A Play in Four Acts* (New York: Macmillan, 1920), https://archive.org/details/johnfergusonplay00ervi/page/n5/mode/2up

Ervine, St John, *How to Write a Play* (London: George Allen & Unwin, 1928)

Famous Plays 1935–6 (London: Victor Gollancz, 1936)

Finn, Clodagh, 'Amanda Coogan: "When I Was Growing Up, We Didn't Sign in Public because It Outed Our family as Different, or Disabled"', *Irish Examiner*, 15 October 2022, https://www.irishexaminer.com/lifestyle/people/arid-40988102.html

Friel, Judy, 'Rehearsing *Katie Roche*', *Irish University Review*, 25.1 (1995), 117–125

Goldsmith, Oliver, 'Retaliation', in *The Miscellaneous Works of Oliver Goldsmith, M.B. Containing All His Essays and Poems* (London: W. Griffin, 1775), https://www.eighteenthcenturypoetry.org/works/o5346-w0060.shtml

Gregory, Augusta, *Lady Gregory's Journals, vol. II, Books Thirty to Forty-four: 21 February 1925–9 May*, ed. by Daniel Murphy (New York: Oxford University Press, 1987)

Houlihan, Barry, 'Introduction: The Potential of the Archive', in *Navigating Ireland's Theatre Archive: Theory, Practice, and Performance*, ed. by Barry Houlihan (Bristol: Peter Lang, 2019), pp. 9–27, https://doi.org/10.1080/23257962.2019.1702004

Houlihan, Barry, 'Outside the Canon: Theatre, Social Change, and Archival Memory' (unpublished doctoral thesis, National University of Ireland, Galway, 2018)

Hong, Moonyoung, 'Women Playwrights at the Crossroads: A Comparative Study of Ireland and Korea in the Mid-Twentieth Century', *Review of Irish Studies in Europe (RISE)*, 7.1 (2024), 77–98, https://doi.org/10.32803/rise.v7i1.3252

Huber, Katherine M., 'Aural Interruptions: The Politics of Sound in Teresa Deevy's Radio Plays', *Review of Irish Studies in Europe*, 7.1 (2024), 7–23, https://doi.org/10.32803/rise.v7i1.3240

Jordan, John, 'Teresa Deevy: An Introduction', *Irish University Review*, 1.8 (1956), 13–26

Kealy, Úna, 'Resisting Power and Direction: *The King of Spain's Daughter* by Teresa Deevy as a Feminist Call to Action', *Estudios Irlandeses*, 15 (2020), 178–192, https://doi.org/10.24162/EI2020-9406

Kealy, Úna, and Kate McCarthy, 'Shape Shifting the Silence: An Analysis of *Talk Real Fine, Just Like a Lady* (2017) by Amanda Coogan in Collaboration with Dublin Theatre of the Deaf, an Appropriation of Teresa Deevy's *The King of Spain's Daughter* (1935)', in *The Golden Thread: Irish Women Playwrights, 1716–2016*, 2 vols, ed. by David Clare, Fiona McDonagh, and Justine Nakase (Liverpool: Liverpool University Press, 2021), I, 197–210 https://doi.org/10.3828/liverpool/9781800859463.003.0015, https://www.liverpooluniversitypress.co.uk/pb-assets/OA%20chapters/Una%20Kealy%20and%20Kate%20McCarthy%20chapter-1710157142.pdf

Kearney, Eileen, 'Current Women's Voices in the Irish Theatre: New Dramatic Visions', *Colby Quarterly, Contemporary Irish Drama*, 27.4 (1991), 225–232, https://digitalcommons.colby.edu/cgi/viewcontent.cgi?article=2849&context=cq

Kearney, Eileen, 'The Plays of Teresa Deevy: A Checklist', *The Journal of Irish Literature*, 14.2 (1985), 16–17

Kearney, Eileen, 'Teresa Deevy (1894–1963)', in *Irish Playwrights, 1880–1995: A Research and Production Sourcebook*, ed. by Bernice Schrank and William W. Demastes (Westport, CT: Greenwood Press, 1997), pp. 80–92

Kearney, Eileen, 'Teresa Deevy (1894–1963): Ireland's Forgotten Second Lady of the Abbey Theatre' (unpublished doctoral thesis, University of Oregon, 1986)

Kearney, Eileen, 'Teresa Deevy: Ireland's Forgotten Second Lady of the Abbey Theatre', *The Theatre Annual*, 40 (1985), 77–90

Kearney, Eileen, and Charlotte Headrick (eds), *Irish Women Dramatists 1908–2001* (New York: Syracuse University Press, 2014)

Kelly, Marie, School of Music and Theatre, University College Cork (researched and compiled), *Abbey Theatre Research Pack: Teresa Deevy: Katie Roche* (Dublin: The Abbey Theatre, 2017), https://www.abbeytheatre.ie/wp-content/uploads/2017/10/KATIE-ROCHE_RESEARCH-PACK-2017.pdfKillen, Dayna, '"I Took Up the Inkpot and Flung It at Her": Women Playwrights and the Domesticated Irish Woman at the Abbey Theatre, 1902–1937' (unpublished doctoral thesis, South East Technological University, 2024)

Kurdi, Mária, 'Taking the "Black Stick": Ageing Husbands and Fathers in the Plays of J.M. Synge and Teresa Deevy', in *Ageing Masculinities in Irish Literature and Visual Culture*, ed. by Michaela Schrage-Früh and Tony Tracy (New York: Routledge, 2022), pp. 17–32, https://doi.org/10.4324/9781003240532-3

Leeney, Cathy, 'Deevy's Leap: Teresa Deevy Re-Membered in the 1990s', in *The State of Play: Irish Theatre in the 'Nineties*, ed. by Eberhard Bord (Germany: Wissenschaftlicher Verlag Trier, 1996), pp. 39–49

Leeney, Cathy, 'Ireland's "Exiled" Women Playwrights: Teresa Deevy and Marina Carr', in *The Cambridge Companion to Twentieth-Century Irish Drama*, ed. by Shaun Richards (Cambridge: Cambridge University Press, 2004), pp. 150–163, https://doi.org/10.1017/CCOL0521804000

Leeney, Cathy, *Irish Women Playwrights, 1900–1939: Gender and Violence on Stage* (New York: Peter Lang, 2010), https://doi.org/10.3726/978-1-4539-0373-5

Leeney, Cathy, 'Themes of Ritual and Myth in Three Plays by Teresa Deevy', *Irish University Review*, 25.1 (1995), 88–116

Leeney, Cathy, 'Women and Irish Theatre before 1960', in *The Oxford Handbook of Modern Irish Theatre*, ed. by Nicholas Grene and Chris Morash (Oxford: Oxford University Press, 2016), pp. 269–285, https://doi.org/10.1093/oxfordhb/9780198706137.001.0001

Leeney, Cathy, 'Women's Traditions in Theatre, 1920–2015', in *A History of Modern Irish Women's Literature*, ed. by Heather Ingman and Clíona Ó Gallchoir (Cambridge: Cambridge University Press, 2018), pp. 312–333, https://doi.org/10.1017/9781316442999

Lusk, Kirsty, and Willy Maley, 'Drama Out of a Crisis: James Connolly's *Under Which Flag* (1916) and Teresa Deevy's *The Wild Goose* (1936)', *Irish Studies Review*, 30.4 (2022), 453–475, https://doi.org/10.1080/09670882.2022.2127642

Maley, Willy, '"She Done *Coriolanus* at the Convent": Empowerment and Entrapment in Teresa Deevy's *In Search of Valour*', *Irish University Review*, 49.2 (2019), 356–369

McCarthy, Kate, and Úna Kealy, 'Writing from the Margins: Re-framing Teresa Deevy's Archive and Her Correspondence with James Cheasty', *Irish University Review*, 52.2 (2022), 322–340, https://doi.org/10.3366/iur.2022.0570

Meaney, Gerardine, *Gender, Ireland and Cultural Change: Race, Sex and Nation* (London: Routledge, 2011), https://doi.org/10.4324/9780203859582

Morash, Chris, '*Katie Roche* (1936) by Teresa Deevy', in *Fifty Key Irish Plays*, ed. by Shaun Richards (Oxon: Routledge, 2023), pp. 56–60, https://doi.org/10.4324/9781003203216

Murphy, Fiona, *The Shape of Sound* (Melbourne: Text Publishing Company, 2021)

Murray, Christopher, 'The Stifled Voice', *Irish University Review*, 25.1 (1995), 1–10

Murray, Stephan, 'The One-Act Plays of Teresa Deevy', *Irish University Review*, 25.1 (1995), 126–132

'New Play', *Evening Herald*, 5 October 1956, p. 6

National Centre for Disability and Journalism, Arizona State University, *Disability Language Guide* (2021), https://ncdj.org/wp-content/uploads/2021/08/NCDJ-STYLE-GUIDE-EDIT-2021-SILVERMAN.pdf

Ní Bheacháin, Caoilfhionn, '"It Was Then I Knew Life": Political Critique and Moral Debate in Teresa Deevy's *Temporal Powers* (1932)', *Irish University Review*, 50.2 (2020), 337–355, https://doi.org/10.3366/iur.2020.0474

Ní Bheacháin, Caoilfhionn, '"The Seeds beneath the Snow": Resignation and Resistance in Teresa Deevy's *Wife to James Whelan*', in *Irish Women Writers: New Critical Perspectives*, ed. by Elke D'hoker, Raphaël Ingelbien, and Hedwig Schwall (New York: Peter Lang, 2011), pp. 91–110, https://doi.org/10.3726/978-3-0353-0057-4

Ní Bheacháin, Caoilfhionn, 'Sexuality, Marriage and Women's Life Narratives in Teresa Deevy's *A Disciple* (1931), *The King of Spain's Daughter* (1935) and *Katie Roche* (1936)', *Estudios Irlandeses*, 7 (2012), 79–91, https://doi.org/10.24162/ei2012-1903

Ochu, Patience, 'Women in Three Plays by Teresa Deevy' (unpublished master's thesis, University of Ottawa, 1981)

O'Doherty, Martina Ann, 'Deevy: A Bibliography', *Irish University Review*, 25.1 (1995), 163–170

O'Doherty, Martina Ann, 'The Representation of Women in the Plays of Teresa Deevy (1894–1963)' (unpublished MA thesis, National University of Ireland, 1992)

O'Doherty, Martina Ann, 'Teresa Deevy and *Wife to James Whelan*', *Irish University Review*, 25.1 (1995), 25–28

O'Doherty, Martina Ann, 'Teresa Deevy Playwright (1894–1936)', *Decies—The Waterford Archaeological and Historical Society Journal*, 51 (1995), 108–113, https://waterfordlibraries.ie/decies-journal-of-the-waterford-archaeological-and-historical-society/decies-no-51

O'Toole, Fintan, '1936: *Katie Roche*', in *Modern Ireland in 100 Artworks*, ed. by Fintan O'Toole with Catherine Marshall and Eibhear Walshe (Ireland: Royal Irish Academy, 2016), pp. 61–63

Richards, Shaun, '"Suffocated in the Green Flag": The Drama of Teresa Deevy and 1930s Ireland', *Literature & History*, 4.1 (1995), 65–80

Roche, Anthony, *The Irish Dramatic Revival 1899–1939* (Bloomsbury: London, 2015)

Roche, Anthony, 'Woman on the Threshold: J.M. Synge's *The Shadow of the Glen*, Teresa Deevy's *Katie Roche*, and Marina Carr's *The Mai*', *Irish University Review*, 25.1 (1995), 143–162

Romera, Andrés, 'Translation of *The King of Spain's Daughter* (1935), by Teresa Deevy', *Estudios Irlandeses*, 15 (2020), 193–221, https://doi.org/10.24162/EI2020-9413

Ryan, Phyllis, *The Company I Kept* (Dublin: Town House, 1996)

Sahal, Nathamal, *Sixty Years of Realistic Irish Drama* (Bombay: Macmillan, 1971)

Sihra, Melissa, 'Coda—Spinning Gold: Threads of Augusta Gregory and Marina Carr', in *The Golden Thread: Irish Women Playwrights, 1716–2016*, 2 vols, ed. by David Clare, Fiona McDonagh, and Justine Nakase (Liverpool: Liverpool University Press, 2021), II, 221–240

'Studio Theatre Club Success: Fine Production of New Play by Teresa Deevy', *Irish Independent*, 5 October 1956, p. 3

Trinity College Dublin, 'Bringing Unseen Irish Drama to the Digital Airwaves—Prof Chris Morash Curates New Abbey podcast', 2 November 2021, https://www.tcd.ie/news_events/articles/bringing-unseen-irish-drama-to-the-digital-airwaves--prof-chris-morash-curates-new-abbey-podcast/

'Two New Plays', *Evening Herald*, 15 April 1949, p. 5

Walshe, Eibhear, 'Lost Dominions: European Catholicism and Irish Nationalism in the Plays of Teresa Deevy', *Irish University Review*, 25.1 (1995), 133–142

Waters, Maureen, 'Lady Gregory's *Grania*: A Feminist Voice', *Irish University Review*, 25.1 (1995), 11–24

Whittle, Nicholas, 'An Appreciation: Teresa Deevy, Playwright', *Waterford News and Star*, 1 Feb 1963, p. 6

ACCESS AND ARCHIVES

1. 'Why Would Anyone Be Interested in My Old Aunt Teresa?':[1] Illuminating Teresa Deevy's Legacy

Eileen Kearney

In one of my favourite moments from Truman Capote's *Breakfast at Tiffany's*, Holly Golightly, while touching up her makeup in the back seat of a New York City cab, remarks that 'certain shades of limelight wreck a girl's complexion'.[2] It is also true that being relegated to the shadows dims one's reputation. I am thrilled to see Teresa Deevy take centre stage as the star of *Active Speech: Critical Perspectives on Teresa Deevy*, and I am confident her complexion will sustain the bright lights shining upon her now. This collection focuses and adds extra illumination to Deevy's well-deserved limelight.

So many aspects of Teresa Deevy's life, plays, and personal challenges merit focus. In reflecting on her embarrassing lack of recognition, I remember attending a lecture in New York City by Thomas Cahill, author of *How the Irish Saved Civilization*.[3] Citing various examples, he pointed out that although many people believe history is made up of major, huge events and movements, it is actually made up of a sequence of many small events, which interconnect and lead to the

---

1 Interview with Jack Deevy, 1984, as part of my PhD research.
2 Truman Capote, *Breakfast at Tiffany's and Three Stories* (New York: Random House, 1958), p. 81.
3 Book signing lecture at New York City's Upper West Side Barnes and Noble bookstore, 83rd and Broadway, in the autumn of 1995; Cahill was promoting his new book, *How the Irish Saved Civilization: The Untold Story of Ireland's Heroic Role from the Fall of Rome to the Rise of Medieval Europe* (New York: Nan A. Talese, Doubleday, 1995).

major event most people remember. Mulling over his words, I recall the considerable kvetching of my university theatre students about being required to study theatre history. They were often frustrated by the thought of memorising centuries of the who, what, when, and where of theatre history, when in fact the why was always far more interesting. And so, the question of why a playwright as talented as Teresa Deevy was kept for so long in the wings instead of onstage still begs to be addressed.

Having devoted much of the past forty years to writing, publishing, and lecturing about Irish women playwrights in general, and Deevy in particular, I have dreamed of the day when she would become known and recognised among scholars, actors, directors, and readers alike. I chronicle now how I ran across the name of this seemingly obscure 1930s Irish playwright, and how I proceeded to unearth information about her life and works.

As my name might suggest, I have had a life-long fascination with my Irish heritage and, subsequently, with Irish theatre for nearly fifty years. After finishing my undergraduate major in theatre studies in 1971, I made the first of what would evolve into a dozen trips to Ireland. Inspired by an unforgettable visit to the Aran Islands, I became fascinated by J.M. Synge's work there, and in 1976 my Master of Arts degree from the Catholic University of America in Washington, DC focused on Synge and his women characters. After a brief stint of acting in Los Angeles and New York City, naively hoping to take the Broadway stage by storm, I decided to refocus my spotlight on an equally lofty, but perhaps more attainable goal. I embarked upon doctoral studies hoping to discover an Irish woman in theatre who merited serious recognition. But if the woman is not already in the spotlight, how might one find her and bring her out of the shadows?

Flash back with me to the early 1980s when I was a graduate student at the University of Oregon searching for an unexplored dissertation subject that would place an unrecognised, but deserving, woman centre stage in Irish theatre. In October 1983, I unexpectedly discovered Teresa Deevy's name in Micheál Ó hAodha's 1974 book, *Theatre in Ireland*. Near the conclusion of the chapter 'The End of the Beginning', which focused on the Abbey Theatre in the 1930s, two sentences at the bottom of the right-hand page caught my eye:

> After the death of Lady Gregory in 1932, several women dramatists vied for a place in the sun. The most interesting was Teresa Deevy, who, in her one-acter, *The King of Spain's Daughter*, and in her full-length *Katie Roche*, wrote sensitively of wilful and romantic young girls who try to come to grips with the workaday realities of a man's world.[4]

My heart skipped a beat. Who was this woman, and why had I never heard of her? Excitedly, I turned the page, eager to read more about this amazing woman whose name I had never encountered, but I disappointedly discovered that the topic had shifted to Frank O'Connor's Abbey Theatre battles with W.B. Yeats. That was it. I saw nothing more about Deevy, or, for that matter, any of those other women who 'vied for a place in the sun'. Hence began my uphill challenge, pushing the rock, like Sisyphus, trying to find information on women in the shadows of Irish theatre history.

In those early 1980s pre-Google, pre-internet days, I looked in the indexes of every book I could find on Irish theatre, in general, and the Abbey Theatre, in particular, but found no mention of Deevy. With the encouragement of Richard Heinzkill, an enthusiastic reference librarian at the University of Oregon, I also consulted the good old *Reader's Guide to Periodic Literature* and came upon a 1956 journal article by Irish poet and critic John Jordan entitled 'Teresa Deevy: An Introduction'.[5] Next, I found Irish poet James Liddy's entry on Jordan in *The Macmillan Dictionary of Irish Literature*.[6] Then, via the almost bygone phenomenon of 'snail mail', I proceeded to write to Liddy, whose Wisconsin whereabouts my sleuthing skills had unearthed. Liddy kindly wrote back and furnished me with Jordan's Dublin address. In December 1983, I wrote to Jordan, and was delighted to receive his gracious reply two weeks later. Hopeful, I opened the letter only to feel my heart sink with the second sentence:

> Dear Miss Kearney,
>
> Thank you for your letter in re T.D., and your kind words about my article. Alas, I can give you little help. I met T.D. only once, in 1955 or 6. The only friend of hers I ever met was Lennox Robinson, who of

---

4   Micheál Ó hAodha, *Theatre in Ireland* (Oxford: Blackwell, 1974), p. 131.
5   *The Readers' Guide Retrospective: 1890–1982*, ed. by H.W. Wilson; John Jordan, 'Teresa Deevy: An Introduction', *Irish University Review*, 1.8 (1956), 13–26.
6   *The Macmillan Dictionary of Irish Literature*, ed. by Robert Hogan (London: Macmillan, 1980), pp. 317–318.

course was to die in 1958 [....]. Micheál Ó hAodha of the Abbey Theatre may also have memories. But at the moment [...] your safest contact is a young Waterford man who has been researching T.D. on [...] a non-academic basis. He is Seán Dunne [....]. He has been in contact with the Deevy family in Waterford [....]. I will let him know by the same post that I have given you his address. It will be up to him of course to decide how cooperative he can be.

I'm sorry not to have been of more help. I would be very glad to hear of your progress.

Yours sincerely,
John Jordan.[7]

The truth is Jordan helped me immensely by putting me in touch with Seán Dunne, the Waterford-born poet and journalist who resided in Cork: I promptly contacted him. At that time, Dunne was working on an article for the *Cork Examiner* entitled 'Rediscovering Teresa Deevy'.[8] With the most wonderful New Year's wishes, Dunne responded in January 1984 and graciously offered to share his wealth of Teresa Deevy materials. He also opened his family's home to me and offered to arrange meetings with any members of the Deevy family. Ecstatic, I started planning a visit to Cork that summer.

Through the openhearted generosity of Dunne, in the summer of 1984 I was introduced to Jack Deevy, Teresa's nephew who lived at Landscape, the lovely Waterford home in which Deevy grew up. After I answered Jack's bewildered question, 'Why would anyone be interested in my old Aunt Teresa?', he graciously granted me access to all of Deevy's estate papers, a treasure trove of letters, documents, scripts, and reviews that had sat for several decades in a suitcase under a bed at Landscape. Although these five men who sequentially guided me, Heinzkill, Liddy, Jordan, Dunne, and Jack Deevy, have 'gone west', I am forever grateful to them.

Thus began the litany of saints and scholars to whom I wrote, whenever possible, including a self-addressed stamped envelope in order to encourage replies. In addition to contacting Liddy, Jordan, Dunne, and Jack Deevy, I corresponded with notable poets, professors, theatre directors, and biographers, among whom were: Robert Hogan, Mary Rose Callaghan,

---

7   Maynooth, Russell Library (RL), Letter from John Jordan to Eileen Kearney, 28 December 1983. My archive of Deevy-related material is now conserved within the Teresa Deevy Archive, Maynooth University.

8   Seán Dunne, 'Rediscovering Teresa Deevy', *Cork Examiner*, 20 March 1984, p. 10.

Richard Fallis, Maurice Harmon, Frank McEvoy, Michael O'Neill, Garry Hynes, Jack and Noeleen Deevy, Miriam Deevy Clarke, Kevin Whelan (National Library of Ireland), Gerald Dawe, and M.J. Molloy. Armed with my faithful pocket tape recorder, I also pursued and was granted interviews with Jack Deevy (Teresa's nephew) and his wife Noeleen; Miriam Deevy Clarke (Teresa's niece and Jack's sister), her husband, Brendan Clarke, and their son, Peter; John Jordan (Dublin poet and critic); Tomás Mac Anna (director at the Abbey Theatre); Christopher Casson (Dublin actor who reminded me, time and again, that he was actress Sybil Thorndike's son!); Phyllis Doolan (Waterford friend of Teresa's); Colbert Kearney (Professor of Literature at University College Cork); Michael J. O'Neill (Lennox Robinson's biographer); and James Cheasty (contemporary playwright and friend of Teresa's).[9] With each inquiry, I asked for research direction and with each reply, I pursued those suggested avenues, along with the many side streets (and sometimes dead ends) to which they invariably led.

I remind those younger scholars and performers that this research process was incredibly slower and more painstaking than that of today's world: writing letters, mailing them to the other side of the pond with expensive international postage, setting up interviews, and walking through the inimitable Irish mist towards a pay phone box, pockets full of heavy coins and lists of phone numbers. It was a different world and a slower process for sure. I emphasise this to illustrate how far removed this experience was from the instant gratification of the internet: weeks and months would pass before I received responses.

When I reflect on how research is conducted, I am struck by its many similarities to directing a play, another enterprise I have done for decades. The director is best served by a play that speaks to her, with which she can identify, and to which she can sense a true connection; she can thereby cast, rehearse, and produce a finished project that moves its audience and inspires insight. The truth is that the more I gathered information about Teresa Deevy in the early 1980s while researching in her family's house in Waterford, the more I felt connected to her. She was one of thirteen children—I was one of nine. She was, like me, educated in Catholic schools, taught by nuns, and won awards for knowing her catechism so well—I think memorising all those long answers is what made me a quick line study! She was a single woman, working in a male-dominated theatre world in which she succeeded

---

9   Recordings of many of these interviews and documents relating to them are conserved within the Teresa Deevy Archive, Maynooth University.

to a certain degree: I had encountered the challenge presented by a male-dominated world in both the theatre and academia. She was fascinated by language and character development—as an actress, these had always been of top importance to me. And, probably most impressive of all, she wrote and published in spite of developing Ménière's disease, which left her totally deaf—I had endured epilepsy throughout my childhood. In essence, I recognised her struggle, was impressed by her ambition, shared many interests with her, and was inspired by her indomitable spirit. But as I got to know her dramatic works, I gained a deep respect and admiration for her quiet, understated, subtle character development of strong, suppressed women who, more often than not, lived in the shadows of the powerful men surrounding them.

As I continued my correspondence sleuth work, I received one of my most memorable replies from Micheál Ó hAodha, RTÉ Radio producer and Abbey Theatre board member. I had referred to his correspondence with Deevy, which I read in her estate papers in Landscape. He sent me this letter in care of Seán Dunne, who once again had graciously invited me to stay in his family's home in Cork during my second summer of Deevy research in 1985.

Dear Eileen Kearney,

Just as I received your letter, I was putting together a collection of Teresa Deevy's correspondence for the National Library. I have found... letters and 4 pages of a manuscript connected to her play *Supreme Dominion* which cover the period 1947–1963. Some of these are the originals which relate to the correspondence from me which you saw at Landscape.

It occurred to me that you may like to purchase these for your own use [...] and later for sale to the University of Oregon or some such institution. Because of your special interest you can have these all for £250, which is less than the going rate.

If you are interested, let me know when you can call here (I suggest some afternoon). I shall be here for a fortnight at least. My personal recollection will be slight in contrast to the importance of this new source material to which you can have exclusive access.

With best wishes,
Micheál Ó hAodha[10]

---

10 Maynooth, Russell Library (RL), Letter from Micheál Ó hAodha to Eileen Kearney, 10 August 1985).

Remember that, at this point, I was still a financially-challenged graduate student who had become accustomed to the culinary limitations of soup and noodles, which is why the Dunne family's hospitality was so greatly appreciated. After Dunne and I had a good laugh about Ó hAodha's sales tactics and asking price (which was roughly equivalent to $800, or €740, today), I declined to answer the man with the treasure. Some folks just aren't into sharing.

Two of my favourite interviews were conducted with Teresa's niece, Miriam Deevy Clarke, and Teresa's nephew, Jack Deevy. After Teresa's well-deserved success at the Abbey was waning, Miriam came to live with her aunts Tessa (as Teresa was called) and Nell in Dublin from 1942–1948. Miriam recalled her Aunt Tessa wearing unfashionable clothing including 'ghastly frocks and mismatched socks'.[11] In horror, Miriam witnessed Tessa riding her bicycle to meet someone in Grafton Street, oblivious of course to any traffic noises, wearing an old woollen coat that still had the wooden hanger on its back. Miriam also recalled her aunt as often so absorbed in her writing that she would only have toast and tea at mealtimes; she described Teresa as a terrible cook and recalled that 'If Tessa's life depended on her cooking, she would have starved': that fact may explain Teresa's life-long slenderness.[12] Her nephew Jack commented that, although Teresa never smoked, she would occasionally 'take a sherry'.[13] Perhaps these idiosyncratic traits resulted from a sense of being disconnected or shut off from the world. Although Teresa's deafness might be considered a challenge, it may have freed her from external distractions and supported her access to her rich interior world.

I remember a story Jack shared with me about his aunt's early days in Landscape when the family was aided by their live-in nurse-servant, Mary Ryan. The maid's room was above the kitchen, and Deevy family legend has it that the room was only accessible by ladder up to the trapdoor in the ceiling of the kitchen; the ladder was promptly removed after the maid's retirement every night, making it impossible for her to

---

11 Maynooth, Russell Library (RL), the Teresa Deevy Archive, Miriam Deevy Clarke, interview with author, 26 August 1984.
12 RL, Miriam Deevy Clarke, interview with author.
13 Maynooth, Russell Library (RL), the Teresa Deevy Archive, Jack Deevy, interview with author.

escape to see her boyfriend. Perhaps this story inspired some of Deevy's future characterisations of frustrated, confined servant girls. By the time I met Jack and his wife Noeleen, the trapdoor had long since been boarded up.

By now, I am quite familiar with the main events which shaped Deevy's childhood, early education, university years, and adulthood.[14] I recall her Catholic upbringing as the youngest of thirteen children in the comfortable surroundings of Landscape, her love of music and sports in her early education, and her hopes of an Arts degree and teaching. I marvel at her not allowing being deafened by Ménière's disease to hinder her ambition. I admire her steadfast determination to learn lip-reading while living with her sister Josie in London in the last days of the First World War, and I share the interest she took in the lively theatre scene during those years. I appreciate her return to Landscape, where she began her serious playwriting. I applaud the success of her six plays at the Abbey, and her decision to live as a writer in Dublin, where she and her sister Nell, who served as Teresa's interpreter until Nell's death in 1954, lived in Waterloo Road, not far from St Stephen's Green.[15] I imagine, through Miriam's recollections, Tessa and Nell's hosting many gatherings with the best of Dublin's theatrical and cultural circles, where guests included playwrights Lennox Robinson and M.J. Molloy; painters Jack B. Yeats and Patrick Hennessy; violinist William Shanahan; writers David Marcus and Terence Smith; and, actress Ria Mooney. Tessa would lip-read, but Nell would often interpret for her, in a sort of code that had developed between the two and which many of their friends found mystifying.[16] And I mourn Deevy's surprise and hurt from the Abbey's 1942 rejection of her next full-length play, *Wife*

---

14 Eileen Kearney, 'Teresa Deevy (1894–1963): Ireland's Forgotten Second Lady of the Abbey Theatre' (unpublished doctoral thesis, University of Oregon, 1986); Martina Ann O'Doherty, 'Teresa Deevy, Playwright (1894–1963)', *The Waterford Archaeological and Historical Society Journal* (1995), 108–113 (p. 111); Martina Ann O'Doherty, 'Deevy: A Bibliography', *Irish University Review*, 25.1 (1995), 163–170; Cathy Leeney, 'Themes of Ritual and Myth in Three Plays by Teresa Deevy', *Irish University Review*, 25.1 (1995), 88–116 (p. 90); Cathy Leeney, 'Ireland's "Exiled" Women Playwrights: Teresa Deevy and Marina Carr', in *The Cambridge Companion to Twentieth-Century Irish Drama*, ed. by Shaun Richards (Cambridge: Cambridge University Press, 2004), pp. 150–163.
15 Dunne, 'Rediscovering Teresa Deevy', p. 10.
16 Ibid.

to James Whelan, realising that when that theatre rejected her work, she successfully redirected her playwriting muse toward the studio theatre network in Dublin and elsewhere, and continued to give voice to her uniquely complex characters who sought to challenge the prevailing and increasingly State-sponsored conversations.[17] I reflect on her decision, as a single woman without children, to write children's stories, among which was 'Strange People', which appeared alongside two other stories, one by Patricia Lynch and one by Helen Staunton, in a collection entitled *Lisheen at the Valley Farm & Other Stories*.[18] During this time, Deevy also published several essays, short stories, and religious-themed radio scripts in *Irish Writing* magazine, alongside such noted contributors as Liam O'Flaherty, Frank O'Connor, Seán Ó'Faoláin, James Stephens, Patrick Kavanagh, and Myles na gCopaleen.[19] Finally, I recall the irony of her ending. Even though in 1956 she received the distinguished honour of being elected to the Irish Academy of Letters, only seven years later she died alone in a Waterford nursing home, during one of the coldest winters in Ireland's history, two days short of her sixty-ninth birthday.[20]

The Abbey had a complex history of fostering new playwrights and then dropping them once the relationship was no longer fresh.[21] Having enjoyed the limelight for most of the 1930s, Deevy was stunned by the rejection of *Wife to James Whelan* in 1942, a play which John Jordan praises for its 'psychological profundity'.[22] It was later produced on radio by both the BBC and Radio Éireann, and received its first stage

---

17   Kate McCarthy and Úna Kealy, 'Writing from the Margins: Reframing Teresa Deevy's Archive and her Correspondence with James Cheasty c.1952–1962', *Irish University Review*, 52.2 (2022), 322–340; see also Chapter 6 in this volume.
18   Patricia Lynch, Helen Staunton, and Teresa Deevy, *Lisheen at the Valley Farm & Other Stories* (Dublin: Gayfield Press, 1945).
19   David Marcus and Terence Smith (eds), *Irish Writing: The Magazine of Contemporary Irish Literature*, 1 (Cork: Irish Writing, 1946).
20   Dunne, 'Rediscovering Teresa Deevy', p. 10.
21   Besides Deevy, these playwrights included Seán O'Casey, Denis Johnston, and Paul Vincent Carroll. Excellent sources which illuminate this trend include Richard Fallis, *The Irish Renaissance* (Syracuse, NY: Syracuse University Press, 1977); Robert Hogan, *After the Irish Renaissance* (Minneapolis, MN: University of Minnesota Press, 1967); Christopher Fitz-Simon, *The Irish Theatre* (London: Thames, 1983); Hugh Hunt, *The Abbey: Ireland's National Theatre, 1904–1979* (Dublin: Gill, 1979); Frank O'Connor, *A Short History of Irish Literature: A Backward Look* (New York: Capricorn, 1967); Ó hAodha, *Theatre in Ireland*; and, Lennox Robinson, *Ireland's Abbey Theatre: A History 1899–1951* (London: Sidgwick, 1951).
22   Jordan, 'Teresa Deevy', p. 25.

production in Madame Cogley's Studio Theatre Club in Dublin on 4 October 1956.[23] Madame Cogley's production was hailed by critics for its 'sturdy homespun quality'[24] as well as its originality, sensitivity, and character-revealing dialogue.[25] But the Abbey's rejection caused Deevy to change tack, evidenced by Jordan describing Deevy's focus between 1939 and 1949 as on writing and adapting her existing plays for radio.[26] However, although Deevy's works virtually disappeared from the Abbey repertoire in her lifetime, the Abbey's experimental Peacock Theatre did produce her stage play, *Light Falling*, in 1948.[27] On the grand scale, however, it is obvious now that by the 1940s Deevy's heyday at the Abbey was over.

Someone once asked me how the rejection of one play could cause the undoing of a playwright; after all, most writers must deal with rejection. But bearing in mind the Abbey's prestigious distinction as Ireland's prominent national theatre, this was much more than a rejection; it was a divorce. In theatre lighting terms, it was the sudden beginning of a slow 'fade to black'. In examining the post-Abbey correspondence from Teresa Deevy to her friend Florence Hackett, we know Deevy understood that Yeats had never been the biggest fan of her work.[28] In fact, years later, Frank O'Connor, who adored her work, recollected what he caustically termed 'the Yeats repair-and-maintenance service'.[29] In discussing Deevy's work once with Yeats and Lennox Robinson, O'Connor recalled:

> Once when he [Yeats] was grumbling to me against the charming plays of Teresa Deevy and muttering that 'she wouldn't let us rewrite them for her', Robinson said rudely, 'Teresa Deevy rewritten by you would be like Chekhov rewritten by Scribe'.[30]

---

23 BBC radio produced *Wife to James Whelan* in 1946; Radio Éireann produced it on 18 May 1947.
24 'Studio Theatre Club Success: Fine Production of New Play by Teresa Deevy,' *Irish Independent*, 5 October 1956.
25 'Teresa Deevy's New Play,' *Evening Mail*, 5 October 1956.
26 Jordan, 'Teresa Deevy', p. 13.
27 *Light Falling* by Teresa Deevy, directed by Seán Mac Shamhrain (Jack McGowran), and produced by the Abbey Experimental Theatre, Dublin, 25–30 October 1948.
28 Dublin, Eavan Boland Library (EBL), Florence Hackett Collection, Teresa Deevy to Florence Hackett (undated), MS 10722, item 13.
29 Frank O'Connor, *A Short History of Irish Literature: A Backward Look* (New York: Capricorn, 1968), p. 169.
30 Ibid., p. 179.

Ironically, while Yeats was alive, most of Deevy's submitted plays were accepted. Only after his death in 1939 did the Abbey reject her work. The arrival of Ernest Blythe as Managing Director of the Abbey in 1941 redirected the theatre's policies and priorities with the result that the theatre produced work that reflected Blythe's own interests in the promotion of the Irish language in particular.[31] As a centre of artistic innovation and experimentation, the Abbey Theatre did not hold under Blythe's management and Deevy's work suffered as a consequence.[32] As Seán O'Casey would wittily express it, 'The terrible beauty', that was the Abbey, began to 'lose her good looks'.[33]

Deevy was and is universally remembered by those who knew her for her kindness, generosity, and unworldliness. Her Catholicism was deeply rooted, and while she had continually challenged Catholic traditions in her plays of the 1930s, her own faith remained unquestioned. For most of her life, she attended daily Mass, said the rosary, made novenas, and, in her later years especially, made pilgrimages alone to Lourdes (where she volunteered her services by carrying invalids on stretchers), and to Italy in honour of Padre Pio. Her later plays have strictly religious themes, and her estate papers contain cards commemorating different saints. Because Deevy rarely made reference to her deafness in her correspondence, and her friends and family simply referenced it as a fact when they spoke to me in the 1980s, it may be that Deevy made peace with being deaf. It is intriguing and impressive that she progressed as far as she did in an art form, which often begins with written verbal expression and manifests in a theatrical production where the sound of dialogue interspersed with silences is at the very core of the performance. It is through writing that she chose to be heard, albeit with a sense of the detachment created by her deafness. As Dunne speculated, this no doubt opened up dimensions to her as a writer.[34] Her interest in other people inspired her

---

31 Tomás Mac Anna, *Theatre and Nationalism in Twentieth Century Ireland*, ed. by Robert O'Driscoll (Toronto: University of Toronto Press, 1971), p. 100.

32 In analysing the Abbey Theatre minute books, Tricia O'Beirne argues that F.R. Higgins'—Blythe's predecessor—approach to theatre management 'was integral to shaping the plodding artistic policies generally associated with Blythe's subsequent tenure'. See Tricia O'Beirne, '"In a Position to be Treated Roughly"', *New Hibernia Review/Iris Éireannach Nua*, 22.1 (2018), 120–134 (p. 134).

33 Seán O'Casey, *Innisfallen, Fare Thee Well*, in *Autobiographies II* (London: Macmillan, 1980), p. 72.

34 Dunne, 'Rediscovering Teresa Deevy', p. 10.

invention of characters who expressed their conflicting desires through her richly subtextual dialogue. It was her gift in expressing the subtle, often unspoken truths of her characters that invited so many to refer to her as 'the Irish Chekhov'.[35]

In thinking of how far we have come in recognising the work of more women playwrights, I am acutely aware of the vast number to whom we yet owe that duty. In the late 1980s, a few years after I had written about Teresa Deevy, my friend Kathleen Quinn asked the sales assistant in Fred Hanna's flagship bookstore on Nassau Street, opposite Trinity College Dublin, where she could find plays written by Irish women. He led her to a lone volume by Lady Gregory, to which she replied that she meant women *other* than Lady Gregory. He chuckled and dismissively replied, 'Women don't write plays', blatantly embracing the stereotypes and strictures inflicted upon women. His response prompted our grand detective challenge, and in a couple of years Quinn and I had unearthed seventy-five of these playwrights, Deevy of course being one of them, and we knew there were many more to come.[36] This launched the project I started with Quinn, which later evolved into the 2014 annotated anthology, *Irish Women Dramatists 1908–2001*, which I co-edited with Charlotte Headrick, and to which Quinn contributed substantially in its critical introduction.[37]

As we celebrate the current resurgence of scholarly (as well as production) interest in Teresa Deevy, we need to ensure that she holds a permanent place in the limelight rather than hovering in the wings. I am privileged to have laid the groundwork in the 1980s for much of this appreciation, and I applaud the creation of the Teresa Deevy Archive at Maynooth University and the *Active Speech: Critical Perspectives on Teresa Deevy* project through which present and future researchers can continue to honour her legacy.

With gratitude, I reflect once again on the providential sequence of events which guided me forty years ago in learning about Teresa Deevy. I acknowledge again Seán Dunne, without whose introductions I would not have been able to research Deevy, and without whose generosity we might not be experiencing this wonderful research celebration. Had Seán

---

35 Ibid. Abbey director Tomás Mac Anna also expressed this in my interview with him on 24 August 1984. See also Chapter 3 in this volume.
36 Eileen Kearney, 'Current Women's Voices in the Irish Theatre: New Dramatic Visions', *Colby Quarterly* 27.4 (1991), 225–232.
37 *Irish Women Dramatists 1908–2001*, ed. by Eileen Kearney and Charlotte Headrick (Syracuse, NY: Syracuse University Press, 2014).

been a territorial academic, or an author looking to cash in on his research by selling it to an interested but impoverished graduate student, he might not have shared it with me. But Seán was a poet, the kindest of sensitive souls, who gladly shared the wealth of his findings with me. Like Deevy herself, he appreciated the detachment of silence and reflection, and was intensely interested in what made people tick—traits evident in his poetry. May we tread softly on those dreams common to both of them.

Perhaps most important, however, is a renewed commitment and determination to recognise the gifts, the 'many small events' as Cahill articulated, that women have contributed to history.[38] It is no coincidence that Deevy's contributions were shelved for so long. It is no coincidence that several academic presses which focused on Irish Studies in the 1980s and 1990s, including that of my MA alma mater Catholic University, rejected the publication of my revised dissertation, dismissing it as unimportant, echoing Jack Deevy's query of why anyone would ever be interested in this unknown and, therefore, to them, unimportant woman. Driven by the necessity of rectifying this pattern of neglect and exclusion, I continue to champion the vast contribution women have made to theatre, and question the tacit requirements implied for membership in what theorist Annette Kolodny once termed the 'canon of "greats"'.[39] And as for the venerable book sales assistant's questionable comment that 'women don't write plays', let me assure him that 'oh yes they do'!

Bibliography

Cahill, Thomas, *How the Irish Saved Civilization: The Untold Story of Ireland's Heroic Role from the Fall of Rome to the Rise of Medieval Europe* (New York: Nan A. Talese, Doubleday, 1995)

Capote, Truman, *Breakfast at Tiffany's and Three Stories* (New York: Random House, 1958)

Dunne, Seán, 'Rediscovering Teresa Deevy', *Cork Examiner*, 20 March 1984, p. 10

Fallis, Richard, *The Irish Renaissance* (Syracuse, NY: Syracuse University Press, 1977)

---

38 Cahill, *How the Irish Saved Civilization*.
39 Annette Kolodny, 'Dancing through the Minefield: Some Observations on the Theory, Practice, and Politics of a Feminist Literary Criticism', *Feminist Studies*, 6.1 (1980), 1–25 (p. 20).

Fitz-Simon, Christopher, *The Irish Theatre* (London: Thames, 1983)

Hogan, Robert, *After the Irish Renaissance* (Minneapolis, MN: University of Minnesota Press, 1967)

Hogan, Robert (ed.), *The Macmillan Dictionary of Irish Literature* (London: Macmillan, 1980)

Hunt, Hugh, *The Abbey: Ireland's National Theatre, 1904–1979* (Dublin: Gill, 1979)

Jordan, John, 'Teresa Deevy: An Introduction', *Irish University Review*, 1.8 (1956), 13–26

Kearney, Eileen, 'Current Women's Voices in the Irish Theatre: New Dramatic Visions', *Colby Quarterly* 27.4 (1991), 225–232, https://digitalcommons.colby.edu/cgi/viewcontent.cgi?article=2849&context=cq

Kearney, Eileen, 'Teresa Deevy (1894–1963): Ireland's Forgotten Second Lady of the Abbey Theatre' (unpublished doctoral thesis, University of Oregon, 1986)

Kearney, Eileen, and Charlotte Headrick (eds), *Irish Women Dramatists 1908–2001* (Syracuse, NY: Syracuse University Press, 2014)

Kolodny, Annette, 'Dancing through the Minefield: Some Observations on the Theory, Practice, and Politics of a Feminist Literary Criticism', *Feminist Studies*, 6.1 (1980), 1–25, https://doi.org/10.2307/3177648

Leeney, Cathy, 'Ireland's "Exiled" Women Playwrights: Teresa Deevy and Marina Carr', in *The Cambridge Companion to Twentieth-Century Irish Drama*, ed. by Shaun Richards (Cambridge: Cambridge University Press, 2004), pp. 150–163, https://doi.org/10.1017/CCOL0521804000.011

Leeney, Cathy, 'Themes of Ritual and Myth in Three Plays by Teresa Deevy', *Irish University Review*, 25.1 (1995), 88–116

Mac Anna, Tomás, *Theatre and Nationalism in Twentieth Century Ireland*, ed. by Robert O'Driscoll (Toronto: University of Toronto Press, 1971)

Marcus, David, and Terence Smith (eds), *Irish Writing: The Magazine of Contemporary Irish Literature*, 1 (Cork: Irish Writing, 1946)

McCarthy, Kate, and Úna Kealy, 'Writing from the Margins: Reframing Teresa Deevy's Archive and her Correspondence with James Cheasty c.1952–1962', *Irish University Review*, 52.2 (2022), 322–340, https://doi.org/10.3366/iur.2022.0570

O'Beirne, Tricia, '"In a Position to be Treated Roughly"', *New Hibernia Review/Iris Éireannach Nua*, 22.1 (2018), 120–134

O'Casey, Seán, *Autobiographies II* (London: Macmillan, 1980)

O'Connor, Frank, *A Short History of Irish Literature: A Backward Look* (New York: Capricorn, 1967)

O'Doherty, Martina Ann, 'Deevy: A Bibliography', *Irish University Review*, 25.1 (1995), 163–170

O'Doherty, Martina Ann, 'Teresa Deevy, Playwright (1894–1963)', *The Waterford Archaeological and Historical Society Journal* (1995), 108–113, snap. waterfordcoco.ie/collections/ejournals/116768/116768.pdf

Ó hAodha, Micheál, *Theatre in Ireland* (Oxford: Blackwell, 1974)

Robinson, Lennox, *Ireland's Abbey Theatre: A History 1899–1951* (London: Sidgwick, 1951)

'Studio Theatre Club Success: Fine Production of New Play by Teresa Deevy,' *Irish Independent*, 5 October 1956

'Teresa Deevy's New Play,' *Evening Mail*, 5 October 1956

2. The Teresa Deevy Archive and the Development of Collections and Curation in Maynooth University Library

Hugh Murphy

Maynooth University (MU) (formerly National University of Ireland Maynooth) is located twenty kilometres west of Dublin. MU provides library services to over 14,000 students registered in both MU and Saint Patrick's Pontifical University, which was founded in 1795 (with the abolition of anti-Catholic penal legislation) as the headquarters of Ireland's Catholic hierarchy and which is commonly referred to as Saint Patrick's College, Maynooth (SPCM). Library services are housed in the John Paul II Library and the Russell Library with the Russell Library acting as a repository for the historical collections of SPCM. Consequentially, Maynooth University Library (MUL) constitutes a key resource for the history of religion in Ireland. Collections conserved in the Russell Library, some of which date to pre-Christian times, include Mesopotamian tablets, medieval manuscripts, early printed books (the earliest printed in 1468), and works published by leading scholars across Europe from the sixteenth to the mid-nineteenth centuries. However, in recent decades, MUL has developed its curatorial holdings and special collections focusing on figures who positioned themselves, or were positioned by others, as outside the parameters of the powerful or the popular. This central tenet of collection development in both policy and practice has led to the creation of a unique archival collection bringing together individuals whose contributions to social, cultural, and political life both within and beyond Ireland's shores is significant. MUL's collections reflect both personal and institutional curatorial biases revealing the legacy of the institution's history and, following a brief contextualising of MUL and MUL archives and special collections, the chapter discusses the rationale for collecting in this manner, the benefits of open access, and the need to acknowledge curatorial bias in the Library's archival work.

MU has a long-standing commitment to social justice established by the work of MU lecturer Father Michael McGreil in the early 1970s and continuing up to the 2020s, which constitutes an exemplary testament to pioneering sociological research into Irish Traveller and Irish prison communities. MU's Department of Applied Social Studies is the longest established provider of education and training in youth and community work in Ireland and seeks to 'promote human rights, social justice and equality, nationally and internationally'.[1] MU's Department of Adult and Community Education is similarly committed to increasing diversity of educational access for all parts of society.[2] This contemporary focus and commitment to social justice both nationally and internationally is rooted in a tradition of social engagement within SPCM, one example of which was the Maynooth Mission to China in the early twentieth century. The Mission aimed, as *The Irish Monthly* reported in 1920, to 'build churches, chapels and schools, […] provide for the teaching of the orphans, and of the young […] higher education for the sons and daughters of the Chinese: [and] a college for the education of native students who will be the future priests and Bishops of China'.[3] While clear aspects of cultural imperialism are evident in the endeavour, it is also recognised that the Maynooth Mission was notable (and untypical) in its clear focus on humanitarian issues and relief work, rather than 'spiritual salvation'.[4] The long-standing commitment to social justice that informed the fabric of research and public engagement within both SPCM and the National University of Ireland, Maynooth has informed the contemporary ethos and activities of MU and, by extension, MUL.

---

1 Maynooth University, 'Maynooth University Department of Applied Social Studies' (2023).
2 Maynooth University, 'Maynooth University Department of Adult and Community Education' (2023).
3 'The Maynooth Mission to China. Sixteen Priests Leave for China in March. Appeal for Ireland's Help', *The Irish Monthly*, 48.561 (1920), 168–170.
4 Peter Kelly, 'An Misean sa tSín [The China Mission]', *History Ireland*, 25.4.

Bringing Order Out of Chaos: Formulating the MUL Collections Management Policy

Pius Olatunji Olaojo and Modupe Akewukereke note that 'a collection development policy can help bring order out of chaos' and that encapsulating a planned and strategic approach to collection development in a formal collections management policy is critical to focus and articulate intent and drive practice.[5] Typically, libraries utilise three primary methods of acquiring collections: donation, long term loan, and purchase. Each has merit, but each also brings challenges. The challenges of funding have ensured that for most Irish libraries, the words of Peter Fox, who notes that 'for the most part it is not the purchases that have made [the Library of Trinity College Dublin] great, but the donations that it has received', remain true.[6] Purchasing archives and archival documents and/or artefacts depends on the financial capability of an organisation, while donations and loaned items depend on the generosity of donors and a degree of synchronicity between donors' wishes and the role and/or capabilities of the library in question. With limits on purchasing and the unpredictability of loans and donations, a clear institutional view on what a library will purchase and/or accept as donations, or on loan, is key.

Historically, MUL's approach to acquiring and developing archival collections was, though never explicitly stated, guided by an ethos that prioritised historical collections associated with the founding institution of St Patrick's College. This approach to primary sources was complemented by the acquisition of secondary source material, which supported the teaching aims of the various departments previously noted. However, aligning with national and international trends recognising the unique role archival collections play in contributing to 'institutional goals for research, learning and public engagement', MUL focused, from 2010, on acquiring primary source material in support of broader teaching and research needs.[7] Such practice had begun in the

---

5   Pius Olatunji Olaojo and Modupe A. Akewukereke, 'Collection Development Policies: Ground Rules for Planning University Libraries', *Library Philosophy and Practice*, 9.1 (2006).
6   Peter Fox, *Trinity College Library Dublin: A History* (Cambridge: Cambridge University Press, 2014), p. 350.
7   Research Libraries UK based on field work carried out by Alison Cullingford,

early 2000's with MUL's acceptance of the donation of the Denis Faul Collection and the Desmond Forristal Archive. While both collections were small, they represented a departure from previous practice, which had focussed on augmenting the existing institutional archive, accepting donations (typically of theological materials), and acquiring specific antiquarian items.

In 2011, a review of MUL services recommended that a collection development approach be codified resulting in a plan to 'develop, curate and open access to collections that meet and anticipate the needs of the academy'.[8] Creating a collections management policy facilitated, within MUL, a process of critical reflection and strategic development. Formulating the policy involved the library team and stakeholders reflecting on strengths and weaknesses of existing resources informed by a thorough review of library collections and their intended audiences. While it may sound axiomatic for an academic library to consider its purpose in this way, such reflection and professional analysis ultimately allows the distillation of certain themes in librarianship and archival practice into policy and the synthesis of these distillations with university ethos. For example, in Maynooth, these include the need for MUL to reckon with and accommodate themes of social justice, decolonisation, and marginalisation, which had become, and remain, central to teaching and research activity within the MU community.

Devising a collections management policy necessitated reflection on how MUL actioned institutional values such as access to the spaces and resources of the university, how to mitigate against bias and threats to academic freedom in relation to the selection of what archival material to collect and, how collections are framed within MUL curatorial practice. This process of reflection and decision-making emphasised the reality that libraries and archives are not neutral spaces. Randall C. Jimerson's argument regarding the political potency of archival collections whereby 'Archives can serve the interests of entrenched power, but they can also empower the marginalised in society'[9] seems increasingly prescient in

---

Unique and Distinctive Collections: Opportunities for Research Libraries, ed. by Caroline Peach and Mike Mertens (RLUK, 2014), pp. 1–57 (p. 5).

8   Maynooth University Library, *Maynooth University Library Strategic Plan, Ollscoil Mhá Nuad An Leabharlann Plean Straitéiseach 2016–2018* (Maynooth University, 2016), 1–16 (p. 3).

9   Randall Jimerson, *Archivists and the Call for Justice*, webcast, University of British

light of recent trends towards the defunding of libraries in countries such as the United States of America.[10] Collection management policy statements that clearly articulate a commitment to academic freedom as a defence against censorship can, as Peggy Johnson argues, help librarians and universities defend and protect intellectual freedom.[11] More practically, as special collections teams encounter an ever-increasing variety of collection, artefact, and document types, the need for an overarching rationale for what to collect is increasingly important. The act of collecting and making archival documents and artefacts available is an act of proactive engagement that is not neutral. As Terry Cook notes, 'claims for that evidence of impartiality and objectivity, of being a mirror of "Truth" to reveal the past as it really was, must ring hollow at best'.[12] More pragmatically, while it is important that a library collection development strategy aligns with the strategic aims of the broader university, it is also critical that it is created in consultation with and serves the user community. By involving a broad cohort of stakeholders in discussion and review of such policy, MUL can flex what soft power is available to it, to encourage consideration of issues of marginalisation and othering from those who teach and research in MU.

It can be argued that there is an obligation on any institution such as a library to endeavour to collect and represent the full breadth of life, but for an academic library this has to be balanced with the requirement to curate and host collections which have some link to the teaching and research endeavours of the university. In 2016, what began as a collections acquisition practice aligning with established MU and SPCM religious, educational and ethical tradition within MU was codified in the *Maynooth University Library Collection Development Policy 2016–2023*.[13] This policy placed traditional collection strengths in the Humanities, Natural Philosophy and Sacred Music, Philosophy, Theology and Canon Law alongside 'more recent strengths' in

---

    Columbia Library and Archives, 27 January 2010.
10 Madeleine Carlisle, 'Public Libraries Face Threats to Funding and Collections as Book Bans Surge', *Time*, 7 September 2022.
11 Peggy Johnson, *Fundamentals of Collection Development and Management*, 2nd edn (Chicago, IL: ALA, 2005), p. 72.
12 Terry Cook, 'Evidence, Memory, Identity and Community: Four Shifting Archival Paradigms', *Archival Science*, 13 (2013), 95–120.
13 Maynooth University Library, *Maynooth University Library Collection Development Policy 2016–2023* (Maynooth University, 2016).

Sociology and Anthropology.¹⁴ The policy, in support of teaching and research aims and 'informed by the research themes of the University (both distinct and interdisciplinary) and the unique research heritage of both Maynooth institutions', proposed the 'multidisciplinary theme' of 'The Outsider'. The theme of 'The Outsider' encompasses 'figures from various backgrounds, who were either marginalised or viewed as existing on the fringes of contemporary society, but whose impact in areas such as literature, history, or social movements is considerable'.¹⁵ This plan encapsulated current practice and formalised it. Thus, while some of the archives which could be considered 'outsider' had already been acquired, the 2016 collection development policy was the first time MUL articulated its intent to develop archives along this broad theme. Informed by the work of the International Council on Archives Section on Archives and Human Rights, the collection development plan sought to put a clear value on archival documents relating to individuals whose life and work connected with social development and justice.¹⁶

'Outsiders': Pearse Hutchinson, Ken Saro-Wiwa, and Teresa Deevy

While it is important to try to formalise curatorial practice in this regard, the reality is that arriving at a conclusive definition for 'outsiders' is impossible and unhelpful as the term and what it can represent is mutable, inherently contentious, and exclusionary.¹⁷ MUL broadly defines 'outsiders' as individuals of any and all nationalities who, during their lifetime, resisted or dissented from mainstream or popular social or political life and those whose work or social/political contribution was marginalised either during, or after, their lives. MUL's ethos of inclusivity motivated this deliberately broad definition which is also informed by Jimerson's encouragement to attend to 'marginalized voices' and open

---

14   Ibid., p. 5.
15   Ibid., p. 6.
16   For more on the Section on Archives and Human Rights within the International Council on Archives, see International Council on Archives, 'Section on Archives and Human Rights—SAHR' (2023).
17   Niall Lucy observes that 'every community is always a gathering of only some at the exclusion of others'. See Niall Lucy, *A Derrida Dictionary* (Oxford: Blackwell, 2004), p. 164.

'the door to the stranger whose concerns enable us to understand the diversity of society'.[18] Arguably, focusing on those who are, or were, regarded as existing on the margins of society is, as Lisa Stead argues, a form of reclamation and, by securing and curating these collections, MUL provides a platform whereby the life and work of such people is brought to increased critical attention and, as a result, can contribute to a better understanding of societal diversity.[19] It should be noted, however, that given how quickly certain trends emerge, a policy can never fully anticipate developments, or be considered fully responsive. As an example, issues of coloniality in library collections have become prominent in recent years, stimulated, in part, by broader discussions of decolonising the curriculum.[20] Consequently, it is important that any collections management policy links to both an overall library and university strategic plan. Doing so reinforces and strengthens the strategy, embedding it in a broader landscape, but equally making it likely that broader developments will need to be reflected in revisions.

In 2023, MUL archival holdings were increased by four hundred percent and included documents relating to artists and activists who dissented from, or focused their personal and/or professional life and/or work outside of mainstream society, ideology, and/or politics. Important MUL archival holdings now include the archives of Irish poet, translator, and broadcaster Pearse Hutchinson (1927–2012), and writer and activist Ken Saro-Wiwa (1941–1995) acquired by MUL in 2013 and 2011, respectively. Hutchinson's archive references his homosexuality, his experience of living in both Ireland and Spain, his empathy for those who did not conform to contemporary expectations and laws relating to sexual orientation, and documents his activism in relation to social justice, racial oppression, and sexual freedom. The archive of Ken Saro-Wiwa, a member of the Ogoni ethnic group from the Niger Delta region of Nigeria, documents his commitment to exposing corruption and environmental damage, until his execution in 1995. His letters, written during his military detention and smuggled out of prison in breadbaskets, manifest what Verne Harris

---

18   Jimerson, *Archivists*, p. 309.
19   Lisa Stead, 'Introduction', in *The Boundaries of the Literary Archive: Reclamation and Representation*, ed. by Carrie Smith and Lisa Stead (London: Routledge, 2013), pp. 1–14.
20   Elizabeth Charles, 'Decolonizing the Curriculum', *Insights: The UKSG Journal*, 32.24, 1–7 (p. 24).

refers to as the 'ghosts' that change the nature and imperative of archival work for all who conserve, curate, and/or access archives.[21] In 2011, the Teresa Deevy Archive containing manuscripts of stage and radio plays, other literary writings, and correspondence was donated by the Deevy family to MUL.[22] In recent years, there has been productive engagement with academic colleagues, which has led to the addition of more archival material related to Deevy.[23] Harris contends that, in providing access to archives, archival documents, and artefacts, librarians, conservators, and special collections library staff do more than simply 'take responsibility for' archives but, rather, take responsibility 'before them', working so that archives can be made meaningful, respected, remembered, and framed for those who access them.[24] The Teresa Deevy Archive was a foundational pillar in MUL's appreciation of how a collection development policy can both provide direction in ensuring a library has a broad representation in its collections, but also in how to engage with colleagues on campus on such matters, particularly as regards trying to mediate the various diverse views on what a library should collect and why. As an example, when the Teresa Deevy Archive came to Maynooth, it was seen primarily as a literary archive, whereas now it can, quite rightly, be regarded through a lens of inclusion and accessibility also. By securing, conserving, and curating such collections, MUL seeks to make available and contextualise the collections and the life and work of their creators, and facilitate the collections to be accessed, considered, and critiqued by scholars and researchers: as stated above, such a strategy is regarded by MUL as a form of reclamation.

---

21 Verne Harris, 'Antonyms of Our Remembering', *Archival Science*, 14 (2014), 215–229 (p. 218).

22 This donation contains the majority of Deevy-related archival holdings. MUL acknowledges the support of Chris Morash in facilitating the donation of the Teresa Deevy Archive.

23 In MUL, newer Deevy-related archival material is contained in the James Cheasty Archive, which was donated to MUL by the Power family in 2022, and in Eileen Kearney's scholarly archive donated in 2023. MUL acknowledges the involvement of Úna Kealy in facilitating the donation of the Cheasty Archive.

24 Harris, 'Antonyms', p. 218. The full quotation is as follows: 'The ghosts demand that we take responsibility before them. Not responsibility *for* them—responsibility *before* them, in front of them, seeing them, seeing them again, and re-specting them. They demand that we work to make our lives meaningful by working to make their lives meaningful. The work of memory, and the work of archive, in these framings, is about just such a taking of responsibility [emphasis in the original]'.

The Teresa Deevy Archive

Living in the 1930s, a time when Irish society was insular and dominated by the Catholic Church's influence on social values, behaviour and politics, Teresa Deevy—an unmarried woman who was deafened in her early twenties and increasingly faced financial hardship—could be defined as an outsider. Born into a family where education, literature, religion, and politics were valued and actively pursued, and living through the First World War, the 1916 Rising, the Irish War of Independence, and the Irish Civil War, as a young woman, it is perhaps unsurprising that Deevy was inspired to explore and critique Ireland's changing social landscape through literature, drama, and theatre. She began her career writing short stories and one-act plays and, by the mid-1930s, was a successful playwright with a number of plays produced and staged at Dublin's national theatre, the Abbey Theatre. In 1937, the Irish Government revised Ireland's constitution, distilling the nascent State's opinion of women's roles and duties into a reductive Article (41.2.1 and 41.2.2) asserting: 'In particular, the State recognises that by her life within the home, woman gives to the State a support without which the common good cannot be achieved', and 'The State shall, therefore, endeavour to ensure that mothers shall not be obliged by economic necessity to engage in labour to the neglect of their duties in the home'.[25] As Chris Morash has observed, the portrayal of women in Deevy's work stood in contrast to this ideological positioning of women as homemakers located within domestic spaces and, through her work, Deevy challenged and exposed the consequences of such a restrictive view of women's contribution to social and political life.[26]

Deevy's critique was, by the standards of the day, radical.[27] Such criticism was not simply manifest in her literary work as is attested to by a letter to the *Irish Times* dated 20 October 1936, in which she questioned the role and competence of Ireland's censors. Eloquent in its brevity, the

---

[25] Government of Ireland (2023), *Bunreacht Na hÉireann* (Dublin: Government Publications Office, 2003), p. 164. Two constitutional referenda concerning the Family [sic] and care in the Irish Constitution took place on 8 March 2024. The second referendum proposed to delete Article 41.2 and replace it with a new text (Article 42B).

[26] Chris Morash, 'Teresa Deevy—an Introduction', *The Teresa Deevy Archive*.

[27] Ibid.

letter offers a clear rebuke to official Ireland.[28] Under the directorship of Ernest Blythe, the Abbey Theatre, Ireland's national theatre, disinclined to continue staging her plays, a decision that seriously reduced her ability to reach theatre audiences. Although her work continued to be produced in smaller studio theatres, albeit sporadically, she increasingly focussed her dramatic practice on creating radio plays.[29] As many scholars have recounted, subsequent to Deevy's work being rejected by the Abbey post-1940, her creative output changed direction and was less subject to critical attention and analysis. Despite this, Deevy never disappeared from the critical lens and a revival of interest in her work over the last two decades—and the donation, by the Deevy family, of her archive to MU in 2011—has acted as a clear stimulus to theatremakers and academics to explore her work through practice and research.[30]

The act of archiving is partly one of preserving and partly an act of appraisal: deciding *what* to archive is making a determination. Thus, by accepting the donation of the archive of Teresa Deevy, MUL made a decision to add this material to what Rebecca Schneider calls 'privileged remains'.[31] In this context, the decision to purchase, or accept a donated archive, is significant. Put simply, by making such a decision, albeit one that may be guided by a policy and ethos, a library makes a determination on the merit and value of the artefacts and/or documents, a corpus of work, and the status of the person or people who created it. In the case of the Teresa Deevy Archive, acquired as a donation rather than through purchase, there was no immediate financial implication. However, the subsequent cataloguing and outreach has incurred considerable investment. Thus, by agreeing to take custody of her archive, MUL, and MU by extension is, in essence, endorsing the life and work of Teresa Deevy.

Coupled with this is the reality that library resources are limited. The hard reality is that collections reflecting the life or work of canonical figures in any discipline are in great demand and will inevitably end up being

---

28 Teresa Deevy, 'The Censorship', *Irish Times*, 20 October 1936, p. 4.
29 See Chapter 6 in this volume.
30 It is worth noting that Deevy's text, *The King of Spain's Daughter*, is listed as one of the prescribed drama texts on the Junior Cycle English (2024–2026) curriculum. See Department of Education, 'Prescribed Material for Junior Cycle English, Circular Letter: 0014/2022' (2022), https://www.gov.ie/en/circular/65046-prescribed-material-for-junior-cycle-english/
31 Rebecca Schneider, *Performing Remains: Art and War in Times of Theatrical Reenactment* (Abingdon: Routledge, 2011).

acquired by institutions with higher profiles, which are typically more financially well-resourced.[32] This means that, for library management teams, there must be an element of pragmatism when devising a collecting strategy as even a donation brings with it significant cost in terms of staff time and expertise, conservation, and ongoing curatorial overheads.[33] As such, there is a clear obligation on curators to make archives visible and frame their contents. To quote Harris, 'The work of memory, and the work of archive, in these framings, is about just such a taking of responsibility'.[34] Framing the lives of those who have been marginalised is a privilege and a responsibility, particularly as, given financial limitations, when a library chooses to acquire, conserve, and share one archive that choice often involves a decision not to acquire another. Thus, there is always a gain and a sacrifice—and the consequences are lasting as, typically, a collection is unlikely to be curated a second time.

The role of the curator has become contested in recent years with the long-held conviction of the importance of aspiring to neutrality, if not objectivity—or more accurately, perhaps, the longstanding diminution of bias is no longer considered by many to be the *sine qua non*.[35] As suggested by Michelle Carswell and Marika Cifor, the relationship between curator and collection requires recognition that the former has an 'affective responsibility' to the latter.[36] In this theory, the archivist or curator is no longer primarily concerned with the authenticity of the collection (which requires detachment and objectivity), but more invested in the collection and the subjects contained, and is willing to engage with them on a deeply empathetic level, acknowledging that this 'radical empathy' hinges on the personal.[37] Issues of curator bias are deeply challenging and important for the MUL team and, as

---

32 The purchase of some 500 letters between W.B. Yeats and his wife Georgiana Hyde-Lees by the National Library of Ireland for some €750,000 in 2017 is an example of an acquisition which would simply be beyond MUL's financial reach.
33 Chela Scott Weber, Martha O'Hara Conway, Nicholas Martin, Gioia Stevens, and Brigette Kamsler, *Total Cost of Stewardship: Responsible Collection Building in Archives and Special Collections* (Dublin: OCLC Research).
34 Harris, 'Antonyms', p. 218.
35 Hilary Jenkinson, *A Manual of Archive Administration Including the Problems of War Archives and Archive Making* (Oxford: Clarendon Press, 1922).
36 Michelle Carswell and Marika Cifor, 'From Human Rights to Feminist Ethics: Radical Empathy in Archives', *Archivaria*, 81 (2016), 23–43 (p. 24).
37 Ibid., p. 25.

practitioners, there is an increasing awareness that it is incumbent upon us to curate, frame, and represent a collection in ways that make the framing and representation process transparent. Globally, such a dramatic recalibration of practice emerged in relation to human rights collections, initially, and can be seen by some as contentious. There are, however, several salient lessons for a library like MUL, notably the realisation that bias of any form that might have impacted curatorial choices should be acknowledged, that the lived experience of those who created the archives within MUL will differ from those who curate it, and, importantly, that views, opinions, and values expressed within existing and future archives may not chime with the personal beliefs and/or values of a curator. Acknowledgement of this is critical in terms of informing the practice of curation on a day-to-day basis.

The act of curatorship is rooted in power, more specifically the power of representation. As such, it is never neutral. Katie Shilton and Ramesh Srinivasan rightly note that 'through arrangement and description of their acquisitions, archivists impart or relay narratives and knowledge structures to explain the relationships among records in a collection', and acknowledging this is critical in MUL's collection management approach and curatorship.[38] To tease this out further, at a very basic level, the gender of the curator of the Deevy archive *will* affect their engagement with the collection, as will the fact that they will most likely not suffer from Ménière's disease. Understanding and acknowledging differences of historical context and language is becoming increasingly common with many repositories in the United States, Canada, and Australia, in particular, making public statements and investigating ways in which descriptive language (which is heavily standardised to ensure consistency) can be remediated.[39] The first steps for MUL were enacted in a public statement related to 'potentially harmful language in cataloguing and archival description', which commits MUL to continue to eliminate and address harmful language, as well as understanding how particular communities describe themselves, while also acknowledging that:

---

38 Katie Shilton and Ramesh Srinivasan, 'Participatory Appraisal and Arrangement for Multicultural Archival Collections,' *Archivaria*, 63.1 (2007), 87–101 (p. 88).
39 See Sustainable Heritage Network, 'Protocols for Native American Archival Materials with notations by NAAS', March 2019 and Sustainable Heritage Network, 'Protocols for Native American Archival Materials'.

Some of the materials in our holdings contain offensive, derogatory or harmful language. Our archival descriptions also include historical language of their time-periods that by today's standards may be considered racist, sexist, or otherwise harmful to racialised and marginalised populations.[40]

Importantly, the statement acknowledges that 'description is not neutral, nor are the individuals who create it', but, naturally, finding ways to further acknowledge and account for such bias is far more challenging than publishing a statement.[41] An adoption of Caswell and Cifor's approach of 'radical empathy' is compelling, and it could be argued that some small steps have been taken in the case of the Teresa Deevy Archive by close liaison with family and friends, as well as engagement with groups such as the Dublin Theatre of the Deaf, but it has to be acknowledged that this remains an organic rather than an embedded process.[42]

Material Documents within the Teresa Deevy Archive

MUL positions Teresa Deevy within the 'outsider' context, as loosely defined above, a category that incurs the risk of framing her as a subject with limited power or agency. The work by various actors (including MUL) to, as Eileen Kearney says elsewhere in this collection, shine a light on Deevy contributes to a reframing of her artistic and social contribution to Irish life and culture.[43] MUL aspires to continually enhance the conditions whereby archivists and scholars can stand before, respect, remember, and contextualise archives that were created as a result of a commitment to a political or aesthetic project in the conservation and curation work applied to all of the archives in the University's collection, none more so than in the conservation, curatorial, and commitment to access applied to the Teresa Deevy Archive. If, as Barry Houlihan suggests, the theatre archive 'is a social history of modern Ireland', then it follows that understanding the lives of those who may have existed on

---

40 Maynooth University Library, 'Statement on Harmful Language in Catalogue Description' (2023).
41 Ibid.
42 Carswell and Cifor, 'From Human Rights to Feminist Ethics', p. 25.
43 See Chapter 1 in this volume.

the fringes of that social history is critical.[44]

The arrival of Deevy's archive, housed in a battered green suitcase and containing documents dating from the early twentieth century, presented MUL with both an opportunity and a challenge. Modern archives are compellingly resonant, the material within them is often within the lived memory of those who engage with them, which can add an additional dimension to such engagement. Suzanne Keen argues that archives, like important physical sites (such as a birthplace, work or social space, or grave site), are situated: unlike people and events, archives, like physical places, continue to exist within geographical locations through time.[45] Like a birth or death place, archives can be visited and, like geographical spaces, resonate with meaning and atmosphere despite the fact that time, situation, context, and life have passed on and/or the geographical location of an archive may have changed. Geraldine Higgins, building on Keen's work and focusing on the materiality of archives, suggests that archives have a conductive connection to the past, which she terms as the 'frisson of "the real thing" [that is] inherent in the materiality of the manuscripts themselves'.[46] Despite the limitations of access and use, archives offer a degree of resonance not necessarily present in their digital equivalents. Higgins writes of 'the shiver I felt',[47] while Sandra Roff writes of the 'thrill of [historical] discovery' when working with original material documents.[48] This charge, thrill, and sense of discovery and the situatedness of documents and artefacts in their materiality ensures that archives continue to be sought by libraries and scholars. Archives provide that direct connection to the archive creator, the people they knew, and the times and the places they experienced, some, or all, of which have may have passed away, or are otherwise inaccessible. Physically holding Deevy's letters, for example,

---

44 Barry Houlihan, *Theatre and Archival Memory: Irish Drama and Marginalised Histories, 1951–1977* (Hampshire: Palgrave, 2021), p. 26.
45 Suzanne Keen, 'Magical Values in Recent Romances of the Archive', in *Libraries, Literatures and Architects*, ed. by Sas Mays (London: Routledge, 2013), pp. 115–129 (p. 116).
46 Geraldine Higgins, 'The Place of Irish Archives', *Irish University Review*, 52.1 (2022), 9–21 (p. 16).
47 Ibid., p. 9.
48 Sandra Roff, 'Archives, Documents, and Hidden History: A Course to Teach Undergraduates the Thrill of Historical Discovery Real and Virtual', *The History Teacher*, 40.4 (2007), 551–558 (p. 551).

can allow those who read them to travel imaginatively back in time, sit inside her home in Landscape, Waterford City, or at her desk in Waterloo Road, Dublin as she mentors her friend and fellow playwright James Cheasty on writing dialogue.[49] As a counterpoint, however, modern archives are often subject to copyright legislation, which can restrict what is permissible to make publicly available. That frisson facilitating an imagined conduit to the past can be interrupted, muted, or obscured by what must be redacted or withdrawn from public view while family, friends, or associates are still alive.[50] The frisson of archival research into Teresa Deevy can be experienced in MUL not only because MUL holds Deevy's archive but also because, in recent times, MUL has acquired the archives of her friend and mentee, Waterford playwright James Cheasty, which contains the largest known extant collection of correspondence authored by Deevy, and of Eileen Kearney, whose pioneering work and crucial scholarship into Deevy's life and dramaturgy in the 1980s is germinal to Deevy scholarship.

Open Access (OA) to Digitised Documents within the Teresa Deevy Archive

OA promotes active scholarship and active citizenship and plays a role in ensuring equity of access to collections that is particularly advantageous to those in the Global South.[51] Furthermore, the potential to disseminate the work of those considered as having existed, either by accident or choice, on the fringes of their communities is accentuated by the possibilities of OA. MUL seeks to engage beyond the walls

---

49 Deevy's letters to James Cheasty are contained within the Cheasty Archive donated by the Power family to MUL in 2022. For more on this archive, see Kate McCarthy and Úna Kealy, 'Writing from the Margins: Re-framing Teresa Deevy's Archive and Her Correspondence with James Cheasty c.1952–1962, *Irish University Review*, 52.2 (2022), 322–340.

50 In the case of Deevy's archive, all documents that arrived in the green suitcase are available to scholars, however, as McCarthy and Kealy note ('Writing from the Margins'), archival documents relating to Deevy are widely dispersed in several different archival collections.

51 Hugh Murphy, 'Whose Story: Working Towards Diversity in the Maynooth University Library Collections', in *I Am a Man of Peace: Writings Inspired by the Maynooth University Ken Saro-Wiwa Collection*, ed. by Helen Fallon (Quebec: Daraja Press, 2020), pp. 116–122.

of the academy: Belinda Battley's point that 'Archival institutional custody can build boundary walls that communities find opaque or even impenetrable' is apposite, and the potential paradox of a library aspiring to highlight 'outsiders', but only within the university walls, is both counterproductive but, more importantly, deeply hypocritical.[52] Unsurprisingly then, MUL's current collections management policy espouses the merit of OA, and future iterations of the policy will, most likely, further that commitment. As part of MUL's commitment to enabling a deeper access to collections, the Library commissioned three online exhibitions examining Deevy, Hutchinson, and Saro-Wiwa through the lens of equality, diversity, and inclusion, making these archives online and OA, in part. MUL aspires to ensure that, in so far as is possible, the Teresa Deevy Archive is accessible, an aspiration informed by MUL's strategy to endorse the merits of OA, generally, and as it applies to scholarly endeavour. By making Deevy-related material more accessible through digitisation, MUL provides access to her work to a wider and more diverse readership, on a global scale.[53] Ensuring that as much of the Teresa Deevy Archive is openly available is indisputably a good thing, although, as noted earlier, the thrill of engaging with the physical object is removed when the document or artefact is digitally accessed. There is also a tension between simply enabling open digital access via images of documents within Deevy's archive, and offering a platform that is truly accessible to a diverse array of readers, using transcription, text to speech, and Irish Sign Language interpretation, for example. OA has, historically, focused on opening up *content* rather than the media to engage with it and has been found lacking in terms of visually impaired user requirements.[54] However, by having far less rights management, OA content should, in theory, lend itself to being engaged with via assistive technologies that reduce or eliminate barriers to people with disabilities. As noted earlier, a relatively modern collection such as the

---

52 Belinda Battley, 'Archives as Places, Places as Archives: Doors to Privilege, Places of Connection or Haunted Sarcophagi of Crumbling Skeletons?', *Archival Science*, 19 (2019), 1–26 (p. 3).

53 MUL note that, to date, this access has been limited to digitising documents so that they can be accessed visually. There is currently no access to digitised Deevy archival material for those who are visually impaired.

54 Raj Kumar Bhardwaj, 'Availability and Preferences for Information Services to Visually Impaired Tertiary Students in Delhi', *Journal of Enabling Technologies*, 16.1 (2022).

Teresa Deevy Archive is comprehended by copyright legislation, which imposes a certain level of restriction upon access, mainly on what can be reproduced, rather than what can be consulted in person. However, it has been possible to ensure that sizeable parts of the archive, and the scholarship which is emerging from it, are becoming available digitally to a broad cohort, which is a very welcome step.

Conclusion

While librarians and archivists have a key role in sourcing, curating, and opening up archival and special collections, they are not and cannot be alone in these endeavours. In a university environment, the support of academic colleagues is essential. Given the nuances across disciplines represented in archives, the involvement of disciplinary experts adds credibility and greater scope for interpretation of archives and collections. Furthermore, such involvement is central to underpinning these collections in teaching and research. As such, it is essential that communities represented and cross-disciplinary scholars, educators, and practitioners are as involved as possible in collection and curatorial decisions from the outset. In many ways, this is an attainable aim, especially in the case of donations which will often come about as a result of representation from such communities and will often involve in-depth discussions about the collections before agreement to accept and conserve a collection is reached. For material acquired in other ways (such as purchase), things may not always be quite as clear, and it may be that the library must proactively find groups with an interest in and relationship to the collection. MUL has seen some success in this regard, using archives in conjunction with local community groups.[55] The very welcome growth in engagement with the Teresa Deevy Archive in recent years, for example, could be said to be reframing both the playwright and MUL special collections. It is a satisfying irony that a collection management policy and strategy that identified 'The Outsider' has resulted in positioning both MUL and Teresa Deevy more centrally

---

55 A leading example is the Saro-Wiwa Archive, which MUL has used as a key tool for engaging with new communities of Nigerian ethnicity by integrating the archive into an undergraduate programme, hosting exhibitions, and welcoming visiting groups of schoolchildren.

into the narrative of twentieth-century literary figures. As far back as 1975, Howard Zinn contended that institutions are ignoring experiences outside of the history of the more powerful in society: as part of its stewardship of collections, MUL is actively working towards redressing that imbalance.[56]

Bibliography

Battley, Belinda, 'Archives as Places, Places as Archives: Doors to Privilege, Places of Connection or Haunted Sarcophagi of Crumbling Skeletons?', *Archival Science*, 19 (2019), 1–26, https://doi.org/10.1007/s10502-019-09300-4

Bhardwaj, Raj Kumar, 'Availability and Preferences for Information Services to Visually Impaired Tertiary Students in Delhi', *Journal of Enabling Technologies*, 16.1 (2022), 1–16, https://doi.org/10.1108/JET-04-2021-0021

Carlisle, Madeleine, 'Public Libraries Face Threats to Funding and Collections as Book Bans Surge', *Time*, 7 September 2022, https://time.com/6211350/public-libraries-book-bans/

Carswell, Michelle, and Marika Cifor, 'From Human Rights to Feminist Ethics: Radical Empathy in Archives', *Archivaria*, 81 (2016), 23–43, https://archivaria.ca/index.php/archivaria/article/view/13557/14916

Charles, Elizabeth, 'Decolonizing the Curriculum', *Insights: The UKSG Journal*, 32.24, 1–7, https://doi.org/10.1629/uksg.475

Cook, Terry, 'Evidence, Memory, Identity and Community: Four Shifting Archival Paradigms', *Archival Science*, 13 (2013), 95–120, https://doi.org/10.1007/s10502-012-9180-7

Cullingford, Alison, *Unique and Distinctive Collections: Opportunities for Research Libraries*, ed. by Caroline Peach and Mike Mertens (RLUK, 2014), pp. 1–57, https://www.rluk.ac.uk/wp-content/uploads/2014/12/RLUK-UDC-Report.pdf

Deevy, Teresa, 'The Censorship', *Irish Times*, 20 October 1936, p. 4

Fox, Peter, *Trinity College Library Dublin: A History* (Cambridge: Cambridge University Press, 2014), https://doi.org/10.1017/CBO9780511894749

Department of Education, 'Prescribed Material for Junior Cycle English, Circular Letter: 0014/2022' (2022), https://www.gov.ie/en/circular/65046-prescribed-material-for-junior-cycle-english/

---

56 Howard Zinn, cited in F. Gerald Ham, 'The Archival Edge', *American Archivist*, 38.1 (1975), 5–13.

Government of Ireland (2023), *Bunreacht Na hÉireann* (Dublin: Government Publications Office, 2003), https://www.irishstatutebook.ie/pdf/en.cons.pdf

Ham, F. Gerald, 'The Archival Edge', *American Archivist*, 38.1 (1975), 5–13, https://doi.org/10.17723/aarc.38.1.7400r86481128424

Harris, Verne, 'Antonyms of Our Remembering', *Archival Science*, 14 (2014), 215–229, https://doi.org/10.1007/s10502-014-9221-5

Higgins, Geraldine, 'The Place of Irish Archives', *Irish University Review*, 52.1 (2022), 9–21, https://doi.org/10.3366/iur.2022.0538

Houlihan, Barry, *Theatre and Archival Memory: Irish Drama and Marginalised Histories, 1951–1977* (Hampshire: Palgrave, 2021), https://doi.org/10.1007/978-3-030-74548-6

International Council on Archives, 'Section on Archives and Human Rights—SAHR' (2023), https://www.ica.org/en/about-archives-and-human-rights

Jenkinson, Hilary, *A Manual of Archive Administration Including the Problems of War Archives and Archive Making* (Oxford: Clarendon Press, 1922), https://archive.org/details/manualofarchivea00jenkuoft

Jimerson, Randall, *Archivists and the Call for Justice*, webcast, University of British Columbia Library and Archives, 27 January 2010, https://ikblc.ubc.ca/history-and-civilization/jimerson/

Johnson, Peggy, *Fundamentals of Collection Development and Management*, 2nd edn (Chicago, IL: ALA, 2005)

Keen, Suzanne, 'Magical Values in Recent Romances of the Archive', in *Libraries, Literatures and Architects*, ed. by Sas Mays (London: Routledge, 2013), pp. 115–129

Kelly, Peter, 'An Misean sa tSín [The China Mission]', *History Ireland*, 25.4, https://www.historyireland.com/misean-sa-tsin-china-mission/

Lucy, Niall, *A Derrida Dictionary* (Oxford: Blackwell, 2004), https://doi.org/10.1002/9780470775752.fmatter

'The Maynooth Mission to China. Sixteen Priests Leave for China in March. Appeal for Ireland's Help', *The Irish Monthly*, 48.561 (1920), 168–170

Maynooth University, 'Maynooth University Department of Adult and Community Education' (2023), https://www.maynoothuniversity.ie/adult-and-community-education/about-us

Maynooth University, 'Maynooth University Department of Applied Social Studies' (2023), https://www.maynoothuniversity.ie/applied-social-studies

Maynooth University Library, *Maynooth University Library Collection Development Policy 2016–2023* (Maynooth University, 2016), https://www.maynoothuniversity.ie/sites/default/files/assets/document/MU%20Library%20Collection%20Development%20Policy%202016_0.pdf

Maynooth University Library, *Maynooth University Library Strategic Plan, Ollscoil Mhá Nuad An Leabharlann Plean Straitéiseach 2016–2018* (Maynooth University, 2016), 1–16, https://www.maynoothuniversity.ie/sites/default/files/assets/document//FINALDraftStrategicPlan20162018Library.pdf

Maynooth University Library, 'Statement on Harmful Language in Catalogue Description' (2023), https://nuim.libguides.com/c.php?g=704856&p=5112548

McCarthy, Kate, and Úna Kealy, 'Writing from the Margins: Re-framing Teresa Deevy's Archive and Her Correspondence with James Cheasty c.1952–1962, *Irish University Review*, 52.2 (2022), 322–340, https://doi.org/10.3366/iur.2022.0570

Morash, Chris, 'Teresa Deevy—an Introduction', *The Teresa Deevy Archive*, https://web.archive.org/web/20210724014250/http://deevy.nuim.ie/about

Murphy, Hugh, 'Whose Story: Working Towards Diversity in the Maynooth University Library Collections', in *I Am a Man of Peace: Writings Inspired by the Maynooth University Ken Saro-Wiwa Collection*, ed. by Helen Fallon (Quebec: Daraja Press, 2020), pp. 116–122, https://mural.maynoothuniversity.ie/id/eprint/13526/1/manofpeaceJan.pdf

Olatunji Olaojo, Pius, and Modupe A. Akewukereke, 'Collection Development Policies: Ground Rules for Planning University Libraries', *Library Philosophy and Practice*, 9.1 (2006), https://digitalcommons.unl.edu/libphilprac/90

Roff, Sandra, 'Archives, Documents, and Hidden History: A Course to Teach Undergraduates the Thrill of Historical Discovery Real and Virtual', *The History Teacher*, 40.4 (2007), 551–558

Schneider, Rebecca, *Performing Remains: Art and War in Times of Theatrical Reenactment* (Abingdon: Routledge, 2011), https://doi.org/10.4324/9780203852873

Shilton, Katie, and Ramesh Srinivasan, 'Participatory Appraisal and Arrangement for Multicultural Archival Collections,' *Archivaria*, 63.1 (2007), 87–101, https://archivaria.ca/index.php/archivaria/article/view/13129

Stead, Lisa, 'Introduction', in *The Boundaries of the Literary Archive: Reclamation and Representation*, ed. by Carrie Smith and Lisa Stead (London: Routledge, 2013), pp. 1–14, https://doi.org/10.4324/9781315614090

Sustainable Heritage Network, 'Protocols for Native American Archival Materials', https://sustainableheritagenetwork.org/cultural-protocol/public-access-11

Sustainable Heritage Network, 'Protocols for Native American Archival Materials with notations by NAAS', March 2019, https://sustainableheritagenetwork.org/system/files/atoms/file/Protocols_NAASmarkup_20190319.pdf

Weber, Chela Scott, Martha O'Hara Conway, Nicholas Martin, Gioia Stevens, and Brigette Kamsler, *Total Cost of Stewardship: Responsible Collection Building in Archives and Special Collections* (Dublin: OCLC Research), https://doi.org/10.25333/zbh0-a044

3. TSI: Teresa Deevy, or What Do We Know about [The] Reapers?

Shelley Troupe

On 18 March 1930, the Abbey Theatre premiered [The] Reapers, the first of Teresa Deevy's plays to receive a professional production.[1] It is a very good example of the ephemerality of the theatre because to consider the question 'What do we know about [The] Reapers?' entails exploring the surviving textual and production evidence. To locate these materials, the researcher must begin a Theatre Studies Investigation (TSI) of Teresa Deevy's three-act play to discover fragments from which we can piece together a hazy picture of the Abbey's production. At present, no known copy of the script has survived and the large-scale efforts at the University of Galway to digitise the Abbey Theatre's archives have revealed only the production programme, a copy of which is also available in Maynooth University's Teresa Deevy Archive. So, what *do* we know about [The] Reapers? At the time of writing this piece in autumn 2022, clues relating to Deevy's play comprise reviews of the play's premiere, academic writing on the play, Deevy's thoughts quoted in that writing, and the Abbey's production programme. From these sources and W.B. Yeats's dramaturgical feedback on a draft of the script, we glean some interesting observations about [The] Reapers such as the interpretation of its title and the play's plot, the Abbey Theatre's production and reception of it, and possible influences on Deevy and her work. Because of the fragmentary nature of available evidence,

---

1   [The] Reapers, directed by Lennox Robinson, the Abbey Theatre, Dublin 18–23 March 1930. The production ran from Tuesday to Sunday evening and included a Saturday matinee.

this chapter does not offer an extensive interrogation of the play or production; rather, it presents responses to and mini-arguments about the surviving archival materials. New evidence uncovered after the final draft was completed is addressed in the coda to this essay and provides some interesting findings.

The Title

The question about the inclusion of the definitive article in the play's title is reminiscent of the academic debate about the location of the altar in ancient Greek theatre. Much prevailing discourse situates the altar in the middle of the orchestra; however, using archaeological evidence, Clifford Ashby theorises that it might have been at the front, along the side, could have been portable, or may not have been located in the orchestra at all.[2] Without a copy of Deevy's script, present-day scholars cannot conclude the title of Deevy's play with absolute certainty, and the use of the play's title in academic work reveals the frailty of theatre historiography when physical evidence is not available.

In her article 'Resisting Power and Direction', Úna Kealy cogently argues that the title is *Reapers* as John Jordan referred to a copy of the script in an essay written for *Irish University Review* in the mid-1950s; Jordan also contended in a later interview that he confirmed the play's title with Deevy herself.[3] In a letter to Lennox Robinson, Deevy's mentor and producer of the Abbey's production of the play, Yeats also refers to the play as *'Reapers'*.[4] In contrast, the physical remnants of the play— the Abbey's programme and existing reviews—refer to the work as *'The Reapers'*. The only other academic known to have consulted a copy of the play, Nathamal Sahal, uses *'The Reapers'* in his analysis of the work and includes a letter from Deevy who he quotes as saying: '....For the

---

2   Clifford Ashby, *Classical Greek Theatre: New Views of an Old Subject* (Iowa City, IA: University of Iowa Press, 1999), pp. 42–61.

3   Úna Kealy, 'Resisting Power and Direction: *The King of Spain's Daughter* by Teresa Deevy as a Feminist Call to Action', *Estudios Irlandeses*, 15 (2020), 178–192 (p. 188, fn. 2).

4   Illinois, Morris Library (ML), Lennox Robinson Papers, W.B. Yeats to Lennox Robinson, 9 March 1929, MS 091 1/5, pp. 1–3 (p. 1). Special thanks to Dayna Killen for generously sharing Yeats's letter to advance this scholarship on Deevy's work.

subject of *The Reapers* blaming the sowers is a very real one, in Ireland'.[5] In response to Sahal's inclusion of the definitive article and citing Willy Maley's criticism of Sahal's misunderstanding of Deevy's plays, Kealy chooses to refer to the play as '*Reapers*'.[6] Further, Temple Lane uses '*Reapers*' in a 1946 article for the *Dublin Magazine*.[7]

The question of the title of Deevy's play as *Reapers* or *The Reapers* seems pedantic and unimportant, particularly since 'the' is such a miniscule word. However, this uncertainty showcases the significance, not only of the word, generally, but of how we understand these few remaining fragments of Deevy's play. With the definite article, *The Reapers* might refer to a specific set of reapers—ostensibly the microcosm of characters in the play. As *Reapers*, however, we can broaden our interpretation of the information left behind in short quotes from the play and from critical responses to it to consider Deevy's reapers as those living in the macrocosm of Ireland. Yeats's dramaturgical note that 'the allusions to the censorship should go and all general statements about religion' points up Deevy's interest in interrogating contemporary issues facing Ireland and, perhaps, foreshadows her exclusion from the Abbey under Ernest Blythe's direction later in her career.[8] To draw attention to this subtle difference in meaning—and without the original typescript, or a copy of it as evidence—I refer to the play as [*The*] *Reapers*. Crucially, physical evidence itself can be flawed. In this instance, say a copy of the script is unearthed in the future, but is a draft of the play rather than a copy of the script as it was presented at the Abbey Theatre in March 1930. We would have no way of knowing what had been changed for production. Even so, a draft would push forward our analysis of [*The*] *Reapers*. In essence, *some*thing is better than *no*thing.

---

5   Nathamal Sahal, *Sixty Years of Realistic Irish Drama* (Bombay: Macmillan, 1971), p. 135. This quotation also points up the fragility of theatre studies when faced with an absence of evidence as Sahal's archive—if it exists—is not available for consultation.

6   Willy Maley, '"She Done *Coriolanus* at the Convent": Empowerment and Entrapment in Teresa Deevy's *In Search of Valour*', *Irish University Review*, 49.2 (2019), 356–369.

7   Temple Lane, 'The Dramatic Art of Teresa Deevy', *Dublin Magazine*, 21.4 (1946), 35–42.

8   ML, MS 091 1/5.

The Play

Without Deevy's script, recounting the play's narrative hinges on critical and academic reports of it. It is, perhaps, significant that a clear-cut plot does not emerge from the reviews since, as one reviewer notes: 'I am under no obligation to spoil an evening's pleasure by retelling the plot where in any event the plot is nothing [...]'.[9] That 'the plot is nothing' was a sentiment echoed in other reviews.[10] Sahal concurs with reviewers' findings on [*The*] *Reapers* noting that '[t]he plot is very meagre', but goes on to argue that the play 'reveals the fatalistic tendency of the Irish people' and includes Deevy's quote that was mentioned above.[11] An argument regarding the play's narrative is found in Jordan's 1955 assessment of Deevy's work: 'This is a play about Catholic "Big Houses", Ballinrea House and Glenbeg House, and the psychological conflict between the two Doherty families which occupy them'.[12] Writing in *Women's Personality Parade*, published in June 1948, R.M. Fox observes that the play 'had a middle-class setting. It dealt with business and family troubles and how these affected various people'.[13] All of these descriptions point to a play in which a group of middle-class, Irish

---

9 Digital Repository of Ireland (DRI), The Teresa Deevy Archive, C.P.C., 'Drama Notes: The Reapers', https://doi.org/10.7486/DRI.95944b571. The review has a handwritten annotation that the excerpt is published in the *Irish Statesman*.

10 See, for example, the *Irish Times*: 'What it was that she [Deevy] wanted to say got so entangled in her method of saying it, that it failed completely to emerge' and *Dublin Opinion*: 'What the play lacks is a thing on which many present-day critics have agreed not to insist, and that is a plot, or rather, a *good* plot'. DRI, The Teresa Deevy Archive, '"The Reapers": First Production at the Abbey Theatre', PP/6/178(3), https://doi.org/10.7486/DRI.5999vb302, and DRI, The Teresa Deevy Archive, 'Stage and Screen', *Dublin Opinion*, PP/6/178(4), https://doi.org/10.7486/DRI.5999vb32m

11 Sahal, *Sixty Years*, p. 135 and p. 136; and Deevy in ibid., p. 135, respectively.

12 John Jordan, 'Teresa Deevy: An Introduction', *Irish University Review* 1.8 (1956), 13–26 (p. 14). This information provides an opportunity for future research as Ballinrea House and Glenbeg House are both actual dwellings. Located in Ballinrea, Carrigaline, County Cork, there is little to no information available about Ballinrea House, which could be a renovated estate house or a newly-built house. Glenbeg House, in Glenbeg, County Waterford, though, is a restored Jacobean Manor included in the National Inventory of Architectural Heritage. If both houses existed when Deevy was writing the play, it would be interesting to study their history and if they were occupied by families with the same surname.

13 Dublin, National Library of Ireland (NLI), Papers of Patricia Lynch and R.M. Fox, R.M. Fox, 'Theatre Personalities, 15—Teresa Deevy', June 1948, MS 40,377/2, pp. 11–12, p. 12.

Catholics are not only affected by the past, but are at odds with each other in the present. These ideas are interesting in terms of the wider sociopolitical context of the play's setting, 1923.

The Abbey's production programme specifies that the action of the play's first and second acts occur on a 'summer afternoon in 1923' and a 'few hours later', while Act Three takes place '[t]hree weeks later'.[14] 1923 is a significant year in Irish history, marking as it does the end of the Irish Civil War. Following on from the Irish War of Independence (1919–1921), the Anglo-Irish Treaty partitioning Saorstát Éireann (the Irish Free State, now known as the Republic of Ireland) from Northern Ireland was signed in London on 6 December 1921. The Irish Civil War began on 28 June 1922 when Anti-Treaty forces were attacked by Pro-Treaty forces in Dublin. Anti-Treaty forces ended the Civil War on 24 May 1923. Setting the play just shortly after the conclusion of the Civil War suggests that [*The*] *Reapers* draws attention to the conflict through Deevy's representation of the two 'big houses' that are owned by people with the same surname. Further, the *Evening Herald* notes that the character 'Ted, a budding patriot [i.e., a member of the IRA (the Irish Republican Army)]' who 'thinks the best way to stop it [the sale of the family mill] is to get some of his pals of the gun game to kidnap the family solicitor. His ruse is frustrated by the arrival of a posse of Saorstat soldiers [sic]'.[15] Perhaps, then, [*The*] *Reapers* is a delicate critique of a nation at war with itself. That the play was presented on the same evening as W.B. Yeats and Lady Gregory's *Cathleen Ni Houlihan*, a staple of Irish nationalist theatre in which a young man leaves his family to fight for Ireland's freedom, provides a unique contrast to this reading of [*The*] *Reapers*. Shaun Richards notes that women writers working in post-Independent Ireland were limited by their circumstances, but 'capable of providing significant insights into the social realities and restrictions which determined both the writers and their characters'.[16]

---

14 Maynooth, Russell Library (RL), The Teresa Deevy Archive, 'The Reapers', production programme, PP/6/42.

15 DRI, The Teresa Deevy Archive, '"The Reapers": Work of New Woman Dramatist at the Abbey', PP/6/178(5), https://doi.org/10.7486/DRI.95944b635. A handwritten annotation notes the publication as the *Evening Herald*.

16 Shaun Richards, '"Suffocated in the Green Flag": The Drama of Teresa Deevy and 1930s Ireland', *Literature and History*, 4.1 (1995), 65–80 (p. 65). Thanks to Shaun Richards for providing me with a copy of his article.

Although it is not possible to support this argument without specific textual evidence, Deevy's subsequent work, such as *The King of Spain's Daughter* (1935) and *Katie Roche* (1936), which Richards interrogates, present discreet assessments of women's position in post-independent Ireland, indicating the playwright's ability to use the theatre as a place from which to reevaluate contemporary issues.

The Performance

Detailed descriptions of set, lighting, or costume designs for [*The*] *Reapers* are not known to exist except for one grainy newsprint pre-production photograph. Researchers have no prompt copy of the script, which might contain clues indicating actors' blocking or other production information such as cues for light and sound. Neither box office reports—determining the size of the audience and related income—nor correspondence regarding Deevy's contract or payment is available for analysis.[17] There is, however, some evidence in the reviews and pre-production material that assists in recouping a little about the production. At least two reviews reveal some evidence regarding set and costume for [*The*] *Reapers*. The *Irish Times* remarks that '[p]eople go in and out a delightfully-set French window, some dressed for tennis, and at least one like a caricature of one of the Misses Bennett, from Jane Austen's novel [*Pride and Prejudice*]'.[18] *Dublin Opinion* adds that:

> There was…a nice-looking boy in flannels, and there was a tennis-racket, and a modern girl and a fine setting of the sitting-room of a country house. That was a very good effect the producer got with those large sunlit glass doors.[19]

These statements certainly support Jordan's and Fox's claims that the play gives a picture of middle-class families who had leisure time to play tennis near a 'big house'. On 17 March 1930, the day before the play's premiere, the *Irish Independent* published a rehearsal photograph of the character Ted Doherty's arrest by Saorstát Éireann soldiers in the

---

17 See Kealy, 'Resisting Power and Direction', pp. 186–88, as an example of the importance of information found in stage management scripts to providing a well-rounded analysis.
18 DRI, PP/6/178(3).
19 DRI, PP/6/178(4).

sitting room of one of the 'big houses'.[20] Although the reproduction of the photograph is grainy and the French doors are not readily apparent, the photo suggests a sitting room with paintings on the walls and a fireplace similar to those found in what Jordan calls 'Catholic "big houses"'.[21] The juxtaposition of a woman character who the *Irish Times* remarks was dressed 'like a caricature of one of the Misses Bennett from Jane Austen's novel' with another woman character that another review described as 'the flapper daughter', perhaps suggests a disconnection between older and younger generations, or in keeping with Deevy's penchant for discreet criticism of contemporary Ireland, between an Ireland repressed under Britain's governance contrasted with a new Irish Free State.[22] The seemingly middle-class set and costuming may also point to those who influenced Deevy as a writer.

The Influences

As Deevy was a new Abbey playwright and [*The*] *Reapers* was a premiere, it is inevitable that the critical reception attempts to tease out the influences on her writing, particularly since [*The*] *Reapers* is not typical of Abbey productions of the late 1920s and early 1930s as it depicts a prosperous middle-class, Catholic 'big house' rather than a peasant's thatched cottage. Well-known critic A.J. (Con) Leventhal saw the play and remarked in a letter to Deevy: 'If there was error in the play then it erred on the side of reality....You gave us an honest to God [illegible, but possibly 'downright'] picture of Irish futility'.[23] Perhaps it is not surprising, then, that the *Irish Times* identified Deevy as 'a student of Tchechov [sic]', while a critic from the *Waterford News and Star* saw the play as 'an attempt to adapt the Tchekov [sic] method to a study of Irish life', identifying comparisons between [*The*] *Reapers* and *The Cherry Orchard*, while another critic found 'the same type of dialogue as one finds in [Chekhov's] *The Three Sisters*'.[24] Disrupting

---

20 'New Abbey Play', *Irish Independent*, 17 March 1930, p. 3.
21 Jordan, 'Teresa Deevy', p. 14.
22 DRI, PP/6/178(3); DRI, PP/6/178(5). The review has a handwritten annotation that the publication is the *Evening Herald*.
23 DRI, The Teresa Deevy Archive, C.J. Leventhal to Teresa Deevy, 22 March 1930, PP/6/6(1-2) (p. 2).
24 DRI, PP/6/178(3); DRI, The Teresa Deevy Archive, 'Waterford Lady's First Play', *Waterford News and Star*, 21 March 1930, PP/6/178(87), https://doi.org/10.7486/

the Chekhovian observations, the *Dublin Magazine* observed that Deevy 'exploited quite unconsciously in the last act Moliere's comedy-trick of a repeated phrase'.[25]

While this evidence supports the assertion that Deevy's work was directly influenced by Anton Chekhov, it is more likely that [*The*] *Reapers* responds to George Bernard Shaw's *Heartbreak House*.[26] Both Eibhear Walshe and Sahal note that, when Deevy attended the theatre in London to help her practice lip-reading, she saw plays by Shaw and Chekhov.[27] Although most critics who mention inspiration specifically note Chekhov's influence on Deevy's dramaturgy, R.M. Fox's overview of Deevy's work supports Shaw as a major influence on Deevy's work:

> In London—where she went for treatment—she studied lip-reading which, incidentally, she does not find so easy to practice in Ireland. She saw many plays there. She read Bernard Shaw's description of his *Heartbreak House* as a play of English life in the Russian manner. She wondered then if she could write plays of Irish life in the Irish manner, for she did not care about the vapid productions which cluttered the London stage with their silly triangle situations and sex themes.[28]

The full title of Shaw's 1919 play is *Heartbreak House, A Fantasia in the Russian Manner on English Themes*. The 'Russian manner' of the title refers to Shaw's adaptation of Chekhov's style, which, when taking Fox's observations into account, suggests that Deevy was more interested in adapting—and perhaps subverting—Chekhov's work in an Irish context to which the critic from the *Waterford News and Star* alludes above.[29] If a copy of Deevy's play is ever rediscovered, a comparative analysis of *Heartbreak House* and [*The*] *Reapers* would greatly advance Deevy scholarship particularly with regard to Deevy's early work.

Of even more importance, perhaps, is the end of Fox's paragraph above, which notes: 'In Ireland, [Deevy] thought, women are concerned with the running of business and farms. They face all kinds of problems.

DRI.95944b71v; DRI, The Teresa Deevy Archive, Wiswayo, 'The Reapers: A Play in Three Acts', *The Irish Sketch*, 1 April 1930, https://doi.org/10.7486/DRI.95944b724

25 Lane, 'The Dramatic Art of Teresa Deevy', p. 35.
26 George Bernard Shaw, *Heartbreak House: A Fantasia in the Russian Manner on English Themes* (London: Constable, 1919).
27 Eibhear Walsh, 'Ineffable Longings: The Dramas of Teresa Deevy', in *Selected Plays of Irish Playwright Teresa Deevy, 1894-1963*, ed. by Eibhear Walshe (Lewiston, NY: Edwin Mellen Press, 2003), pp. 1–16 (p. 5); Sahal, *Sixty Years*, p. 134.
28 NLI, MS 40,377/2, p. 11.
29 DRI, PP/6/178(87).

Why can't all this be put on stage?'.[30] This information helps us pinpoint Deevy's theatrical experiences in London as the motivator for her work—not only as a playwright, but, as a playwright committed to representing onstage the concerns of Irish women. Indeed, if a copy of the script is ever found, an analysis of the play's women characters could illuminate the role of them in 'the running of [the] business' of the mill, particularly the sale of it, which the reviews indicate is at the heart of the play's conflict.

Yeats observes that [*The*] *Reapers* is 'very much indebted' to Lennox Robinson's *The White Blackbird* (1925) and notes that 'a young author must imitate somebody and it is better for him [sic] to imitate you than some other writier [sic] further away'; Yeats also declares: 'I don't see any Chekov [sic], except perhaps just the idea of futility and the hating to sell'.[31] A short synopsis of Robinson's play on *Playography Ireland* notes that 'William, the eldest son in the Naynoe household was left everything by his late father. He therefore has financial control over his mother, stepfather and step siblings, who detest him for meddling in their lives'.[32] Control—financial and otherwise—is certainly a theme that recurs in Deevy's oeuvre. Returning to the microcosm/macrocosm aspect of Deevy's play addressed earlier, a draft or final copy of the script would advance an analysis of both Deevy's and Robinson's plays to help us determine how, if at all, they interrogate power struggles on local, national, and—perhaps—international levels.

The Programme

There is also an additional fragment of source material that can augment this Theatre Studies Investigation of Deevy's [*The*] *Reapers*: the Abbey Theatre's production programme. Can any conclusions be drawn regarding the Abbey actors that were cast in both *Cathleen Ni Houlihan* and [*The*] *Reapers*? For example, how might Arthur Shields's work as an actor in both plays *and* his work as the Abbey's Assistant Producer

---

30   NLI, PP/6/178(87), p. 11.
31   ML, MS 091 1/5, p. 2. With the dearth of women playwrights at this time, it is little wonder Yeats referred to the author as 'him'. Yeats's assumption may also suggest Robinson gave him a draft of the play without the author's name attached.
32   'The White Blackbird', *Playography Ireland*.

and Stage Manager impact upon an interpretation of [*The*] *Reapers*, and what do his multiple roles and responsibilities suggest about the Abbey Theatre's production process? At what point of the evening were the selections of Beethoven, Wagner, and J.F. Larchet performed—during *Cathleen Ni Houlihan*, [*The*] *Reapers*, or the 'interval of twelve minutes' between the plays—and did the music reflect, resonate, or detract from the conflicts or concerns of the play?[33]

The Inconclusive Conclusion

Overall, the fragmentary nature of available information related to [*The*] *Reapers* raises more questions than it answers about the play and the Abbey Theatre's production of it. In particular, the absence of the final script—or even slivers of drafts—impedes rigorous analysis of the play. Even so, the small traces of evidence, the breadcrumbs, that are left behind provide us with enough information to make mini-arguments about aspects of the play, the production, Deevy's influences, and provide a number of avenues for future study.

Coda, September 2023

New evidence discovered between the time of writing and the time of final editing in autumn 2023 gives readers the opportunity to see academic discourse in action as these breadcrumbs refine some of the mini-arguments discussed above. In November 2022, Raidió Teilifís Éireann (RTÉ) aired *Tribute: The Teresa Deevy Story*, a documentary in which performance artist Amanda Coogan traces Deevy's artistic journey as part of Coogan's own creative endeavour to stage a version of Deevy's unproduced ballet, *Possession*.[34] Two pieces of evidence in RTÉ's programme help progress this chapter's scholarship on [*The*] *Reapers*: (1) a quote from the original typescript of an autobiographical note Deevy wrote for inclusion in the American publication *Catholic*

---

33 RL, PP/6/42.
34 *Tribute: The Teresa Deevy Story* was produced by Bernadine Carraher for Mind the Gap Films for RTÉ, directed by Claire Dix, shot by Andrew Cummins, and edited by Cara Holmes. Claire Dix, *Tribute: The Teresa Deevy Story*, online documentary, RTÉ Player, 10 November 2022.

Authors: Contemporary Biographical Sketches,³⁵ and (2) an additional pre-production photo of [*The*] *Reapers* with a handwritten annotation stating that it was published in the *Evening Herald* on 17 March 1930. (It was, in fact, published in the 18 March edition.)³⁶ These sources allow us to draw some conclusions about the mini-arguments presented above, particularly the questions about the play's title and Deevy's influences.

The autobiographical note puts an end to the question of the play's title: '*Reapers*, I had called my piece'.³⁷ This definitive title underscores the mini-argument above that the play examines the macrocosm of the country in the early days of the post-Irish Civil War period, a point I will return to shortly.

Deevy also cements the thought that Shaw's work was her inspiration—if not for *Reapers*, for a precursory draft of it:

> One night returning from the theatre I felt very strongly the urge to put the sort of life we live in Ireland into a play. The piece, we had just seen, depicted English life, and I felt how very different these are from the people I know. About this time one of the plays I read was *Heartbreak House*. Shaw had called it a fantasy in the Russian manner about English themes, and I said proudly to myself my play will be 'a fantasy in the Russian manner on Irish themes'. But there was a long way to go. I returned to Ireland—this was in 1919, and Ireland faced the Terror. My play was pushed to the background [...].³⁸

The Terror, undoubtedly, references the Irish War of Independence and the Irish Civil War mentioned above and, possibly, the guerrilla warfare tactics used during them including ambushes, assassinations, arson—and kidnappings. Set on the precipice of the First World War, *Heartbreak House* shows, according to Shaw, 'cultured, leisured Europe before the war' underscoring the occupants' obliviousness to the tragedy awaiting the country.³⁹ Set in the immediate aftermath of two back-to-back wars, *Reapers* brings the conflict *into* the home with the presumed IRA member Ted, his kidnapping attempt, and the arrival of the Saorstát

---

35   Matthew Hoehn, 'Teresa Deevy 1894—', in *Catholic Authors: Contemporary Biographical Sketches*, ed. by Matthew Hoehn (Newark, NJ: St Mary's Abbey, 1952), pp. 121–122 (p. 121).
36   Dix, *Tribute*, timestamp: 9:30.
37   Hoehn, 'Teresa Deevy', p. 121.
38   Dix, *Tribute*, timestamp: 6:41.
39   Shaw, *Heartbreak House*.

Éireann soldiers, which was depicted in the photo mentioned above. These events, combined with the sale of the family-owned mill, and the possibility of two feuding families, showcase Deevy's inclination for providing critical insight into contemporary Irish life.

The second piece of evidence, the *Evening Herald's* pre-production photograph, is different from, and of much better quality than, the *Irish Independent's* photo. Showing four characters—two women and two men—startled as one man draws a gun on the other, it presumably represents the moment when Ted attempts kidnapping the family solicitor. The *Irish Independent* photo includes the edge of the stage's apron, giving us some clues about the space. Although there is still no sign of the French doors mentioned in the reviews, the wood-panelled walls, adorned with two large paintings, highlight the middle-class setting. The set is cramped with the table surrounded by at least three chairs, an armchair, and the four actors. So, was the stage very small, or was it split into two separate performance areas depicting a room in each of the houses? We also see some of the footlights used to light the stage, which appear to contribute to the gunman's shadow, enhancing the ominous incident.

Reverting to Deevy's autobiographical note gives us her perspective on some of the reviews of her first professional production, which:

> [...] declared that the play showed 'promise'—Promise! No word could have seemed more deadly to me!....This had seemed to me the outcome of my life's work, and they talked of 'promise'! It took some time to realize that this was the start of a journey, not the road's end, as I had thought.[40]

She goes on to express her gratitude to her mentor Lennox Robinson and 'others to whose wise words, whether spoken to me, or written, I owe much', and ends by paraphrasing a J.M. Synge quote she found inspiring: '[D]rama, to be worth the name, must nourish imagination'.[41] Likewise, Deevy's work has nourished our imaginations as we tease out the fragmented history of her play *Reapers* through this TSI.

---

40 Hoehn, 'Teresa Deevy', p. 122.
41 Ibid.

Bibliography

Ashby, Clifford, *Classical Greek Theatre: New Views of an Old Subject* (Iowa City, IA: University of Iowa Press, 1999)

Dix, Claire, *Tribute: The Teresa Deevy Story*, online documentary, RTÉ Player, 10 November 2022, https://www.rte.ie/player/movie/tribute-the-teresa-deevy-story/326740520026

Hoehn, Matthew, 'Teresa Deevy 1894—', in *Catholic Authors: Contemporary Biographical Sketches*, ed. by Matthew Hoehn (Newark, NJ: St Mary's Abbey, 1952), pp. 121–122

Kealy, Úna, 'Resisting Power and Direction: *The King of Spain's Daughter* by Teresa Deevy as a Feminist Call to Action', *Estudios Irlandeses*, 15 (2020), 178–192, https://doi.org/10.24162/EI2020-9406

Jordan, John, 'Teresa Deevy: An Introduction', *Irish University Review* 1.8 (1956), 13–26

Lane, Temple, 'The Dramatic Art of Teresa Deevy', *Dublin Magazine*, 21.4 (1946), 35–42

Maley, Willy, '"She Done *Coriolanus* at the Convent": Empowerment and Entrapment in Teresa Deevy's *In Search of Valour*', *Irish University Review*, 49.2 (2019), 356–369, http://dx.doi.org/10.3366/iur.2019.0411

'New Abbey Play', *Irish Independent*, 17 March 1930, p. 3

Richards, Shaun, '"Suffocated in the Green Flag": The Drama of Teresa Deevy and 1930s Ireland', *Literature and History*, 4.1 (1995), 65–80, https://doi.org/10.1177/030619739500400104

Sahal, Nathamal, *Sixty Years of Realistic Irish Drama* (Bombay: Macmillan, 1971)

Shaw, George Bernard, *Heartbreak House: A Fantasia in the Russian Manner on English Themes* (London: Constable, 1919), https://www.gutenberg.org/files/3543/3543-h/3543-h.htm

Walsh, Eibhear, 'Ineffable Longings: The Dramas of Teresa Deevy', in *Selected Plays of Irish Playwright Teresa Deevy, 1894-1963*, ed. by Eibhear Walshe (Lewiston, NY: Edwin Mellen Press, 2003), pp. 1–16

'The White Blackbird', *Playography Ireland*, https://www.irishplayography.com/play.aspx?playid=31923

4. Mysteries of the Teresa Deevy Archive: Reconsidering the plays of D.V. Goode

Caoilfhionn Ní Bheacháin Mitchell[1]

Between 1983 and 1984, the journalist and poet Seán Dunne corresponded with Teresa Deevy's nephew, Jack Deevy. Dunne was researching an early and important retrospective on the playwright's career and biography, and his efforts culminated in an extended article in the *Cork Examiner* and a special issue of *The Journal of Irish Literature*, which published Deevy's award-winning play *Temporal* Powers for the first time.[2] He concludes one letter to Jack in 1984 by noting that his search for biographical information on the playwright made him 'feel like Sherlock Holmes at this stage!'.[3] Identifying with Dunne's emotion and recognising that I have retraced some of his investigative journeys some four decades later, I am conscious that there is value in recounting incomplete and partial stories for others embarking on similar work in the future. Thus, in this chapter, I tentatively present an investigation in progress, a summary map of an unsolved mystery that may help another to reach a firmer conclusion than I can at present. I reconsider the body of work by D.V. Goode that is held in the Teresa Deevy Archive at

---

1 Caoilfhionn Ní Bheacháin Mitchell also publishes on Teresa Deevy as Caoilfhionn Ní Bheacháin. I would like to thank Jacqui Deevy, Edward Deevy, Cyril Deevy, Christopher Morash, Jonathan Bank, Kathryn Laing, and Angus Mitchell for enjoyable and provocative conversations about various aspects discussed in this chapter.
2 This special issue of *The Journal of Irish Literature*, 14.2 (1985), included an introduction by Seán Dunne, a checklist of Deevy's plays, and the script of the three-act play *Temporal Powers*. The checklist of Deevy's plays does not include the three plays by D.V. Goode.
3 Maynooth, Russell Library (RL), The Teresa Deevy Archive, Seán Dunne to Jack Deevy, 19 December 1983, PP/6/1-30.

Maynooth University. The D.V. Goode materials comprise the manuscripts of three complete plays authored under what is clearly a pseudonym. Undated, unsigned, and not presented in a particular sequence, these plays are entitled *The Firstborn* (a one-act radio play), *Let Us Live* (a three-act stage play set in Dublin), and *Practice and Precept* (a three-act stage play set in England).[4] Included in the Deevy papers since Teresa Deevy's death in 1963, these plays have not received critical attention to date, and this study seeks to categorically redate the texts, introduce them, and explore different theories regarding authorship.[5] More generally, this chapter considers Deevy's literary legacy, her archival presence (understood in its broadest sense), and her surviving correspondence, scattered across various sites, including Maynooth University Library, Trinity College Dublin, the National Library of Ireland, University College Dublin, and Waterford Central Library.

The contemporary theatre historian is no stranger to archives. Whether housed in virtual spaces or built environments, the archive directs attention and presents a multitude of treasures to contemplate and investigate. A fortunate researcher may reconstruct specific productions with the aid of scripts, sketches, prompt books, financial accounts, inventories of props, correspondences, and all manner of other clues; or they may find materials to identify the full complement of theatremakers in a professional company, exploring the creative networks and collaborative practices that underpin theatrical partnerships. However, archives are not neutral spaces and their curation and collections both influence and are influenced by what is studied and what is memorialised. Such an outcome is unsurprising: the word archive derives 'from the Latin "archivum", meaning the "residence of the magistrate and those who command", which in turn comes from the Greek *arkhe*, a word that signifies both "commencement" and "commandment"'.[6] This etymology hints at the canon-formation and state-sanctioned aspects of official archives, and numerous studies

---

4   Maynooth, Russell Library (RL), The Teresa Deevy Archive, *Let us Live*, PP/6/82 (1-37); Maynooth, Russell Library (RL), The Teresa Deevy Archive, *Practice and Precept*, PP/6/81 (1-41); Maynooth, Russell Library (RL), The Teresa Deevy Archive, *The Firstborn*, PP/6/85, pp. 1–12.

5   I have briefly presented the case for redating the plays in a newspaper article: See Caoilfhionn Ní Bheacháin, 'Teresa Deevy and the Secrets of the Green Suitcase', *Irish Times*, 3 April 2021.

6   Neeraj Bhatia, 'Reassembling the Archive', *AA Files*, 77, ed. by Maria Sheherazade Giudici (2020) (italics in the original).

have illuminated the role of those museums and archives as instruments of control, power, and legacy formation.⁷ Mutually defining, official archival practices combine with literary and cultural canons to shape understanding of who or what is valued. Whether by accident or design, the historic omission and occlusion of women within many formal cultural archives, literary anthologies, and official commemorations has reflected their marginalisation within the public sphere.⁸ Theorising the concept of archive, illuminating patterns of collection and curation, learning to read archives 'against the grain', and identifying conventions that have marginalised or overlooked particular groups or individuals, will facilitate and support revision, retrieval, and redress.⁹ In this sense, archives and cultural practices must also be considered in terms of the mechanisms of exclusion and occlusion which structure and delimit their reach. This chapter highlights the consequences of the longstanding neglect of leading Irish women writers and their networks, whose archives are often scattered and fragmented, and their influence and achievements obscured or misunderstood.

A writer's sense of their own importance is critical for how they curate or plan for their archive; indeed, it determines whether they recognise their papers as a tangible archive at all. Ondrej Pilný, Ruud van den Beuken, and Ian R. Walsh highlight how the 'consummate

---

7   See, for example, *Refiguring the Archive*, ed. by Carolyn Hamilton, Verne Harris, Jane Taylor, Michele Pickover, Graeme Reid, and Razia Saleh (Amsterdam: Kluwer Academic Publishers, 2002); Dan Hicks (ed.), *The Brutish Museums: The Benin Bronzes, Colonial Violence and Cultural Restitution* (London: Pluto Press, 2020); Marisa J. Fuentes (ed.), *Dispossessed Lives: Enslaved Women, Violence, and the Archive* (Philadelphia, PN: University of Pennsylvania Press, 2018).

8   Recent special issues have illuminated the complex and ambivalent position of women within official archives. See, for example, the following special issues and their introductory essays, which highlight some of the scholarly and archival challenges intrinsic to researching feminist, LGBTQ+, and intersectional histories: Laura Engel and Emily Ruth Rutter, 'Women and Archives', *Tulsa Studies in Women's Literature*, 40.1 (2021), 5–13; Kathryn Laing, Sinéad Mooney, Caoilfhionn Ní Bheacháin, Anna Pilz, Whitney Standlee, and Julie Anne Stevens, 'Connecting Voices: An Introduction to Irish Women Writers' Collaborations and Networks, 1880–1940', *English Studies*, 104.6 (2023), 843–864; and Jane Freeland and Christina von Hodenberg, 'Archiving, Exhibiting, and Curating the History of Feminisms in the Global Twentieth Century: An Introduction', *Women's History Review*, 33.1 (2023), 1–6.

9   For a recent example of how theatre archives can fruitfully illuminate the histories of marginalised groups, see Barry Houlihan, *Theatre and Archival Memory: Irish Drama and Marginalised Histories, 1951–1977* (Hampshire: Palgrave Macmillan, 2021).

professionalism' of Hilton Edwards and Micheál mac Liammóir ensured they 'meticulously documented production details in prompt scripts, set and costume designs, lighting plots, photographs and sketches';[10] but such a professional identity was not as readily available to a woman contemporary such as Teresa Deevy who struggled financially to attend premieres of her own work and who, it seems, did not believe her papers were of interest to a regional or national archive. In this instance, gender intersects with provincial location and physical disability (her deafness), so that at times Deevy was positioned on the margins of Dublin's cultural scene. For example, in a letter to Florence Hackett, Deevy debates attending the Abbey premiere of her play *The King of Spain's Daughter*:

> I'm afraid now I shan't be up to see it in Dublin. Fares are so high, and the play is so tiny a thing—Then it would mean staying a night or so in Dublin—all runs to so much money. If Willie happens to be motoring up—which does not seem very likely—of course we'll go.[11]

Ultimately, Deevy did travel for the premiere and, although she was unhappy with the production, a subsequent letter to Hackett reveals she was 'delighted' with her visit to the capital city as this propelled her, briefly, into a social whirl meeting writers and artists including Signe Toksvig, Francis Hackett, Seamus O'Sullivan, Estella Solomons, Lennox Robinson, Rosamond Jacob, and Frank O'Connor.[12] This letter reveals her precarious inclusion in the literary scene of the day, dependent as it was on lifts, offers of accommodation, her sister Nell's willing presence, and so forth. Furthermore, Deevy's circumstances dictated her ability to have her manuscripts typed, copied, circulated, or published. In relation to her later life, Edward Deevy (the playwright's grandnephew) recalls that Teresa 'wasn't living like a

---

10 Ondrej Pilný, Ruud van den Beuken, and Ian R. Walsh, *Cultural Convergence: The Dublin Gate Theatre, 1928–1960* (Cham: Palgrave Macmillan, 2021), p. 5. The editors use the spelling 'mac Liammóir' following Cathy Leeney and Deirdre McFeely's use of this spelling at the request of the executors of mac Liammóir's estate (see Maura Laverty, *The Plays of Maura Laverty: Liffey Lane, Tolka Row, A Tree in the Crescent*, ed. by Cathy Leeney and Deirdre McFeely (Liverpool: Liverpool University Press, 2023), p. 6).
11 Dublin, Eavan Boland Library (EBL), Florence Hackett Collection, Teresa Deevy to Florence Hackett (24 April 1935), MS 10722/6.
12 Dublin, Eavan Boland Library (EBL), Florence Hackett Collection, Teresa Deevy to Florence Hackett, 8 May 1935, MS 10722/6.

professional writer' in Waterford in the 1950s and that she 'had no air of self-importance'.[13] After her death in 1963, her papers were gathered together (but not catalogued) and remained within the family home.

In this regard, Teresa Deevy was not unusual: Lucy Collins notes that women poets frequently 'do not systematically collect their manuscripts, either because they have not been encouraged to think of these as valuable, or because periods of comparative creative inactivity may prevent them from seeing their artistic career in a singular or continuous way'.[14] Such negative value judgements can be worryingly pervasive, equally affecting an author's friends and family who may not realise the importance of correspondence, ephemera, or manuscripts: for example, in a transcript of an important early lecture on Teresa Deevy, the scholar Frank McEvoy noted that 'on a chance visit to Florence Hackett a few years ago, she handed me a bundle of letters [from Teresa Deevy] which she was about to consign to the fire'.[15] This startling statement goes some way to explaining the archival lacunae that currently exist in understandings of Deevy's biography and literary achievement; it also gives reason to hope that, someday, other correspondence or the missing manuscript of the 'epoch-making' play, *The Reapers*, will turn up in an ancillary collection or a house clearance.[16] The occasional restitution or recovery of women to the public archive and to popular memory results from the determined

---

13 Interview with the author, 8 December 2022.
14 Lucy Collins, 'Hidden Collections: The Value of Irish Literary Archives', *Irish University Review*, 50.1 (2020), 187–197 (pp. 193–194).
15 Maynooth, Russell Library (RL), The Teresa Deevy Archive, Lecture Transcript, PP/6/176. Frank McEvoy (1925–2012) was a prominent intellectual in the literary, historical, and cultural life of Kilkenny and its environs. As honorary secretary of the Kilkenny Arts Society and associate editor of the *Kilkenny Magazine*, McEvoy was a critical figure in promoting and nurturing the work of many writers. His early research on Teresa Deevy, his 1966 public lecture on her work, and his preservation of this critical correspondence between Deevy and Hackett demonstrate the importance of local scholarship and regional networks. The Deevy-Hackett correspondence is now held in the Manuscripts Collection at Trinity College Dublin. Jonathan Bank recalls discussing the Deevy papers with McEvoy in 2010, and the latter recalled promptly returning the script of *Wife to James Whelan* after his public lecture, suggesting the manuscript was subsequently mislaid within the Deevy family home, Landscape, for over a decade (correspondence with the author, January 2023).
16 Described in a letter (22 March 1930) by Con Leventhal as 'epoch-making', the script of *The Reapers* has been missing since Deevy's death. See DRI, The Teresa Deevy Archive, C. J. Leventhal to Teresa Deevy, 22 March 1930, PP/6/6(1-2), p. 1. Furthermore, much of Deevy's correspondence is lost or destroyed.

efforts of numerous agents; however, belated recovery work is not without specific challenges. The fate of Teresa Deevy's archival legacy, and its fragmentary nature, illuminates the complex forces which have distorted the reputation and influence of Irish women writers more generally.

Teresa Deevy's papers were stored in suitcases under a spare bed in the family home, Landscape, in Waterford for decades after her death; this makeshift archive was managed by her family who shared its contents with a singular but steady stream of interested critics and scholars. Now deposited in Maynooth University, one can read the fascinating correspondence between Jack Deevy (Teresa's nephew) and Frank McEvoy, P. Chika Ochu, Séan Dunne, Eileen Kearney, Martina Ann O'Doherty, and others. The letters reveal the efforts of these intrepid researchers and the critical significance of unofficial archivists such as Jack and Noleen Deevy (and, subsequently, their daughter Jacqui Deevy) in preserving the playwright's reputation and legacy through multiple cycles of remembrance and forgetting. Such literary executors and familial gatekeepers demonstrate the importance of alternative, non-official, archivists and archives in ensuring the survival of an author's oeuvre and shaping its critical reception. It was Jacqui Deevy in collaboration with Chris Morash (then Professor of English at Maynooth University, Kildare, Ireland) and Jonathan Bank (of the Mint Theater in New York) who finally found a formal home for the papers in Maynooth University, and archivists there have since catalogued and digitised much of the collection, making it accessible to scholars nationally and internationally.

Redating the Plays: The Blackheath Address

When the Deevy papers (that are now held in Maynooth University) were first catalogued in Martina Ann O'Doherty's bibliography for the *Irish University Review* in 1995, the D.V. Goode plays were attributed to Teresa Deevy, but dated to her extended stay in Blackheath in London between 1914 and 1919.[17] An address for 96 Kidbrooke Park Road in Blackheath in London is handwritten on the front page of the manuscript

---

17 Martina Ann O'Doherty, 'Deevy: A Bibliography', *Irish University Review*, 25.1 (1995), 163–170.

of D.V. Goode's *The Firstborn*, and the assumption that these plays were written between 1914 and 1919 probably gained credence because of this English address, as it is well known that Teresa spent those five years in London with her sister Josie.[18] In recent years, the Maynooth archive lists the plays in a folder entitled 'Plays by D.V. Goode 1914 to 1919'. According to the archive catalogue,

> A number of early works may have been written by Deevy under the pseudonym 'D.V. Goode', although the authorship remains unclear. These include 'Practice and Precept', 'Let Us Live' and 'The Firstborn', written between 1914 and 1919.
>
> There is some speculation that they could be the work of Deevy's sister, Josie, with whom she lived in Blackheath in South East London.[19]

Digital mapping of the Blackheath area now allows us to identify and visualise the property at the Kidbrooke Park Road address, and all is not as was originally assumed. It is a detached house in an architectural style that suggests it is from the 1930s, located in a suburb that was largely undeveloped in the years when Deevy first lived in England. A local history society in London states that there was substantial acreage remaining in agricultural use in the Kidbrooke area until the 1920s; a section was sold to the RAF in 1921 and then Kidbrooke Park Road was developed for residential use between 1925 and 1938:

> From 1925 the process of developing the remaining agricultural lands began in earnest, with ribbon developments beyond St James' Church in Kidbrooke Park Road. These development [sic] continued through the late 1920s up to 1938.[20]

Therefore, this is not the house where Teresa and Josie lived during the First World War. A trawl through the correspondence of Deevy to Florence Hackett reveals that Teresa and Nell stayed with Josie in December 1948 and January 1949 with two letters addressed from 96 Kidbrook Park Road contained within this collection.[21] Furthermore, on

---

18 Maynooth, Russell Library (RL), Teresa Deevy Archive, Manuscript of *The Firstborn: A Short Play for Broadcasting*, PP/6/84 (I).
19 Digital Repository of Ireland (DRI), The Teresa Deevy Archive, '"The Firstborn": A Short Play for Broadcasting by D.V. Goode', https://doi.org/10.7486/DRI.95944c691-1
20 The Blackheath Society, 'Archive: Kidbrooke' (2021).
21 Dublin, Eavan Boland Library (EBL), Florence Hackett Collection, Teresa Deevy

at least one occasion, Teresa used this address to send out her work for review in England. She notes to Hackett in the 1949 letter that 'I have written a story and sent it in for a B.B.C. competition. Some day I must ask you to read it [sic]'.[22] According to Jacqui Deevy, Teresa's sister Josie lived and worked in south-east London for decades, but never owned a house there: she rented a few different properties during her time in England and so it is probable that the Kidbrooke Park Road address was written on the playscript in the late 1940s or early 1950s, the period when it is certain that Josie was based there.[23] The Blackheath area had been devastated by bombing during the Second World War. In the 1948 letter to Hackett, Teresa writes of 'getting quite a lot through the customs, meat, butter, eggs, chocolates' and notes that parts of London 'are still terrible'.[24]

Redating the Plays: The Advent of Radio Drama and Reference to Deevy's 1932 Abbey Prize

On the title page of *The Firstborn* is the typed subheading 'A Short Play for Broadcasting'. This reveals D.V. Goode to be writing at a much later date than previously believed: the BBC did not begin broadcasting (and then initially for short periods each day) until 1922, so it is impossible that this play could have been written during Teresa Deevy's stay in London between 1914 and 1919. As far as we know, Teresa Deevy did not write for radio for some two decades after this period. This timeline accords with the fact that regular radio broadcasting begins in Ireland from 1926, and it was several more years before plays were written specifically for that medium with all the adaptations and innovations that the genre demands.[25] Radio was a new and exciting platform in

---

to Florence Hackett (17 December 1948), MS 10722, item 45; Dublin, Eavan Boland Library (EBL), Florence Hackett Collection, Teresa Deevy to Florence Hackett (4 January 1949), MS 10722, item 56. Many thanks to TCD archivist Estelle Gittins who scanned these two letters for me in February 2021, when pandemic restrictions limited my access to Dublin archives.
22   EBL, MS 10722, item 56.
23   Interview with the author, November 2021.
24   EBL, MS 10722, item 45.
25   The Free State's radio service began on 1 January 1926 and, from 1935, radio drama and variety programmes at Radio Éireann were handled by the Productions Office. The archive of RTÉ Radio Drama and Variety Scripts, 1931–2000 is held in University

the 1930s, and it is only from that period that authors begin thinking about the possibilities and reach of the medium. D.V. Goode was clearly crafting the play for a radio audience: the opening lines do not describe a physical set, but rather the sounds of a kitchen scene: 'Woman humming a hymn, moving about, chopping with a knife on a board, then frying pan placed on stove and spluttering of fat. Latch of door lifted and young girl's voice speaking'.[26] These directions suggest an author conscious of the atmospheric power of radio soundscapes.

The three-act play, *Let Us Live*, is also from a much later date than previously assumed. A play about Catholic and Protestant marriages, it has a positive resolution for the younger generation in the 1930s moving beyond the divisions of the past. Most striking in the play are the debates about the importance of women's freedom and their right to continue to work after marriage: these were key concerns and debates in the 1930s as legislation was being enacted that restricted women's rights in these areas. Most strikingly, a character in the play references a prize that Teresa Deevy herself won in 1932, again revealing beyond doubt that the play was scripted significantly later than previously designated.[27]

> The Abbey Co. offered a £50 prize for the best play and the judges divided it between two—a man in Glasgow and a lady in Ireland.
> And she got it because her name was Deevy, so like Dev—Up Dev. every time![28]

This reference, a form of in-joke, is both confusing and revealing. It provides an incontrovertible sign that the play was written much later than previously thought because Deevy's play *Temporal Powers* was awarded joint first prize in the 1932 Aonach Tailteann Dramatic Arts competition when she tied for first place with Paul Vincent Carroll, an Irish playwright then living in Glasgow. While such a joking self-

---

College Dublin, https://www.ucd.ie/archives/collections/depositedcollections/
26 Digital Repository of Ireland (DRI), The Teresa Deevy Archive, 'The Firstborn', PP/6/84 (2), https://doi.org/10.7486/DRI.95944c691-1
27 Teresa Deevy's third play, *Temporal Powers*, tied for first place with Paul Vincent Carroll's *Things That Are Caesar's* in 1932. See Digital Repository of Ireland (DRI), The Teresa Deevy Archive, 'Abbey Theatre Play Contest: Man and Woman Tie for Big Prize: Judge's Comments', PP/6/178(82), *Irish Press*, 2 July 1932, p. 7.
28 Digital Repository of Ireland (DRI), The Teresa Deevy Archive, 'Play in Three Acts by D.V. Goode: "Let Us Live"', PP/6/82 (31), https://doi.org/10.7486/DRI.95944c313-1

reference is distracting and incongruous, unlike anything that Teresa Deevy incorporates into the dramatic writing that is confirmed as her own, it unequivocally reveals the play was written after 1932.

The Three Plays

In D.V. Goode's three plays, the author explores the lives of working women, demonstrates an openness to new technologies, and celebrates social change and modernisation. There is an engagement with class issues and gender, and with questions of religious and individual freedom. D.V. Goode is consciously writing for different platforms (radio and stage) and audiences (English and Irish), and these are not first drafts but complete manuscripts replete with intricate plotlines and defined contexts. While the play scripts are complete, it is unclear if they are finished and professional versions; as will be highlighted below, paratextual elements such as pagination suggest these were not uniformly edited, polished, and ready for submission to a production company. Furthermore, Deevy's sharp editing (whether for herself or others) would not seem to have been completed. For example, the speech of some characters is not distinctly individualised, and the action is at times overplotted, something which would suggest an accomplished author such as Deevy had not finished with them.[29] The theme of modernisation is foregrounded in D.V. Goode's plays. All three plays make extended and very specific reference to automobiles, to working women, and to societal change. For D.V. Goode, the car serves as a symbol of modernisation, and there are serious motorcar collisions in both *The Firstborn* and *Practice and Precept*, and an extended conversation about motorcars and motoring in *Let Us Live*.

The three-act play, *Let Us Live*, opens in 1904 in the drawing room of a Dublin house in 'one of the streets off Merion [sic] Square, such as Mount St' where a mother and son discuss the imminent arrival of

---

29 McCarthy and Kealy highlight Deevy's skill in individualising dialogue and aligning specific speech patterns with characters. See Kate McCarthy and Úna Kealy 'Writing from the Margins: Re-framing Teresa Deevy's Archive and her Correspondence with James Cheasty c.1952–1962', *Irish University Review*, 52.2 (2022), 322–340. For example, through the Deevy-Cheasty correspondence, they reveal how Deevy advised the younger playwright that 'each individual should have his own length of sentence... his own turn of words' (p. 331).

Catholic Molly Healy, a 'paying guest' whose contributions will support the dwindling family income of this Protestant teacher and her law student son, Claud Read.[30] The next scene flashes forward a year and the intimacy between the three is quickly apparent, and so too is the Reads' need to keep up appearances within their social circles. The second act opens in 1932 with Claud Read now father to three sons, one of whom is engaged to a Catholic woman called Finola Fanning. Claud calls to the Fanning home and, after a heated discussion about mixed marriages and working women, realises that Finola is the daughter of Molly Healy, who had married a judge and settled for a time in Australia. The remainder of the play explores the relationships within the two families and reflects on women's roles within marriage. It is a type of problem play, meditating on the issue of women's financial and emotional independence, intergenerational conflict, and on marriage as an institution. Its happy resolution sees Molly Healy insist to Claud that 'they [their respective children] have as much right to live their own way as we have'.[31] This acceptance of difference and the affectionate familial context results in the soon-to-be-married John exclaiming 'Sweetheart, let's live – you and me, happily ever after'.[32] Such parental support and this straightforwardly happy ending are unlike the ambiguous resolutions to be found in Deevy's best-known stage plays such as *Katie Roche*, *The King of Spain's Daughter*, or *Wife to James Whelan*; however, this conclusion does echo the closing lines of *The Reapers* when the marriage between two warring families is marked with the phrase 'life must be lived'.[33] In the extant manuscript of *Let Us Live*, the scenes are paginated separately, so that each one begins on page one, allowing for more discreet editing. The opening stage set is described on the first page of the first scene and inserted again separately with minor adjustments on

---

30 DRI, *Let Us Live*, PP/6/82 (4), I. 1. 4.
31 DRI, *Let us Live*, PP/6/82 (35), III. 2. 35.
32 DRI, *Let us Live*, PP/6/82 (37), III. 2. 37.
33 Teresa Deevy, 'Katie Roche', in *Teresa Deevy Reclaimed*, 2 vols, ed. by Jonathan Bank, John P. Harrington, and Christopher Morash (New York: Mint Theater, 2011), I, 57–102; Teresa Deevy, 'The King of Spain's Daughter', in *Teresa Deevy Reclaimed*, 2 vols, ed. by Jonathan Bank, John P. Harrington, and Christopher Morash (New York: Mint Theater, 2017), II, 17–26, and Teresa Deevy, 'Wife to James Whelan', in *Teresa Deevy Reclaimed*, I, 109–158; This phrase is quoted in a review of *The Reapers*, see DRI, The Teresa Deevy Archive, 'Waterford Lady's First Play', *Waterford News and Star*, 21 March 1930, PP/6/178(87), https://doi.org/10.7486/DRI.95944b71v

a separate page after the title page and list of characters page. These paratextual elements suggest this is not a finished and polished script, although it is complete in terms of plot resolution and was at a stage where an author may feel it could be circulated for critique and feedback.

The second three-act play considered here is entitled *Practice and Precept* and it is set in suburban England in the Swift family home. It opens with an account of a fatal car crash, an incident which involves one of the characters, David, who is married to Joyce Swift. In this busy, complicated script, there are references to alternative medicine, women smoking, divorce, astrology, and several crimes including burglary and manslaughter. David, the young husband, has a shadow side having fled the scene of the hit-and-run accident caused by a criminal friend which opens the play. Eventually, he goes to prison and the final act of the play opens after he has served his sentence. During this time, Joyce gets a job and becomes financially independent, and she begins to dread his return. Feeling ashamed and fearing that she will never trust her husband again, she is supported by friends and family who encourage her to give David an opportunity to redeem himself. In the final act, Joyce decides to accept her husband back into her life and the play concludes with a sense of optimism that the marriage and this family's situation might work itself out. The manuscript for *Practice and Precept* includes insertions, missing pages, and inconsistent pagination, giving the impression of an unfinished piece, or of different versions fused together. There are seemingly unconnected handwritten notes on the back of the final page; random phrases and words are used, possibly as an aid for an accompanying conversation.[34] Along with isolated phrases and questions suggesting low spirits and ill health, the note includes a figure of £2.10 and a sequence of numbers, presumably a date: 31.12.62 or New Year's Eve, 1962, which is less than three weeks before Teresa Deevy's death.[35] The notes reference illness, an operation, 'no visitors',

---

[34] Deevy was known for this practice of writing notes on scraps of paper as an aid for understanding conversation. In his article for the *Cork Examiner*, Séan Dunne records the memory of Deevy's friend, Mary O'Regan: 'when she was too tired to lip-read she'd write on pieces of paper and next morning there'd be reams of paper all over the place after her visit'. See 'Rediscovering Teresa Deevy', *Cork Examiner*, 20 March 1984, p. 10.

[35] DRI, *Practice and Precept*, PP/6/81, https://doi.org/10.7486/DRI.5999vb76p-1

and a letter from a Fr Burke in Ibadan in West Nigeria.[36] Whatever the explanation for these fragmentary words and sentences, their very existence suggests a casual attitude to manuscripts as the back sheet had been repurposed for making notes, most likely in the weeks before Deevy's death when she was quite feeble and suffering from vertigo.

D.V. Goode's *The Firstborn* is a one-act radio play set in a gate lodge a mile from a 'big house'.[37] In the opening sentences of dialogue between Mary (an older woman) and the visiting young woman Ellen, we learn that a baby is due to be born in the demesne and, in anticipation, the family had built an extension to catch the sunlight at all times of the day. This wealthy family designed this beautiful room so the child would see the world as a happy place, and this confident planning is wryly considered by the locals gathered in the gate lodge. This short play has a dark, tragic end as the baby dies ten minutes after birth. Foreshadowing the infant's death is a dramatic collision when a truck crashes into the gatepost of the estate. There is confusion in the closing lines when the death of the child is announced, and Mary assumes the death being discussed is related to the motoring accident. In this play there is a dramatic confrontation between different worlds and temporalities with an explicit theme of societal change as the forces of modernisation mean that old social structures are being swept away.

There are similarities and differences between the D.V. Goode plays and Teresa Deevy's confirmed works. Deevy's skilful use of pauses, silences, and insinuation are not evidenced in the D.V. Goode stage plays where thoughts, feelings, backstories, and context are frequently articulated, leaving less to the imagination. Characters are more likely to expound a set perspective or to represent a 'type'. Most notable is the absence of Deevy's signature ellipsis although, in this context, it is significant that some acknowledged plays like the fragmentary *The Finding of the Ball* include few ellipses.[38] Deevy's expressionistic techniques and what Lennox Robinson

---

36 Fr William (Liam) Burke SMA (1926-2013) was an influential member of the Society of African Missions. Over a long career, he cultivated positive interfaith relationships within the archdiocese and hosted Pope John Paul II on his visit to Nigeria in 1982. From a Kilkenny family embedded in religious, civic, and business networks, his connection to Teresa Deevy is not surprising as both her parents originated from similar Kilkenny families.

37 DRI, *The Firstborn*, PP/6/84.

38 Digital Repository of Ireland (DRI), The Teresa Deevy Archive, "The Finding of the Ball: A Play in One Act", PP/6/119 (1-13), https://doi.org/10.7486/DRI.95944g52g

described as her 'half-realistic' style are distinct from the detailed realism of D.V. Goode's two stage plays.[39] However, there are some echoes too, although this is not to confirm a clear linguistic fingerprint. For example, both D.V. Goode and Teresa Deevy use the problem play genre. In Deevy's *Temporal Powers,* she brought to life a contemporary social and political problem, exploring different views on that issue as the drama unfolds.[40] This technique, or format, is deployed in D.V. Goode's *Let Us Live* and in *Practice and Precept,* as these dramas centre on social or moral dilemmas. In both, the issue of married women working and earning their own money is explored and debated. Both plays conclude with the young married women working for personal satisfaction and financial independence. Furthermore, like *Temporal Powers*, *Practice and Precept* is concerned with the question of forgiveness in personal relationships.

Another similarity between the D.V. Goode stage plays and Deevy's *Wife to James Whelan* is the use of a technique where several years pass between the first act and the two subsequent acts where the action plays out. *Let Us Live* has Act One in 1904 and 1905 and Acts Two and Three in 1932, a challenging structure in terms of production; *Practice and Precept* concludes two and a half years after it opens in Act One. Similarly, Act One in Deevy's *Wife to James Whelan* is separated by seven years from the later Acts Two and Three. There are some resemblances in language and the use of colloquialisms within the D.V. Goode dramas and Teresa Deevy's confirmed work. For example, in *Wife to James Whelan*, a character notes that Nan's husband's pension 'died with him' while in *Practice and Precept,* a character says, 'but a pension dies with you'.[41] There are echoes too with the titles used. *Temporal Powers* has a religious signification; it refers to worldly power, as contrasted with spiritual power. Even though the play itself is not explicitly about religion, there is an ethical and moral dimension to the debates presented within the drama. *Practice and Precept* has a similar kind of resonance. The phrase is often used to discuss religious rules (like the Ten Commandments) that become principles and that should be practised in everyday life. *Let Us Live* is different—it

---

39   Lennox Robinson described Deevy's style as 'half-realistic' in his review of her *Three Plays* in *The Dublin Magazine*, 15 (April–June 1939), 71–72.
40   Caoilfhionn Ní Bheacháin, '"It Was Then I Knew life": Political Critique and Moral Debate in Teresa Deevy's *Temporal Powers* (1932)', *Irish University Review*, 50.2 (2020), 337–355. Teresa Deevy, 'Temporal Powers', in *Teresa Deevy Reclaimed*, I, 7–50.
41   Deevy, *Wife to James Whelan*; DRI, *Practice and Precept*, PP/6/81.

echoes a Latin phrase which in English goes 'while we are alive, let us live', a sentiment which resonates with the closing lines of Deevy's missing debut, *The Reapers*: 'Life must be lived, not simply accepted'.[42]

As discussed above, the opening directions of the radio play, *The Firstborn*, demonstrate the author's consciousness and understanding of the medium, and this is something that is also evident in confirmed works of Teresa Deevy, such as in her radio play *Going Beyond Alma's Glory*. This latter play contains the following sound directions in its opening lines:

> Subdued, indistinct voices. Then—clearly—a man's step coming to a table, a chair pulled out, a newspaper opened noisily, and folded at a chosen place. A girl's step.[43]

Going Beyond Alma's Glory was broadcast by Radio Éireann in October 1951 and published that December in *Irish Writing* (No. 17). If the Blackheath address on the front cover of *The Firstborn* is from Deevy's visit in 1948/49, this timeframe would suggest both plays were written during the same period. Of the three D.V. Goode plays, the atmosphere and language of *The Firstborn* most closely resemble that of Teresa Deevy's known work, and its themes and setting are familiar. Indeed, in *The Firstborn,* the character of Stephen critically refers to Ellen as 'More like larkin' around with the boys and she missed her chance',[44] a line that could have come from one of Deevy's best-known stage plays. However, these synergies and echoes do not resolve the question of authorship, as they could be the result of mentorship, influence, or editorial suggestions.[45] In other words, the D.V. Goode plays could have been written by a protégé or sibling of Teresa Deevy.

---

42 An unidentified critic in the *Irish Times* quoted this line from *The Reapers*. DRI, The Teresa Deevy Archive, '"The Reapers": First Production at the Abbey Theatre', PP/6/178(3), https://doi.org/10.7486/DRI.5999vb302

43 Teresa Deevy, 'Going Beyond Alma's Glory', in *Teresa Deevy Reclaimed*, II, 97–107 (p. 97).

44 Deevy, *The Firstborn*, PP/6/85(8).

45 Deevy mentored numerous writers and made suggestions on how they could improve their technique. For example, it has been argued that Deevy's influence is evident in James Cheasty's stage directions and dialogue. See McCarthy and Kealy, 'Writing from the Margins', pp. 329–330.

Provenance and Authorship of the Plays

When originally assessed when stored in Landscape, these plays were likely to have received less attention because they are not part of Deevy's performed work for the Abbey in the 1930s and neither are they part of her portfolio of radio plays produced by the BBC and RTÉ in her later career. They were not included in her published works and there are no obvious references to them in the correspondence which is currently available for consultation.[46] Infused with realism, containing some unwieldy dialogue, occasionally didactic, and devoid of her signature ellipsis, these plays are not straightforwardly like Deevy's published or performed work. However, the scripts contain echoes and resonances of her dramaturgical style; furthermore, that these manuscripts were included with Deevy's papers at the time of her death and the pseudonym 'D.V. Goode' suggest they can be attributed to either Teresa Deevy or someone in the Deevy family.

This question of provenance raises questions about which Deevy, other than Teresa, could have authored the plays. According to her grandniece Jacqui Deevy, none of the Deevy siblings were known to have been creative writers. She notes that Teresa Deevy's sisters did occasionally help with the typing and sorting of her papers.[47] Similarly, Edward Deevy, a grandnephew and a frequent visitor to Landscape in the 1950s, recalls these elderly aunts being regular letter writers, but states that only Teresa was known to write fiction or drama.[48] From Teresa's correspondence with Florence Hackett, it is clear that Nell was very interested in the theatre. However, when Teresa died in 1963, her sister Frances Deevy (who was deaf and blind) was the only sister still living in the family home; therefore, with all but one of her sisters having predeceased her, can it be assumed that Teresa would have separated a sibling's work from her own papers or, at a minimum, identified manuscripts as belonging to herself or a particular sister? Within the archive, many of Deevy's confirmed scripts, pseudonymous essays from

---

46 However, it is notable that several performed plays by Deevy had not been published until the Mint Theater released two volumes of her collected plays (*Teresa Deevy Reclaimed*, ed. by Bank, Harrington, and Morash).
47 Interview with the author, March 2021.
48 Interview with the author, December 2022.

Will 'o' the Wisp, and a short story entitled 'Brian of the Boers'[49] have Teresa Deevy's handwritten signature on the typescript, suggesting she made some efforts to identify these works as hers. Other documents include handwritten notes, edits, and annotations. However, there is a dearth of information on how the papers were originally arranged or grouped within the suitcase archive, and there are instances of other files or manuscripts being consulted or borrowed by friends and scholars at different junctures.[50] To complicate matters, the archive also contains writings by authors such as Gerard Westby and David Marcus.[51]

The Penname: D.V. Goode

Using a pseudonym is not uncommon among writers: Mark Twain, the Brontës, and George Orwell all used pseudonyms. So, too, did some of Deevy's Irish contemporaries, including Rosamond Jacob, Una Troy, and Flann O'Brien. *The Firstborn, Let Us Live,* and *Practice and Precept* all appear under the pseudonym D.V. Goode. The first part of this nom de plume clearly relates to the surname Deevy, and it also recalls a well-known abbreviation of the Latin phrase Deo Volente. In English, Deo Volente, or 'DV', means 'God willing' or 'if it is meant to be', and it was a common expression in twentieth-century Ireland. The second part of the surname, 'Goode', complements the first, and again is an interesting choice. Surnames such as 'Goode', 'Goody', 'Goodwife', and 'Goodman' are rooted in 'good' or 'God'. 'Goode' is a synonym for virtuous or exemplary, although there are other resonances. Its etymology can be traced back to the Middle Ages, but it is most associated with the

---

49 DRI, The Teresa Deevy Archive, Deevy, Teresa, 1894–1963, 'Brian of the Boers', PP/6/164, https://doi.org/10.7486/DRI.5999vj14x. A second version of this story is also included in the Maynooth Depository, and this includes the following handwritten note: '1300 words - as sent to U.S.A., Jan. 12th '31'. See DRI, The Teresa Deevy Archive, Deevy, Teresa, 1894–1963, 'Brian of the Boers', PP/6/163(1-6), p. 1, https://doi.org/10.7486/DRI.5999vj08s

50 For example, as mentioned above, Frank McEvoy borrowed a manuscript of the stage play *Wife to James Whelan* when preparing his talk for the Kilkenny Literary Society.

51 A minor playwright, Gerard Westby is best known for his one-act play, *Kevin Barry*, published by Bourke in 1953. Cork-born intellectual, David Marcus (1924–2009), was an influential author, journalist, and editor who mentored generations of Irish writers. These two are just some of the writers known to have sent their work to Teresa Deevy for feedback.

Puritans in America as a generic form of respectful address or title. Together, as a penname, D.V. Goode suggests spirituality and the author's commitment to Christian values. It could also be read as an invocation, a petition to God, or as a writerly luck charm. The D.V. Goode penname could have been used by Teresa Deevy or, indeed, by one of her siblings although, as noted earlier, there is no evidence to suggest that any of them were secretly writing to the extent that they could produce a few substantial scripts, including one that is specifically written for radio. Of course, if the plays are Teresa Deevy's, then it raises questions about why a published and successful author would write plays under this pseudonym. One possibility is that Deevy was trying to write commercially or to a formula, for a different audience. Could Deevy, living in increasingly straitened circumstances, have been writing for the burgeoning amateur circuit, an outlet which was lucrative in these mid-century years, while simultaneously protecting her reputation as an 'epoch-making' playwright? However, this seems unlikely as Deevy was already known for working with amateur authors and theatremakers, and preliminary searches in catalogues of Irish and UK archives have not yielded evidence of either D.V. Goode or the three plays. Therefore, it seems unlikely that they were produced.

The Teresa Deevy Archive in Maynooth also contains short stories that are authored under the pseudonym 'Chris. Devoy.' [sic] and the typed address of the apartment in Waterloo Road in Dublin that Deevy shared with her sister Nell.[52] The 'Chris. Devoy.' penname is important in that it has a similar resonance to D.V. Goode: a first name that is gender neutral and a Christian reference in the name 'Chris.'. The surname Devoy is close to Deevy and evokes the famous Irish nationalist, the Fenian John Devoy. Are D.V. Goode and Chris. Devoy the same person? Is Chris. Devoy a penname for Teresa Deevy? Could Nell, who shared the Waterloo Road flat, be Chris. Devoy? Or could it be someone else?

---

52 DRI, The Teresa Deevy Archive, 'Alen.' by Chris. Devoy., Deevy, Teresa, 1894–1963, PP/6/161(1-13), p. 1, https://doi.org/10.7486/DRI.5999vj01v. It is noteworthy that both '"Man Proposes --- "'[sic] and 'John Potter's Story' have a similar layout, but with Teresa Deevy's name and the Waterloo Road address in a similar position. See DRI, The Teresa Deevy Archive, '"Man Proposes --- "' by Teresa Deevy, Deevy, Teresa, 1894–1963, PP/6/172 (1-17), https://doi.org/10.7486/DRI.5999vj423; DRI, The Teresa Deevy Archive, '"John Potter's Story"' by Teresa Deevy, Deevy, Teresa, 1894–1963, PP/6/166(1-5), https://doi.org/10.7486/DRI.5999vj156

Significantly, there are two versions of the short story 'Alen' by Chris. Devoy and one shows evidence of decisive and thoughtful editing; this careful work involved excising several sections from the story, eliminating unnecessary detail, and explanation of character; it is unclear if this is self-editing or the expert editing of a more accomplished writer (for example, Teresa critiquing the work of a sibling). Another story attributed within the archive to Teresa Deevy, published in the *Weekly Examiner,* appears under the penname T.D. O'Toole (significantly another gender-neutral penname). If using pennames, it is possible that Deevy was either experimenting with form, disguising her work for some reason, or writing for different audiences. Whatever the case may be, from this evidence, it cannot be conclusively determined whether Teresa Deevy was using the penname D.V. Goode. Neither has it been recorded why or how these different materials were included with her papers at the time of her death. However, this ambiguity does highlight the need to re-examine these different texts with a fresh lens and new methodologies to identify stylistic idiosyncrasies, material aspects (such as font, paper, and margins), annotations and paratextual elements, and so forth.[53]

Could (an) Edward Deevy be D.V. Goode?

The initial discovery of the mystery surrounding the dating of the D.V. Goode plays was enabled by the digitisation project undertaken by Maynooth University and prompted by the research conditions that emerged during the Covid-19 pandemic; public health restrictions meant physical libraries and archives were inaccessible, and so I found myself trawling through the online Deevy archive, reading these little-known manuscripts with a growing sense of surprise and interest. At that juncture, it seemed most probable that either Teresa or one of her closest sisters (Nell or Josie) had written the D.V. Goode plays: what

---

53 There are graphic design elements (use of capitals in the titles and repeated use of the @ symbol to structure the layout) on one of the D.V. Goode manuscripts (*The Firstborn*, PP/6/84 (1)) that match those on one of the manuscripts of *The King of Spain's Daughter*. See DRI, The Teresa Deevy Archive, *The King of Spain's Daughter*: A One-Act play, PP/6/97 (1-10), https://doi.org/10.7486/DRI.95944d41j. Furthermore, both scripts seem to have been printed on similar watermarked bond paper. This is intriguing and warrants further investigation.

else could explain the pseudonym, the Blackheath address on *The Firstborn* script, and their original inclusion in the green suitcase that partly housed Teresa's archive. The key issue was provenance: who else could have written the 'D.V.' plays that were in Teresa Deevy's archive? However, one of the challenges of online archives is what gets omitted, either because of the focus of specific digitisation projects, copyright issues, funding limitations, or plain bad luck. Therefore, as the pandemic restrictions eased, I journeyed to Maynooth to work in person at the archive there, and another possibility emerged. What if there was another author with the surname Deevy? What if this figure, Edward Deevy, shared his work with Teresa? What if he wrote for stage and radio? What if he had spent time in England? What if Teresa had advised him on how to improve his scripts and he had adopted all her recommendations? Within the Deevy collection, there is a single letter which provides a credible alternative for authorship.

In a letter penned in 1954, Edward Deevy (not a family member) wrote to Teresa Deevy thanking her for sharing her work with him and offering sympathy regarding her health after she had suffered a setback. He prays (using the Latin abbreviation D.V.) that Teresa will 'hear some time in the future'.[54] He gratefully acknowledges her feedback on his work, revealing that he has made the changes that she suggested and confiding that he has submitted the play (apparently to Radio Éireann) for consideration:

> Also, thanks a lot for having read my play. I noted your comments and could see where I made mistakes. I retyped the play and made the alterations you suggested. It is now in the hands of R.E. and fate...!!!
> All your comments were of great value to me.[55]

In this letter, Edward mentions that a poem he had previously sent her had been written while he was in England. He also references his 'case full of returned and scrapped mss'.[56] These details lend credibility to the theory that he could be D.V. Goode. Searches for a writer called Edward Deevy (distinct from her grandnephew) have not yet yielded

---

54 DRI, The Teresa Deevy Archive, Edward Deevy to Teresa Deevy, 29 April 1954, PP/6/10.
55 DRI, PP/6/10.
56 DRI, PP/6/10.

results.⁵⁷ The 1954 letter was sent from an address at 'Light House Cross, Patrickswell, Co. Limerick', a location not mentioned on the Ordnance Survey Ireland map, but a site which receives a single mention in a school's submission to the National Folklore Collection.⁵⁸ Teresa's brother, Fr John Aloysius Deevy, was a Jesuit priest at nearby Mungret College (the parish adjoining Patrickswell) until his death in 1969, and could possibly have been the connector between Teresa Deevy and this writer bearing the family surname.⁵⁹ Could D.V. Goode's plays and Edward Deevy's letter have been stored together and accidentally separated? Is it significant that Edward Deevy used 'D.V.' or Deo Volente when asking after his mentor's health? These questions present a hypothetical alternative to the identity of D.V. Goode. If this Edward Deevy is D.V. Goode, it would explain the differences between the latter's work and that of Teresa Deevy. It would also explain some echoes between the two authors in that Edward admired Teresa, possibly emulating her themes, language, dramatic structure, titles, and style, and he, apparently, took her advice on how to improve his scripts.

Conclusion

While all archives are incomplete, Teresa Deevy's literary legacy—fragmentary in terms of surviving correspondence and scripts, and spread across several institutions—is particularly inchoate, because much of her correspondence has not survived, material has been lost, and there are no diaries to consult. The main repository for Deevy

---

57   However, Teresa Deevy's grandnephew, Edward, remembers her critiquing his short stories (written when a schoolchild), and her encouragement of his efforts. Interview with author, December 2022.

58   National Folklore Collection, The Schools' Collection, 'Lurga, Patrick's Well', https://www.duchas.ie/en/cbes/4922108/4852764. A fieldtrip to the area eventually led to my identifying the address, a crossroads on the old Cork to Limerick Road where buses would stop outside a small house (that, according to a neighbour, always had a light on) that is far from any lighthouse. The area was part of the old Attyflynn Estate, a 250-acre farm between Patrickswell and Adare.

59   Jacqui Deevy suggests this could have been a possible connection. As manager of the agricultural estate at Mungret College, Fr John was responsible for its 240 acres of farmland and would have been well known in the area. For a description of the Mungret Estate and Seminary, see Sharon Slater, 'Mungret College, 1882–1974, History and Photograph Book', *Limerick's Life*, 1 September 2015, http://limerickslife.com/mungret-college/

scholars is located at the Teresa Deevy Archive at Maynooth University, and this critical resource was established several decades after her death, so it is unclear how the papers were arranged in 1963. Significantly, the Teresa Deevy Archive is still dynamic and in flux.[60] Overlooked for many years, Deevy's papers were stored in the family home and cared for by dedicated relations. Despite her authoring of six Abbey plays throughout the 1930s, occasional revivals on stage, and a steady stream of interested scholars, Deevy was obscured in the public imagination. A manuscript of her first play, *The Reapers*, has yet to be discovered. Furthermore, missing or unarchived correspondence means Teresa Deevy's role as a mentor to amateur and emerging playwrights has also been overlooked or underestimated.

There are various scenarios which could explain the opaque origins of the D.V. Goode plays and the reason for using a pseudonym that echoes the Deevy name but obscures the exact identity of the author. Could they have been by a sister emulating her sibling's craft? This would explain the common addresses included on manuscripts, the interest in politics and social issues, and some of the echoes between the authors. Indeed, if one of Teresa's sisters was the mysterious D.V. Goode, it would be intriguing, further complicating our understanding of the family and, more broadly, of women's cultural production and political critique during this era. Could an elderly Teresa Deevy have written as D.V. Goode, attempting something different from her better-known dramas? Could she have been seeking new audiences or income streams, but abandoning this project in these uneven scripts? If Deevy herself used this pseudonym for these plays, that raises questions about stylistic differences within the manuscripts, why none of them are signed, and why these three scripts are apparently not referenced elsewhere. And what about Edward Deevy? Could he have used this pseudonym to disguise his identity as he developed his craft? If this amateur playwright was D.V. Goode, it would reveal something fascinating about Teresa Deevy's influence as an intellectual and a mentor. Or could

---

60 The Eileen Kearney papers and the Deevy-Cheasty correspondence are now conserved within the Deevy Archive at Maynooth University. While not available for consultation while research was being undertaken for this chapter, these resources are sure to illuminate lesser-known aspects of Deevy's life and work. They may also include additional clues to the mystery of D.V. Goode.

D.V. Goode be the creation of another writer, yet unknown? Ultimately, this is a 'whodunit' about Irish writers, intellectual networks, archives, and cultural memory. The fragmentary evidence currently available is tantalising and suggestive, and this chapter offers an account of an investigation in progress. What is categorically proven here is that the D.V. Goode plays are significantly later than previously believed. Furthermore, there are intriguing possibilities regarding authorship: D.V. Goode was either Teresa Deevy herself exploring an alternative authorial voice, a sibling secretly writing, or an unrelated Deevy who we know had written radio plays, but who has yet to be positively identified. As Teresa Deevy receives more scholarly and archival attention, and as additional correspondence and records become publicly available, some of these archival conundrums and biographical mysteries may finally be solved.

Bibliography

Bank, Jonathan, John P. Harrington, and Christopher Morash (eds), *Teresa Deevy Reclaimed,* 2 vols (New York: Mint Theater, 2011 and 2017)

Bhatia, Neeraj, 'Reassembling the Archive', *AA Files*, 77, ed. by Maria Sheherazade Giudici (2020), https://www.theopenworkshop.ca/publications/re-assembling-the-archive/

The Blackheath Society, 'Archive: Kidbrooke' (2021), https://www.blackheatharchive.org/f466378646

Collins, Lucy, 'Hidden Collections: The Value of Irish Literary Archives', *Irish University Review,* 50.1 (2020), 187–197, https://doi.org/10.3366/iur.2020.0445

Dunne, Seán, 'Rediscovering Teresa Deevy', *Cork Examiner,* 20 March 1984, p. 10

Dunne, Seán, 'Teresa Deevy, an Introduction', *The Journal of Irish Literature,* 14.2 (1985), 3–15

Engel, Laura, and Emily Ruth Rutter, 'Women and Archives', *Tulsa Studies in Women's Literature*, 40.1 (2021), 5–13, https://tswl.utulsa.edu/uncategorized/women-and-archives-spring-2021-vol-40-no-1/

Freeland, Jane, and Christina von Hodenberg, 'Archiving, Exhibiting, and Curating the History of Feminisms in the Global Twentieth Century: An Introduction', *Women's History Review*, 33.1 (2023), 1–6, https://doi.org/10.1080/09612025.2023.2208401

Fuentes, Marisa J. (ed.), *Dispossessed Lives: Enslaved Women, Violence, and the Archive* (Philadelphia, PN: University of Pennsylvania Press, 2018)

Hamilton, Carolyn, Verne Harris, Jane Taylor, Michele Pickover, Graeme Reid, and Razia Saleh (eds), *Refiguring the Archive* (Amsterdam: Kluwer Academic Publishers, 2002), https://doi.org/10.1007/978-94-010-0570-8

Hicks, Dan (ed.), *The Brutish Museums: The Benin Bronzes, Colonial Violence and Cultural Restitution* (London: Pluto Press, 2020)

Houlihan, Barry, *Theatre and Archival Memory: Irish Drama and Marginalised Histories, 1951–1977* (Hampshire: Palgrave Macmillan, 2021), https://doi.org/10.1007/978-3-030-74548-6

Laing, Kathryn, Sinéad Mooney, Caoilfhionn Ní Bheacháin, Anna Pilz, Whitney Standlee, and Julie Anne Stevens, 'Connecting Voices: An Introduction to Irish Women Writers' Collaborations and Networks, 1880–1940', *English Studies*, 104.6 (2023), 843–864, https://doi.org/10.1080/0013838X.2023.2243968

Laverty, Maura, *The Plays of Maura Laverty: Liffey Lane, Tolka Row, A Tree in the Crescent*, ed. by Cathy Leeney and Deirdre McFeely (Liverpool: Liverpool University Press, 2023)

McCarthy, Kate, and Úna Kealy, 'Writing from the Margins: Re-framing Teresa Deevy's Archive and Her Correspondence with James Cheasty c.1952–1962', *Irish University Review*, 52.2 (2022), 322–340, https://doi.org/10.3366/iur.2022.0570

Ní Bheacháin, Caoilfhionn, '"It Was Then I Knew life": Political Critique and Moral Debate in Teresa Deevy's *Temporal Powers* (1932)', *Irish University Review*, 50.2 (2020), 337–355, https://doi.org/10.3366/iur.2020.0474

Ní Bheacháin, Caoilfhionn, 'Teresa Deevy and the Secrets of the Green Suitcase', *Irish Times*, 3 April 2021, https://www.irishtimes.com/culture/stage/teresa-deevy-and-the-secrets-of-the-green-suitcase-1.4522873

O'Doherty, Martina Ann, 'Deevy: A Bibliography', *Irish University Review*, 25.1 (1995), 163–170

Ondrej Pilný, Ruud van den Beuken, and Ian R. Walsh, *Cultural Convergence: The Dublin Gate Theatre, 1928–1960* (Cham: Palgrave Macmillan, 2021), https://doi.org/10.1007/978-3-030-57562-5

Robinson, Lennox, 'Review of Three Plays by Teresa Deevy', *The Dublin Magazine*, 15 (April–June 1939), 71–72

Slater, Sharon, 'Mungret College, 1882–1974, History and Photograph Book', *Limerick's Life*, 1 September 2015, http://limerickslife.com/mungret-college/

DEEVY'S IRELAND:
A COUNTRY IN CONTEXT

5. 'Very Seldom Are Messages Properly Given':[1] Teresa Deevy's Dark Matter

Chris Morash

In the summer of 2017, the Mint Theater in New York staged a very belated premiere of one of Teresa Deevy's late plays, the one-act *In the Cellar of My Friend*, where it made up a four-play bill entitled *The Suitcase under the Bed* with *Holiday House*, *Strange Birth*, and *The King of Spain's Daughter*.[2] Before that, however, apart from a rehearsed reading in August of 2011, it had only been performed once before, for a brief two-day run in 1957,[3] and only existed in two manuscript copies, one in the Maynooth archive and the other in the National Library of Ireland; and before that, it had been part of the pile of papers that had been gathering dust under a bed in Teresa Deevy's family home in Waterford, Landscape since her death in 1963.

Dot … dot … dot …

Like many of her later short plays, *In the Cellar of My Friend* appears deceptively simple, almost hopelessly naïve. The world of the play seems to be a sleepy little world in a realist box set, in this case made up of the

---

[1] Teresa Deevy, 'In the Cellar of My Friend', in *Teresa Deevy Reclaimed*, 2 vols, ed. by Jonathan Bank, John P. Harrington, and Christopher Morash (New York: Mint Theater, 2011 and 2017), II, 111–122 (p. 114).

[2] *The Suitcase under the Bed,* dir. by Jonathan Bank, Mint Theater, New York, 21 July–23 September 2017. Texts of the plays were published in the accompanying volume: *Teresa Deevy Reclaimed*, II.

[3] Kate McCarthy and Úna Kealy, 'Writing from the Margins: Re-framing Teresa Deevy's Archive and Her Correspondence with James Cheasty c. 1952–1962', *Irish University Review*, 52.2 (2022), 322–340 (p. 333).

drawing room of a large house in the Irish countryside, Grantsthorn House, in which 'it is a July morning—about nine thirty and through the window can be sensed some of the loveliness of the morning'.[4] This world of suffused sunlight is a signature in Deevy's work, its very intensity signalling to us to mistrust the textures of the material world, as much as we revel in their materiality. It is a world we recognise from the opening of *Wife to James Whelan* on the sun-soaked bench behind the garage that they call 'the South of France'.[5] We find Deevy reflecting on this quality in her work in the letter to Florence Hackett written after the opening night of *The King of Spain's Daughter* in 1935, when Deevy declared that 'the whole play had turned for me on the April day atmosphere'; she subsequently dedicated the play 'To an April Day'.[6] This quality of 'atmosphere' is explored most explicitly in the 1948 play, *Light Falling*, where the character of Mr Leslie at one point says: 'For me truth is embodied in light falling… (*Speaks with quiet intensity.*) if I can get that down on canvas others will see in it the eternal mystery, the beneficence—oh, damn it all,—there's nothing new'.[7]

In the Cellar of My Friend begins, then, with a quality of light. Into this glowing world enters the character of Belle Dobbyn, where her friend Patty Keane and her family live. As the play opens, Patty compliments Belle on her dress, telling her 'you look like a summer morning'. To which Belle replies:

> Well isn't it summer—and a lovely morning…the most lovely— (*Breaks off.*)…See, this basket—nothing really but a platform for the roses to rest on…and the great handle arching over them like a rainbow…no sides, nothing to hold them…but they hold on.[8]

There are a couple of things worth noting here. In the first place, there is the way in which the phenomenological world—the summer's morning—is constantly veering towards becoming a signifier of some unspoken significance, just as the roses manage to be both roses, and

---

4   Deevy, 'In the Cellar of My Friend', p. 111.
5   Teresa Deevy, 'Wife to James Whelan', in *Teresa Deevy Reclaimed*, I, 109–158 (p. 109).
6   Maynooth, Russell Library (RL), The Teresa Deevy Archive, Frank McEvoy, Teresa Deevy: Her Plays: Read to the Kilkenny Literary Society, 25 March 1966, p. 7, PP/6/III/176 16.
7   Teresa Deevy, 'Light Falling', in *Teresa Deevy Reclaimed*, II, 63–75 (p. 69).
8   Deevy, 'Cellar', p. 112.

seem to be straining towards some other meaning. However, perhaps most striking, when we see the passage on the page, is the fragmentation of the language in a stage world that otherwise seems so whole. In a passage that is only forty-five words long, there are no fewer than five ellipsis, and three long em-dashes; or, on average, one irregular break in syntax every six and a half words. There is, in short, as much silence as sound, and this feature is central to the way in which Deevy's theatre language works. What is more, were we to go back to Deevy's plays of the 1930s, we would find multiple examples of this kind of broken syntax. Nor is this accidental; in fact, it can be argued that the same shattered syntax can stand as an image of *In the Cellar of My Friend* as a whole, where it appears that we are looking at a theatrical world that is basking in its own fullness and completeness, but which on closer examination turns out to be as splintered as the speech.

In the first instance, objects in the play's world have a habit of breaking into fragments. As Belle looks at a basket full of roses, the basket itself effectively disappears, becoming, in her perception '—nothing really but a platform for the roses to rest on... [...] no sides, nothing to hold them ...'. The basket becomes, in phenomenological terms, a tool, an object of which the sole purpose is to accomplish a task, and thereby erases itself as an object. At the same time, the roses both become more fully present as roses, but as she sees the roses as having an intensity of presence that is almost like a kind of immanence, they too cease to become pure objects, instead becoming available as symbols. So, when the character of Tom, Patty's brother, pricks his finger on them, he immediately veers away from the actual rose before him to an unspoken idea: 'Ah-h...those roses are treacherous... I often think it...hidden thorns always in them—' (a line, it is worth noting, with fourteen words, three ellipses, and an em-dash).[9] He goes on to ask Belle what she once said to him about red roses, 'What did you once say about them? Drops of the Precious Blood, you told me, scarcely heeded, yet making for gladness...'—to which Belle replies: 'Did I say that? Then I was cribbing—not my own words at all, but Barney's...'.[10]

In the same way, we can also think of the plot of *In the Cellar of My Friend* as being like one of Deevy's sentences where what looks like an

---

9   Ibid., p. 114.
10   Ibid., pp. 114–115.

ordinary, innocuous sentence is broken up and the real significance of what is happening resides in the pieces that are missing—in the silences. The character of Barney mentioned here is the play's fourth character, Tom's son (and hence, Patty's nephew), a young man of about twenty-one. We first hear of him when Tom enters raging about Barney's 'latest idea! ...so absurd...so preposterous', upon which Belle cuts her finger on a rose, startled because she believes—as does Patty—that Barney's 'latest idea' is to propose marriage to Belle.[11] And this is what Belle (and, indeed, the audience) think is happening right up until the play's final scene, when we discover that Barney's great epiphany of the previous night was not that he should ask Belle to marry him: it was that he should join a religious order, live in a monastery, and commit his life to God. Indeed, it is not until the play's final moments that Tom actually states what is taking place—that Barney is leaving Grantsthorn 'to be a monk'—leaving the audience with the sense that they had been distracted by some other play, and have somehow missed the real play that was taking place unseen in front of their eyes.[12] Or, to put it another way, it is as if the words in the sentence suddenly appear like shining irrelevances, and the real meaning lies in the silence of the ellipsis.

'Exultant'

When Barney first appears in *In the Cellar of My Friend*, he is described as being 'exultant and charged with eagerness'.[13] This might not seem like a remarkable set of stage directions; however, it is worth paying particular attention to the word 'exultant'. In *The King of Spain's Daughter*, the same word is used at the play's end, when Annie Kinsella has decided—inexplicably from the audience's perspective (and, indeed, from that of the other characters)—to marry Jim Harris, after hearing that Jim has been busily saving his shillings week by week. Having seen the grubby savings book of the man she is to marry, Annie exclaims: 'He put by two shillin's every week for two hundred weeks. I think he is a man that—supposin' he was jealous—might cut your throat'. At that point,

---

11 Ibid., p. 114.
12 Ibid., p. 122.
13 Ibid., p. 116.

the stage directions describe her as '*Quiet, exultant* [...]'.¹⁴ The same word appears in the stage directions for the closing lines of Deevy's best-known play, Katie Roche. Again, a woman trapped in the domestic cage of a realist set chooses to marry a man she does not love, but in her final lines announces (exultantly): 'I *will* be brave! [...] I was looking for something great to do—sure now I have it'.¹⁵

This suggests that there is a kind of precision in Deevy's writing that extends even to her stage directions. The moments of Annie Kinsella's exultation, and Katie Roche's exultation are, on one hand, the products of their particular situations as women in an Irish society of the 1930s, a situation so precisely and theatrically encapsulated by the 'Road Closed' sign that dominates the stage in The *King of Spain's Daughter*. However, with Deevy's use of the word 'exultant', we glimpse the curious paradox at the heart of her work. For both characters, this moment of 'exultation' erupts at the moment they are, in dramatic terms, resigned to a particular fate. At the same time, their male counterparts in two of these plays—Jim Harris in *The King of Spain's Daughter* and Stanislaus Gregg in *Katie Roche*—end their respective plays curiously defeated, even though they have gained what they desired, or thought they desired. In *Wife to James Whelan*, Deevy plays a variation on the theme by extending this understanding of acceptance as a kind of ecstasy. In that at the play's conclusion Whelan accepts that he will never marry Nan, and he ends the play '(*Soaring.*)', then '([...] *with his head thrown back,* [...] *gazing into his own future.*)'.¹⁶

In a letter, possibly written in 1939, about an unidentified lost (or perhaps re-titled) play that Deevy called 'Port of Refuge', she wrote to one of her most trusted confidantes, Florence Hackett: 'Tell me what you think of 'Port of Refuge'— I liked the way it brought out the disillusionment that follows on getting what we have put too much store on having'.¹⁷ It could be said that we have the coordinates of Deevy's theatrical world in that letter: that which can be possessed can only

---

14 Teresa Deevy, 'The King of Spain's Daughter', in *Teresa Deevy Reclaimed*, II, 17–26 (p. 26).
15 The stage direction is '(*Grows exultant.*)'. Teresa Deevy, 'Katie Roche', in *Teresa Deevy Reclaimed*, II, 57–102 (p. 102).
16 Deevy, 'Wife to James Whelan', p. 158.
17 Dublin, Eavan Boland Library (EBL), Florence Hackett Collection, Teresa Deevy to Florence Hackett , 2 February 1939(?) [sic], MS 10722, item 24.

produce disappointment, whereas when we renounce possession, the result is a kind of exultation. However, the nature of this renunciation—and this is the paradox of Deevy's theatre—is not a renunciation of the phenomenological world. Instead, in accepting that one cannot possess that world, that world becomes more fully present in its own terms.

In *In the Cellar of My Friend*, it is this complex dynamic of renunciation and exultation that is at work, but the gender roles are reversed. Where *The King of Spain's Daughter*, *Katie Roche*, and *Wife to James Whelan* are all—quite rightly—now widely studied and respected as plays about women's experience in Ireland in the mid-twentieth century, in *In the Cellar of My Friend*, that elusive central role—the Annie Kinsella, the Katie Roche, the Nan Bowers—is occupied (as is the case in *Wife to James Whelan*) by a male character: Barney Keane. This does not suggest that gender is irrelevant in relation to the earlier characters. It is not. However, we can say that their gender puts those earlier characters in a position in which Deevy can use them to explore a particular relation between acceptance and freedom. In the later plays—*Wife to James Whelan*, and to an even greater extent, *In the Cellar of My Friend*—Deevy begins to explore the possibility that this relation can be extended to her male characters as well. In this respect, Barney Keane is effectively a development of those earlier characters; indeed, he is not Deevy's first protagonist to have imagined his life in terms of entering a religious order. There is a curious line in *Katie Roche*, where the character of Reuben asks Katie if she loves Stanislaus: 'I didn't know that was love till he asked me now, and I said to myself, "there's your convent"'.[18] In other words, for Katie, marrying Stanislaus involves the same renunciation—and the same 'exultation'—as entering a convent.

This passage in *Katie Roche* is pivotal for understanding Deevy's work. It opens with the entrance of Reuben, who in performance is a menacing, dangerous character, who disrupts not only the fictional world of the play, but also *Katie Roche*'s dramatic form, grating against its surface realism, like a character who has wandered in from some dark fairy tale. He is about as close as Deevy ever comes to creating a character who is less an individual, and more the embodiment of an idea. So, when he first enters, and Stanislaus says, innocuously enough: 'Good

---

18   Deevy, 'Katie Roche', p. 62.

evening'—Reuben replies: 'It is a fine evening. It is one of these golden evenings that God still lavishes on a sinful world'.[19] Now, this might seem like a line that is simply there to establish him as a puritanical old curmudgeon, but in the context of Deevy's insistence on atmosphere and the quality of light as 'the eternal mystery, the beneficence', it suggests something more far-reaching.[20] In the scene from *Katie Roche* that opens with Reuben referring to the 'golden evening that God still lavishes on a sinful world', he goes on to state his theological position unambiguously: 'Christ left no doubt. He was at war with this world, worldly thoughts, and worldly values', and Reuben as a wandering 'holy man' (as he is described) thus embodies a theological view of the phenomenological world as inherently sinful and fallen, and hence to be rejected in every way possible.[21] Katie takes a different view: 'Ah, you couldn't go very much by the Bible; what's said in one place is unsaid in another, and that's the great puzzle; —often you'd think you had an answer'.[22] Again, in performance this can seem like one of those moments when Katie is simply being vague, but again it is a case of doing something serious with something apparently casual. In fact, Deevy seems to be setting up an opposition, in which Reuben represents a form of Catholicism that is dogmatic, and which is founded on a kind of dualism, for which the world is evil, and only that which is not of the world can be good—in short, a strain that ran strongly through the Catholic dogmatic theology that was so influential in the early decades of the Irish state. Whereas for Katie, goodness—or God—can be immanent in the world—as it can be immanent in light falling for Kenneth Leslie in *Light Falling*, or in an April morning. And here is the important thing: that immanence can never really be known, only experienced; it remains 'a great puzzle', although 'often you'd think you had an answer'.

In the Cellar of My Friend thus comes into a focus as a pivotal play because through it we glimpse the deeply unfashionable idea that Teresa Deevy's theatrical aesthetic is at least partly engaged with a very particular form of Catholic mysticism. By mysticism, we can take a line from William James, in which he writes that it is about a kind of

---

19   Ibid.
20   Deevy, 'Light Falling', p. 69.
21   Deevy, 'Katie Roche', p. 63, p. 61, respectively.
22   Ibid., p. 63.

'transport', and, furthermore, 'the incommunicableness of the transport is the keynote of all mysticism'.[23] Or, to put it in Deevy's language, religious mysticism is 'exultant', but sprinkled with ellipses.

To put this in context, all of the scant biographical writing we have about Deevy mentions her deeply-held religious beliefs. Her nephew Jack Deevy claimed that she made a pilgrimage to meet Padre Pio, who 'was apparently rather rude to her on account of her deafness'.[24] Martina Ann O'Doherty reports that she was told by a family member that Deevy 'was a daily communicant and embarked on pilgrimages to Lisieux, Lourdes, Fatima, Assisi, San Giovanni and Rome', and was 'an active member of the Legion of Mary in Dublin'.[25] Catherine Rynne, writing in *The Story of the Abbey Theatre* in 1967, noted: 'Miss Deevy has travelled extensively on the Continent and can speak and lip-read French fluently. She used to act as brancardière during her annual visits to Lourdes'.[26] Going beyond such third-person testimony, however, we see a deep religious conviction in Deevy's most unguarded moments. In particular, there is a letter to her close friend Patricia Lynch, written in 1954 shortly after the death of her sister, Nell, apparently responding to Lynch writing that she still considered Nell as part of a 'gathering of friends around a fire'. 'It is just what I feel too', responds Deevy, '... and I love to know that Nell is in your fireside group. The great fire we gather at is the glowing heart of God—pulsating with love... I do feel that Nell is living her life somewhere else'.[27]

This religious sensibility becomes more pronounced in Deevy's later work. For instance, the late radio play, *Supreme Dominion*, about seventeenth-century Irish priest, Fr Luke Wadding (who was founder of the Irish College in Rome, and who was from Deevy's hometown of Waterford), is very much about the incommunicable nature of

---

23 William James, *Varieties of Religious Experience*, Library of America (New York: Vintage, 1990), p. 343, p. 366, respectively.
24 Maynooth, Russell Library (RL), The Teresa Deevy Archive, Jack Deevy in interview with Frank McEvoy, 3 November 1983, PP/6/176.
25 Martina Ann O'Doherty, 'Teresa Deevy, Playwright (1894–1963)', *The Waterford Archaeological and Historical Society Journal* (1995), 108–113 (p. 111).
26 Catherine Rynne, 'The Playwrights', in *The Story of the Abbey Theatre*, ed. by Sean McCann (London: Four Square, 1967), pp. 69–100 (p. 88).
27 Dublin, National Library of Ireland (NLI), Papers of Patricia Lynch and R.M. Fox, Teresa Deevy to Patricia Lynch, undated 1954, MS 40,327 /2.

certain kinds of religious experience.²⁸ 'I think of Luke always as very spiritual', she wrote to a radio producer at the time, '– this is hard to convey. [...] About Luke Wadding himself my idea, when writing, was to reveal him more by the reactions of others to his personality than by any "wonderful" sayings or doings of his. This makes your job (on the air) hard'.²⁹ By the time we reach one of Deevy's final works, *One Look and What it Led To*, this incommunicable mysticism has become the clear focus of the work.³⁰ Broadcast posthumously on Radio Éireann in 1964, but dating from that same later period as *Supreme Dominion* and *In the Cellar of My Friend*, the play opens in the time of Christ, and features Jesus and his disciples, before moving to a final scene in contemporary France, in which a seemingly immortal Mary Magdalen is still living on a mountainside in France as a kind of bride of Christ, speaking to him through the birds. 'Of late we've had so many interruptions… In the beginning You spoiled me,—those lovely years when no one came, only the birds,—and *You…You, my beloved…*'. The 'You' here, in the script, has an upper case 'Y': in other words, Mary Magdalen is addressing the absent Christ as her 'beloved'.³¹ The play ends with the two French characters, Pierre and Antoinette, marvelling at a shooting star, and a fragrance in the air. It is about as close to a theatre of religious experience as you will find in Irish theatre.

What makes *In the Cellar of My Friend* such a key work in this group of late plays is that it helps to place the Catholicism of Deevy's theatre in a very particular theological tradition, quite distinct from the dualist dogmatic theology that predominated in Irish Catholic teaching at the time (and of which Reuben can be taken as a kind of exemplar and a rejection). Instead, this is a mystical tradition predicated on the immersion in religious experience. The key to this reading is the title of the play, *In the Cellar of My Friend*, which comes from the *Spiritual Canticle* of the Spanish saint and mystic, St John of the Cross:

---

28 Teresa Deevy, 'Supreme Dominion', in *Selected Plays of Irish Playwright Teresa Deevy, 1894–1963*, ed. by Eibhear Walshe (Lewiston, NY: Edwin Mellen Press, 2003), pp. 207–252.
29 Dublin, NLI, Teresa Deevy to Philip Rooney, 22 August 1955 and 7 September 1955, MS 33,665.
30 Teresa Deevy, 'One Look and What It Led To', in *Teresa Deevy Reclaimed*, II, 125–114.
31 Ibid., p. 114.

In the inner cellar
Of my Beloved have I drunk;
Over all the plain I knew nothing,
And lost the flock I followed and when I went forth before.[32]

The image of Christ as the 'beloved' is, it will be noted, picked up in Mary Magdalen's address to the absent Christ in *One Look and What it Led To*. St John of the Cross' *Spiritual Canticle* had a profound influence on a certain brand of Catholic mysticism—particularly that of St Thérèse of Lisieux, which was one of the sites of pilgrimage that Deevy is reputed to have visited during her life. The *Spiritual Canticle* was written when its author (Juan de Yepes y Álvarez)—known as St John of the Cross—a Carmelite monk who was a disciple of St Teresa of Ávila was imprisoned for heresy in a cell barely large enough to hold him and brought out only for weekly scourgings; it is about suffering, and spiritual revelation through suffering. The *Canticle* is a remarkable work, with no real equivalent in English literature, taking the dramatic form of a dialogue between the Soul (as a bride) and Jesus (the bridegroom), in which the Soul ultimately enters into full communion with Christ. St John of the Cross later wrote his own analysis of the *Canticle*, in which he glossed the passage that Deevy uses as being about the irrelevance of knowledge to love (particularly love of God). He writes, that 'God can infuse love without specific knowledge of the thing loved'.[33] The suggestion of a wine cellar in the title of Deevy's play (and hence of drunkenness), hints at the idea of going beyond rationality, particularly when we realise that the 'Friend' (the equivalent of the 'Beloved') is Christ. In short, the play's title signals that it is about spiritual revelation; and yet, the nature of the revelation can only be spoken in Barney's halting explanation, which ultimately turns to another passage from St John of the Cross:

BARNEY: Last night something happened... I was... invited... (*Slow—looking for words to describe an experience.*) to come nearer... Not the first time... but always before I had drawn

---

32　St John of the Cross, 'A Spiritual Canticle of the Soul and the Bridegroom Christ', in *The Mystical Doctrine of St John of the Cross*, ed. by R.H.J. Steuart (London: Continuum International Publishing, 2006), p. 169.
33　Ibid.

> back—dreading. Last night, being happy, I went on, in spirit I mean... I opened the door—or it was opened for me... Something was offered... How foolish is all our dreading! (*Exultant.*) ...our withdrawals... hesitations—how utterly foolish![34]

Capped by the tell-tale direction '*Exultant*', this is perhaps the closest Deevy comes to a mystical vision—which is, ironically, not very close at all; because once more we are back in the world of broken syntax, of language that is inadequate to the task of communication. 'Last night something happened'. What? Neither the characters nor the audience ever really know.

And this is what makes this play so fascinating, perhaps more than the more straight-forward religious world of the later *One Look and What it Led To*. *In the Cellar of My Friend* is not just about mystical revelation. It is about how easy it is to misread—or to miss—the signs of this revelation all around us, and, in this regard, we can consider the play to be a comedy, at least in terms of the way in which Teresa Deevy understood comedy. *In the Cellar of My Friend* is a comedy in the same sense that *The King of Spain's Daughter* is a comedy, in that it is a play about misreading the world. The entire play hinges around an unseen, offstage moment the night before, when Barney has had a moment of religious epiphany powerful enough to convince him to join a monastery and devote his life to God. But when he attempts to write down this revelation in a letter, drawing on one of the most powerful texts in the Catholic mystical tradition, the *Spiritual Canticle* of St John of the Cross, all that remains are some broken pieces of misunderstood sentences, chewed by the family's puppy. 'It doesn't make one bit of difference...', Barney says, 'Maybe the puppy had some wisdom...'.[35] The chewed letter, of course, is the visual equivalent of the fractured syntax of Deevy's spoken dialogue. All that his father Tom can make out, as he and Belle pour over the letter is the word 'explanation', followed by some puppy chew, are a few broken lines from St John of the Cross, ending: 'And coming forth knew nothing of all this plain | And lost—'.[36]

---

34 Deevy, 'Cellar', p. 119.
35 Ibid., p. 121.
36 Ibid., p. 122.

Dark Matter

The welcome resurgence of theatrical and critical interest in the work of Teresa Deevy that has emerged over the past ten years has resituated her in Irish theatre both as a woman, writing at a time when women's experience was largely occluded in Irish culture; and, more recently, as a deafened artist, again working at a time when disability was often invisible in Irish society. However, in the shell-game of blindness and insight, these new (and welcome) perspectives produce their own occlusions. And one of these, I am suggesting here, concerns religious experience. The reasons for this are complex and have much to do with the involvement of the Catholic Church as an institution in determining, and restricting, the lives both of women in Irish society, and of those with disabilities. The result of this has been a tendency to sort repressed experiences and identities to one side of the equation, and to sort anything to do with religion to the other side of the equation. The reality, however, was often more complex. It was possible—as we see with Teresa Deevy—to be deafened, to be a woman, and to take seriously certain forms of religious experience. What is more, not only is Teresa Deevy all of these things, she was also a playwright, fascinated by what theatre could, and could not, do: and it is on stage that the disparate elements of her identity collide in productive tension.

Read in this way, the later religious plays—*In the Cellar of My Friend, One Look and What it Led To, Light Falling*, and *Supreme Dominion*—are not a departure from the concerns of her earlier, better-known plays, such as *Katie Roche*; they are entirely consistent with them. In Deevy's work, there are pivotal moments of experience that are, to use William James' term, 'incommunicable'; and in the later plays, these moments are most often associated with religious experience. What is more, because they are fundamentally incommunicable, these moments are intensely private; they belong the individual alone. It is this that constitutes the pivotal point of intersection between a Catholic (or, indeed, any other kind) of mysticism, and something even the most secular amongst us can recognise as a very modern sensibility. Indeed, one of the ways in which we recognise this existential solitude in modern literature is through the failures of language; we need only think of Beckett here, from the collapse of syntax in *The Unnameable* to the drift towards silence in the late plays.³⁷ Similarly, *In the Cellar of My Friend* is a play about the failures of language. Indeed, we are more or less told as much. Very early in the play, when Tom makes his first entrance, he asks Patty why she did not wait for him in the meadow. She must not have received his message, she tells him: 'Very seldom are messages properly given'.³⁸ In some respects, indeed, the entire play is summed up in what could be read as a throw-away line from the play's fifth character, the gardener Martin, who is something like the old retainer Firs in Chekhov's *The Cherry Orchard*: 'It do seem to me there is no two people can to the full com-pre-hend one another. Not fully... not as I sees it'.³⁹

If the source of these failures of vision and language is a kind of religious mysticism in *In the Cellar of My Friend*, and if it finds its language from a very particular tradition within Catholic mysticism— one that runs from St John of the Cross through Thérèse of Lisieux—such failures, as Beckett learned, are also profoundly theatrical. All that an actor has to work with is what can be seen or heard: voices, bodies, light, objects on the stage. And yet, from this, they must construct an inner state, an inner life. In *Dark Matter*, Andrew Sofer uses the term 'dark matter' to refer to 'the invisible dimension of theater that escapes visual detection, even though its effects are felt everywhere in performance. [...] No less than physical actors and objects, such invisible presences matter very much indeed, even if spectators, characters, and performers cannot put their hands on them'.⁴⁰ All theatre involves 'dark matter' of some sort; however, some theatre manages to make the paradox of dark matter not just a condition of production, but its subject matter. This is the case with Teresa Deevy's theatre, where we are working with a medium that is fundamentally visual, and fundamentally about speech. That visual world is both as fully present as the sunshine on a July day, and as elusive; and speech is ever-present, but full of gaps and elisions, little more than the chewed bits of a letter eaten by a dog. It is thus

---

37   Samuel Beckett, *The Unnameable* (London: Faber & Faber, 2010).
38   Deevy, 'Cellar', p. 114.
39   Dublin, NLI, Manuscripts, Teresa Deevy, 'In the Cellar of My Friend', MS 29,169. The lines published in *Teresa Deevy Reclaimed*, II, differ slightly, as follows: MARTIN 'To my way of seeing there's no two people who can to the full com-pre-hend one another...not fully...as I sees it— (*He goes.*)'. See Deevy, 'Cellar', p. 120.
40   Andrew Sofer, *Dark Matter: Invisibility in Drama, Theater, and Performance* (Ann Arbor, MI: University of Michigan Press, 2013), p. 3.

theatre that stages the comedy of a world in which the possibility of certain forms of experience—including religious experience—can only be intimated. Equally, we can now begin to see that acknowledgement of religious experience as the dark matter of Deevy criticism.

Bibliography

Bank, Jonathan, John P. Harrington, and Christopher Morash (eds), *Teresa Deevy Reclaimed*, 2 vols (New York: Mint Theater, 2011 and 2017)

Beckett, Samuel, *The Unnameable* (London: Faber & Faber, 2010)

James, William, *Varieties of Religious Experience*, Library of America (New York: Vintage, 1990)

McCarthy, Kate, and Úna Kealy, 'Writing from the Margins: Re-framing Teresa Deevy's Archive and Her Correspondence with James Cheasty c.1952–1962', *Irish University Review*, 52.2 (2022), 322–340, https://doi.org/10.3366/iur.2022.0570

O'Doherty, Martina Ann, 'Teresa Deevy, Playwright (1894–1963)', *The Waterford Archaeological and Historical Society Journal* (1995), 108–113, snap.waterfordcoco.ie/collections/ejournals/116768/116768.pdf

Rynne, Catherine, 'The Playwrights', in *The Story of the Abbey Theatre*, ed. by Sean McCann (London: Four Square, 1967), pp. 69–100

Sofer, Andrew, *Dark Matter: Invisibility in Drama, Theater, and Performance* (Ann Arbor, MI: University of Michigan Press, 2013), https://doi.org/10.3998/mpub.3186316

St John of the Cross, 'A Spiritual Canticle of the Soul and the Bridegroom Christ', in *The Mystical Doctrine of St John of the Cross*, ed. by R.H.J. Steuart (London: Continuum International Publishing, 2006), p. 169

Walshe, Eibhear (ed.), *Selected Plays of Irish Playwright Teresa Deevy, 1894–1963* (Lewiston, NY: Edwin Mellen Press, 2003)

6. 'I Must Just Make an Opening Elsewhere': Teresa Deevy's Involvement with Studio Theatre Practice, 1934–1958[1]

Úna Kealy and Kate McCarthy

An established narrative of Teresa Deevy's career is that, after six productions of her plays at the Abbey during the 1930s, her three-act play *Wife to James Whelan* was 'rejected' for an Abbey production in 1942, an event that, thereafter, significantly reduced her ambition as a dramatist for the theatre, directing her towards writing and adapting existing work for radio.[2] This chapter argues that Deevy was interested

---

1 The authors acknowledge the contribution and support of Deirdre Power and the Power family in providing access to the Cheasty Archive in advance of its conservation by Maynooth University; SETU Research Connexions and the School of Humanities for funding support; and colleagues who attended the Women in Irish Writing in the 1930s conference in the University of Almería in 2023. We acknowledge the support of the Letters from the Margins project team in 2015: Helen Byrne, Ricky Croke, Orla Foley, Lorna Grant, Jean Kealy, Dayna Killen, Aisling O'Meara, Frances Ryan, Niamh Ryan, Mary Smart, Shelley Troupe, and Annette Wyse. The project was further supported by David Fallon, Aisling O'Byrne, Norberta O'Gorman, and Lorna Grant who took part in the Letters from the Margins WIT Summer Research Project in 2019. The quotation in the title is taken from an undated letter fragment sent by Teresa Deevy to Florence Hackett, catalogued within the Hackett Archive alongside two other pages of a separate and complete letter itemised as number '33' within the Florence Hackett Archive, Trinity College Dublin, Ms. 10722. The authors also acknowledge the editorial advice of the anonymous reviewers of the *Active Speech* manuscript.

2 Caoilfhionn Ní Bheacháin, 'The Seeds Beneath the Snow': Resignation and Resistance in Teresa Deevy's *Wife to James Whelan*', in *Irish Women Writers: New Critical Perspectives*, ed. by Elke D'hoker, Raphaël Ingelbien, and Hedwig Schwall (New York: Peter Lang, 2011), pp. 91–109; Eibhear Walshe, 'Ineffable Longings', in *Selected Plays of Irish Playwright Teresa Deevy, 1894–1963*, ed. by Eibhear Walshe (Lewiston: Edward Mellen Press, 2003), pp. 9–10.

and enthusiastic in radio drama as a medium for her work as early as the mid-1930s. We argue that, although Deevy was disappointed at what she correctly perceived of as the loss of the Abbey mainstage as a production venue for her work post 1940, she was not uncritical of the Abbey's managerial and production practices during the 1930s and 1940s. Rather than being a final terminus within her career, we argue that the 1940s was a decade when Deevy pursued radio *and* theatre productions of her work with energetic ambition. In order to establish the importance and relevance of Deevy's interest and involvement in studio theatre practice in Dublin in the 1940s and 1950s, we contextualise and chart the evolution of that milieu in the early decades of the twentieth century. We then consider how, in the mid-1930s, Deevy sought theatre productions of her work outside the Abbey in Dublin, London, Waterford, and New York, and radio productions of her work in Ireland and Britain. Building on recent analysis of Deevy's correspondence[3] and Irish studio theatre practice during the 1950s,[4] we analyse excerpts from letters, conserved

---

[3] Kate McCarthy and Úna Kealy, 'Writing from the Margins: Re-framing Teresa Deevy's Archive and Her Correspondence with James Cheasty c.1952–1962', *Irish University Review*, 52.2 (2022), 322–340. As documents composed by Hackett and Cheasty are absent from the Deevy, Cheasty, and Hackett archives, analysis here considers only documents authored by Deevy.

[4] Christopher Fitz-Simon, *The Boys* (Dublin: Gill and Macmillan, 1994); Gus Smith and Des Hickey, *John B: The Real Keane* (Cork: Mercier Press, 1992); Gerard Whelan with Carolyn Swift, *Spiked: Church-State Intrigue and The Rose Tattoo* (Dublin: New Island, 2002); Christopher Morash, *A History of Irish Theatre 1601–2000* (Cambridge: Cambridge University Press, 2002); Ciara O'Farrell, *Louis D'Alton and the Abbey Theatre* (Dublin: Four Courts Press, 2004); Ian Walsh, *Experimental Theatre After W.B. Yeats* (Houndmills: Palgrave, 2012); Siobhán O'Gorman, 'Scenographic Interactions: 1950's Ireland and Dublin's Pike Theatre', *Irish Theatre International*, 3.1 (2014), 25–42; Siobhán O'Gorman, '"Hers and His": Carolyn Swift, Alan Simpson, and Collective Creation at Dublin's Pike Theatre', in *Women, Collective Creation, and Devised Performance: The Rise of Women Theatre Artists in the Twentieth and Twenty-First Centuries*, ed. by Kathryn Mederos Syssoyeva and Scott Proudfit (New York: Palgrave Macmillan, 2016), pp. 129–144; Lionel Pilkington, 'The Little Theatres of the 1950s', in *The Oxford Handbook of Modern Irish Theatre*, ed. by Nicholas Grene and Chris Morash (Oxford: Oxford University Press, 2016), pp. 286–303; Christopher Collins, 'Other Theatres', in *The Palgrave Handbook of Contemporary Irish Theatre and Performance*, ed. by Eamonn Jordan and Eric Weitz (London: Palgrave, 2018), pp. 221–232; Ondřej Pilný, Ruud van den Beuken, and Ian R. Walsh (eds), *Cultural Convergence: The Dublin Gate Theatre, 1929–1960* (London: Palgrave Macmillan, 2021); Chris Morash, '"Somehow It Is Not The Same": Irish Theatre and Tradition', in *Irish Literature in Transition, 1940–1980*, ed. by Eve Patten (Cambridge: Cambridge University Press, 2020), pp. 134–149; Paige Reynolds, 'Theatrical Ireland: New Routes from the Abbey Theatre to the Gate Theatre', in *Irish Literature in Transition,*

in/by Trinity College Dublin and Maynooth University, written by Teresa Deevy to her friends and fellow playwrights Florence Hackett and James Cheasty. This correspondence powerfully evidences that Deevy worked hard during the 1940s and 1950s, and with some success, to make stage productions of her work outside the Abbey a reality. The chapter concludes that, while Deevy is primarily recalled as an Abbey dramatist—albeit one who was ousted—and that she did write 'mainly, and successfully, for radio' during the 1940s, her interest, ambition, and involvement in theatre practice extended throughout her career.[5] Research into Deevy's radio dramas and broadcast performances demands separate and detailed scholarship and is not attempted here.[6] Rather, our analysis considers Deevy's ambition for her theatre work outside the Abbey Theatre and expands scholarship outwards from select institutions and literary texts, which are, in the main, the focus of Irish theatre scholarship of that period.

Development of Studio Theatre Practice in Ireland

Studio theatres were inspired by the late 1800s and early 1900s European tradition of art house theatre that promoted creative experimentation in an attempt, as James Joyce put it, to 'protest against the sterility and falsehood of the modern stage'.[7] The phenomenon of the little, pocket, or studio theatre was international and was characterised by innovation that challenged conventions of genre, performance style, and dramaturgy: theatremakers were encouraged to experiment and innovate for audiences who expected and welcomed artistic risk-taking and accepted material compromises. The 'Foreword' to the first issue of *Theatre Arts Monthly*, published in America, outlines the mission of

---

1880–1940, ed. by Marjorie Elizabeth Howes (Cambridge: Cambridge University Press, 2020), pp. 55–72; Maura Laverty, *The Plays of Maura Laverty: Liffey Lane, Tolka Row, A Tree in the Crescent*, ed. by Cathy Leeney and Deirdre McFeely (Liverpool: Liverpool University Press, 2023).

5 John Jordan, 'Teresa Deevy: An Introduction', *Irish University Review*, 1.8 (1956), 13–26 (p. 13).

6 Some of this work has been initiated by Emily Bloom. Emily Bloom, 'Looking In: Teresa Deevy, Deafness, and Radio', *Modernism/Modernity*, 30.2 (2023), 279–299.

7 James Joyce (1901), 'The Day of the Rabblement', in *Handbook of the Irish Revival: An Anthology of Irish Cultural and Political Writings 1891–1922*, ed. by Declan Kiberd and P.J. Mathews (Dublin: Abbey Theatre Press, 2015), pp. 164–165 (p. 164).

the magazine as an attempt 'to help conserve and develop craetive [sic] impulse in the American theatre', describing the little theatre movement as artist-centric and committed to 'establishing its own experimental playhouses, and small but appreciative audiences'.[8]

Studio, little, or pocket theatres, sometimes configured as dramatic societies, became a feature of the Irish theatre landscape in the late 1800s offering Irish artists and audiences alternative theatrical experiences to contemporaneous popular, large-scale, commercially-driven productions.[9] Like European and American studio theatre practice, studio theatres in Ireland curated artistic programmes inspired by, and borrowing from, avant-garde theatre practice, producing work that was political, experimental, unknown or, as yet, unproduced in Ireland. Operating as private members' clubs, studio theatres and dramatic societies evaded the need for theatre licences by including club membership within the ticket price. Studio theatre club tickets could be purchased either from production venues (typically spaces or rooms in community, disused, or derelict spaces), or from local businesses. The Irish Literary Theatre, the Ormond Dramatic Society, Inghinidhe na hÉireann, the National Theatre Society, the Irish Language Theatre of Ireland, and the Irish National Theatre Society can be regarded as key organisations that contributed significantly to early studio theatre activity in Ireland.[10] Máire Nic Shiubhlaigh positions the National Theatre Society as one of 'a number' of emerging small theatre groups in Ireland and England, while Annie Horniman describes the Abbey as 'the first of the many "little theatres" which are sprinkled all over the world'.[11]

The 'matter of money' to produce work was a perennial problem for

---

8 'Foreword', *Theatre Arts Magazine*, 1 (1916), 11.
9 Christopher Fitz-Simon, *The Irish Theatre* (London: Thames and Hudson, 1983); Morash, *A History of Irish Theatre*.
10 Inghinidhe na hÉireann is included in this list due to the tableaux vivants it created, which directly contributed to the aesthetic of scenography and performance within the Ormond Dramatic and the National Theatre Societies.
11 Máire Nic Shiubhlaigh, 'The Irish National Theatre Society', extracted from *The Splendid Years: Recollections of Máire Nic Shiubhlaigh; as Told to Edward Kenny* (Dublin: James Duffy, 1955), p. 43, and republished in *The Abbey Theatre: Interviews and Recollections*, ed. by Edward H. Mikhail (London: Macmillan Press, 1988), pp. 40–48 (p. 29); Annie E.F. Horniman, 'The Origin of the Abbey Theatre', originally published in *John O'London's Weekly*, 20 August 1932, p. 741 and republished in *The Abbey Theatre*, pp. 28–30 (p. 29).

studio theatre clubs and societies.[12] Studio theatres did not necessarily pay company members or, if remuneration was available, earnings unrelated to theatre practice were required to supplement that income and to pay for production materials. Acknowledging that finance, and sometimes, expertise were not always available to newly formed groups, Alice Milligan advised stage managers in amateur drama societies and clubs that 'Simplicity of make will be found to be quite compatible with artistic beauty, and stage magnificence can be attained without extravagance'.[13] Descriptions of the premiere of *Kathleen Ni Houlihan* on a tiny stage with unsteady cottage walls suggest production standards that might have appeared 'unprofessional', but a potent combination of energy, ambition, and resourcefulness ensured that reduced finances and cramped performance spaces did not compromise ambition or artistic integrity.[14] Despite warped flats and ill-fitting curtains, studio theatre clubs were recognised by those within the profession as important in terms of providing emerging playwrights and audiences with alternatives to productions that were motivated primarily by commercial success.[15]

As the 1910s progressed, studio theatre companies became synonymous with experimental theatre practice. Founded in 1918 by Lennox Robinson with the support of W.B. Yeats, and described as 'a shadow network' of the Abbey, the Dublin Drama League used the Abbey stage on Sunday and Monday evenings to offer a programme of new and recent European drama.[16] In the 1920s, Désirée Bannard Cogley founded the Studio Arts Club; Mary Manning founded the company, Anomalies; John Lodwick established a stage society; the Dublin Jewish Dramatic Society was founded, and Eveline Kirkwood Hackett and Lyle Donaghy also staged studio theatre productions.[17] These studio clubs, groups,

---

12 Frank Fay (1901), 'The Irish Literary Theatre', in *Handbook of the Irish Revival*, p. 166.
13 Alice Milligan (1904), 'Staging and Costume in Irish Drama', *Ireland's Own*, 30 March 1904, in *Handbook of the Irish Revival*, pp. 160–161 (p. 161).
14 Morash, *A History of Irish Theatre*, p. 123; Nic Shiubhlaigh, *The Splendid Years*, p. 41.
15 Winifred Letts, 'My First Abbey Play', condensed from an original publication in *Irish Writing* (Cork), 16 (September 1951), 43–46 (pp. 35–39).
16 Nora Moroney, 'The Women Behind the Abbey: Dolly Robinson and Irish Theatrical Networks', *English Studies*, 104.6 (2023), 1037–1054 (p. 1042).
17 Elaine Sisson suggests that the Studio Arts Club was founded in either 1924 or 1925. Elaine Sisson, 'Experiment and the Free State: Mrs Cogley's Cabaret and the Founding of the Gate Theatre 1924–1930', in *The Gate Theatre: Inspiration and Craft*,

societies, and individuals—which were not allied or in agreement in terms of artistic output or priority—created an infrastructure of artists, producers, and audiences that contributed to a dynamic cultural and artistic 'cross-pollination' within Dublin theatre practice.[18] The concept of the Abbey Experimental Theatre (AET) (which became the Peacock) emerged in the 1920s, but it was not until 1937 'that the idea took formal shape' with Ria Mooney's students at the helm.[19] Described by Ernest Blythe as 'a little theatre which would be used for the production of works of young dramatists', the AET provided an 'experimental [...] testing ground for new ideas'.[20] The founding of the Gate Theatre in 1928, by Hilton Edwards and Micheál mac Liammóir with support from Bannard Cogley and Gearóid Ó Lochlainn, and of the Dublin Little Theatre Guild, co-founded by Liam O'Leary, Seán O'Meadhra, and Patrick Fitzsimons, establishes the first two decades of the twentieth century as a particularly fruitful time in Irish studio theatre practice.[21] However, as Lionel Pilkington and Siobhán O'Gorman suggest, because these groups frequently banded and disbanded, merged and separated, and because documents are not always archived or are dispersed across multiple private and public collections, the history of individual studio theatre groups, clubs, and societies is challenging to determine, delineate, and chart.[22]

---

    ed. by David Clare, Des Lally, and Patrick Lonergan (Dublin: Carysfort Press, 2018), pp. 11–27. For more on Jewish theatre practice see Irina Ruppo Malone, 'Synge, An-Sky, and the Irish Jewish Revival', *The Irish Review*, 48 (2014), pp. 17–27 and Barry Montgomery, 'Jewish Drama on the Irish Stage: The Socio-Political and Cultural Milieu of the Dublin Jewish Amateur Operatic Society (1908–1910) and the Dublin Jewish Dramatic Society (1924–1954)', *Studi Irlandesi. A Journal of Irish Studies*, 10.10 (2020), 133–152.

18 Mary Trotter, *Modern Irish Theatre* (Cambridge: Polity Press, 2008), p. 98.
19 Ciara O'Dowd, *Wild-Looking but Fine: Abbey Theatre Actresses of the 1930s* (Dublin: University College Dublin Press, 2024), p. 67.
20 'Dáil Éireann Debate—Wednesday, 6 Jul 1927', *5th Dáil*, 20.6 (1927), Orduithe an Lae. Orders of the Day. Vote 21—Miscellaneous Expenses, https://www.oireachtas.ie/en/debates/debate/dail/1927-07-06/16/; Robert Welch, *The Abbey Theatre 1899–1999: Form and Pressure* (Oxford: Oxford University Press, 1999), p. 101.
21 Sisson, 'Experiment and the Free State'; Fitz-Simon, *The Boys*; Mícheál Ó hAodha, *Theatre in Ireland* (Oxford: Basil Blackwell, 1974). We use the spelling 'mac Liammóir' following Leeney and McFeely's use of this spelling at the request of the executors of mac Liammóir's estate (see Leeney and McFeely (eds), *The Plays of Maura Laverty*, p. 6).
22 Pilkington, 'Little Theatres'; O'Gorman, 'Scenographic Interactions'.

New Directions for Deevy in the 1930s

The Abbey 'adopted' six Dublin Drama League productions in the 1920s, staging them as Abbey productions in what Clarke and Ferrar maintain were 'fruits of the League's seeds that blossomed for a brief moment and wilted as the Abbey speedily rejected innovation'.[23] Arguably, Ninette de Valois' work at the Abbey, the production of O'Casey's *The Plough and the Stars*, and Denis Johnston's production of *King Lear* go some way to contradicting that assertion, as such productions evidence notable moments of artistic risk-taking at the Abbey during the 1920s. Nevertheless, as Lauren Arrington and Pilkington argue, a complex mesh of multifarious influences diminished artistic innovation and experimentation on the main Abbey stage as the 1930s approached.[24] Deevy's first play, *Reapers*, was produced by the Abbey in 1930; thereafter, the Abbey produced *A Disciple* in 1931, *Temporal Powers* in 1932, *The King of Spain's Daughter* in 1935, and *Katie Roche* and *The Wild Goose* in 1936. There was a hiatus of twelve years before another new play by Deevy was premiered there when, in 1948, *Light Falling* was produced on the Peacock stage. The Abbey found, in what Johnston describes as 'kitchen comedies', a dramaturgical formula and realist aesthetic that was relatively economical to produce and adequately commercially successful but which, by the mid-1930s, had become somewhat stale.[25] In an undated letter to Hackett, Deevy wrote, 'There is a theatre group calling itself The Abbey Experimental Theatre—or A.E.T—which is looking for short plays—one actors'.[26] The comment attests to the fact that Deevy was interested in how nuances in performance and experimentation in theatre convention might be applied to short plays, such as those she had either already created, or would create, thus positioning her during this period as a playwright open to theatrical

---

23 Brenna Katz Clarke and Harold Ferrar, *The Dublin Drama League, 1918–41*, The Irish Theatre Series 9, ed. by Robert Hogan, James Kilroy, and Liam Miller (Dublin: Dolmen Press, 1979), p. 19.

24 Lauren Arrington, *W.B. Yeats, The Abbey Theatre, Censorship, and the Irish State: Adding the Half-Pence to the Pence* (Oxford: Oxford University Press, 2010); Pilkington, 'Little Theatres'.

25 Denis Johnston, *Orders and Desecrations: The Life of the Playwright Denis Johnston*, ed. by Rory Johnston (Dublin: Lilliput Press, 1992), p. 50.

26 Dublin, Eavan Boland Library (EBL), Florence Hackett Collection, Teresa Deevy to Florence Hackett, undated, MS 10722, item 20.

innovation and experimentation.

Replying to Hackett in January 1935, Deevy articulates what seems to have been a shared sense of crisis in relation to the Abbey, 'Yes, don't things seem hopeless about the Abbey'.[27] Her next paragraph continues, 'Something will have to be done about the theatre in Ireland. It's appalling'.[28] While it is unclear as to whether Deevy is making reference to theatre, in general, or the Abbey, in particular, it seems that her concern relates to the quality of acting within the Abbey; she suggests that Abbey players rotate, residency-style, with 'tip-top' actors in the London-Irish Players, because the Abbey company has 'become "localised"'.[29] This comment may suggest that either Dublin-based actors were restricted in their range, and/or deliberately focused their skills on a narrow set of performance conventions. Alternatively, or additionally, the comment may suggest that the introduction of new actors from London would benefit the Dublin theatre scene. In the same letter, Deevy writes, 'it seems to me that any scheme that does not prioritise first-rate players is out of the question'[30]—an unsurprising prioritisation of acting excellence given the detailed stage directions, subtext, gesture, and movement in her own dramatic work.

By the mid-1930s, Deevy was actively engaged in seeking productions of her work outside the Abbey and, indeed, outside of Ireland. In 1934 Deevy advises Hackett to send a script to the Irish Players in London who 'sometimes want a short play'[31] and, in a letter sent soon thereafter, she mentions that Ernest Wilton, a producer with connections to 'the New York Theatre Guild and also in London', might produce *The King of Spain's Daughter*.[32] It seems that in early 1935, the Abbey had not yet

---

27 Dublin, Eavan Boland Library (EBL), Florence Hackett Collection, Teresa Deevy to Florence Hackett, 31 January 1935(?) [sic], MS 10722, item 5.
28 EBL, MS 10722, item 5.
29 Ibid.
30 Ibid. For more on Deevy's detailed attention to blocking, see Úna Kealy, 'Resisting Power and Direction: *The King of Spain's Daughter* by Teresa Deevy as a Feminist Call to Action', *Estudios Irlandeses*, 15 (2020), 178–192, https://doi.org/10.24162/EI2020-9406
31 Dublin, Eavan Boland Library (EBL), Florence Hackett Collection, Teresa Deevy to Florence Hackett 12 November 1934(?) [sic], MS 10722, item 3.
32 Dublin, Eavan Boland Library (EBL), Florence Hackett Collection, Teresa Deevy to Florence Hackett, 27 September (1935), MS 10722, item 9. Wilton did not produce *The King of Spain's Daughter* but, in that same letter, Deevy mentions that he was particularly interested in producing 'ballets, and Shakespearian plays', a seemingly

accepted *The King of Spain's Daughter*, but Deevy was already seeking its publication. She confesses her desire to 'get it tidied up, with less stage directions', revealing her strong inclination to imagine and curate actors' bodies, writing, 'I think I always have too many stage directions'.[33] Deevy did 'tidy up' *The King of Spain's Daughter* and *Theatre Arts Monthly* agreed to publish it later that year.[34] The *Dublin Magazine* followed suit scheduling a publication in 1936. Deevy was 'awfully pleased', but longed for a production: 'I wish it would be produced before being published'.[35] She did not have long to wait: the Abbey produced *The King of Spain's Daughter* in April 1935. It was not, however, the production for which she had hoped. She wrote in dispirited tones to Hackett of 'wretched' audience numbers and that the programme stated the play was set on a 'summer's day' when 'the whole play had turned, for me, on the April day atmosphere. I missed the gay air that, to my mind, was essential'.[36] Deevy was not alone in her contention that the Abbey was not attuned to subtleties within her work: one critic wrote of the Abbey production of the play (that was remounted the following year) that 'Its subtlety is too much for the Abbey, and the staging was the last word in bathos'—remarks that suggest that the nuanced social and ideological critique within Deevy's work was not realised.[37]

In the context of less-than-ideal productions of her work at the Abbey,

---

inconsequential comment, but one which might suggest the timeframe of *Possession*, Deevy's ballet interpreting the story of *The Táin*.

33   Dublin, Eavan Boland Library (EBL), Florence Hackett Collection, Teresa Deevy to Florence Hackett, 11 October (1935?) [sic], MS 10722, item 10. The full quotation reads: 'I think I always have too many stage directions, and that is what makes my work so untidy and amateurish', suggesting that she did not see this tendency as a strength.

34   Teresa Deevy, 'The King of Spain's Daughter', *Theatre Arts Monthly*, June 1935, 459–466.

35   Dublin, Eavan Boland Library (EBL), Florence Hackett Collection, Teresa Deevy to Florence Hackett, [1935] 1936 (?) [sic], MS 10722, item 12.

36   Dublin, Eavan Boland Library (EBL), Florence Hackett Collection, Teresa Deevy to Florence Hackett, 8 May 1935, MS 10722, item 8. Scholars have considered how the Abbey's 1935 premiere of *The King of Spain's Daughter* may have impacted contemporary critics' interpretation of the play's conclusion. See Lisa Fitzpatrick, 'Taking Their Own Road: The Female Protagonists in Three Plays by Irish Women', in *Women in Irish Drama: A Century of Authorship and Representation*, ed. by Melissa Sihra (Houndmills: Palgrave Macmillan, 2007), pp. 69–86 and Kealy, 'Resisting Power and Direction'.

37   Seán Ó Meadhra, *Ireland Today*, 1.4 (1936), p. 63, in Fitzpatrick, 'Taking Their Own Road', p. 72.

Deevy may have held out hope that she might find other, more sensitive, interpreters of her work. She may have already been taking note of the formation of the Waterford Dramatic Society in 1935 and of Longford Productions formed in 1936. Deevy's next play, *Katie Roche*, was produced by the Abbey and, possibly because the Abbey directors were 'Inspired, perhaps even alarmed [...] by the Gate's now unassailable superiority in the visual and technical aspects of stage presentation', Hugh Hunt directed and Tanya Moiseiwitsch designed the production.[38] Deevy, who attended rehearsals, records how the production team had worked to realise her vision of the play, writing to Hackett that: 'they were all so eager to have it just as I wanted it'.[39] The production was a success and Deevy began to seek productions in the little theatre network in London writing to Hackett that:

> [...] the London Times gave an excellent criticism with the result that I got several applications from Agents in London wanting to handle the play. I have now given it in charge to one of them—a McGolding Bright who has, I believe, a great name. He is hoping to get it produced in London![40]

In fact, Hunt was also keen to produce *Katie Roche* in London and Deevy's hopes were realised—*Katie Roche* was staged there and, later, in America.

Concurrently, Deevy's interest in radio drama was piqued, possibly by Hackett whose dramatic work had been produced for radio and/or by the fact that Deevy's friends and family were avid radio drama listeners. Deevy vicariously experienced and reacted to radio dramas by either attending recordings of radio dramas, or watching her friends and family listening to broadcasts. Describing her family's reaction to the broadcast of a radio play written by Hackett, she writes, 'It was splendid—at least if I can judge by the family reactions'.[41] In another letter, Deevy writes, 'Nance, Nell and Phyllis listened last night—and I watched their amusement. Then Nell told me the story of it'.[42] In any

---

38 Fitz-Simon, *The Boys*, p. 97. The Abbey first produced *Katie Roche* on 16 March 1936.
39 Dublin, Eavan Boland Library (EBL), Florence Hackett Collection, Teresa Deevy to Florence Hackett, 5 April 1936, MS 10722, item 15.
40 Ibid.
41 EBL, MS 10722, item 23.
42 Dublin, Eavan Boland Library (EBL), Florence Hackett Collection, Teresa Deevy to Florence Hackett, 2 February 1939(?) [sic], MS 10722, item 24. While this evidence of Deevy's experience of radio broadcasts exists, we have not found an account of

case, Deevy submitted *The Wild Goose* to the BBC as a possibility for radio production. It was accepted, prompting Deevy to attend a radio production in Belfast to better understand the conventions of the medium. In a letter to Hackett she confesses:

> When going up I felt doubtful as to whether I could ever be really enthusiastic over writing for radio—now that's settled. I loved the place—and their way of production. [...] There is nothing formal about them—a really theatre atmosphere—everyone friendly and casual. [...] I was fascinated watching it all.[43]

In the radio studios in Belfast, and at home watching family and friends listen to radio drama, Deevy discovered a medium and an environment in which she and her work were welcome. Her decision to investigate radio drama production may also have been motivated by an organisational culture in the Abbey that was injurious to women. Tricia O'Beirne argues there existed in the Abbey a culture of discrimination against women artists and that a 'determinedly patriarchal' modus operandi operated within the managerial hierarchy that resulted in artists being unofficially sanctioned if they would not accept direction or reprimand.[44] Additionally, Deevy was aware, informed by Frank O'Connor, that Yeats did not admire her work. In an undated letter to Hackett she reflects,

> Yeats does not care at all for my plays. Not very encouraging, but it is better to know. [O'Connor] said that is the reason my work was not brought on more at the Abbey.[45]

Deevy does not mention whether she and O'Connor discussed her refusal to allow the Abbey directors 'rewrite [her plays] for her', but the fact that she did refuse to submit to this suggests her confidence in the integrity of her writing and her artistic voice.[46] Perhaps Deevy sought

---

whether, or how, she experienced the BBC television broadcasts of *The King of Spain's Daughter* and *In Search of Valour*, both of which were directed by Denis Johnston in 1939.

43   EBL, MS 10722, item 23.
44   Tricia O'Beirne, '"In a Position to Be Treated Roughly"', *New Hibernia Review/Iris Éireannach Nua*, 22.1 (2018), 120–134 (p. 131).
45   Dublin, Eavan Boland Library (EBL), Florence Hackett Collection, Teresa Deevy to Florence Hackett, undated, MS 10722, item 13. We acknowledge the help of Aisling Lockhart of Trinity College Dublin Libraries for confirming that this letter fragment is undated.
46   Frank O'Connor, *The Backward Look: A Survey of Irish Literature* (London: MacMillan,

alternative producers and outlets for her work rather than choosing to continue to rely on favour from an organisation managed by those who did not favour her work and who had no compunction in treating her less equally than her male counterparts.

Deevy's Involvement with Studio Theatre Practice in the 1940s and 1950s

As the 1930s ended, Deevy's work had been published, broadcast on radio, toured regionally in Ireland and to London and America, and the Abbey had optioned *Holiday House* for production.[47] With her career prospects promising much, and an expanded network of professional and personal contacts in Dublin and London, Deevy took the next step to progress her career. With her sister, Nell, Deevy settled in a 'little house in Dublin', initially house-sitting for Lennox and Dolly Robinson before settling in Waterloo Road.[48] However, the 1940s was unexpectedly disappointing. As Morash notes, the Abbey production of *Holiday House* did not materialise and the directors were not forthcoming as to the reason why.[49] In a letter to Hackett in 1940, Deevy writes that her next play is not progressing as she would like, 'I had hoped to finish my new play long ago, but it came to a standstill [...] I have great plans

---

1967), p. 179.
47 Martina Ann O'Doherty, 'Deevy: A Bibliography', *Irish University Review*, 25.1 (1995), 163–170. O'Doherty suggests that Deevy's work was televised during the 1930s, but Phyllis Ryan recalls recording Deevy's work for television 'when the war was over'—a comment that, given that Ryan was born in 1920, suggests the recording took place post 1945. Phyllis Ryan, *The Company I Kept* (Dublin: Town House, 1996), p. 108. *Katie Roche* was presented at the Torch Theatre in Knightsbridge, London in 1938. See DRI, The Teresa Deevy Archive, 'Irish Comedy in Knightsbridge: Production by the Torch Theatre'. In a letter to Hackett, Deevy mentions an Abbey regional tour that visited Waterford city to stage a production of *The King of Spain's Daughter*. See Dublin, Eavan Boland Library (EBL), Florence Hackett Collection, Teresa Deevy to Florence Hackett, 2 February 1939, MS 10722, item 27. O'Doherty also records that this production toured to Cork.
48 Dublin, Eavan Boland Library (EBL), Florence Hackett Collection, Teresa Deevy to Florence Hackett, 1937, MS 10722, item 18. From her correspondence with Hackett, it seems that Deevy and her sister, Nell, moved to 16 Waterloo Road c. 1941. Deevy moved to 20 Clyde Road in 1955.
49 Christopher Morash, 'Teresa Deevy: Seeing the World', in *Teresa Deevy Reclaimed*, 2 vols, ed. by Jonathan Bank, John P. Harrington, and Christopher Morash (New York: Mint Theater, 2011 and 2017), II, ix–xx (pp. xi–xii).

for [it]'.⁵⁰ While she was reworking it, Ernest Blythe became managing director of the Abbey initiating what Brian Fallon describes as an Abbey programming policy 'associated indelibly with kitchen farce, unspeakably bad Gaelic pantomimes, compulsory Irish and insensitive bureaucracy'.⁵¹ As has been frequently documented, when Deevy did eventually finish her play—*Wife to James Whelan*—and submitted it to the Abbey in 1941 it was rejected, leading her to conclude that the Abbey had 'no further use' for her plays.⁵² As managing director of the Abbey, and signatory of the letter rejecting *Wife to James Whelan*, Blythe's name is synonymous with this moment within Deevy's career but, as Melissa Sihra and O'Beirne contend, Blythe may simply have continued the 'plodding artistic policies' and communicated a prevailing conservative ethos that was 'highly restrictive artistically'.⁵³ O'Beirne cogently argues that the misogynistic and 'megalomaniacal tendencies' of Fredrick Higgins, who disliked what he referred to as Deevy's 'dull' work, contributed to diminishing Deevy's relationship with the Abbey.⁵⁴

However, far from being a pessimistic acceptance of defeat and rejection, Deevy's attitude to Blythe's letter rejecting *Wife to James Whelan* is stoical, if not optimistic. Deevy immediately asserts that she will look for an alternative producer, writing, 'I am trying to get [*Wife to James Whelan*] done elsewhere it is very much an "Abbey" play so I feel rather handicapped'.⁵⁵ Her shaken confidence materialises in her interchanging use of the past and present tense, 'I feel the play was good, and felt very confident of it', but her contestation of Blythe's assertion that 'the characters were too like Katie Roche' evidences her confidence in its value; she argues: 'No one else could see the resemblance', contending

---

50   Dublin, Eavan Boland Library (EBL), Florence Hackett Collection, Teresa Deevy to Florence Hackett, 1940, MS 10722, item 28.
51   Brian Fallon, *An Age of Innocence, Irish Culture 1930–1960* (Dublin: Gill and Macmillan, 1998), p. 134. The 1940s was also a time when numbers of amateur dramatic societies increased nationally. See Morash, *A History of Irish Theatre*.
52   Dublin, Eavan Boland Library (EBL), Florence Hackett Collection, Teresa Deevy to Florence Hackett, undated, MS 10722, item 33.
53   Ibid.; O'Beirne, '"In a Position to Be Treated Roughly"', p. 134; Sihra, *Women in Irish Drama*, 87–96.
54   O'Beirne, '"In a Position to Be Treated Roughly"', p. 130; F.R. Higgins in ibid., p. 130. O'Beirne singles out Higgins as particularly villainous in his sexism, misogyny, and duplicity.
55   Dublin, Eavan Boland Library (EBL), Florence Hackett Collection, Teresa Deevy to Florence Hackett, MS 10722, item 33.

that Abbey actors, Cyril Cusack in particular, shared her opinion of its worth. Regret at being 'finished' with the Abbey sits alongside a dogged determination to find another producer:

> I suppose every play by an author has a certain resemblance—the author's viewpoint—but that was all. However, I must just make an opening elsewhere, and it may be a good thing to be finished with the Abbey. Yet I love the Abbey, & their actors are fine.[56]

These sentiments, contained in an undated letter fragment, express Deevy's disappointment, but also her commitment to pursue alternative production opportunities.

Alternative producers in Dublin were potentially plentiful as Irish studio theatre practice continued as an important and dynamic phenomenon through the 1940s and 1950s. A new incarnation of Desirée Bannard Cogley's Studio Club emerged in the early 1940s with Cogley's son, Fergus, taking on substantial production work. Concurrently, Richards-Walsh Productions was co-founded by Shelah Richards and Michael Walsh. The extent of studio theatre production is demonstrated in Eoin O'Brien's summary of dramatic commentary written by A.J. Leventhal for publication in the *Dublin Magazine* during the 1940s and 1950s, which includes reviews of productions by an astonishing number of studio and theatre clubs including: the Players Theatre; Dublin University Players; Austin Clarke's Lyric Theatre Company; Earlsfort Players; the Abbey Experimental Theatre (which Leventhal first refers to as the Peacock in 1950); Longford Productions; the Dublin Marionette Group; University College Dublin Dramatic Society; Dublin University Modern Language Society; '37' Theatre Club; the Fortune Society; Pilgrim Productions; the Pike Theatre Club; the Arts Theatre; the Dublin Globe Theatre; and Cyril Cusack Productions.[57] Absent from this list, but contributing to theatre production in Dublin during this era were: the Dublin Dance Theatre Club; Erina Brady's Irish School of Dance Art;

---

56 EBL, MS 10722, item 33.
57 Eoin O'Brien, 'II. Dramatic Commentary: *The Dublin Magazine*, 1943–1958', in *A. J. Leventhal 1896–1979: Dublin Scholar, Wit and Man of Letters* (Dublin: The Con Leventhal Scholarship Committee, 1984). A letter written by Leventhal to Deevy in 1930 (dated 22 March) is contained within the Teresa Deevy Archive in Maynooth. See DRI, The Teresa Deevy Archive, 'Letter from C.J. Leventhal', PP/6/6(1), https://doi.org/10.7486/DRI.95944c09k

the Dublin Verse Speaking Society; and amateur theatre companies such as the Bernadette Players.[58]

Deevy approached the Players Theatre, founded in 1944 'by a few disaffected members' of the Abbey—an unsurprising choice given her admiration for the acting skills of Abbey actors.[59] Writing enthusiastically to Hackett, Deevy asserts:

> At the opening meeting of The Players Theatre I gave your name as one who might be interested. [...] I think they will really do good stuff. [...] I am sending my 'rejected Abbey' am, [sic] hoping they may like it! I have been working hard re-writing it.[60]

The Players *were* interested in *Wife to James Whelan* (which Deevy had renamed and submitted under the title *All on a Sunny Day*). Unfortunately, while they awarded the play a prize of £50 in 1945, they did not produce it. In 1944, Deevy wrote to Hackett that 'broadcasting is what I am thinking of',[61] and in 1946 the BBC broadcast a radio production of *Wife to James Whelan* with Radio Éireann later broadcasting an abridged version of the same play. Deevy attended Longford Productions' staging of G.B. Shaw's *In Good King Charles's Golden Days* and Molière's *The School for Wives*, admiring the company's production values.[62] At this time, she remarks that she has 'not been to the Abbey for ages'.[63] She may not have felt particularly welcome there given that, in the previous year in 1947, *The Irish Press* published her complaint at the Abbey's rejection of B.G. MacCarthy's *The Raven of Wicklow* in which Deevy railed: 'Are we not all to blame if we fail to protest when our National Theatre gives yet another proof of the downward path it is choosing'.[64] Despite Deevy's public denunciation of the Abbey, Ria Mooney produced *Light Falling* at

---

58 Deirdre Mulrooney, *Irish Moves: An Illustrated History of Dance and Physical Theatre in Ireland* (Dublin: The Liffey Press, 2006); Pilkington, 'Little Theatres'.
59 Jonathan Bank, 'Introduction', in *Teresa Deevy Reclaimed*, I, 105–107 (p. 105).
60 Dublin, Eavan Boland Library (EBL), Florence Hackett Collection, Teresa Deevy to Florence Hackett, 28 February 1945 (?) [sic], MS 10722, item 39.
61 Dublin, Eavan Boland Library (EBL), Florence Hackett Collection, Teresa Deevy to Florence Hackett, Saturday 1944, MS 10722, item 36.
62 Dublin, Eavan Boland Library (EBL), Florence Hackett Collection, Teresa Deevy to Florence Hackett, undated, MS 10722, item 35 (in which Deevy mistitles Shaw's play) and item 40.
63 EBL, MS 10722, item 40.
64 Teresa Deevy, 'New Historical Play', *Irish Press*, 15 February 1947, p. 9. We gratefully acknowledge Aaron Kent for bringing this letter to our attention.

the Peacock in 1948 the same year that Deevy sent *Wife to James Whelan* to Christine and Edward Longford. Longford Productions could not produce *Wife to James Whelan* as they did not have a 'suitable cast'.⁶⁵ The decade closed with some success for Deevy, however, as, in 1949, Josephine Albericci produced Deevy's *In Search of Valour* (originally staged by the Abbey as *A Disciple* in 1931) for the Dublin School of Acting. These radio and theatre productions constitute positive staging points in the jagged trajectory of Deevy's career during 1940s.

Deevy continued to seek theatre productions of her work within the studio theatre scene, which remained vibrant throughout the 1950s, and also sought productions of her work within the 'thriving amateur movement'.⁶⁶ Fallon offers a truncated list of landmark events demonstrating the vibrancy of cultural, social, and political life in the 1950s which, he argues, opposed 'the last great counter-offensive of the old guard and the obscurantists, whose days in almost every area were outnumbered'.⁶⁷ In 1951, Nora Lever and Barry Cassin co-founded the '37' Club; American actor-producer Jack Aronson staged work in Dublin and London; Carolyn Swift and Alan Simpson co-founded The Pike Theatre in 1953; Godfrey Quigley, Denis Brennan, and Michael O'Herlihy formed the Dublin Globe Theatre in 1954; and, in 1957, Phyllis Ryan formed Orion Productions.⁶⁸ Also, in the 1950s, Albericci, having left the Abbey School of Acting, founded Pilgrim Productions, sometimes also collaborating with Stanley Ilsley and Leo McCabe, managers of the Gaiety and co-founders of Ilsley-McCabe Productions. In the days before Christmas 1953, Deevy mentions that she had attended the Abbey productions (produced at the Queen's Theatre) of *This Other Eden* and *The Devil a Saint Would Be* by Louis D'Alton and G.B.

---

65 Dublin, Eavan Boland Library (EBL), Florence Hackett Collection, Teresa Deevy to Florence Hackett, 17 December 1948, MS 10722, item 45.
66 Ó hAodha, *Theatre in Ireland*, p. 136.
67 Fallon, *Age of Innocence*, p. 258.
68 During 1953 and 1954, Aronson produced Tennessee Williams' *The Glass Menagerie*, Arthur Miller's *All My Sons*, August Strindberg's *Miss Julie* (entitled *Lady Julie*), and evenings of scenes from William Shakespeare, Oscar Wilde, and Samuel Taylor Coleridge. Aronson achieved international fame with his one-man show, *Moby Dick*, which toured extensively throughout the United States in the late 1970s. Lawrence van Gelder, 'Moby Dick, a Test of Actor's Versatility', *New York Times*, 7 January 1979; Ryan, *The Company I Kept*; Dublin, National Library of Ireland (NLI), 'Description', Records of the Lantern Theatre 1957–1975, https://catalogue.nli.ie/Collection/vtls000229597

Shaw's *Saint Joan*, but that she had 'not been to "37"'.[69] This she quickly remedied, becoming a member of the club (referring to it as 'the Barry Cassin Theatre') and enthusiastically welcoming it as 'new life in the stage world', describing the quality of the acting in an 'expressionistic' production of Maurice Meldon's *Aisling* as '<u>very</u> good'.[70]

In 1954, Nell Deevy, who 'had been [Teresa's] ears […] for many years', died; an event Phyllis Ryan describes as Teresa Deevy's 'great tragedy'.[71] In a letter acknowledging condolences on Nell's death, Deevy wrote, 'I do not find it easy to write about her. We were so very close to one another I am desolate now. But that is to be faced,—and she would not have us sad'.[72] Showing that same resilience as she had in the early 1940s, when disappointed at the loss of the Abbey as producer for her work, Deevy continued to work and attend studio theatre productions—without Nell by her side—including those at the Studio Theatre, appreciating the production values and the 'intelligent' audiences who frequented them.[73] In 1954, Deevy writes that she is 'Glad to see the Behan play is well attended', a reference to Brendan Behan's *The Quare Fellow* produced at the Pike Theatre.[74] In 1955, finding the flat in Waterloo Road 'too lonely' without Nell, Deevy moved to 20 Clyde Road.[75]

In 1956, the same year that *Wife to James Whelan* was produced by the Studio Theatre, Josephine and Patrick Funge and Liam Miller founded the Lantern Theatre. While production values had improved since the early decades of the twentieth century, audience numbers for studio theatre productions remained small; attending a production of James Cheasty's *The Lost Years* at the Studio, Deevy notes the 'very poor audience—about 12 or 15 people the night I was there—'.[76] She

---

69   Maynooth, Russell Library (RL), Teresa Deevy to James Cheasty, 22 December 1953. The Deevy-Cheasty correspondence was deposited at the Russell Library in 2023. The James Cheasty Archive is available for consultation in the Russell Library under the reference code PP43.

70   Maynooth, Russell Library (RL), Teresa Deevy to James Cheasty, 21 January [year unknown]; Maynooth, Russell Library (RL), Teresa Deevy to James Cheasty, 24 April 1953.

71   Ryan, *The Company I Kept*, p. 108.

72   Maynooth, Russell Library (RL), Teresa Deevy to Ellen Cheasty, 10 March 1954.

73   Maynooth, Russell Library (RL), Teresa Deevy to James Cheasty, 3 June 1957.

74   Maynooth, Russell Library (RL), Teresa Deevy to James Cheasty, 22 October 1954.

75   Dublin, National Library of Ireland (NLI), John Jordan Papers 1945-1988, Teresa Deevy to John Jordan, 13 October 1955, MS 35,072.

76   Maynooth, Russell Library (RL), Teresa Deevy to James Cheasty, 3 June 1957.

mentions, by name, theatre critics who attended Studio Theatre productions and references published theatre reviews suggesting these productions received careful, critical consideration and that a Studio Theatre production was a cultural event of import. Good news came unexpectedly for Deevy in 1957 when she received word from:

> 'Madame' [Cogley] telling me that Studio is putting on my one-act play 'In the Cellar of my Friend' next Sat (31st) and Sunday (Sept 1st)—I had forgotten she had a script! Must have it for the last 12 mths. She says now the play is 'a gem.'—It has not been done on stage, nor broadcast.[77]

As argued elsewhere, this restores a production history of *In the Cellar of My Friend* that was, until recently, lost.[78]

Concurrently, Deevy was also investigating production opportunities offered by regional studio theatre companies which sometimes employed Dublin-based practitioners. Waterford Dramatic Society, for example, employed Godfrey Quigley, Tomás Mac Anna, Don O'Connell, Nora Lever, Barry Cassin, and Shelah Richards.[79] Other Waterford-based theatre companies, such as the Smith School of Acting, founded in 1955 by Jo Moylan, and the Waterford Drama Circle, formed in the late 1950s, point to a lively, regional studio theatre scene. The formation and productions of these regional drama clubs and studio theatres were of interest to Deevy: in a postcard to Cheasty, she writes, 'Got tickets from Drama Circle—thank you—Want to be subscriber this year too'.[80] Recognising that clubs such as the Drama Circle offered production opportunities for her work, Deevy sent the Drama Circle *Supreme Dominion* in 1957. The play was rejected, but was produced the following year as part of Luke Wadding Centenary celebrations.[81] Thus, the 1950s

---

77 Maynooth, Russell Library (RL), Teresa Deevy to James Cheasty, 28 June 1957.
78 McCarthy and Kealy, 'Writing from the Margins'.
79 *Waterford Dramatic Society 60th Anniversary Production, The Passing of Morgan Carey: A New Play by James Cheasty, Souvenir Programme* (Waterford: Waterford Dramatic Society, 1995), p. 8. The Drama Circle in Waterford produced Cheasty's *A Stranger Came* in February 1957, while the Smith School of Acting, also in Waterford, produced Cheasty's *The Calamaun* in 1961. The importance of these regional productions is evident in the fact that *The Calamaun* was taken up by Illsey-McCabe productions, retitled *Francey*, and produced at the Olympia in 1962 featuring Leo McCabe in the title role. Another indicator of the importance of regional theatres in the Irish theatre landscape was Blythe's visit to Waterford in 1964 to open, with Anna Manahan, Waterford Dramatic Society Theatre Club in Henrietta Street.
80 Maynooth, Russell Library (RL), Teresa Deevy to James Cheasty, 6 February 1958.
81 Maynooth, Russell Library (RL), Teresa Deevy to James Cheasty, 31 October 1957;

was a decade when Deevy worked hard, and with some success, to find production opportunities for her work outside the Abbey.

Conclusion

Primarily, Deevy has been long associated with the Abbey, but her relationship and interaction with theatre practice and theatre practitioners is more complex and varied. During her lifetime, nine premieres of Deevy's theatre work were staged—five on the main Abbey stage and four on the stages of studio and theatre clubs.[82] By her own admission, Deevy wrote plays particularly suited to the company and performance style of the Abbey players, a company she esteemed but, from the 1930s through the 1950s, the Abbey was dominated by those who either disliked, or could not perceive the value of, her work—a fact of which she was well aware. Added to this, during the late 1930s and early 1940s, influential supporters of her work, including Hugh Hunt, Frank O'Connor, and Denis Johnston, departed the Abbey, some considerably acrimoniously, leaving her short of powerful allies. Deevy needed to find one or more alternative venues and/or producers for her work and the studio theatre scene presented opportunities. Demonstrating a consistent artistic integrity, tenacity, and an indomitable entrepreneurial spirit, Deevy actively sought out studio theatre producers for her work as early as the mid-1930s. It was partly by necessity, but also partly by her own design, that Deevy's career as a dramatist for theatre reoriented from the Abbey in the 1940s and 1950s towards studio theatre practice which was, in those decades, particularly vibrant and flourishing at a time when distinctions between professional, studio, and amateur drama often blurred. Details from Deevy's correspondence, collated and synthesised with scholarship of studio theatre practice during the 1930s, 1940s, and 1950s, reveal her as engaged, throughout her career, with agents, literary magazines, artists, and producers of theatre, radio, and television drama. Alongside her work for radio in the 1940s and 1950s, Deevy energetically sought studio theatre productions of her work within a community of theatre practitioners that had impressed and interested her since the mid-1930s. Deevy's criticism of the

---

Maynooth, Russell Library (RL), Teresa Deevy to James Cheasty, 3 June 1957.
82 We count the Abbey Experimental Theatre stage as a studio space here.

Abbey Theatre during the 1930s, 1940s, and 1950s in concert with her attendance at studio theatre productions, her frequent references to personalities, audiences, and the critical reception of those productions evidence a playwright confidently articulate of her own artistic and creative paradigm, tenacious in her ambition for her theatre work right up to the end of her life, and consistently entrepreneurial in creating opportunities for her work regionally, nationally, and internationally.

Bibliography

Arrington, Lauren, *W.B. Yeats, The Abbey Theatre, Censorship, and the Irish State: Adding the Half-Pence to the Pence* (Oxford: Oxford University Press, 2010), https://doi.org/10.1093/acprof:oso/9780199590575.001.0001

Bank, Jonathan, 'Introduction', in *Teresa Deevy Reclaimed*, I, ed. by Jonathan Bank, John P. Harrington, and Christopher Morash (New York: Mint Theater, 2011), pp. 105–107

Bank, Jonathan, John P. Harrington, and Christopher Morash (eds), *Teresa Deevy Reclaimed*, 2 vols (New York: Mint Theater, 2011 and 2017)

Bloom, Emily, 'Looking In: Teresa Deevy, Deafness, and Radio', *Modernism/Modernity*, 30.2 (2023), 279–299, https://doi.org/10.1353/mod.2023.a913149

Clarke, Brenna Katz, and Harold Ferrar, *The Dublin Drama League, 1918–41*, The Irish Theatre Series 9, ed. by Robert Hogan, James Kilroy, and Liam Miller (Dublin: Dolmen Press, 1979)

Collins, Christopher, 'Other Theatres', in *The Palgrave Handbook of Contemporary Irish Theatre and Performance*, ed. by Eamonn Jordan and Eric Weitz (London: Palgrave, 2018), pp. 221–232, https://doi.org/10.1057/978-1-137-58588-2_14

Deevy, Teresa, 'The King of Spain's Daughter', *Theatre Arts Monthly*, June 1935, 459–466, https://archive.org/details/sim_theatre-arts_1935-06_19_6

Deevy, Teresa, 'New Historical Play', *Irish Press*, 15 February 1947, p. 9

Fallon, Brian, *An Age of Innocence, Irish Culture 1930–1960* (Dublin: Gill and Macmillan, 1998)

Fay, Frank, 'The Irish Literary Theatre', in *Handbook of the Irish Revival: An Anthology of Irish Cultural and Political Writings 1891–1922*, ed. by Declan Kiberd and P.J. Mathews (Dublin: Abbey Theatre Press, 2015), p. 166

Fitz-Simon, Christopher, *The Boys* (Dublin: Gill and Macmillan, 1994)

Fitz-Simon, Christopher, *The Irish Theatre* (London: Thames and Hudson, 1983)

Fitzpatrick, Lisa, 'Taking Their Own Road: The Female Protagonists in Three Plays by Irish Women', in *Women in Irish Drama: A Century of Authorship and Representation*, ed. by Melissa Sihra (Houndmills: Palgrave Macmillan, 2007), pp. 69–86, https://doi.org/10.1057/9780230801455

'Foreword', *Theatre Arts Magazine*, 1 (1916), 11, https://babel.hathitrust.org/cgi/pt?id=mdp.39015004831163&seq=11

Horniman, Annie E.F., 'The Origin of the Abbey Theatre', in *The Abbey Theatre: Interviews and Recollections*, ed. by Edward H. Mikhail (London: Macmillan Press, 1988), pp. 28–30

Johnston, Denis, *Orders and Desecrations: The Life of the Playwright Denis Johnston*, ed. by Rory Johnston (Dublin: Lilliput Press, 1992)

Jordan, John, 'Teresa Deevy: An Introduction', *Irish University Review*, 1.8 (1956), 13–26

Joyce, James, 'The Day of the Rabblement', in *Handbook of the Irish Revival: An Anthology of Irish Cultural and Political Writings 1891–1922*, ed. by Declan Kiberd and P.J. Mathews (Dublin: Abbey Theatre Press, 2015), pp. 164–165

Kealy, Úna, 'Resisting Power and Direction: *The King of Spain's Daughter* by Teresa Deevy as a Feminist Call to Action', *Estudios Irlandeses*, 15 (2020), 178–192, https://doi.org/10.24162/EI2020-9406

Kiberd, Declan, and P.J. Mathews (eds), *Handbook of the Irish Revival: An Anthology of Irish Cultural and Political Writings 1891–1922* (Dublin: Abbey Theatre Press, 2015)

Laverty, Maura, *The Plays of Maura Laverty: Liffey Lane, Tolka Row, A Tree in the Crescent*, ed. by Cathy Leeney and Deirdre McFeely (Liverpool: Liverpool University Press, 2023)

Letts, Winifred, 'My First Abbey Play', in *Irish Writing* (Cork), 16 (September 1951), 43–46 (pp. 35–39)

Malone, Irina Ruppo, 'Synge, An-Sky, and the Irish Jewish Revival', *The Irish Review*, 48 (2014), 17–27

McCarthy, Kate, and Úna Kealy, 'Writing from the Margins: Re-framing Teresa Deevy's Archive and Her Correspondence with James Cheasty c.1952–1962', *Irish University Review*, 52.2 (2022), 322–340, https://doi.org/10.3366/iur.2022.0570

Mikhail, Edward H. (ed.), *The Abbey Theatre: Interviews and Recollections* (London: Macmillan Press, 1988)

Milligan, Alice, 'Staging and Costume in Irish Drama', Ireland's Own, 30 March 1904, in *Handbook of the Irish Revival: An Anthology of Irish Cultural and Political Writings 1891–1922*, ed. by Declan Kiberd and P.J. Mathews (Dublin: Abbey Theatre Press, 2015), pp. 160–161

Montgomery, Barry, 'Jewish Drama on the Irish Stage: The Socio-Political and Cultural Milieu of the Dublin Jewish Amateur Operatic Society (1908–1910) and the Dublin Jewish Dramatic Society (1924–1954)', *Studi Irlandesi. A Journal of Irish Studies*, 10.10 (2020), 133–152, https://doi.org/10.13128/SIJIS-2239-3978-11757

Morash, Christopher, *A History of Irish Theatre 1601–2000* (Cambridge: Cambridge University Press, 2002)

Morash, Chris, '"Somehow It Is Not The Same": Irish Theatre and Tradition', in *Irish Literature in Transition, 1940–1980*, ed. by Eve Patten (Cambridge: Cambridge University Press, 2020), pp. 134–149, https://doi.org/10.1017/9781108616348.009

Morash, Christopher, 'Teresa Deevy: Seeing the World', in *Teresa Deevy Reclaimed*, II, ed. by Jonathan Bank, John P. Harrington, and Christopher Morash (New York: Mint Theater, 2017), pp. ix–xx

Moroney, Nora, 'The Women Behind the Abbey: Dolly Robinson and Irish Theatrical Networks', *English Studies*, 104.6 (2023), 1037–1054, https://doi.org/10.1080/0013838X.2023.2256609

Mulrooney, Deirdre, *Irish Moves: An Illustrated History of Dance and Physical Theatre in Ireland* (Dublin: The Liffey Press, 2006)

Ní Bheacháin, Caoilfhionn, 'The Seeds Beneath the Snow': Resignation and Resistance in Teresa Deevy's *Wife to James Whelan*', in *Irish Women Writers: New Critical Perspectives*, ed. by Elke D'hoker, Raphaël Ingelbien, and Hedwig Schwall (New York: Peter Lang, 2011), pp. 91–109, https://doi.org/10.3726/978-3-0353-0057-4

Nic Shiubhlaigh, Máire, *The Splendid Years: Recollections of Máire Nic Shiubhlaigh; as Told to Edward Kenny* (Dublin: James Duffy, 1955)

O'Beirne, Tricia, '"In a Position to Be Treated Roughly"', *New Hibernia Review/Iris Éireannach Nua*, 22.1 (2018), 120–134, https://dx.doi.org/10.1353/nhr.2018.0008

O'Brien, Eoin, 'II. Dramatic Commentary: *The Dublin Magazine*, 1943–1958', in *A. J. Leventhal 1896–1979: Dublin Scholar, Wit and Man of Letters* (Dublin: The Con Leventhal Scholarship Committee, 1984), http://www.eoinobrien.org/wp-content/uploads/2008/11/ajleventahl-1896-1979.pdf

O'Connor, Frank, *The Backward Look: A Survey of Irish Literature* (London: MacMillan, 1967)

O'Doherty, Martina Ann, 'Deevy: A Bibliography', *Irish University Review*, 25.1 (1995), 163–170

O'Dowd, Ciara, *Wild-Looking but Fine: Abbey Theatre Actresses of the 1930s* (Dublin: University College Dublin Press, 2024)

O'Farrell, Ciara, *Louis D'Alton and the Abbey Theatre* (Dublin: Four Courts Press, 2004)

O'Gorman, Siobhán, '"Hers and His": Carolyn Swift, Alan Simpson, and Collective Creation at Dublin's Pike Theatre', in *Women, Collective Creation, and Devised Performance: The Rise of Women Theatre Artists in the Twentieth and Twenty-First Centuries*, ed. by Kathryn Mederos Syssoyeva and Scott Proudfit (New York: Palgrave Macmillan, 2016), pp. 129–144, https://doi.org/10.1057/978-1-137-55013-2

O'Gorman, Siobhán, 'Scenographic Interactions: 1950's Ireland and Dublin's Pike Theatre', *Irish Theatre International*, 3.1 (2014), 25–42

Ó hAodha, Mícheál, *Theatre in Ireland* (Oxford: Basil Blackwell, 1974)

Pilkington, Lionel, 'The Little Theatres of the 1950s', in *The Oxford Handbook of Modern Irish Theatre*, ed. by Nicholas Grene and Chris Morash (Oxford: Oxford University Press, 2016), pp. 286–303, https://doi.org/10.1093/oxfordhb/9780198706137.001.0001

Pilný, Ondřej, Ruud van den Beuken, and Ian R. Walsh (eds), *Cultural Convergence: The Dublin Gate Theatre, 1929–1960* (London: Palgrave Macmillan, 2021), https://doi.org/10.1007/978-3-030-57562-5

Reynolds, Paige, 'Theatrical Ireland: New Routes from the Abbey Theatre to the Gate Theatre', in *Irish Literature in Transition, 1880–1940*, ed. by Marjorie Elizabeth Howes (Cambridge: Cambridge University Press, 2020), pp. 55–72, https://doi.org/10.1017/9781108616379.005

Ryan, Phyllis, *The Company I Kept* (Dublin: Town House, 1996)

Sisson, Elaine, 'Experiment and the Free State: Mrs Cogley's Cabaret and the Founding of the Gate Theatre 1924–1930', in *The Gate Theatre: Inspiration and Craft*, ed. by David Clare, Des Lally, and Patrick Lonergan (Dublin: Carysfort Press, 2018), pp. 11–27, https://doi.org/10.3726/b14576

Smith, Gus, and Des Hickey, *John B: The Real Keane* (Cork: Mercier Press, 1992)

Trotter, Mary, *Modern Irish Theatre* (Cambridge: Polity Press, 2008)

van Gelder, Lawrence, 'Moby Dick, a Test of Actor's Versatility', *New York Times*, 7 January 1979, https://www.nytimes.com/1979/01/07/archives/new-jersey-weekly-moby-dick-a-test-of-actors-versatility.html

Walsh, Ian, *Experimental Theatre After W.B. Yeats* (Houndmills: Palgrave, 2012), https://doi.org/10.1057/9781137001368

Walshe, Eibhear, 'Ineffable Longings', in *Selected Plays of Irish Playwright Teresa Deevy, 1894–1963*, ed. by Eibhear Walshe (Lewiston: Edward Mellen Press, 2003), pp. 9–10

Waterford Dramatic Society 60th Anniversary Production, The Passing of Morgan Carey: A New Play by James Cheasty, Souvenir Programme (Waterford: Waterford Dramatic Society, 1995), https://waterfordtheatrearchive.com/wp-content/uploads/2017/03/1995-WDS-The-Passing-Of-Morgan-Carey.pdf

Welch, Robert, *The Abbey Theatre 1899–1999: Form and Pressure* (Oxford: Oxford University Press, 1999)

Whelan, Gerard, with Carolyn Swift, *Spiked: Church-State Intrigue and The Rose Tattoo* (Dublin: New Island, 2002)

7. 'It Is Myself I Seen in Her': Points of Departure in Teresa Deevy's *The King of Spain's Daughter* (1935)

Willy Maley

Careless Talk Costs Little

Assessing the drama of J.M. Synge and Seán O'Casey, Raymond Williams spoke of the 'pressing poverty' behind 'that endless fantasy of Irish talk'.[1] In other words, talk is cheap. You get a lot of overcompensating active speech in a Teresa Deevy play, or 'poet's talking', as Pegeen Mike calls it in Synge's *Playboy*.[2] Exorbitant utterance is characteristic of Deevy's women. They do not depend on men to deliver them from poverty through poetry. Nor is talkativeness tied to powerlessness in quite the way Williams suggests.

The conjunction between poetic speech and poverty of opportunity is one Deevy dwells on. She plays with an Irish tradition of the servant who refuses to be servile. Eighteenth-century philosopher George Berkeley bemoaned the impudence of a servant girl: 'In my own Family a Kitchen-wench refused to carry out Cinders, because she was

---

1   Raymond Williams, *Drama from Ibsen to Brecht* (Oxford: Oxford University Press, 1969), p. 137 and p. 153. Williams overlooks women playwrights.
2   'And what is it I have, Christy Mahon, to make me fitting entertainment for the like of you that has such poet's talking, and such bravery of heart?' J.M. Synge, *The Playboy of the Western World and Other Plays*, ed. by Ann Saddlemyer (Oxford: Oxford University Press, 1995), p. 137. Deevy's Annie Kinsella, like her other heroines, isn't waiting on a man for bravery and poetry. She has it in herself.

descended from an old *Irish* stock'. Berkeley remarks of this effrontery: 'Never was there a more monstrous Conjunction than that of Pride with Beggary; and yet this Prodigy is seen every Day in almost every Part of this Kingdom'.[3] Here the philosopher of immaterialism sounds remarkably like the founder of cultural materialism.

Robust verbal resistance to authority characterises Deevy's female protagonists. As well as endless talk they deliver formidable backtalk. bell hooks speaks about the force of talking back:

> In the world of southern black community I grew up in 'back talk' and 'talking back' meant speaking as an equal to an authority figure. It meant daring to disagree and sometimes it just meant having an opinion.[4]

Speaking of her own community, in contrast to more privileged white women, hooks insists that:

> our struggle has not been to emerge from silence into speech but to change the nature and direction of our speech. To make a speech that compels listeners, one that is heard. Our speech, 'the right speech of womanhood', was often the soliloquy, the talking into thin air, the talking to ears that do not hear you—the talk that is simply not listened to.[5]

Without erasing race as a structuring aspect of hooks' argument, mindful of a tradition of comparing Irish and African American dramatic forms, I want to suggest that the Irish context also offers examples of active and engaged backtalk.[6]

---

3   George Berkeley, *A Word to the Wise: Or, the Bishop of Cloyne's Exhortation to the Roman Catholic Clergy of Ireland* (Dublin: George Faulkner, 1749), p. 4.

4   bell hooks, 'Talking Back', *Discourse: Journal for Theoretical Studies in Media and Culture*, 8 (1986–1987), 123–128 (p. 123). For a compelling discussion of the need to talk back by Irish playwright and Traveller Rosaleen McDonagh, see 'Talking Back', in *(Re)searching Women: Feminist Research Methodologies in the Social Sciences in Ireland*, ed. by Anne Byrne and Ronit Lentin (Dublin: Institute of Public Administration, 2000), pp. 237–246.

5   hooks, 'Talking Back', p. 124. As a child, hooks was rebuked for 'crazy talk, crazy speech' (p. 125).

6   See Megan Sullivan, 'Folk Plays, Home Girls, and Back Talk: Georgia Douglas Johnson and Women of the Harlem Renaissance', *CLA Journal*, 38.4 (1995), 404–419 (p. 404).

Missing the Boat—and the Point

In *Ulysses*, James Joyce has 'Old Gummy Granny' present herself as 'Ireland's sweetheart, the king of Spain's daughter'.[7] Later, Stephen tells Bloom that Kitty O'Shea is 'The king of Spain's daughter'.[8] Neither allusion appears favourable. Here I want to pursue another Joycean connection. In a podcast on *Dubliners* in January 2013, Sebastian Barry said: 'I chose "Eveline" [...] because, 40 years later, I am still not over it. [...] The scene at the dockside. I am still inclined to cry out the same thing I cried out the first time I read it, aged 17: "Get on the bloody boat, Eveline"'.[9] Thanks to the work of Katy Mullin and others we now know Eveline was wise to resist going aboard, as she could have been pressed into service of a particularly demeaning kind by Frank, her sailor suitor.[10] As Mullin argues, Joyce's fusion of 'antiemigration fiction with [...] the white slave cautionary tale' serves 'to complicate his heroine's renunciation of' her apparent escape route.[11] Joyce recognises intersecting aspects of life experience particular to women that lead directly to a specific form of paralysis engendered by repetition. The paragraph in Joyce's story, beginning with the line 'Home! She looked

---

7   'Circe', *Ulysses*, 15.4585.
8   'Eumaeus', *Ulysses*, 16.1414.
9   Sebastian Barry, 'Sebastian Barry Reads "Eveline" by James Joyce', podcast, *The Guardian*, 2 January 2013, http://www.theguardian.com/books/audio/2013/jan/02/sebastian-barry-james-joyce-eveline. Of course, Barry's youthful wish that Eveline 'get on the bloody boat' does not simply miss the point that for Eveline to do so was risky (even though he might have missed that point as a seventeen-year-old), but acknowledges and regrets the feeling of sorrow and missed opportunity that multiple forces combine to create a particular net that traps Eveline. Barry's own approach as a writer and editor has been to push the boat out against the current, venturing beyond 'inherited boundaries'. See *The Inherited Boundaries: Younger Poets of the Republic of Ireland*, ed. by Sebastian Barry (Mountrath: Dolmen Press, 1986).
10 See Katherine Mullin, 'Don't Cry for Me, Argentina: "Eveline" and the Seductions of Emigration Propaganda', in *Semicolonial Joyce*, ed. by Derek Attridge and Marjorie Howes (Cambridge: Cambridge University Press, 2000), pp. 172–200.
11 Ibid., p. 193. There was a white slave trade at home as well as abroad, as Anthony Roche notes in discussing Deevy's *Katie Roche*: 'Katie's experience of the nuns would derive from the long-prevalent practice in Ireland of farming out illegitimate young women to work as unpaid labour in convents. [...] The stigma of illegitimacy can be erased in only a few instances: entering a convent she imagines to be one of them'. Anthony Roche, 'Woman on the Threshold: J. M. Synge's *The Shadow of the Glen*, Teresa Deevy's *Katie Roche* and Marina Carr's *The Mai*', *Irish University Review*, 25.1 (1995), 143–162 (p. 154).

round the room, reviewing all its familiar objects which she had dusted once a week for so many years, wondering where on earth all the dust came from', suggests the curiosity-dulling impact of endlessly repetitive domestic duties echoed by Deevy's Katie Roche in the lines, 'The bread and the butter and to fill the jug...' and later articulated by Simone de Beauvoir in *The Second Sex* when she writes: 'Few tasks are more like the torture of Sisyphus than housework, with its endless repetition: the clean becomes soiled, the soiled is made clean, over and over, day after day'.[12] Arguably, not only is Eveline paralysed by her sense of duty towards her parents (living and dead) and the children for whom she cares, but her paralysis (Joyce uses the words 'passive' and 'helpless') is compounded by her awareness that, should she leave for Buenos Ayres, she might, as a woman, face a worse fate than she might in Ireland.[13] In the final moments of Joyce's story Eveline, 'set[s] her white face' and stares with expressionless eyes, becoming statuesque; a plaster saint in whose body the paralysing forces of social expectations and domestic duties are reified. This compounded paralysis results in Eveline not simply being petrified on the quay, but also doomed to inarticulacy. She is silent; incapable of back talk, capable only of a single paralinguistic utterance—'a cry of anguish'—which is never heard but immediately lost 'amid the seas'.[14]

In a comparative and intersectional essay exploring class, race, and gender in relation to domestic service, Danielle Phillips-Cunningham observes: 'Of all the ethnic and racial groups of women who migrated to northeastern cities in the late nineteenth and early twentieth centuries, Irish immigrant, southern Black, and Afro Caribbean women were most likely to be concentrated in domestic service'.[15] The spectre of servitude

---

12   James Joyce, 'Eveline', in *The Essential James Joyce*, ed. by Harry Levin (St Albans: Granada, 1977), pp. 40–44 (p. 41); Teresa Deevy, 'Katie Roche', in *Teresa Deevy Reclaimed*, 2 vols, ed. by Jonathan Bank, John P. Harrington, and Christopher Morash (New York: Mint Theater, 2011 and 2017), I, 58; Simone de Beauvoir, *The Second Sex* (London: Random House, Vintage Classics, 1997), p. 470. I cite the recent Mint edition of *Katie Roche* here, but the 1939 edition has an ellipsis after 'butter' and pauses are always pertinent in Deevy's work. See Teresa Deevy, *Three Plays: Katie Roche, The King of Spain's Daughter, The Wild Goose* (London: Macmillan, 1939), p. 10.
13   Joyce, 'Eveline', p. 44.
14   Ibid. I owe this and the previous point to Úna Kealy.
15   Danielle Phillips-Cunningham, 'Slaving Irish "Ladies" and Black "Towers of Strength in the Labor World": Race and Women's Resistance in Domestic Service', *Women's History Review*, 30.2 (2021), 190–207. In this context one wonders

loomed at home as well as abroad.[16] A remarkable essay published in 1929 by Signe Toksvig sheds light on 'Eveline' and on Deevy, whom Toksvig knew, with whom she corresponded, and to whom she showed work-in-progress.[17] Toksvig tells of 'a walk on a soft day in a southern Irish county' and an encounter with three sisters of her maid Moll:

> I looked at Katie [...] dressed in rags, and with little naked blue-grey feet in the cold deep mud. Katie was very dirty. Katie was a sight. [...] But my thoughts took a juster turn. When this little Katie grew up and became some other housekeeper's problem, would they really see her? No, no more than I was doing, although I knew all the facts. But the facts, so tangibly dramatized, of my own troubles had put the others out of my mind. Katie-in-the-mud, however, knocked them back in again. And the answer is: Why wouldn't they go to America, and why wouldn't they be 'raw' when they get there![18]

The word 'raw' refers back to Toksvig's friends talking of getting 'a raw Irish girl' as a servant.[19] As Marie Clarke observes, young women in rural Ireland had little choice but to join the servant class:

> Unqualified rural girls had few chances of employment outside the domestic and agricultural sectors [...] where the labour market was very strongly gender segregated. They had little choice as to whether or not they went into domestic service [...] viewed as more stigmatising than work carried out by male farm labourers.[20]

---

if Eveline's 'white face' denotes more than her pallor and panic.
16 As Beckett's Mrs. Rooney says: 'It is suicide to be abroad. But [...] what is it to be at home? A lingering dissolution'. Samuel Beckett, *All That Fall* (1956), in *Collected Shorter Plays* (London: Faber, 1984), p. 15.
17 See Signe Toksvig, 'Why Girls Leave Ireland', *The Survey*, 1 August 1929, pp. 483–486 and 509. See also Signe Toksvig, 'A Visit to Lady Gregory', *The North American Review*, 214.789 (1921), 190–200 (p. 190): 'Here and there [...] the madder-red of a Galway petticoat gleamed in a small yellow cornfield, and girls let their sickles fall to look at us'. On Toksvig's literary relations with Deevy see Lis Pihl, '"A Muzzle Made in Ireland": Irish Censorship and Signe Toksvig', *Studies: An Irish Quarterly Review*, 88.352 (1999), 448–457 (p. 453). On Toksvig as a writer forced by Irish censorship to return home to Denmark, see Sandra McAvoy, 'All about Eve: Signe Toksvig and the Intimate Lives of Irish Women, 1926–1937', *The Irish Review*, 42 (2010), 43–57.
18 Toksvig, 'Why Girls Leave Ireland', p. 483.
19 Molly 'is the type who aims for America [...] it has dawned on me now what my friends meant when they said with such queer expressions that they had got '"a raw Irish girl"'. Toksvig, 'Why Girls Leave Ireland', p. 483.
20 Marie Clarke, 'Education for the Country Girls: Vocational Education in Rural Ireland 1930–1960', *History of Education* (2021), 1–16 (p. 6).

Emigration was one alternative to domestic servitude, thought to be encouraged by education: 'Some were of the view that vocational schools encouraged young girls to emigrate'.[21] Key to the predicament of young women was the cultural isolation they faced: 'Girls in rural Ireland were not in a position to live independently and did not have the same access to popular culture as their urban peers'.[22] This last point is worth pondering. There were no limits to the dreams of leaving or fantasies of escape that rural women entertained, and the question of 'popular culture' is complicated by the fact that such culture could materialise in the remotest of places, like the all-female production of *Coriolanus* Ellie Irwin witnessed in one of Deevy's earliest dramas.[23]

In Joyce's 'Eveline' the romantic adventurer is male. Eveline is speechless throughout, never uttering a solitary syllable. She makes herself heard just once, her exit line: 'Amid the seas she sent a cry of anguish'.[24] The ending of 'Eveline' is much debated. Deevy's drama possesses the same degree of poetic depth and deserves the same assiduous attention. Úna Kealy's essay on *The King of Spain's Daughter*, a brilliant example of the kind of subtle and theoretically informed criticism Deevy demands, invites us to think more deeply about the play's ending.[25] Eveline Hill was a domestic drudge with a brutal father who dreamt of getting away. Like Joyce—and yet not like Joyce—Deevy approached her would-be escapees unsentimentally.

From Christy Mahon to Roddy Mann

The King of Spain's Daughter opens with Annie Kinsella, an adventurous young woman of twenty with a great imagination, giving a long kiss to Roddy Mann, while resisting the advances of Jim Harris, her would-be suitor, and the threats of her father that he'll sign her over to the factory for five years if she does not settle down and behave herself. Jim is a

---

21 Ibid., p. 7.
22 Ibid., p. 6.
23 See Willy Maley, '"She Done *Coriolanus* at the Convent": Empowerment and Entrapment in Teresa Deevy's *In Search of Valour*', *Irish University Review*, 49.2 (2019), 356–369.
24 Joyce, *The Essential James Joyce*, p. 44.
25 Úna Kealy, 'Resisting Power and Direction: *The King of Spain's Daughter* by Teresa Deevy as a Feminist Call to Action', *Estudios Irlandeses*, 15 (2020), 178–192.

saver, and one of the things Jim wants to save is Annie *as she is*, not as a reluctant gift from her father. She's as she is, Jim says, a dreamer and a desirer of other men, because 'she must; she's made that way, she can't help it'.[26] Jim is painted in flattering tones in the play's opening, standing up for Annie in her absence against both her father and Mrs Marks, the neighbour. Annie's philandering, as her father calls it, is in stark contrast to Jim's apparent steadfast love. When Mrs Marks urges him to give up on Annie, Jim retorts: 'Give up me life, is it?'.[27] But when Annie appears with Roddy Mann in tow, we see another side of Jim—jealous, petty, and willing to stand by while Annie is beaten by her father. And there's something else. In an early exchange with Mrs Marks, Jim is advised against pursuing Annie because 'her head is full of folly and her heart is full of wile'.[28] Mrs Marks appeals to his sense of domestic responsibility—'You have two good sisters, can't you settle with them, or get a sensible girl'—which Jim dismisses as 'a lot of old talk'.[29]

Jim's 'two good sisters' come back into the play, mentioned by name, when Annie reluctantly agrees to marry him and Jim says distractedly, 'I'll tell them look out for a place so: they can get a room in the town'. 'Tell who?', asks Annie: 'Molly and Dot. 'Tis I have the house: they knew they'd have to go'. Annie's response demonstrates her ability to see beyond herself:

> ANNIE: Well, then, they needn't. Let them stop where they are. What would I do without a woman to talk to?
>
> JIM: I want you to myself.
>
> ANNIE: I never heard the like! A good 'man' he'd make to begin by turnin' his two sisters on the road! And they after mindin' the place since his mother died.[30]

The disagreement escalates when Jim takes Annie's reaction as a marriage deal-breaker:

---

26 Teresa Deevy, 'The King of Spain's Daughter', in *Teresa Deevy Reclaimed*, II, 17–26 (p. 18).
27 Ibid., p. 19.
28 Ibid.
29 Ibid.
30 Ibid., p. 23.

JIM: Will you go back on me so?

ANNIE: Leave Molly and Dot stay where they are.

JIM: I will not.

ANNIE: What great harm would they do?

JIM: They'd be in it—spoilin' the world.

ANNIE: Spoilin' the world! I think you're crazy.

JIM: When we shut the house door I'll have no one in it but you and me.[31]

Jim begins to sound worryingly familiar to Annie, so much so that she says, 'I think I'll stop with my father'.[32] Gerardine Meaney makes precisely this point: 'Jim, who offers to throw his sisters out of his house to facilitate the marriage, seems more like her father than initial appearances had suggested'.[33] Molly and Dot are even more disadvantaged than Eveline in that they are completely silenced. They are not given an opportunity to 'talk back' or even, like Eveline, cry out in anguish at being cast out of their house. The exchange between Annie and Jim above exposes how the shelter provided by an Irish home was provisional for women whose male relations could, upon a whim, remove or restrict that shelter. Molly and Dot's 'room in the town'[34] could be but a stopgap until either or both leave Ireland to become the 'raw' domestic servants described so vividly in Signe Toksvig's account previously quoted. Jim's true colours come out: the same prison grey as those of the bride's dress that Annie splashed with rainbow romance.

Jim points out that with her father comes the factory, so Annie suggests she might run away, to which Jim counters: 'He'd go after you: he'd have you crippled'.[35] This is the point at which Jim pulls out the savings account notebook and mentions the twenty pounds he has

---

31 Ibid.
32 Ibid.
33 Gerardine Meaney, 'The Sons of Cuchulainn: Violence, the Family, and the Irish Canon', Éire-Ireland, 41.1/2 (2006), 242–261 (p. 254).
34 Deevy, 'The King of Spain's Daughter', p. 23.
35 Ibid.

scraped together over four years, money for him and Annie, but money too that Molly and Dot, minding the house, could have done with. If Jim is a saver rather than a saviour, and mean with it, then Molly and Dot are two of the unseen, unheard characters in Deevy's drama, mentioned by name, spoken of by Jim, and spoken for—in sisterhood and solidarity—by Annie.

Joanna Luft points out that while readers of Joyce's 'Eveline' have assumed that 'the two young children [...] left to her charge' are her siblings, the text makes clear that 'her brothers and sisters were all grown up', leading Luft to observe: 'The absence of an immediate familial tie between Eveline and her charges reduces her obligation to remain in Dublin, yet they are certainly part of the "home" that her mother enjoins her to keep together'.[36] Luft's observation of the notion of a reduced obligation is problematic. Family ties are complex. In Deevy's play, Annie rebukes Jim for being prepared to abandon his sisters in taking on Annie as his new exclusive family. Annie's compassion is not fuelled by 'an immediate family tie', yet she is ready to break off her prospective tie to Jim due to his cold-heartedness towards Molly and Dot. Unlike Eveline, Annie is not taken by—in the broadest sense—a single man. She is taken by the bride with the dress of many colours, just as Ellie Irwin was not enamoured of any man but beguiled by another girl, Charlotta Burke, playing a man using only her voice, performing active speech out of costume.[37] Annie feels an affinity and the need for female friendship at Jim's suggestion that he'll turn his sisters out of the house when he marries her, but it transpires that she fears the factory more than she fears settling down.

Synge's shadow is always in the background of Deevy's deft storytelling. Gerardine Meaney regards *The King of Spain's Daughter* as

---

36 Joanna Luft, 'Reader Awareness: Form and Ambiguity in James Joyce's "Eveline"', *The Canadian Journal of Irish Studies*, 35.2 (2009), 48–51 (p. 48).

37 'Annie has made for herself out of this bride's departure by water a symbol of passage into happiness, and since it is no more than a symbol, she may, like all poets, be annoyed when taxed with discrepancy in her account of the symbol's colour-properties. The bride is variously dressed, according to Annie, in "flamin' red from top to toe," in "shimmerin' green from head to foot," and "in pale, pale gold." [...] We learn that in fact the bride was dressed in grey, and that there is some suspicion about her husband's motives in marrying her'. John Jordan, 'Teresa Deevy: An Introduction', *Irish University Review*, 1.8 (1956), 13–26 (p. 18). See Teresa Deevy, 'In Search of Valour', in *Teresa Deevy Reclaimed*, II, 3–13.

an 'occluded parody of *The Playboy of the Western World*'.[38] The echoes of Synge's *Playboy* are as intriguing as those of Joyce's 'Eveline', but the matchup of Annie as Pegeen Mike, Roddy Mann as Christy Mahon, and Jim Harris as Shaun Keogh is complicated by the fact that Annie is the playgirl and she doesn't lose her only playboy, for behind Roddy is another beau, Jack Bolger, unseen and unimportant to Annie but pulled out of the hat by others as proof of her unreliability. As Jim says, 'We're all the wan! You have no heart'.[39] 'We're all the wan!' All men are the same, that's Jim's fear, fleshed out when he morphs into a replica of Annie's father, hoist by his own patriarchal petard.

The King of Spain's Daughter opens with a stage direction that locates Annie in a grassy space between a sign saying 'No Traffic' and another saying 'Road Closed'.[40] Later, Annie laments: 'Where would I ever find a way out of here?'[41] It looks like there's no way out, except for the fields beyond, or the river where the by turns envied and pitied new bride sets sail. The title of Deevy's play comes from a poem by Padraic Colum entitled 'A Drover' (1922).[42] At one point Annie recites a verse softly to herself, and Jim barks back: 'I'm sick of that thing! Who's the King of Spain's daughter?' Annie answers: 'It is myself I seen in her—sailin' out into the sun, and to adventure'.[43] At the play's end,

---

38 Meaney, 'Sons of Cuchulainn', p. 253.
39 Deevy, 'The King of Spain's Daughter', p. 22.
40 Ibid., p. 17.
41 Ibid., p. 24
42 'Study for a moment the third verse in "The Drover": Then the wet, winding roads,/ Brown bogs with black water;/ And my thoughts on white ships/ And the King of Spain's daughter. It is redolent of Gaelic tradition, suggestiveness, indefiniteness, colouring and alliteration. [...] Thomas MacDonough has reminded us, to isolate the phrase "King of Spain's daughter" from tradition would render it almost meaningless'. James F. Cassidy, 'The Poetry of Padraic Colum. II', *The Irish Monthly*, 49.587 (1921), 314–318 (p. 314). See also Edward Sapir, 'The King of Spain's Daughter and the Diver', *Poetry*, 16.4 (1920), 179–182, in which a siren lures a sailor to his death. Behind these verses lies 'The Little Nut Tree', a nursery rhyme supposedly about Katherine of Aragon's arrival at the court of Henry VII in 1501 to marry Prince Arthur, viewed as alluding to how a Spanish alliance promised access to the spice trade. See Emrys Chew, *Arming the Periphery: The Arms Trade in the Indian Ocean during the Age of Global Empire* (London: Palgrave Macmillan, 2012), pp. 101–102. See also Pam Jarvis, 'Not Just "Once" Upon a Time', *Genealogy*, 3.44 (2019), 1–14 (pp. 7–8), https://doi.org/10.3390/genealogy3030044 and, for some serious poetic detective work, see Patrick Gillespie, 'I Had a Little Nut Tree...', *PoemShape*, 4 June 2012.
43 Deevy, 'The King of Spain's Daughter', p. 22.

Annie reacts to the suggestion that Jim is a good boy and she should be a good girl by saying: 'He put by two shillin's every week for two hundred weeks. I think he is a man that—supposin' he was jealous—might cut your throat'.[44] The stage direction reads: '(*Quiet, exultant, she goes*)', leaving Mrs Marks, the neighbour, to lament 'The Lord preserve us! That she'd find joy in such a thought!'[45] Úna Kealy has addressed this ending with considerable clarity and integrity of purpose.[46] Is it all talk, or active speech? Annie can usefully be set alongside Joyce's Eveline, as someone whose dreams of leaving are dashed—but how far and to what effect?

According to Cathy Leeney, 'reasons for the extraordinarily low marriage rate in Ireland in the nineteen twenties and nineteen thirties' included the 'legacy of the famine' as well as 'primogeniture, fear of poverty involved in having a large family, lack of means and of employment, and the likelihood of emigration', while for women '[…] marriage usually meant loss of financial independence, and emotional and physical vulnerability to the will of their husbands'.[47] Speaking of Deevy's drama, Leeney observes:

> Annie Kinsella imagines marriage as a rite of passage into adventure. This vision of her transforming imagination is necessary in enabling her to survive the reality of matrimony—the loss of herself. Her instinctive understanding of this danger is the very stuff of the play.[48]

For one of her biographers: 'A central preoccupation in much of Deevy's drama is the condition of high-spirited, imaginative young women in rural Ireland, who are forced to reject romantic aspirations in the face of an unglamorous, unchanging reality'.[49] An early review of the published version of the play concluded with a familiar misogynist trope: '*The King of Spain's Daughter* is the one-act taming (perhaps) of one of Miss Deevy's temperamental shrews'.[50] Is Annie tamed? Stephen Murray says

---

44 Ibid., p. 26.
45 Ibid.
46 Kealy, 'Resisting Power and Direction', pp. 186–188.
47 Cathy Leeney, 'Themes of Ritual and Myth in Three Plays by Teresa Deevy', *Irish University Review*, 25.1 (1995), 88–116 (p. 90).
48 Ibid., p. 91.
49 Frances Clarke, 'Deevy, Teresa (1894–1963)', *Dictionary of Irish Biography*, 2009.
50 J.J.H., 'Review of *Three Plays by Teresa Deevy*, Studies: An Irish Quarterly Review', 29.113 (1940), 156–158 (p. 157).

of *The King of Spain's Daughter* that 'the central theme is that marriage is a disappointment but that by numbing one's sensibilities, one can put up with it'.[51] Is Annie numb at the end? Or, conversely, perversely, is she still romancing, still fantasising passionately about a different life? It's been argued that Annie 'wishes for a romantic epic life and this dreaming is scorned by the other characters'.[52]

The lamentation of Synge's Pegeen—'Oh my grief. I've lost him surely. I've lost the only playboy of the western world'—is supplanted in Deevy's play by Annie's exultation: 'I think he is a man that— supposin' he was jealous—might cut your throat', a statement that echoes the reception of Christy Mahon rather than his departure.[53] This is where we came in with Synge, for when Pegeen hears of Christy's propensity for violence she says, 'if I'd that lad in the house, I wouldn't be fearing the loosed khaki cut-throats, or the walking dead'.[54] Annie dreams of a dramatic departure from the life she leads—from her father, the factory, and an emotionally frugal husband—even if it means a dramatic death. Gerardine Meaney puts it nicely and icily when she remarks drily: 'Instead of pretending to be a murderer, Annie Kinsella can ultimately hope only to be interestingly murdered'.[55] But is her final wish for a man who would cut her throat through jealousy part of Annie's dream?

I began with Eveline at the gangway clinging to the guardrail. Did she stay or did she go? What should she have done? We still do not know. The jury is out on Annie too. Is she in the end another victim of male violence wishing fatalistically for more, or an imaginative and independent-minded woman looking out for other women, and talking back to men? Drama at its most dynamic encourages diversity of interpretation.

---

51 Stephen Murray, 'The One-Act Plays of Teresa Deevy', *Irish University Review*, 25.1 (1995), 126–132 (p. 127).
52 Caoilfhionn Ní Bheacháin, 'Sexuality, Marriage and Women's Life Narratives in Teresa Deevy's *A Disciple* (1931), *The King of Spain's Daughter* (1935) and *Katie Roche* (1936)', *Estudios Irlandeses*, 7 (2012), 79–91 (p. 86).
53 Synge, *The Playboy of the Western World*, p. 146; Deevy, 'The King of Spain's Daughter', p. 26.
54 Synge, *The Playboy of the Western World*, p. 107; 'loosed khaki cut-throats' is a reference to the British Army veterans of the Boer War (1899–1902).
55 Meaney, 'The Sons of Cuchulainn', p. 255.

Speech Acts

The power of speech that Joyce denies Eveline is what marks Annie out as unconstrained. The simple act of talking back is speech at its most active:

> Moving from silence into speech is for the oppressed, the colonized, the exploited, and those who stand and struggle side by side, a gesture of defiance that heals, that makes new life, and new growth possible. It is that act of speech, of 'talking back' that is no mere gesture of empty words, that is the expression of moving from object to subject, that is the liberated voice.[56]

As Úna Kealy and Kate McCarthy contend: 'Annie refuses to be silenced and she alone, within the world of the play, demonstrates the capacity to imagine something more vibrant than the grey life on offer'.[57] Mary Louise Pratt observes that certain strands of speech-act theory consider deviant language that is playful rather than productive, including 'some forms of expression primarily associated with women, such as gossip, small talk, or euphemism; and other forms like circumlocution, indirectness, or deliberate ambiguity, that are associated with communication across hierarchy and across lines of conflict'.[58] Pratt calls for:

> a theory of linguistic representation which acknowledges that representative discourse is always engaged in both fitting words to world and fitting world to words; that language and linguistic institutions in part construct or constitute the world for people in speech communities, rather than merely depicting it. Representative discourses, fictional or nonfictional, must be treated as simultaneously world-creating, world-describing, and world-changing undertakings.[59]

---

56 hooks, 'Talking Back', p. 128.
57 Úna Kealy and Kate McCarthy, 'Shape Shifting the Silence: An Analysis of *Talk Real Fine, Just Like a Lady* by Amanda Coogan in Collaboration with Dublin Theatre of the Deaf, an Appropriation of Teresa Deevy's *The King of Spain's Daughter*', in *The Golden Thread: Irish Women Playwrights, 1716–2016*, 2 vols, ed. by David Clare, Fiona McDonagh, and Justine Nakase (Liverpool: Liverpool University Press, 2021), I, 197–210 (p. 205).
58 Mary Louise Pratt, 'Ideology and Speech-Act Theory', *Poetics Today*, 7.1 (1986) 59–72 (p. 69).
59 Ibid., p. 71.

For Raymond Williams, verbal excess in Irish drama is a sign of material lack, a stand-in or understudy for the main protagonist of economic power. But the belittlement of backtalk undervalues the efficacy of such speech. For hooks and Pratt, words are world-changing and talking back is worldmaking. Fusing defiance and deviance, Deevy's aim is not to parody the empty talk of the powerless but to show that speech acts, speech performs, speech liberates.

Robert F. Panara, a Deaf poet who adapted plays for Deaf actors and audiences and was a key figure behind the National Theater of the Deaf (NTD) established in Waterford, Connecticut in 1967, famously asked:

> And what of tomorrow?—and the future? Shall we live to see a deaf writer emerge from the shadow of obscurity and assume the stature of a Robert Frost or an Ernest Hemingway or a Tennessee Williams?[60]

Deevy is a writer of such stature. One aim of the NTD was the provision of 'adequate apprenticeship to Deaf directors, writers, and technicians'.[61] Writers like Panara and Deevy who were deafened in their youth—Deevy from Ménière's disease, Panara from spinal meningitis—acted as door-openers for others. As a woman writer, Deevy is a trailblazer of particular note, exemplary in her understanding of the power of fantasy and the transformative nature of impassioned speech. Deevy has not had the criticism she deserves. Despite acknowledging that 'Deevy's female protagonists [...] occupy the dominant, rather than subordinate, position in terms of the Activity/Passivity opposition', Shaun Richards still regards her plays as characterised by 'conservatism in both form and theme'.[62] Likewise, Christopher Murray sees in Deevy's work a

---

60 Robert F. Panara, 'The Deaf Writer in America from Colonial Times to 1970: PART II', *American Annals of the Deaf*, 115.7 (1970), 673–679 (p. 679). I capitalise the 'd' here in accordance with the positive values within the Deaf community and Deaf culture associated with varying levels of audiological hearing. The NTD capitalise Deaf (https://ntd.org/) and so, it seems appropriate to capitalize the D in the phrase 'Deaf actors' when making reference to NTD. For more on d/Deaf see the entry on 'Deaf, deaf', in the Centre for Integration and Improvement of Journalism, *The Diversity Style Guide* (2024), and the entry for 'Deaf' in The National Centre for Disability and Journalism, Arizona State University, *Disability Language Guide* (2021).

61 David Hays, 'The National Theatre of the Deaf: Present and Future', *American Annals of the Deaf*, 112.4 (1967), 590–592 (p. 590).

62 Shaun Richards, '"Suffocated in the Green Flag": The Drama of Teresa Deevy and 1930s Ireland', *Literature & History*, 4.1 (1995), 65–80 (p. 71, p. 77).

'pragmatic accommodation with Irish social conditions', in keeping with a compliant tradition: 'The stifled voice is at once the condition and the distinction of women's drama in Ireland'.[63] Stifling and suffocation are arguably actions of gatekeepers, including reading committees, producers, critics, and publishers, rather than women playwrights. Silent voices turn out to be silenced voices.[64]

The insight and sophistication of Deevy's social criticism and the parallels and contrasts between Joyce's Eveline and her character of Annie Kinsella serve to underline her significance as a writer who gives active speech to her women protagonists at moments of crisis—remembrance, recognition or resignation, the latter always overlaid by defiance. Like Gretta in another of Joyce's stories, 'standing near the top of the first flight, in the shadow [...] leaning on the banisters, listening', Eveline is 'a symbol of something'.[65] While Gretta stands stock still listening to Mr D'Arcy singing 'The Lass of Aughrim', Eveline's ear catches the boat's 'long mournful whistle into the mist' and '[a] bell clanged upon her heart', a clang which echoes as a 'knell' in Annie Kinsella's soul when Jim talks about marriage and settling down.[66] The stillness and speechlessness of Joyce's female characters at these tipping points, seen through the eyes of their male partners, is at variance with the enduring desire for adventure articulated by Deevy's heroines. What Annie admires most, and finds in Jim's notebook, is perseverance, resilience, determination. These are the qualities she holds dear. Her relentless quest for passionate engagement, even if it manifests as jealousy and danger, deviates from Eveline's—and Gretta's—passivity. Annie ends the play reading and musing, showing she can wring romance from a savings book. Deevy's defiant heroines are not a symbol of something; they are something.

---

[63] Christopher Murray, 'Introduction: The Stifled Voice', *Irish University Review*, 25.1 (1995), 1–10 (p. 9, p. 10).
[64] See Kathleen Quinn, 'Silent Voices', *Theatre Ireland*, 30 (1993), 9–11: 'The voices of women dramatists will be silent no more' (p. 11).
[65] Joyce, 'The Dead', in *The Essential James Joyce*, p. 163.
[66] Joyce, 'Eveline', p. 44; Deevy, 'The King of Spain's Daughter', p. 24.

Bibliography

Bank, Jonathan, John P. Harrington, and Christopher Morash (eds), *Teresa Deevy Reclaimed*, 2 vols (New York: Mint Theater, 2011 and 2017)

Barry, Sebastian (ed.), *The Inherited Boundaries: Younger Poets of the Republic of Ireland* (Mountrath: Dolmen Press, 1986)

Barry, Sebastian, 'Sebastian Barry Reads "Eveline" by James Joyce', podcast, *The Guardian*, 2 January 2013, http://www.theguardian.com/books/audio/2013/jan/02/sebastian-barry-james-joyce-eveline

Beauvoir, Simone de, *The Second Sex* (London: Random House, Vintage Classics, 1997)

Beckett, Samuel, *Collected Shorter Plays* (London: Faber, 1984)

Berkeley, George, *A Word to the Wise: Or, the Bishop of Cloyne's Exhortation to the Roman Catholic Clergy of Ireland* (Dublin: George Faulkner, 1749)

Cassidy, James F., 'The Poetry of Padraic Colum. II', *The Irish Monthly*, 49.587 (1921), 314–318

Centre for Integration and Improvement of Journalism, *The Diversity Style Guide* (2024), https://www.diversitystyleguide.com/glossary/deaf-deaf/

Chew, Emrys, *Arming the Periphery: The Arms Trade in the Indian Ocean during the Age of Global Empire* (London: Palgrave Macmillan, 2012), https://doi.org/10.1057/9781137006608

Clarke, Frances, 'Deevy, Teresa (1894–1963)', *Dictionary of Irish Biography*, 2009, https://doi.org/10.3318/dib.002500.v1

Clarke, Marie, 'Education for the Country Girls: Vocational Education in Rural Ireland 1930–1960', *History of Education* (2021), 1–16, https://doi.org/10.1080/0046760X.2020.1856944

Deevy, Teresa, *Three Plays: Katie Roche, The King of Spain's Daughter, The Wild Goose* (London: Macmillan, 1939)

Gillespie, Patrick, 'I Had a Little Nut Tree…', *PoemShape*, 4 June 2012, https://poemshape.wordpress.com/2012/06/04/i-had-a-little-nut-tree/

Hays, David, 'The National Theatre of the Deaf: Present and Future', *American Annals of the Deaf*, 112.4 (1967), 590–592

hooks, bell, 'Talking Back', *Discourse: Journal for Theoretical Studies in Media and Culture*, 8 (1986–1987), 123–128

Jarvis, Pam, 'Not Just "Once" Upon a Time', *Genealogy*, 3.44 (2019), 1–14, https://doi.org/10.3390/genealogy3030044

J.J.H., 'Review of *Three Plays* by Teresa Deevy, *Studies: An Irish Quarterly Review*', 29.113 (1940), 156–158.

Jordan, John, 'Teresa Deevy: An Introduction', *Irish University Review*, 1.8 (1956), 13–26

Joyce, James, *The Essential James Joyce*, ed. by Harry Levin (St Albans: Granada, 1977)

Kealy, Úna, 'Resisting Power and Direction: *The King of Spain's Daughter* by Teresa Deevy as a Feminist Call to Action', *Estudios Irlandeses*, 15 (2020), 178–192, https://doi.org/10.24162/EI2020-9406

Kealy, Úna, and Kate McCarthy, 'Shape Shifting the Silence: An Analysis of *Talk Real Fine, Just Like a Lady* by Amanda Coogan in Collaboration with Dublin Theatre of the Deaf, an Appropriation of Teresa Deevy's *The King of Spain's Daughter*', in *The Golden Thread: Irish Women Playwrights, 1716–2016*, 2 vols, ed. by David Clare, Fiona McDonagh, and Justine Nakase (Liverpool: Liverpool University Press, 2021), I, 197–210 (p. 205), https://doi.org/10.3828/liverpool/9781800859463.003.0015, https://www.liverpooluniversitypress.co.uk/pb-assets/OA%20chapters/Una%20Kealy%20and%20Kate%20McCarthy%20chapter-1710157142.pdf

Leeney, Cathy, 'Themes of Ritual and Myth in Three Plays by Teresa Deevy', *Irish University Review*, 25.1 (1995), 88–116

Luft, Joanna, 'Reader Awareness: Form and Ambiguity in James Joyce's "Eveline"', *The Canadian Journal of Irish Studies*, 35.2 (2009), 48–51

Maley, Willy, '"She Done *Coriolanus* at the Convent": Empowerment and Entrapment in Teresa Deevy's *In Search of Valour*', *Irish University Review*, 49.2 (2019), 356–369, https://doi.org/10.3366/iur.2019.0411

McAvoy, Sandra, 'All about Eve: Signe Toksvig and the Intimate Lives of Irish Women, 1926–1937', *The Irish Review*, 42 (2010), 43–57

McDonagh, Rosaleen, 'Talking Back', in *(Re)searching Women: Feminist Research Methodologies in the Social Sciences in Ireland*, ed. by Anne Byrne and Ronit Lentin (Dublin: Institute of Public Administration, 2000), pp. 237–246

Meaney, Gerardine, 'The Sons of Cuchulainn: Violence, the Family, and the Irish Canon', *Éire-Ireland*, 41.1/2 (2006), 242–261 (p. 254), https://doi.org/10.1353/eir.2006.0009

Mullin, Katherine, 'Don't Cry for Me, Argentina: "Eveline" and the Seductions of Emigration Propaganda', in *Semicolonial Joyce*, ed. by Derek Attridge and Marjorie Howes (Cambridge: Cambridge University Press, 2000), pp. 172–200

Murray, Christopher, 'Introduction: The Stifled Voice', *Irish University Review*, 25.1 (1995), 1–10

Murray, Stephen, 'The One-Act Plays of Teresa Deevy', *Irish University Review*, 25.1 (1995), 126–132

The National Centre for Disability and Journalism, Arizona State University, *Disability Language Guide* (2021), https://ncdj.org/wp-content/uploads/2021/08/NCDJ-STYLE-GUIDE-EDIT-2021-SILVERMAN.pdf

Ní Bheacháin, Caoilfhionn, 'Sexuality, Marriage and Women's Life Narratives in Teresa Deevy's *A Disciple* (1931), *The King of Spain's Daughter* (1935) and *Katie Roche* (1936)', *Estudios Irlandeses*, 7 (2012), 79–91, https://doi.org/10.24162/EI2012-1903

Panara, Robert F., 'The Deaf Writer in America from Colonial Times to 1970: PART II', *American Annals of the Deaf*, 115.7 (1970), 673–679

Phillips-Cunningham, Danielle, 'Slaving Irish "Ladies" and Black "Towers of Strength in the Labor World": Race and Women's Resistance in Domestic Service', *Women's History Review*, 30.2 (2021), 190–207, https://doi.org/10.1080/09612025.2020.1757864

Pihl, Lis, '"A Muzzle Made in Ireland": Irish Censorship and Signe Toksvig', *Studies: An Irish Quarterly Review*, 88.352 (1999), 448–457

Pratt, Mary Louise, 'Ideology and Speech-Act Theory', *Poetics Today*, 7.1 (1986) 59–72 (p. 69), https://doi.org/10.2307/1772088

Quinn, Kathleen, 'Silent Voices', *Theatre Ireland*, 30 (1993), 9–11

Richards, Shaun, '"Suffocated in the Green Flag": The Drama of Teresa Deevy and 1930s Ireland', *Literature & History*, 4.1 (1995), 65–80, https://doi.org/10.1177/030619739500400104

Roche, Anthony, 'Woman on the Threshold: J. M. Synge's *The Shadow of the Glen*, Teresa Deevy's *Katie Roche* and Marina Carr's *The Mai*', *Irish University Review*, 25.1 (1995), 143–162

Sapir, Edward, 'The King of Spain's Daughter and the Diver', *Poetry*, 16.4 (1920), 179–182

Sullivan, Megan, 'Folk Plays, Home Girls, and Back Talk: Georgia Douglas Johnson and Women of the Harlem Renaissance', *CLA Journal*, 38.4 (1995), 404–419

Synge, J.M., *The Playboy of the Western World and Other Plays*, ed. by Ann Saddlemyer (Oxford: Oxford University Press, 1995)

Toksvig, Signe, 'A Visit to Lady Gregory', *The North American Review*, 214.789 (1921), 190–200

Toksvig, Signe, 'Why Girls Leave Ireland', *The Survey*, 1 August 1929, pp. 483–486 and 509

Williams, Raymond, *Drama from Ibsen to Brecht* (Oxford: Oxford University Press, 1969)

DRAMATURGY, GENRE, AND THEORY

8. Finding Money in the Walls: Uncovering the Feminist Power of Teresa Deevy's Dramaturgy through an Embodied, Practice-Based Approach

Ann M. Shanahan

The recent renewal of attention in Teresa Deevy's plays has included embodied, practice-based approaches, methodologies that are uniquely useful to appreciating her work as an artist, and her feminism, in particular. As a scholar-artist, I apply a method of analysis to plays about women and houses in performance founded on inclusion of my personal lived experience that situates my own body centrally as a source of knowing and site of authority. Drawing from my specific physical experience, including the pain experienced from endometriosis, led me to develop a method of practice-based analysis emanating from my pelvis, from my 'gut', which I apply to reading the spaces and overall meanings of plays in performance.[1] As opposed to using traditional

---

[1] This work is summarised in: 'Making Room(s): Staging Plays About Women and Houses', in *Performing the Family Dream House*, ed. by Emily Klein, Jennifer-Scott Mobley, and Jill Stevenson (London: Palgrave Macmillan, 2019), pp. 87–105; 'The Gender Politics of Spectacle in Staging Sarah Ruhl's Adaptation of Virginia Woolf's *Orlando* and ATHE 2018: Theatre of Revolution', *SDC Journal*, 6.2 (2018), 37–39; Ann M. Shanahan, Prudence A. Moylan, Betsy Jones Hemenway, Bren Ortega Murphy, Jacqueline Long, Susan Grossman, Hector Garcia, and Mary Dominiak, 'Performance: An Approach to Strengthening Interdisciplinarity in Women's Studies and Gender Studies', *PARtake: Performance as Research*, 1.1 (2016), 1–41; 'Playing House: Staging Experiments About Women in Domestic Space', *Theatre Topics*, 23.2 (2013), 129–144; 'Un-"blocking" Hedda and Medea through Feminist "Play" with Traditional Staging Forms', *Theatre Topics*, 20.1 (2011), 61–74.

models that separate conceptual analysis from practical aspects in production, I move back and forth between theory and practice in order to engage feminist, experiential methodologies explicitly and reveal how material circumstances, including limits, can inspire artistic choices, thereby exposing resonances between the fictitious conflicts in the plays and the real-life constrictions that artists often face when producing them. Working from both of these feminist principles—the personal and the embodied—has yielded an understanding of Deevy's larger project across her career. I believe that embodied methods of analysis particularly illuminate Deevy's dramaturgy because of their synergy with her similar approach to writing. Deevy wrote from her personal life and created the plays from the experiences of her specific body in a way that was radical for a woman of her time. A sort of alchemy occurs when the content of her plays meets with an embodied approach to analysing them; the uniquely creative, even generative materialist features of her dramaturgy come to life.

An assessment that Deevy wrote from her personal experience is shared by Judy Friel, Caoilfhionn Ní Bheacháin, and Gerardine Meaney who argue that Deevy's characters and dramaturgy arise from her material experiences. For example, directing *Katie Roche* at the Abbey Theatre in 1994, Friel describes how she recognised in the character of Amelia Gregg, 'a mocking self-portrait' of Deevy and that Deevy had also 'actively written herself into the script as director, fine-tuning the dialogue with countless stage directions'.[2] Ní Bheacháin and Meaney compare Deevy as playwright to the bravely transgressive, imaginative women in her plays, including Annie Kinsella, Katie Roche, and Ellie Irwin. The centrality of the personal in my approach resonates with Deevy's dramaturgy.[3] Foregrounding a personal and embodied approach also resonates with the artistic goals Deevy formed after seeing Shaw's *Heartbreak House* in London: 'One night returning from the theatre I felt very strongly the urge to put "the sort

---

2   Judy Friel, 'Rehearsing *Katie Roche*', *Irish University Review*, 25.1 (1995), 117–125 (p. 117 and p. 118); Teresa Deevy, 'Katie Roche', in *Teresa Deevy Reclaimed*, 2 vols, ed. by Jonathan Bank, John P. Harrington, and Christopher Morash (New York: Mint Theater, 2011 and 2017), I.

3   Caoilfhionn Ní Bheacháin, '"It Was then I Knew Life": Political Critique and Moral Debate in Teresa Deevy's *Temporal Powers* (1932)', *Irish University Review*, 50.2 (2020), 337–355; Geradine Meaney, 'The Sons of Cuchulainn: Violence, the Family and the Irish Canon', *Eire-Ireland*, 41.1 (2006), 242–261.

of life we live in Ireland" into a play'.[4] This seemingly casual but specific construction of 'putting' life '*into* a play' (emphasis mine), and 'the sort of life we live', suggests Deevy's recognition of the material power of the theatre, her role as a playwright, and the significance of inserting Irish subjects, including women, into this potent medium. Bodies—Irish bodies, women's bodies, her own body—could be put into, i.e., materialised in a play, making it a container of life. Additionally, Deevy's phrase acknowledges the meaningful interplay between lives onstage and those in the audience. Analysis of Deevy's dramaturgical project, when interpreted thus, necessitates a material reading that prioritises her proprioception of bodies as they interact with each other and with the material world in which they are situated, both inside the plays and across the proscenium line in the theatre. Application of feminist approaches, such as mine, reveals the interactive materialism of Deevy's dramaturgy. Drawing upon the specifics of her embodied experience as woman as she aged, who became deafened, who remained single, and had no children, she forged a radically material theatre spanning stage and radio plays, one in which she both implanted and gestated matter in the theatre, foreshadowing embodied, feminist methods decades ahead of their time.

This chapter considers Deevy's style and use of space, then explicates the personal and embodied methodological approach applied here to Deevy's work. Initial analysis considers Deevy's use of domestic and liminal spaces and material objects, before defining how Deevy incorporates embodied meta-audiences into her drama. The latter section of the chapter illustrates this practice-based approach through reference to *Strange Birth* (1946) and *Light Falling* (1947), two especially beautiful plays, written when Deevy was in her mid-fifties, writing both for radio and stage.[5] The chapter concludes by arguing that a practice-based approach is uniquely valuable in illuminating Deevy's feminist dramaturgy, expressed in a body of work designed to evoke connective, embodied experiences of healing, reconciliation, and love for audiences both inside and outside her dramas.

---

4 Teresa Deevy, 'Autobiographical Note', in *Teresa Deevy Reclaimed*, II, xxi–xxiii (p. xxi).

5 Teresa Deevy, 'Strange Birth', in *Teresa Deevy Reclaimed*, I, 53–59; Teresa Deevy, 'Light Falling', in *Teresa Deevy Reclaimed*, II, 63–75.

Style, Setting, and the Personal in Deevy's Dramaturgy

Theatre critics in the 1930s identified Deevy's dramas as stylistically complex, mixing elements of realism with other styles: as Ní Bheacháin outlines, reviews in 1930 describe *Reapers* as 'a crazy farce', a 'fantasy' with the 'paraphernalia of realism', which she argues prevents 'any easy categorization' and makes 'for an unsettling theatrical experience'.[6] Several critics since, including Lennox Robinson, Seán O'Casey, Judy Friel, Christopher Morash, and Ní Bheacháin, have identified the stylistic ambiguity and meta-theatricality of Deevy's plays.[7] In light of her dramatic influences—Chekhov, Ibsen, and Shaw—Deevy's stylistic references to realistic tropes are perhaps unsurprising. Morash notes the generic subversions of the standard peasant play that would have been familiar to audiences at the Abbey in 1932, while Ní Bheacháin highlights that contemporary critics noted 'Deevy's Chekhovian technique' and concerns in *Reapers*.[8] Developing the argument for Deevy's stylistic ambiguity, Ní Bheacháin maintains the setting for *Temporal Powers* 'is expressionist' and that the few objects noted in stage directions become symbols—such as the packet of money, stolen from the state, that is hidden in the ruin's walls; debate over the proper use of which becomes the material centre of the conflict.[9] Ní Bheacháin cogently argues that Deevy's dramaturgical project is one of 'uneasy realism' that deliberately references other plays and styles to 'disrupt the sense of verisimilitude experienced by an audience'.[10]

The setting of a house is central to Deevy scholarship, which treats the home as a symbol of marriage and its restrictions. As

---

6   Ní Bheacháin, 'Political Critique and Moral Debate', p. 339.
7   Digital Repository of Ireland (DRI), The Teresa Deevy Archive, Robinson, Lennox 1886–1958, 'Review of Three Plays by Teresa Deevy', PP/6/178 (22), https://doi.org/10.7486/DRI.95944b60b; Seán O'Casey to George Jean Nathan, 14 February 1938, in *The Letters of Seán O'Casey 1910–1941, Volume 1*, ed. by David Karuse (London: Cassell, 1975), p. 703; Friel, 'Rehearsing *Katie Roche*'; Christopher Morash, *A History of Irish Theatre 1601–2000* (Cambridge: Cambridge University Press, 2002), p. 121; Ní Bheacháin, 'Political Critique and Moral Debate'.
8   Morash, *History of Irish Theatre*, p. 342; Ní Bheacháin, 'Political Critique and Moral Debate', p. 342.
9   Teresa Deevy, 'Temporal Powers', in *Teresa Deevy Reclaimed*, I, 7–50; Ní Bheacháin, 'Political Critique and Moral Debate', pp. 342–343.
10 Ní Bheacháin, 'Political Critique and Moral Debate', p. 351.

one example, Cathy Leeney considers the setting of the ruin a metaphor for the lives of Min and Michael Donovan in *Temporal Powers*.[11] Several scholars focus on the liminality of settings, notably Christie Fox, Anthony Roche, and Úna Kealy, with the features of the often domestic settings mirroring the social liminality of the period following the Irish Civil War—a period between constitutions, and particularly of regression from promises of equality for women in the early 1900s.[12] In her illuminating analysis of *The King of Spain's Daughter*, Kealy reviews scholars whose work has positioned and considered the nuanced ways that Deevy's work has responded to 'the social, political and cultural context of Irish life in the 1920s and 1930s', but further asserts that:

> [...] additional critical opportunities emerge when historiographic and cultural-materialist methodologies are supplemented with analysis of a playwright's proprioception of actors' bodies, of scenography and of stage properties and costume. Deevy's proprioception, particularly her awareness and manipulation of the resonance of kinesthesis and stage properties, demonstrates a highly-refined skill in activating non-verbal communication.[13]

In alignment with practice-based approaches, Kealy highlights the detail of Deevy's stage directions, the role of physical expression within her work, and her meticulous attention to physical detail in her dramaturgy. Kealy's embodied spatial analysis of *The King of Spain's Daughter* concludes with a reading of Mrs Marks' last line—'The Lord preserve us! that she'd find joy in such a thought!'—thus:

> In the final moments of the play Deevy undermines the conventions of realism by making direct comic appeal to the audience. Mrs Marks'

---

11 Cathy Leeney, 'Teresa Deevy—Themes in Context', in *Abbey Theatre Research Pack: Teresa Deevy: Katie Roche*, researched and compiled by Marie Kelly, School of Music and Theatre, University College Cork (Dublin: Abbey Theatre, 2017), pp. 21–27.

12 Christie Fox, 'Neither Here nor There: The Liminal Position of Teresa Deevy and Her Female Characters', in *A Century of Irish Drama: Widening the Stage*, ed. by Stephen Watt, Eileen Morgan, and Shakir Mustafa (Indianapolis, IN: Indiana University Press, 2001), pp. 193–203; Anthony Roche, 'Woman on the Threshold: J.M. Synge's *The Shadow of the Glen*, Teresa Deevy's *Katie Roche*, and Marina Carr's *The Mai*', *Irish University Review*, 25.1 (1995), 143–162; Úna Kealy, 'Resisting Power and Direction: *The King of Spain's Daughter* by Teresa Deevy as a Feminist Call to Action', *Estudios Irlandeses*, 15 (2020), 178–192.

13 Kealy, 'Resisting Power and Direction', p. 181.

last speech constitutes a deliberate breaking of the fourth wall, a comic device that facilitates this 'messenger' character to deliver the final stark warning that, if women and men are directed to live repressed both physically and psychologically dysfunction will ensue.[14]

Kealy's assessment of the play's conclusion correlates with Brechtian strategies of direct address and breaking of the fourth wall, through which theatre can create a thinking, critical audience by promoting thinking actors, critiquing characters' choices as they show them. Brecht wanted audiences to observe and compare possible alternative choices, and to understand them within specific material contexts. For example, Brecht's concept of 'not-but' (showing something as '*not* this, *but* that') involves the actor metaphorically standing alongside of, and adopting a critical stance towards, the character they play, demonstrating both the choice the character makes and all the choices they do not, simultaneously.[15] Through making the familiar strange, the plot, the space, and the style(s) of performance are revealed as constructs so that they, and ultimately the world they reflect, can be changed.

Whereas Brecht aims to foster a thinking audience, Deevy wants a physically free audience (including women's sexuality). Kealy ties this to what bell hooks called a 'community of resistance' in what Kealy labels as the play's 'feminist call to action'.[16] According to Fox, 'what is searched for in Deevy is legitimacy itself, the space to be free'.[17] The methodology I have developed, based on Ibsen's plays (also tying hooks to Brecht), likewise centres on climaxes and lines spoken in denouement, such as Judge Brack's famous last line in *Hedda Gabler* after Hedda's suicide (precipitated by a similar conflict to that experienced by Annie Kinsella), translated variously as 'God in Heaven! People don't do such things'.[18] This closing line, similar to that of Mrs Marks', pressures the fourth wall and forges a space of resistance at realism's definitive proscenium line.

Scholars comment that Deevy's plays sometimes end in ambiguous,

---

14 Teresa Deevy, 'The King of Spain's Daughter', in *Teresa Deevy Reclaimed*, II, 17–26 (p. 26); Kealy, 'Resisting Power and Direction', p. 188.
15 *Brecht on Theatre: The Development of an Aesthetic*, trans. by John Willet, 13th edn (New York: Hill and Wang, 1964), p. 174.
16 Kealy, 'Resisting Power and Direction', p. 188.
17 Fox, 'Neither Here nor There', p. 194.
18 This is a paraphrase of the gist of various translations.

dramatically unsatisfying ways. Meaney writes: 'Like Annie, Deevy's play can reference the mythological but not realize it [...Deevy's work] refuses to mythologize and remains uncanonical'.[19] Likewise, Friel considers that 'Katie Roche [...] is on the threshold of being a revolutionary young feminist [...] but in the end she goes quietly with her husband', an ending Friel argues is 'too abrupt and tidy'.[20] Deevy's drama, and particularly her endings, were criticised by playwrights and critics such as O'Casey as being 'vague, ingenuous, and incomplete'.[21] However, when using a practitioner's, embodied approach, which takes into account the material of actors' and audiences' bodies as they interpret these 'vague' and 'incomplete' plot reversals, experienced within the specific spatial architecture of performance, and in context of the social, political, and corresponding stylistic transitions in which Deevy was writing, I, like Kealy and Ní Bheacháin, reach a different conclusion. Deevy's plays only complete themselves in embodied performance, in material collaboration with an audience.

For its depiction of women's sexuality and physicality, and treatment of the crisis of landlessness, combined with its stylistic mix, Ní Bheacháin calls *Temporal Powers* a 'political intervention on the national stage', arguing the fact that *Temporal Powers* as produced by the Abbey 'underlies the subversive and challenging nature of her project'.[22] As Leeney argues, Deevy's plays centre on characters who, at profound moments, struggle to express the inexpressible.[23] Rather than being about the impossibility of humans to fully comprehend one another's inner lives, as some scholars have observed, I sense, rather, that Deevy's plays mine the potential and the role of bodies in communication.[24] Deevy inserts breadcrumbs of *matter* into her plays: scones, potatoes, roses, turf, letters, dogs, bodies in contact. Through physical identification with it, this matter invokes bodily experiences in each audience member which are personal to them, but which allow for powerful connection to others in the audience who experience a similarly personal embodied experience.

---

19 Meaney, 'The Sons of Cuchulainn', p. 255.
20 Friel, 'Rehearsing *Katie Roche*', p. 123.
21 *Letters of Seán O'Casey*, p. 703.
22 Ní Bheacháin, 'Political Critique and Moral Debate', p. 342 and p. 349.
23 Leeney, 'Teresa Deevy'.
24 See Christopher Morash, 'Teresa Deevy: Between the Lines', in *Teresa Deevy Reclaimed*, I, ix–xiv.

This method evokes experiences that are both personal *and* collective, drawn out by a unique set of layered, materialist, embodied strategies which Deevy revised, but which remained essentially consistent throughout her career. This dramaturgy occurs in liminal spaces, in a style I call liminal materialism, one best discerned through an embodied approach. Deevy's goal is that we, as audiences, experience the content of her plays *in our bodies* so that—beyond merely seeing, understanding, or feeling the content—like Sara hugging a love letter to her breast at the end of *Strange Birth*, we 'have something'.[25]

Applying Practice-Based Analysis of Plays about Women and Houses to Deevy's Work

The conclusions about Deevy's work drawn by scholars and practitioners working from an embodied perspective resonate with the findings of my research into plays about women and houses. By applying the feminist criticism of Sue-Ellen Case to stage space, as well as criticism by Hanna Scolnicov, I have traced a pattern in plays—notably also inspired by plays of Ibsen—linking a woman's creativity and agency, and conflicts concerning these, to domestic space in plays.[26] I read the house as the central woman character's body. The plays' climaxes usually involve violence inflicted by the central woman character against herself and/or her children. Thwarted by social limits, she is left with no agency over her creative power except to kill herself or her offspring, or abruptly leave. Playwrights often script a reaction to the climax by the members of the surrounding community. These reactions in denouement either re-inscribe social and gender norms or suggest new possibilities given their obvious inadequacy in answering or containing what has just occurred.

Tracking the action of such plays through an embodied approach leads to liminal spaces—either literally spaces between, i.e., a threshold (limen) or wall, or stylistically, such as the fourth wall, at the proscenium, separating real life from stage fiction, or where mixed styles such as

---

25   Deevy, 'Strange Birth', p. 57.
26   Sue-Ellen Case, *Feminist Theatre* (London: Routledge, 1988); Hanna Scolnicov, *Women's Theatrical Space* (New York: Cambridge University Press, 1994).

abstraction and realism intersect. For example, I understood the action of *Hedda Gabler* because I placed myself—specifically all of my five-foot two-inch body (including the parts that Judge Brack would not have us talk about)—*in* the frame, disrupting and defying the male gaze, both literally in the rehearsal hall and through projecting my body through an actor's imaginative approach. I used this approach as a way of learning about space and style within the play, learning, for example, where Hedda felt restricted, trapped, afraid of being penetrated, impregnated, and where she felt she had agency and breathing room. The latter was largely found in liminal spaces, doors, and windows, between audience and actors and the stylistic divides between realism and abstraction. In turn, this embodied, experiential approach to interpreting space from within the play illuminated design and staging choices in other plays about women and houses. The practice-based method supplied the same illuminating results with Deevy's plays: I think Deevy was doing the same thing, imaginatively occupying the stage with her body, facing limits (often of domestic space), and mining liminal spaces in the setting and between styles to expose oppressions and make room on stage and in the lives of the audience for alternative realities.

Women are at the centre of most of Deevy's plays: there are several women in their fifties (I have never encountered as many women in their fifties in plays by any writer in the Western canon). This is, in itself, meaningful, but is especially so in relation to my argument about her dramaturgy. Strikingly, unlike the plays by Ibsen and others that formed my methods, relatively few of Deevy's central women protagonists have children, and while their childlessness is sometimes a factor (as in the case of Min Donovan and Mary Scully, for example), the symbolic and real creative conflict (or destruction) of children does not figure overtly in the action of the plays. While they do not have children, Deevy's women character's sexuality figures large in relation to houses, notably in *Katie Roche, The King of Spain's Daughter*, and *Light Falling*.

Deevy's Use of Domestic and Liminal Spaces and Material Objects

The majority of Deevy's plays are set in a domestic space or a space which includes architectural features of a house. *Temporal Powers*, for example, is set within a ruined house with partial walls, while *The King of Spain's Daughter*, though set on a roadside, is enclosed by a wall with a doorway to fields beyond. From *Temporal Powers* to *In the Cellar of My Friend*, the defining characteristic of most of the spaces Deevy suggests is *liminality*.[27] There is an open door, or full-length window, or door with a mail slot in the upstage centre of most of the plays under consideration here. With rare exception, most of the plays surround a question of marriage, proposed or actual, and a conflict between men and women, often across generations in marriages. In *Temporal Powers*, the characters' relationship to the house is unstable and, in the main, transience, hardship, and/or trauma characterise the domestic spaces in Deevy's plays written in the 1930s. Women's relationship to the house is more stable in Deevy's later plays, though central questions about women's relationship to the house remain. In several plays, maiden sisters determine the changing relationship of a central woman character's relationship to, or situation within, a house. Related to this instability is the role of food in the plays, and a centrally placed table: potatoes in *Temporal Powers*, scones in *Katie Roche*, Patricia's insistence on eating breakfast in *In the Cellar of My Friend*, and the fettling of the dogs and potatoes in *Light Falling*, lunch arriving in *The King of Spain's Daughter*, serving breakfast in *Dignity*, and crumbs for the birds in *One Look and What It Led To*.

Similar to the plays that informed my method, the climaxes of Deevy's plays often involve a woman working out a profound decision in relation to a house.[28] Scholars have observed how interior experience is not spoken: Deevy's plays 'do their work with what happens between the lines', she had 'conflicted feelings about the limits of language in translating visual phenomenon'.[29] Making sense of those moments of transition, decision, and struggle at the end of each of the plays requires an engagement by the spectator, listener, and/or reader to interpret in these non-verbal spaces between, and experience or *feel alongside* the

---

27 Teresa Deevy, 'In the Cellar of My Friend', in *Teresa Deevy Reclaimed*, I, 111–122.
28 Through my practice-based work as a director staging a series of plays with women and houses as subjects, I have discovered similar features in both plot and spatial dramaturgy that are expressed either explicitly through stage directions, or implied by conventions of the time (see Shanahan, 'Making Room(s)').
29 Christopher Morash, 'Teresa Deevy: Between the Lines', p. xvi; Emily Bloom, *Blindness and Insight in Teresa Deevy's Radio Plays*, online video recording, Active Speech Conference: Sharing Scholarship on Teresa Deevy, 19 February 2021.

characters. Reading *Temporal Powers* for the first time I was fascinated, *super*-engaged reading and imagining the reckoning between Min and Michael Donavan at the end of the play. An American, unaccustomed to the Irish syntax and colloquialisms in Deevy's texts, I read parts aloud to aid my understanding, imagining the lilt and cadence of the speech as I read, and listened to myself. By the time I got to the final reckoning I was engaged bodily, reinforced by Deevy's materialisation of domestic space in the play, and the liminal materialism of its ending. As Min and Michael reckon, Min gathers belongings, the stuff of their home (a stool, etc.), into her shawl, which Michael has just asked her to take off her back. As they leave their liminal lodging—disconnected and resigned to separate—Michael puts over his back the shawl that just shortly before had warmed Min's body; their temporal home becoming even more liminal as it is shifted across gendered bodies as they leave the ruin and cross the border of the stage frame.

In *The King of Spain's Daughter,* the resolution is worked out between two women of different generations, Annie Kinsella and Mrs Marks, in a likewise complicated dance of the material and liminal as described powerfully by Kealy above. The climax in *Katie Roche* echoes this end of *The King of Spain's Daughter*, and also occurs between two women, but as a bond between them, not rupture. Katie is separated from the house for being 'too free with the boys'; her older sister-in-law, Amelia, tries to comfort her with the thought that at least she and her husband will be together.[30] When Katie complains that she would rather be together there, in the house: 'There's no grandeur in this! Taken away…my own fault', Amelia replies: 'If you're brave, you can make it grand. My dear, you must!' After a look at Amelia, Katie agrees 'I *will* be brave!', and they clasp hands and make a pact between them both to be brave. Katie acknowledges, 'I think *you* were, always… 'Tis a promise between us—whatever'll come, good or bad'.[31] Making that bond with Amelia to be brave, within limits of the restricted and mundane, Katie finds her grandeur. As Katie leaves, she declares, 'I won't forget. I'll keep my word…', and leaving, wishes the boys, with whom she was too free, 'a good night'.[32] Amelia, her sister in bravery, watches her from the

---

30 Deevy, 'Katie Roche', p. 101.
31 Ibid., p. 102, original emphasis.
32 Ibid.

threshold of the centre door—the matron-maiden holding down the limen in a pact of courage; both women finding strength and meaning (grandeur) to sustain them in their shared endurance of limits.

The climactic moment of *In the Cellar of My Friend* is a reverse to *Katie Roche*—the staging starts where *Katie Roche* leaves off. The plot moves in the reverse order: as the play opens, the older Patricia, alone in the house, is joined by and clasps hands with Belle. The ending is also a reverse to *Katie Roche* when Belle, the younger women, agrees to take over as the woman of the house. More than any of the other plays considered here, the characters' motivations driving the climax of *In the Cellar of My Friend* are unclear. Belle does not speak her thoughts fully, leaving many gaps to fill. Deevy connects us to her and the play, in general, through material objects: Belle wraps a piece of paper from a letter around her finger, breakfast food, a bowl of strawberries, a basket of flowers.[33] The term 'matter' is used regularly in this play (and increasingly in later plays), for example, Belle says, 'Need that matter?' and then, 'It doesn't matter'.[34] These items tie Belle's thoughts and feelings to her body; at the same time, the bodies of the audience are engaged.

Living through each of those climactic moments, I experienced the transformations physically. I think this experience was instigated by the centrality of other women characters in these moments, specifically Amelia at the end of *Katie Roche*, mirrored at the beginning of *In the Cellar of My Friend* when Patty and Belle 'catch hands'.[35] In each of the plays other women figure in what will be the future of and how it will be understood by the central women characters. I used an embodied approach to select *Strange Birth* and *Light Falling* as examples of plays for in-depth focus here because they move me more than most plays I have read, by anyone; similar to John Jordan with *Temporal Powers*, I was almost 'unbearably moved'.[36] He calls *Light Falling* 'very nearly a gem',

---

33 Christopher Morash and Emily Bloom illuminate the significance of this basket as a container in their papers included in the Active Speech Conference. See Christopher Morash, 'Knew Nought of All This': Teresa Deevy's Dark Matter', Active Speech Conference: Sharing Scholarship on Teresa Deevy, 19 February 2021, https://web.archive.org/web/20210610101001/https://activespeech2021.org/keynotes/; Emily Bloom, *Blindness and Insight*.

34 Deevy, 'Cellar', p. 121.

35 Ibid., p. 111.

36 John Jordan, 'Teresa Deevy: An Introduction', *Irish University Review*, 1.8 (1956), 13–26 (p. 16).

placing both plays in a period when 'Deevy began to work in a field of pure, unexplicated, poetic statement'.[37] In this sense, he thought these plays were 'unactable'.[38] Rather than being unactable, I think the power of these plays requires (and evokes) the collaboration, an embodied co-enactment, by the audience. Deevy accomplishes this by inserting meta-audiences, sometimes multiple, within her hybrid style.

Embodied Meta-Audiences

Working within a feminist, personal, and embodied approach, I read the plays as reconciling and healing for women, in particular in the moment of performance. This reconciling happens in a liminal space between the ideal and the material, which the highly imaginative women in limiting circumstances occupy, and is experienced within their bodies. In several cases, the reconciliation is fostered by an exchange with another woman who also occupies and holds the tensive, liminal space within her body, and this encounter between the two women forms yet another liminal space between. The women form an embodied audience to each other. Importantly, the plays themselves (all of them) offer meta-examples of Deevy's unique, layered dramaturgy and how it functions, internally. They do this by offering physical, experiential signs to guide the liminal material dramaturgy of form and style, modelling and internally mirroring the intended overall effect. This liminal material dramaturgy has two elements. Firstly, it presents a complex moral question or piece of art or writing at the centre of the story, which encapsulates or mirrors the concerns of the play. Secondly, it offers audiences stand-in bodies inside the play/container to encounter and attempt to make sense of the play's question, artwork, or experience, which encapsulates or mirrors the encounter/experience of a live audience of the play. For example, the plot in *Temporal Powers* centres on a complex moral question (material versus spiritual priorities) with audiences internal to the play, i.e., the villagers, observing the courtroom below and Michael and Min's trials in the ruin, while in *The King of Spain's Daughter* and *Katie Roche* the audiences within the play are the older women, Mrs Marks and Amelia

---

37   Ibid., p. 21 and p. 22.
38   Ibid., p. 24.

Gregg. In *Dignity*, Mrs Hally creates her youthful self to Mr Wade in a flashback, *Within a Marble City* centres on an advertisement with multiple audiences and, in *Beyond Alma's Glory*, the radio audience is embodied within the play.[39] In the section below, I outline how this liminal material dramaturgy works in *Strange Birth* and *Light Falling* as chief examples.

Strange Birth and *Light Falling*

Significantly, *Strange Birth* was written for live theatrical production, and was first published in 1946; produced as a radio play in 1948, but was not presented on stage until the Mint Theater produced it in 2018.[40] Just as Jordan called the play 'unactable', it is challenging to encapsulate the 'unexplicated, poetic statement' of the play in written criticism, outside of its intended form of performance experienced by an audience.[41] *Strange Birth* is about the birth (note the material word) of love, love born through creation of a work of art, shared and interpreted between two people. The setting is inherently liminal, at the threshold between public and private—a hallway with multiple doors, including a main door with a mail slot (note vaginal connotations), which people enter to come and go, and receive letters. The work of art/writing is a letter delivered (inserted) through the slot—addressed to an imaginary future person, 'Mrs. Kirwan'. Imagining a future thing in material form brings into existence something that has been there all along: *a strange birth*.

---

39 See *Teresa Deevy Reclaimed*, I.
40 *Strange Birth* is published in the following sources: *Irish Writing*, 1 (1946), ed. by David Marcus and Terence Smith, F129; DRI, The Teresa Deevy Archive, Teresa Deevy, *The King of Spain's Daughter and Other One-Act Plays* (Ireland: New Frontiers, 1947), pp. 17–23, PP/6/97A. (1), https://doi.org/10.7486/DRI.5999vb55x; DRI, The Teresa Deevy Archive, *Life and Letters and the London Mercury*, Irish Writers, 61.140 (1949), ed. by Robert Herring, pp. 22–30, PP/6/100 (B), https://doi.org/10.7486/DRI.95944b899; *Teresa Deevy Reclaimed*, II; *Strange Birth* was first broadcast on Home Service Northern Ireland on 28 February 1947, see Martina Ann O'Doherty, 'Deevy: A Bibliography', *Irish University Review*, 52.1 (1995), 163–170. Produced by Mint Theater Company, the world premiere of *Strange Birth* (dir. by Jonathan Bank) ran from 21 July–30 September 2017 at the Beckett Theatre, New York. Public performances of *Strange Birth* in Ireland include a rehearsed play reading on 22 September 2017 at Garter Lane Arts Centre, Waterford, as part of Ireland's national Culture Night programme (dir. by Rebecca Phelan).
41 Jordan, 'Teresa Deevy: An Introduction', p. 24 and p. 22.

Deevy's dramaturgy explores the interrelationship of the material and immaterial world; how immaterial things, such as feelings and future people, can be realised through the creation of and interaction with material objects (in this play, Bill Kirwan's letter to Sara). These material objects, when encountered and interpreted by bodies, give 'birth' to new experiences—in Sara's case, love. Deevy's dramaturgy—her use of the liminal space of the play's setting and the arrival into this space of material objects in the form of letters—illustrates how people read each other's intent through physicalised constructs of imagination, a work of art or, in this case, a letter given and interpreted, making from something abstract something real, which can be held to the body. Love is born because of a letter addressed to a Mrs Kirwan, who, as Sara says, does not exist in the house. However, Mrs Kirwan is brought nearer to existence by the letter. In a short exchange, Bill and Sara discuss this possibility:

SARA: Do I live here Bill-the-post?

BILL: Don't you come here daily working?

SARA: Sara Meade—if you could make a Mrs. Kirwan out of that...

(*Silence: they look at one another.*)

BILL: It might be made... It might very well be.

(*Silence.*)[42]

The love letter from Bill to Sara creatively materialises a possible future and, in so doing, gives 'strange birth' to a feeling within Sara that has been there all along, although she 'didn't know' it.[43]

Deevy's stage directions are, as noted previously, crucial in enacting her dramaturgical project. Her embedded direction of Sara and Bill's bodies and their interaction with Bill's letter (as if it was a child) enacts how people interact with material objects as a means to aid and express difficult, but intensely important moments of communication. Sara and Bill fight over it:

---

42 Deevy, 'Strange Birth', p. 56.
43 Ibid., p. 58.

SARA: Here! Give it to me! (*Springs forward, seizes the letter.*)

BILL: Did I give it? or did you take it?

(SARA, *arms crossed on breast, the letter clasped tightly in one hand, stands facing him.*)

SARA: I took it Bill. I'll keep it now—come rain or sorrow. Tell it to me—all you said.[44]

The full meaning of the layered, material dramaturgy is impossible to convey in a form other than in embodied performance. Bill described the letter, intermingling acts of imagination and abstraction with physical, emotional, and sexual references:

BILL: I said you were a mine of wisdom—

SARA: *Me*, is it? (*A happy laugh.*)

BILL: I said I didn't know you yet.

SARA: And you don't either. (*A shadow.*)

BILL: But that I know you're the mine I could dig in forever.

SARA: That is queer—

BILL: I said you had nature; kindness and depth in your easy ways, and you are happy.

SARA: If you shut the door Bill, we could have a kiss.

BILL: But then you'd be destroyed entirely, since I'm not going to marry you.

SARA: (*After an instant.*) For a minute that went stabbing through me... I knew this is the way I'd be if love got born.[45]

But love has been there all along:

BILL: Got born! (*Roughly catching her wrist, and drawing down her*

---

44 Ibid.
45 Ibid.

arm—uncrossing the arms.) You have loved me for a long time past. I have seen it often in your eyes.

SARA: I think you're right. I didn't know. Now I'll keep a hold on it always. (*With great gentleness.*)[46]

This poetic, choreographed communication—where abstract ideas are born with the aid of material objects—is sexual and elementally creative, creating experiences which materialise in both the bodies on stage and the bodies in the audience, in simultaneously personal and profoundly connective ways. The significance of the interpretive processes described above goes beyond illuminating the play's content to include meta-theatrical references to its form and style as a play for live production and radio. This process of understanding a letter sent to a future person is the same creative process—bridging idea and matter, real and imaginary—as an audience appreciating the physical world of a radio play. For a radio play, *Strange Birth* makes substantial references to sight and seeing, and to physical engagement with place and things, including the letters: there are references to eyes, eyeglasses, light, and blinds. Deevy requires audiences to create material objects in their minds but, by connecting the visual elements with material elements in the play, she also engages their bodies. Sara and Bill's experience of birthing love as something material which can be held to the body is a meta-example of the imaginative process audiences undergo to create the props, settings, and characters' bodies in radio plays, and of the potent transformative implications to their lives as they do so. As Bill leaves with a promise to return the next day to ask Sara to marry him, Sara sits down holding his letter, 'her arms crossed again as though hugging a treasure to herself, the envelope held tightly in her hand'.[47] When Mr Bassett, a lodger in the house, returns to the hall, ready to complain at a slight he has received from a woman who did not write him, Sara replies: 'What matter…what matter…(*Quietly*) you *have* something'.[48] This poetic line, which can only be understood along with the stage directions, suggests that even expressed by its absence, communication between people produces something material you can have and hold. *Strange Birth* makes human feelings material, by a layered,

---

46 Ibid.
47 Ibid., p. 59.
48 Ibid.

shared physical encounter with a piece of writing, a work of art (or its absence). In this, the play is a metaphor for Deevy's whole project, a map for understanding the plays and their aims that come before and after.

Written in the same year as *Strange Birth*, *Light Falling* contains a similar metaphor for the way Deevy's plays are intended to work on an audience. Again, love is shared and/or expressed via matter and, similar to *Strange Birth*, the climax surrounds birthing and negotiations of the use of words referring to a future person, namely the use of the word 'Grandpa', which Mary, the central woman in the play, hopes her father-in-law, Pat, will be when she has a child. Like *Strange Birth*, *Light Falling* is about a shared experience of love between a man and a woman: the play offers a counterpoint to the disintegration of the marriage in *Temporal Powers*, an ultimate reconciliation and affirmation of deep love and mutual commitment between Mary and John, although it must be noted, following instances of what we would, today, call abuse.

The setting of *Light Falling* contains all the hallmark liminal elements: a middle door, this time on the front of a house; a dancing board (like an ancient Greek dancing circle) set on the grass, importantly in front of a house (skene); a hill; at the seaboard; a chair. There are repeated references to material items (potatoes); importantly, Mary has flour on her hands, which gets on other things, including Pat, a physical symbol of her impact on him; she bemoans 'the flour from my hands is on you now'.[49] Pat replies: 'No matter, no matter' (note the precise same line as in *Strange Birth*), then: '(*To himself.*) The flour from her hands...and the whole blossoming flower of her around me...'.[50] Deevy's construction toggles the material flour to a metaphor for the feeling of Mary's affect on Pat—the smell of a blossoming flower—by changing a word through spelling, but not sound (or physical formation in the mouth). The flour/flower exists physically and abstractly arousing him in mind and body: 'Old,—and not old enough. God give me grace. (*Brushes the flour from his clothes.*)'.[51] Like the choreopoem that is *Strange Birth*, *Light Falling* weaves a similarly complex spell, as communicatively complicated as expressing and experiencing smell in a radio play. Pat urges John to see Mary's love for him:

---

49   Deevy, 'Light Falling', p. 65.
50   Ibid.
51   Ibid.

PAT: Often I see her all a-flower opening to you, but you don't see it…

JOHN: Fragrance…a-flower… What's on you, old man?[52]

This lack of awareness to the truth of love also refers to the larger, central idea of the play's title, 'light falling', which is 'always' there 'but very often we don't see it'.[53] The painter, Mr Leslie, describes:

> For me truth is embodied in light falling… (*Speaks with quiet intensity.*) if I can get that down on canvas others will see in it the eternal mystery, the beneficence—oh, damn it all,—there's nothing new. Others have said it, thousands of others, yet I must say it my own way: I *must* capture the moment.— [sic]

PAT: I think, Mr. Leslie, what a man captures he'll destroy.[54]

Making repeated references to the actors' physicality and their interaction with material items, Deevy's text precisely directs the actors' bodies and emotions: they laugh, move, bend, breathe, catch, jump, and brush off one another. There is a climactic moment of dancing where bodies in collision create powerful change and the final, carefully choreographed moments of the play express the truth of love which, like in *Strange Birth*, has been there all along. At the end of the play, John and Mary argue over her right to use that word 'Grandpa':

MARY: Grandpa, isn't that a nice way he'd treat me?

JOHN: 'Grandpa' is a queer word in your mouth.

MARY: John! (*In sudden pain.*)

JOHN: 'Grandpa'—he isn't as you know well.[55]

This prompts Pat to stand and lunge at John, causing Pat to fall. Having worked together to lift and make Pat comfortable after he has fallen, Mary and John arrive at a moment when they are gentle and can '*laugh*

---

52 Ibid., p. 66.
53 Ibid., p. 70.
54 Ibid., p. 69, emphasis in original.
55 Ibid., p. 73.

joyfully, standing close together'.[56] John expresses his love for Mary through his body and his words:

> JOHN: He'd say I don't prize you. How can he tell? (*He grips her arm.*) You, and none other, it is for me. And you know that?[57]

In the physicality of the dance, the collision, the restoration of Pat to his chair and, in the examining of potatoes, Deevy's hallmark dramaturgical approach is enacted as a precise choreography of text, voice, sight, emotion, bodies, and material objects. Furthermore, the exchange between John and Mary is experienced aurally (like a radio drama) by Pat, positioned as an embodied meta-audience. Pat sees and hears John's expression of love for Mary, and then shares this with Mr Leslie who has returned for his pipe, accidentally left behind:

> PAT: [...] I *saw* what you were *saying*, Mr. Leslie [emphasis added].
>
> [...]
>
> What's this you called it—'light falling' and we don't see it. (*Very eager.*) It was when they were talking, usual-like, about the turf and potatoes... then I saw it...falling around them.
>
> MR LESLIE: (*Kindly.*) You've had a rare moment, Mr. Scully. [...]
>
> PAT: (*To himself.*) A 'rare' moment. Very clear...[58]

Pat's narration to Mr Leslie forms another act of meta-theatre, toggling between aural and visual. The play dramatises light falling in a way an audience can see it, and feel it, by means of a stand-in audience to a layered experience. Could such a rare moment be staged so that we see this in the standard live theatre, without Deevy's layered, liminal materialism? Could light falling in this poetic sense be adequately designed by a theatrical lighting designer? Or must this existential idea be expressed in a theatre that casts our bodies into the drama, so we experience the play's events along with the characters? Deevy's theatre draws our bodies in, places potatoes in our hands, and moves our bodies with the characters

---

56   Ibid., p. 75.
57   Ibid., p. 74.
58   Ibid., p. 75.

as they dance and collide and sit on the grass, and fall. The 'rare moment' is presented in a liminal frame that marries the experience of the radio play for Pat with an audience experience in the theatre seeing John and Mary embodied, speak, in front of, not *in*—i.e., the liminal (and inherently theatrical) house. In Pat, Deevy creates a meta-audience who serves as a stand-in, in and between, both media. This marriage of modes—visual, aural, and embodied—enacts the ideal dramaturgy of Deevy's project for the theatre, creating a rare moment that captures the truth of things in a dramatic form, designed to express and promote experiences of the 'sort of life we live in Ireland today', experiences of connection, union, and love.[59]

Conclusions

As an artist working in a method focused on my own and other women's reproductive bodies, I recently followed a hunch and did the math to discern that Deevy was fifty-three and fifty-four when she wrote these plays, the age I was when I read them, in my first year of menopause. While we perhaps can never know when Deevy experienced the cessation of her menses, that she is writing plays about the pains of childlessness and births through other means in her fifties seems significant. First, literally, in *Temporal Powers*, and then in her unique material abstractions in plays for theatre and radio written after that, Deevy impregnates the walls of her plays with matter, with bodies, with herself; simultaneously, she holds this creative matter within herself in the containers of her plays, in a way whereby audiences share this dual experience of inserting/implanting (inseminating) and gestating, carrying, and bearing, also. Perhaps she was investigating the potential products of her writing at this point of her life and her ability to generate material (to make people) outside the means of live production of the Abbey mainstage. Inserting audiences into the plays is its own strange birth: an embodied experience of love for audiences, which in later plays extended even to the experience of the love of God. In *One Look and What It Led To*, with several stand-in audiences including the Virgin Mary, Mary Magdalen, and Jesus Christ, Deevy completes her project of evoking joy,

---

59 Teresa Deevy, 'Autobiographical Note', in *Teresa Deevy Reclaimed*, II, xxi–xxiii (p. xxi).

happiness, and union between a man and a woman, woman to woman, and human and God.[60] In Deevy's theatre, God's love is born, materialised by watching, hearing, and feeling it born in other people.

Reading the plays in this way, the radio plays can be understood as a continuation of, indeed an *advancement* of, the dramaturgical goals of Deevy's earlier plays, and driving her whole career.[61] In the radio plays Deevy forges a dramaturgy informed by material limitation, including her deafness. I propose that in addition to the visual elements of the dramatic world that the words of the radio dramas reference, Deevy is also conjuring the embodied, the material of the stage drama—the physical realm, shared with an audience. Just as I experienced physically, as a reader, the experiences of Min, Annie, Katie, Belle, Amelia, and Patty, listeners and readers are prompted and/or encouraged to not only imagine the visual scene of the plays' climactic moments, but also their physical *experience* of actors embodying those moments while watching from the auditorium of the theatre. It is as if Deevy is mining the potential of radio to render ('birth') the same truth ('light falling') that she was exploring for the live stage—as if she is trying to provide the experience more directly through the potentialities and limitations of radio. This is achieved chiefly by inserting material elements, such as the money in the walls, that are crucial to the plot: food, animals, and *bodies* (falling, dancing), and a meta-audience within the drama that become a 'stand-in' for the live audience, so that they cast themselves, their bodies, within the play, experiencing the story. This trend reaches a crescendo in the radio plays. One might even posit that the liminal material space of the radio plays was a better container for the experiential truth Deevy strove to convey, that *imagining* the embodiment/embodied experience in the theatre as more expressive of the truth than seeing it enacted in the theatre—as it engages our/an audiences' own unique body truth—we construct and fill it in ourselves. The theatre cannot 'contain' it (like the houses, paintings, and flower baskets). A liminal medium is required to contain the truth—to show light falling on the experience of Deevy and Irish women.

This chapter takes its title from the metaphor of finding money in walls, and the political potency that Ní Bheacháin identifies in Deevy's

---

60 Teresa Deevy, 'One Look and What It Led To', in *Teresa Deevy Reclaimed*, II.
61 Bloom, *Blindness and Insight*.

hybrid-realism.[62] In *Temporal Powers*, the money stolen from the state, over which the Donovans fight, evolves into larger material embodiments of theatre's potential to affect real life, i.e., theatre's ability to effect individual and/or social change; the walls evolve to include those containing the audiences' experiences of plays beyond the Abbey, including Deevy's radio plays. In *Temporal Powers*, the matter wedged into the, importantly, *ruined* walls, of the traditional box set can be read as a larger metaphor for the power of an embodied feminist dramaturgy, which Deevy wedges into the materiality of realist staging, i.e., the apparent trappings of realism's walls (including fourth walls between actor and audience). This 'money' is the creative, material potential of Deevy's embodied approach to affect change in the lives of Irish people in the audience—a potential employed or inserted in between mixed dramaturgical styles, which include expressionist abstraction and fantasy. In this, Deevy employs a complex, embodied, feminist strategy, inserting her specific woman's body in split/mixed styles, decades ahead of materialist feminist playwrights inspired by Brecht, such as Caryl Churchill and Timberlake Wertenbaker, and the application of embodied hybrid styles by playwrights of colour, women, and queer artists, situated between dance and poetry, such as the choreopoems of Ntozake Shange, the 'spells' of Suzan-Lori Parks, and the mix of realism and expressionism of María Irene Fornés and Latine playwrights in her tradition. As testament to Audre Lorde's idea that 'The master's tools will never dismantle the master's house',[63] Deevy creates new stylistic tools, similarly to these later women poets and playwrights who seek to make more space on stage for the experiences of people who have been historically marginalised and oppressed: people of colour, women, people with disabilities, queer folks, and more.

Applying a personal, feminist analysis based in the body has proven revelatory of the power of Deevy's dramaturgy across her career. Deevy's theatre evokes a truth about communication in the theatre that could only have been generated by a person who could hear and became deafened, who remained single, without children, who was writing as a woman in a specific period of Irish history and theatre history, likewise who experienced

---

62   Ní Bheacháin, 'Political Critique and Moral Debate'.
63   Audre Lorde, 'The Master's Tools Will Never Dismantle the Master's House', in *Sister Outsider: Essays and Speeches* (Freedom, CA: Crossing Press, 1984), pp. 110–114.

a shift in access to production from the live stage to radio. In each of Deevy's plays, the central women assume into their bodies the impossible social and material contradictions, often in connection with other women. Love is not only inclusive of limits, but achieved *through* limits. Deevy works in recognition of these limits, in a unique, liminal materialist dramaturgy, which is based in the personal, and in concert with a collective (and with God in later plays), in a way that heals the audience, and brings them joy. Deevy places our bodies in the container of the play; like Pat Skully experiencing light falling and Sarah birthing love, ultimately, we are made the money in the walls.

Bibliography

Bank, Jonathan, John P. Harrington, and Christopher Morash (eds), *Teresa Deevy Reclaimed*, 2 vols (New York: Mint Theater, 2011 and 2017)

Bloom, Emily, *Blindness and Insight in Teresa Deevy's Radio Plays,* online video recording, Active Speech Conference: Sharing Scholarship on Teresa Deevy, 19 February 2021, https://wayback.archive-it.org/org-1444/20210610134822/https://activespeech2021.org/dramaturgy-genre-theory/

Case, Sue-Ellen, *Feminist Theatre* (London: Routledge, 1988)

Fox, Christie, 'Neither Here nor There: The Liminal Position of Teresa Deevy and Her Female Characters', in *A Century of Irish Drama: Widening the Stage*, ed. by Stephen Watt, Eileen Morgan, and Shakir Mustafa (Indianapolis, IN: Indiana University Press, 2001), pp. 193–203

Friel, Judy, 'Rehearsing *Katie Roche*', *Irish University Review*, 25.1 (1995), 117–125

Jordan, John, 'Teresa Deevy: An Introduction', *Irish University Review*, 1.8 (1956), 13–26

Karuse, David (ed.), *The Letters of Seán O'Casey 1910–1941, Volume 1* (London: Cassell, 1975)

Kealy, Úna, 'Resisting Power and Direction: *The King of Spain's Daughter* by Teresa Deevy as a Feminist Call to Action', *Estudios Irlandeses*, 15 (2020), 178–192, https://doi.org/10.24162/EI2020-9406

Leeney, Cathy, 'Teresa Deevy—Themes in Context', in *Abbey Theatre Research Pack: Teresa Deevy: Katie Roche*, researched and compiled by Marie Kelly, School of Music and Theatre, University College Cork (Dublin: The Abbey Theatre, 2017) pp. 21–27, https://www.abbeytheatre.ie/wp-content/uploads/2017/10/KATIE-ROCHE_RESEARCH-PACK-2017.pdf

Lorde, Audre, *Sister Outsider: Essays and Speeches* (Freedom, CA: Crossing Press, 1984)

Meaney, Geradine, 'The Sons of Cuchulainn: Violence, the Family and the Irish Canon', *Eire-Ireland*, 41.1 (2006), 242–261, https://doi.org/10.1353/eir.2006.0009

Morash, Christopher, *A History of Irish Theatre 1601–2000* (Cambridge: Cambridge University Press, 2002)

Morash, Christopher, 'Knew Nought of All This': Teresa Deevy's Dark Matter', Active Speech Conference: Sharing Scholarship on Teresa Deevy, 19 February 2021

Ní Bheacháin, Caoilfhionn, '"It Was then I Knew Life": Political Critique and Moral Debate in Teresa Deevy's *Temporal Powers* (1932)', *Irish University Review*, 50.2 (2020), 337–355, https://doi.org/10.3366/iur.2020.0474

O'Doherty, Martina Ann, 'Deevy: A Bibliography', *Irish University Review*, 52.1 (1995), 163–170

Roche, Anthony, 'Woman on the Threshold: J.M. Synge's *The Shadow of the Glen*, Teresa Deevy's *Katie Roche*, and Marina Carr's *The Mai*', *Irish University Review*, 25.1 (1995), 143–162

Scolnicov, Hanna, *Women's Theatrical Space* (New York: Cambridge University Press, 1994)

Shanahan, Ann M., 'The Gender Politics of Spectacle in Staging Sarah Ruhl's Adaptation of Virginia Woolf's *Orlando* and ATHE 2018: Theatre of Revolution', *SDC Journal*, 6.2 (2018), 37–39, https://issuu.com/sdcjournal/docs/sdc_journal_6.2_winter_2018

Shanahan, Ann M., 'Making Room(s): Staging Plays About Women and Houses', in *Performing the Family Dream House*, ed. by Emily Klein, Jennifer-Scott Mobley, and Jill Stevenson (London: Palgrave Macmillan, 2019), pp. 87–105, https://doi.org/10.1007/978-3-030-01581-7_5

Shanahan, Ann M., 'Playing House: Staging Experiments About Women in Domestic Space', *Theatre Topics*, 23.2 (2013), 129–144, https://doi.org/10.1353/tt.2013.0028

Shanahan, Ann M., 'Un-"blocking" Hedda and Medea through Feminist "Play" with Traditional Staging Forms', *Theatre Topics*, 20.1 (2011), 61–74, https://doi.org/10.1353/tt.2011.0000

Shanahan, Ann M., Prudence A. Moylan, Betsy Jones Hemenway, Bren Ortega Murphy, Jacqueline Long, Susan Grossman, Hector Garcia, and Mary Dominiak, 'Performance: An Approach to Strengthening Interdisciplinarity in Women's Studies and Gender Studies', *PARtake: Performance as Research*, 1.1 (2016), 1–41, https://doi.org/10.33011/partake.v1i1.331

Willet, John, trans., *Brecht on Theatre: The Development of an Aesthetic*, 13th edn (New York: Hill and Wang, 1964)

9. Becoming a Domesticated Irish Woman: Teresa Deevy's Critique of Idealised Representations of Womanhood in *Katie Roche*

Dayna Killen and Úna Kealy[1]

This chapter reads *Katie Roche* as Teresa Deevy's critique of idealised representations of Irish womanhood, in particular, the hegemonic, ideologically inflected, representation that we define as the 'domesticated Irish woman'. We conceive of the domesticated Irish woman as a representation, or conceptual mould, which formed, and into which Irish women were pressed, during the first half of the twentieth century. The domesticated Irish woman is an idealised representation of womanhood expressed as a heteronormative, married mother who is located primarily inside a domestic space. We argue that the trope of the domesticated Irish woman formed as a result of abstract, ideological codifications of women popular in the late nineteenth and early twentieth centuries that combined to shape, reshape, and restrict Irish women playwrights and their contemporaries physically, socially, and creatively. Drawing on literature theorising the creation

---

1 South East Technological University, formerly Waterford Institute of Technology (WIT), funded, through the WIT/SETU PhD Scholarship Fund, the Performing the Region: Performing Women project undertaken by Dayna Killen and led by Úna Kealy. Co-supervisors on the project were Richard Hayes and Jacinta Byrne-Doran. The project was also supported by the Higher Education Authority and D/FHERIS Covid-19 costed extension. The authors also acknowledge Shonagh Hill and the anonymous reviewers of the *Active Speech* manuscript whose editorial advice supported revisions.

and perpetuation of idealised archetypes of women and synthesising these with historiographic analyses of socio-cultural aspects of Irish society, the chapter opens by discussing the influences and ideologies that underpinned and shaped representations of Irish women, as well as characteristics associated with these representations.

Simone de Beauvoir posits that 'Woman is not a fixed reality but a becoming' and we employ the word 'domesticated' to suggest that female bodies in Ireland during the early decades of the twentieth century were subject to, and at times enacted, a domestication process through which they *became* domesticated Irish women.[2] Referring to Judith Bulter's theories on gender as performative, Elin Diamond asserts that 'Performance [...] is the site in which performativity materializes in concentrated form'.[3] In this chapter, we synthesise the work of gender constructivist theorists, such as de Beauvoir and Butler, with Michel Foucault's discussion of how individuals are shaped into 'docile bodies', to argue that Deevy's dramaturgy, within *Katie Roche*, deploys space, characters' physicality, and language (within dialogue and stage directions) to create a protagonist who, over three acts, is shaped into a representation of womanhood that aligns closely with representations of the domesticated Irish woman.[4] In so doing, this chapter reveals how Deevy found creative possibilities in deconstructing and interrogating a developmental process whereby young women and girls in Ireland during the early decades of twentieth century were shaped into idealised representations of Irish womanhood.

---

2   Simone de Beauvoir, *The Second Sex*, trans. by Constance Borde and Sheila Malovany-Chevallier with an introduction by Sheila Robotham (London: Vintage Classics Kindle edition, 2015), loc. 1187.
3   Elin Diamond, *Unmaking Mimesis: Essays on Feminism and Theatre* (Abingdon: Routledge, 1997), p. 47.
4   Simone de Beauvoir, *The Second Sex*; Judith Butler, 'Performative Acts and Gender Constitution: An Essay in Phenomenology and Feminist Theory', *Theatre Journal*, 40.4 (1988), 519–531; Judith Butler, *Gender Trouble: Feminism and the Subversion of Identity*, 2nd edn (Abingdon: Routledge, 1990); Michel Foucault, *Discipline and Punish: The Birth of the Prison* (London: Penguin Random House Kindle edition, 2020).

The Domesticated Irish Woman

Although the early decades of the twentieth century were characterised, in the West, by social, political, and ideological fracture, Catherine Jagoe attests that idealised representations of women crossed international borders, shaped, defined, and supported by shared bourgeois ideologies that agreed upon an 'essence of natural womanhood'.[5] In Victorian Britain, women were frequently idealised to the point of divinity in representations that were, typically, inextricably linked to qualities of docility and domesticity. Women were, as Coventry Patmore conceived of them, celestially domesticated—a collective angelic host located within their husband's houses. Patmore's poetry popularised the phrase 'the angel in the house'—a conceptualisation that 'came to represent nothing less than the ideal of womanhood in the age of Queen Victoria'.[6] In Ireland, however, during the early decades of the twentieth century, a period of tremendous social, political, and cultural change, Revivalists sought to remember, discover, and imagine an Irish cultural identity that differentiated Ireland from England—an aspect of which involved creating representations of women and womanhood.[7] Eleanor Hull, Sidney Gifford, Hanna Sheehy-Skeffington, Dora Mellone, and members of Inghinidhe na hÉireann, amongst others, looked to historical and legendary women—Maeve, Macha, and Brigit—to locate 'a female genealogy outside the traditional realm of hearth and home' to serve 'as inspirational role models'.[8] Hull emphasised 'the high estimate that was placed in Ireland upon woman's influence', describing Irish mythological heroines as 'very human' and comparable neither to 'the Titanic women of the Northern Saga', nor 'the morbid, luxurious ladies of Southern romance'.[9] Describing legendary Irish women as sprightly,

---

5   Catherine Jagoe, *Ambiguous Angels: Gender in the Novels of Galdós* (Los Angeles, CA: University of California Press, 1994), p. 14.

6   Joan Hoffman, '"She Loves with Love That Cannot Tire": The Image of the Angel in the House across Cultures and across Time', *Pacific Coast Philology*, 42.2 (2007), 264–271 (p. 264).

7   Declan Kiberd, *Inventing Ireland: The Literature of the Modern Nation* (London: Vintage Books, 1996).

8   Shonagh Hill, *Women and Embodied Mythmaking in Irish Theatre* (Cambridge: Cambridge University Press, 2019), p. 29.

9   Eleanor Hull, *The Cuchullin Saga in Irish Literature* (London: David Knutt, 1898), p. xlvii.

spirited, self-respecting, piquant, malicious, capricious, provoking, dignified, and heroic, Hull conceived of them as imperfect, powerful women who acted independently and demanded equality from men.[10] In such assertions and descriptions of legendary Irish women, Louise Ryan recognises:

> a strategy to position feminism back into a pre-colonial past of gender equality, where strong women like Queen Maeve exerted authority in Irish society [… and] constructed a Janus-quality for feminism by simultaneously looking back to a 'glorious' Gaelic past and forward to a bright future of women's rights and equality.[11]

Sadly, it was a strategy doomed to fail. Even while arguing for the independence and important influence of legendary women, Hull recognised a reshaping of women characters by successive scribes and scholars which had infantilised them and 'softened' their 'savagery […] into the coy shyness' of romantic girls.[12] The characters of Irish mythology were, as Joseph Valente argues 'unmistakably filtered and softened through the defining literary and social institutions of Great Britain' in a process of reinterpretation that controverted 'invidious gender stereotypes' into representations that were deemed authentically Irish.[13] Thus, despite early twentieth-century ideological fracture and attempts by Irish Revivalists to reject British cultural mores and social values, representations of women in Irish culture were ideologically inflected by British idealised representations of women. Furthermore, despite the efforts of contemporaneous Irish feminists, these idealised representations were integrated into Irish culture and further inflected with Irish particularities.

In Ireland in the late nineteenth and early twentieth centuries the importance of woman's domestic and familial orientation was powerfully propagated and idealised by nationalist rhetoric, nationalist

---

10   Ibid.
11   Louise Ryan, 'Nationalism and Feminism: The Complex Relationship between the Suffragist and Independence Movements in Ireland', in *Women and the Irish Revolution: Feminism, Activism, Violence*, ed. by Linda Connolly (Kildare: Irish Academic Press, 2020), pp. 36–55 (p. 54).
12   Hull, *The Cuchullin Saga*, p. xlvii.
13   Joseph Valente, 'Lost (and Found) in Translation: The Masculinity of O'Grady's Cuculain', in *Standish O'Grady's Cuculain: A Critical Edition*, ed. by Gregory Castle and Patrick Bixby (New York: Syracuse University, 2016), pp. 210–225 (p. 213 and p. 214).

political parties, and Catholic teaching.[14] In the late 1800s the Catholic Church, in Britain and Ireland, in a bid to fortify Catholic influence and combat increasing secularisation within life and culture, sought to sanctify women through the character of the Blessed Virgin Mary. The glorification of the Virgin Mary constituted a 'supreme masculine victory' that de Beauvoir contends was but a ploy to further subjugate women. She argues that:

> [Woman] will be glorified only by accepting the subservient role assigned to her. 'I am the handmaiden of the Lord.' For the first time in the history of humanity, the mother kneels before her son; she freely recognises her inferiority. The supreme masculine victory is consummated in the worship of Mary: it is the rehabilitation of woman by the achievement of her defeat.[15]

Ireland embraced the 'Marian century' enthusiastically: many religious observances, sodalities, and devotions sanctifying the Blessed Virgin were introduced to Catholic worship including the popularisation of novenas and the centralisation of the rosary as a daily family observance.[16] As Cara Delay argues, the early twentieth century saw women and girls 'bombarded with messages on Catholic womanhood from an early age' by a Catholic hierarchy determined to 'define the ideal woman'.[17] Through this plethora of structured devotional activities, and the 'steady democratization of devotional material culture', the Catholic Church created in the Blessed Virgin an idealised version of

---

14 Libreria Editrice Vaticana, 'Rerum Novarum: Encyclical of Pope Leo XIII on Capital and Labor' (1891); Mary Butler, 'Irishwomen and the Home Language (Continued)', *All Ireland Review*, 1.51 (1900), 4–5; Susan Cannon-Harris, *Gender and Modern Irish Drama* (Indiana, IN: Indiana University Press, 2002); Paul Murphy, '"That a Black Twisty Divil Could Be Hiding under Such Comeliness": *Woman* versus *woman* in Early Twentieth-Century Irish Theatre', *Theatre Journal*, 60.2 (2008), 201–216; Tanya Dean, 'Staging Hibernia: Female Allegories of Ireland in *Cathleen Ni Houlihan* and *Dawn*', *Theatre History Studies*, 33.1 (2014), 71–82.

15 Susan O'Brien, 'The Blessed Virgin Mary', in *The Oxford History of British and Irish Catholicism, Volume IV: Building Identity, 1830–1913*, ed. by Carmen M. Mangion and Susan O'Brien (Oxford: Oxford University Press, 2023), pp. 154–172; de Beauvoir, *The Second Sex*, loc. 3965.

16 O'Brien dates the Marian Century as 1850–1950. The first Irish pilgrimage to the Marian shrine in Lourdes involving 2,000 pilgrims occurred in 1913 and was filmed and shown to 'packed audiences' at the Rotunda in Dublin that year. Ibid., p. 168.

17 Cara Delay, *Irish Women and the Creation of Modern Catholicism, 1850–1950* (Manchester: Manchester University Press, 2018), p. 7.

womanhood centred within a domestic space that was identified as her 'natural sphere'.[18]

In 1936, the year that *Katie Roche* premiered, Bunreacht na hÉireann was drafted. Although opposition vociferously articulated the draft Constitution as unfair to women, and as lacking in respect for the Catholic Church's teachings on 'the position, the sphere, the duties of women'.[19] During the drafting process, legislation fused with Catholic teaching to form a mould which would shape Irish women.[20] In 1937, the Constitution was published using language explicitly locating women within domestic spaces and identifying them as mothers.[21] Article 41, sections 2.1 and 2.2, of the 1937 Constitution stated (and continues to state) that:

> 41.2.1 In particular, the State recognises that by her life within the home, woman gives to the State a support without which the common good cannot be achieved.
>
> 41.2.2 The State shall, therefore, endeavour to ensure that mothers shall not be obliged by economic necessity to engage in labour to the neglect of their duties in the home.[22]

---

18   O'Brien, 'The Blessed Virgin Mary', p. 170; see also Libreria Editrice Vaticana, 'Rerum Novarum: Encyclical of Pope Leo XIII on Capital and Labor'.

19   *Irish Press*, 17 December 1937, in Siobhán Mulally, 'Presentation by Prof. Siobhan Mullally, UCC', in *Second Report of the Convention on the Constitution*, May 2013, pp. 14–18, https://citizensassembly.ie/wp-content/uploads/Role-of-Women-Woemn-in-Politics.pdf; Dorothy Macardle articulated her opposition to the text of the draft 1937 Constitution in a private letter to Éamon de Valera, see Dublin, National Archives of Ireland (NAI), 'Letter to Éamon de Valera', 21 May 1937, DTS 9880; see also, Rosemary Cullen Owens, *A Social History of Women in Ireland 1870–1970* (Dublin: Gill and Macmillan, 2014); Jennifer Molidor, 'Dying for Ireland: Violence, Silence, and Sacrifice in Dorothy Macardle's *Earth-Bound: Nine Stories of Ireland* (1924)', *New Hibernia Review*, 12.4 (2008) 43–61; Maria Luddy, *Hanna Sheehy Skeffington* (Dundalk: Dundalgan Press, 1995); Maria Luddy, 'A "Sinister and Retrogressive" Proposal: Irish Women's Opposition to the 1937 Draft Constitution', *Transactions of the Royal Historical Society*, 15 (2005), 175–195; Gerard Hogan, *The Origins of the Irish Constitution: 1928–1941* (Dublin: Royal Irish Academy, 2012).

20   John Cooney's *John Charles McQuaid: Ruler of Catholic Ireland* (Dublin: Paperview in association with the *Irish Independent*, 2006) evidences the extent and impact of the influence of the Catholic Church hierarchy upon the creation of Bunreacht na hÉireann 1937.

21   Melissa Sihra, 'Introduction: Figures at the Window', in *Women in Irish Drama: A Century of Authorship and Representation*, ed. by Melissa Sihra (Hampshire and New York: Palgrave, 2007), pp. 1–22; Hill, *Women and Embodied Mythmaking*.

22   Government of Ireland, *Constitution of Ireland*, January 2020; John Cooney in *John Charles McQuaid* argues cogently for this conspiratorial relationship.

Conceptualising the role and place of women as support workers within domestic spaces and as mothers was contemporaneously politically practical. The context of the Western economic depression of the 1930s, the rejection of international capitalism and isolationist ideology of the Cumann na nGaedheal government created a decline in living standards.[23] In order to pursue a policy of fiscal retrenchment, and to mitigate against the inevitable slowing or decline in what were, for many, already poor living standards, a cohort of people devoted to working within Irish domestic spaces—i.e. women—was essential.[24] It was necessary, as Katie Roche reiterates, for women to be given responsibility to make the bread, churn the butter, and 'fill the jug'.[25]

Within a social and political context ostensibly intent on differentiating itself from British ideology and cultural references, idealised representations of womanhood took on particular Irish and Catholic attributes. Irish women's duty was to sustain the family—a social unit, which, as Maryann Valiulis contends, was 'privileged in Irish political thought as the source of order and stability'.[26] Valiulis argues that the 1937 Constitution describes the family as 'the necessary basis of social order and as indispensable to the welfare of the Nation and the State'.[27] The Constitution closed gaps in existing legislation, further

---

23 Mary E. Daly 'The Irish Free State and the Great Depression of the 1930s: The Interaction of the Global and the Local', *Irish Economic and Social History*, 38 (2011), 19–36 (p. 32).

24 Although living standards in Ireland generally increased from the mid-nineteenth century, improvements varied according to geography and class. Living standards for many rural Irish people remained low well into the twentieth century. For an overview of consumption, living conditions, frugality, food crises, health, and welfare in Ireland during the early decades of the twentieth century, see 'Consumption and Living Conditions, 1750–2016' by Andy Bielenberg and John O'Hagan, 'Food in Ireland Since 1740' by Juliana Adelman, and 'Health and Welfare, 1750–2000' by Catherine Cox in *The Cambridge Social History of Modern Ireland*, ed. by Eugenio F. Biagini and Mary E. Daly (Cambridge: Cambridge University Press, 2017), pp. 195–211, 233–243, and 261–281, respectively.

25 Teresa Deevy, 'Katie Roche', in *Teresa Deevy Reclaimed*, 2 vols, ed. by Jonathan Bank, John P. Harrington, and Christopher Morash (New York: Mint Theater, 2011 and 2017), I, 57–102 (p. 59).

26 Maryann G. Valiulis, 'Virtuous Mothers and Dutiful Wives: The Politics of Sexuality in the Irish Free State', in *Gender and Power in Irish History*, ed. by Maryann G. Valiulis (Dublin: Irish Academic Press, 2008), pp. 100–114 (p. 102). A referendum to change the wording of the Irish Constitution on 8 March 2024 was rejected and the family remains privileged as a social grouping within Irish constitutional law.

27 Ibid., p. 102.

inhibiting and restricting women's involvement in decisions relating to family planning, their bodies, and their futures, and, as is illustrated in the sections of Article 41 quoted above, unambiguously directed Irish women towards marriage, motherhood, and domestic service.[28] The infantilisation, filtering, and softening of representations of mythic Irish women, the transnational icon of the Angel in the House, the devotional revolution within the Catholic Church, the fiscal strategy of the Free State government, and the language and implicit ideology relating to women's role and place within the Free State as articulated within Bunreacht na hÉireann, constituted mutually reinforcing practices and ideologies during the Irish Revival. Conceptions of Irish women and womanhood were shaped into an idealised representation that Paul Murphy describes as a 'fantasy object of patriarchal nationalist desire'—a representation of womanhood that was 'self-sacrificing, bound by the confines of the home and [accepting of] her place in society in the service of the male élite'.[29] As Marian devotee, impecunious housewife, and mother, the Angel in the House recited the Rosary, blessed herself, and set the table for dinner—in so doing, consciously or otherwise, she reshaped as the domesticated Irish woman.

Katie Roche: A Critique of Representations of Irish Womanhood

Deevy's *Katie Roche* can be read as the tale of one young woman's resistance to the mould of the domesticated Irish woman and her eventual capitulation to it. Constructed in three acts and set in the living-room of a 'time-worn' cottage, *Katie Roche* foregrounds a collective fear of, and a determined attempt to control, a young woman's unregulated sexuality. The play dramatises the process, but also the consequences, of shaping women to fit behavioural and ideological representations in ways that

---

28 This legislation included the Juries Acts (1924) and (1927), the Civil Service Regulation Act (1924), and the Censorship of Publications Act (1929). Caitriona Beaumont, 'Women, Citizenship and Catholicism in the Irish Free State, 1922–1948', *Women's History Review*, 6.4 (1997), 563–585; Maria Luddy, 'Sex and the Single Girl in 1920s and 1930s Ireland', *The Irish Review*, 35 (2007), 79–91; Valiulis, 'Virtuous Mothers and Dutiful Wives'.
29 Paul Murphy, '*Woman* versus *woman*', p. 202; Paul Murphy, *Hegemony and Fantasy in Irish Drama, 1899–1949* (Houndsmills: Palgrave Macmillan, 2008), p. 152.

maintain an existing power and socio-economic hierarchy; one wherein unmarried mothers and their children occupy a place at the bottom.[30] It appears, in Act One, that Katie and a young man, Michael Maguire, are attracted to one another and that Katie might marry him. However, despite the fact that Michael promises to marry Katie, his mother's 'bitter tongue' dissuades him from proposing to her.[31] That bitterness was the prevailing practice of shaming and ostracising children born to unmarried women during the twentieth century and it paralyses him. He admits to Stanislaus that because of Katie's 'want of a name', i.e., her birth to an unmarried woman, his 'mother would die if [he] were to bring her in the door'.[32] Emasculated by the threat of social censure, Michael offers no escape to Katie. Unlike Michael, however, Katie, at the play's opening and before her marriage to Stanislaus, is not cowed by her awareness of contemporaneous conceptions of how she should behave. Her 'inward glow' continuously 'breaks out' 'either in delight or desperation' and she dances and interacts with men, unashamed of her sexual appeal and charisma.[33]

Unabashed and unregulated sexual appeal and activity is, Deevy suggests, problematic within Irish society. Woven into the opening act of *Katie Roche* are details of Katie's life and that of her parents, notably her mother, Mary Halnan. It transpires that Mary, like Katie, had lived with Amelia Gregg but had become pregnant outside marriage, given birth and, subsequently, died. As an unmarried mother, had she lived, Mary's status in Ballycar would, as Lindsey Earner-Byrne contends was true for unmarried mothers in the Irish Free State, have been 'regarded [...] as morally untenable and socially undesirable'.[34] However, as time in Ballycar has passed, Mary Halnan is conceptually reconstructed by Stanislaus as an ideal representation of womanhood, inextricably linked to beauty and sacrifice. The result is that the memory of Mary, like her namesake the Blessed Virgin Mary, becomes an ideologically

---

30 Deevy, 'Katie Roche', p. 57; *Katie Roche* premiered at the Abbey theatre on the 16 March 1936. Abbey Theatre, 'Katie Roche 1936', *Abbey Theatre*, 2022.
31 Deevy, 'Katie Roche', p. 93.
32 Ibid., p. 69, p. 70.
33 Ibid., p. 57.
34 Lindsey Earner-Byrne, 'The Boat to England: An Analysis of the Offical Reactions to the Emigration of Single Expectant Irishwomen to Britain, 1922–1972', *Irish Economic and Social History*, 30 (2003), 52–70 (p. 53).

loaded reconstructed representation of womanhood that is employed by Stanislaus, the stand-in for the patriarchal elite, to shape Katie and young women like her. Stanislaus advocates that Katie must reshape her speech and her behaviour, so as to more closely fit with the idealised Mary who is more beautiful and 'wonderful' than Katie.[35] Stanislaus has intensified Mary in his memory making her taller, more beautiful, refined, polite, and articulate than Katie. In Stanislaus's memory, Mary exists, as de Beauvoir might describe her, as eternally feminine—'unique and changeless' while Katie is 'dispersed, contingent, and multiple'— or, as Jo describes her, 'vegarious'.[36] Stanislaus's comparison of the perfect, but deceased, Mary with the imperfect living Katie exposes how women who fail to perform idealised behaviours during their lifetime can be reconstructed as self-contradictory, pseudo-divine abstractions after their death. The comparison suggests that women, such as Katie, whose attitudes and behaviours threaten the stability of the family and the home, are vulnerable to being shaped and/or reshaped through comparisons with falsified representations of dead women that are impossible for living women to emulate.

Cathy Leeney contends that Stanislaus substitutes Katie for her mother, thereby attempting to put 'Katie in her place'.[37] That place is both physically constructed through the Gregg cottage and imaginatively constructed in Stanislaus's mind. Leeney argues that Stanislaus is 'disappointed' in Katie, perceiving her as an inferior copy of her mother Mary.[38] Having idealised Mary, Stanislaus employs that ideal in an attempt to shape and remake Katie. He utilises shame as a tool to do this telling Katie, 'It's a great shame for you not to better yourself, it's a shame—the way you speak'.[39] Shame induced by proximity to idealised representations of womanhood and criticisms of her language reads as Stanislaus's attempt to keep Katie 'in line, in her place' and an attempt to fit Katie into the place in his mind where an idealised representation of womanhood resides.[40] Stanislaus does not specify

---

35 Deevy, 'Katie Roche', p. 60.
36 Ibid., p. 87.
37 Cathy Leeney, 'Themes of Ritual and Myth in Three Plays by Teresa Deevy', *Irish University Review*, 25 (1995), 88–166 (p. 104).
38 Ibid., p. 104.
39 Deevy, 'Katie Roche', p. 60.
40 Robin Lakoff, 'Language and Woman's Place', *Language in Society*, 2 (1973), 45–80

what 'shame' exists in Katie's language, but his correction of her occurs when she adopts syntactical or idiomatic patterns of Hiberno-English drawing attention to her social class, her status as his social inferior, and her Irishness. Stanislaus's reprimands and grammatical corrections of Katie's language and idiom subtly infer that the idealised constructions of Irish women in the Free State were inflected by class and behavioural ideology imported from Britain. *Katie Roche* thus highlights the irony of political and religious power brokers in the fledgling Irish Free State who sought to direct or reshape the speech, behaviours, and desires of Irish women in ways that aligned with anglicised gendered norms and idealised representations.

Unlike Katie, Stanislaus performs his gender role in accordance with idealised, anglicised representations: the ideal he attempts to embody is one of chivalrous masculinity. Like a mythic knight, he left Ballycar in Katie's youth to resolve the conundrum of how to fit her into his conceptualisation of an acceptable wife. He returns to claim her, having triumphed in his task by deconstructing her and selecting from that deconstruction the parts of her that he imagines he can shape into the contours of an ideal woman. He proposes marriage to Katie, explaining to Amelia that 'I went away….But afterwards I came again and I found she was what I wanted. Her heart and her mind were what I wanted'.[41] After saying this, he '*Bows to* KATIE', an action that recalls an idealised chivalric physicality and which invites her to respond in kind, that is, with a similarly idealised performance of femininity. Such a performance, it seems, will signal Katie's acquiescence to adopting the shape and values of the domesticated Irish woman.[42] However, Katie is not so easily snared: in a retort of stunning, elliptical brevity that rejects performances of masculinity as chivalrous, exposing instead the violence of deconstructing and remaking women as ideals of femininity, Katie replies, 'My heart and my mind! A queer way to love! … taking a body to pieces!'.[43]

Alongside his linguistic and gestural direction, Stanislaus directly attempts to shape Katie according to his ideal woman, regulating her

---

(p. 47).
41   Deevy, 'Katie Roche', p. 71.
42   Ibid.
43   Ibid.

physically by putting his hand on her shoulder, while simultaneously infantilising her, calling her a 'dear little girl'.[44] Katie's reaction to this is one of physical and intellectual disgust and she 'Flings from him', crying: 'If you're asking to marry me, show me respect. I won't marry you now, not if you'd go on your knees. I flout you—the same as she did'.[45] During Stanislaus's marriage proposal and Katie's eventual acceptance, Deevy's stage directions detail Katie's physicality—she fumes, 'flings', laughs 'wildly', and lashes out with 'sudden spite'.[46] Presciently, she fears that the marriage will be a mistake: colliding with Stanislaus as she rushes from the room after his proposal, she expresses that fear physically and verbally:

> KATIE: Oh—(*In turmoil.*)—who knows what they wish! (*Clasps her hands—then, seeking strength.*) "One false step and you're over the precipice, one bad link and the chain goes snap, one wrong act and a life is ruined, one small...one small...one... one" (*Trying to concentrate.*)—ach!—(*Turns to run from the room, meets* STANISLAUS *coming in. He opens his arms, takes her.*) Oh-h...Oh-h... (*In ecstasy.*).
>
> STANISLAUS: I couldn't wait. (*Kisses her.*)
>
> KATIE: Oh! (*Overcome. Then frees herself; stands back from him.*) Yes, I'll give you my hand.
>
> STANISLAUS: That's right. That's a good girl. Now don't be nervy. Don't be upset. It's only the strain. (*Pats her shoulder reassuringly.* KATIE *stiffens.*) Why—even I felt it. We'll be sensible. We'll get married very soon. My sister will live with us—if you don't mind. She'll go away sometimes. (KATIE *looks at him now with the anger of a child at a clumsy companion.*)[47]

Quoting from something that she cannot quite remember, but ominous in tone, Katie's emotions and physicality flash from dread to ecstasy to anger. The collision, the kiss, and the exchange between Katie and

---

44 Ibid., p. 61.
45 Ibid.
46 Ibid.
47 Ibid., p. 72.

Stanislaus immediately thereafter exemplifies how Deevy's dramaturgy exquisitely combines space, physicality, and language. As Katie runs from the room that symbolises the drudgery of domesticity, she collides with Stanislaus who, taking advantage of her 'false step', physically 'takes' her and kisses her. Significantly, Stanislaus's embrace is not consented to by Katie—he imposes it upon her and contains her within it. The changing nature of the subtext within this moment is complex and open to multiple interpretations but the embrace ends with Katie accepting Stanislaus's proposal. Subsequently, and in a phrase that jars with her Hiberno-Irish dialect thus far in the play, Katie says, 'I'll give you my hand'.[48] In her acceptance, it seems that Katie interprets the embrace as indicative of a hitherto hidden but deep well of passionate impetuosity within Stanislaus, which suggests that marriage to him will provide her with a passion-filled life. Stanislaus's interpretation of her acceptance is, however, quite different. There is a brief moment of mutual misunderstanding before Katie realises her mistake. Immediately after Katie has accepted his proposal, Stanislaus begins the process of reshaping her into a domesticated Irish woman. He calls her a 'good girl', cautions her against being 'nervy', and pats her shoulder. It is a moment that encapsulates, through dialogue and physicality, how idealised romantic language and physicality, infantilising terminology, and restraining gestures combine to entrap and then reshape young women to accord with idealised and gendered behavioural norms.

The effect of Stanislaus's actions and language on Katie is that she 'stiffens' and 'does not move' for some minutes.[49] It is only when prompted by Amelia to sit down that Katie moves 'slowly to the table, and sits down'—the pace and action suggesting submission and defeat. Michel Foucault argues that, by the eighteenth century, a soldier had 'become something that can be made; out of a formless clay, an inapt body'.[50] The stiffness within Katie's body suggests that her 'inapt' body is slowly forming to fit or align with the representational mould of a domesticated Irish woman. Later in the play, Reuben, a holy man whom it transpires is Katie's father, more forcefully pressures Katie's rebellious body into the physical and behavioural

---
48 Ibid.
49 Ibid.
50 Foucault, *Discipline and Punish*, loc. 2498.

contours of the domesticated Irish woman when he beats her with a stick. Stanislaus and Reuben attempt to humiliate and reduce Katie physically and intellectually in order to recreate her as a domesticated Irish woman who is demure, humble, and obedient to male suitors, fathers, and husbands. In an epiphanic flash, Katie realises that 'Oh, we must be humble, but 'tis hard!... The bread and the butter and to fill the jug...'.[51] Butler claims that 'the ground of gender identity is the stylized repetition of acts through time, and not a seemingly seamless identity'—Katie's epiphany is her perception that by endlessly and repetitively performing domestic tasks, 'enclosed' in repetitive 'daily life rituals', she will regulate and reshape her body, mind, and ambition and become a domesticated Irish woman: a woman disciplined by 'the cycles of repetition' within a set of domestic chores that begin anew every day.[52] Humility, in this context, is simply another word for docility—to become a domesticated Irish woman Katie must allow her body to be 'used, transformed and improved' by the disciplined and endless routine of domestic service.[53]

In Act Two, Deevy reveals what Iris Marion Young argues as 'the deeply ambivalent' nature of women's relationship to domestic spaces.[54] Leeney argues that 'It is not the physical setting in which she lives that confines her [...]. It is the social environment that entraps Katie' and that social environment—that oppressive darkness on the other side of the drawn curtains—is impossible to shut out because it exists in Stanislaus's mind.[55] As Leeney argues, 'Deevy is aware of the playing space as an external image of the internal life of the characters', and the changes in the Gregg cottage in Act Two manifest Katie's ambition to retain some autonomy and individuality within her marriage.[56] Katie's glow—her sexual, creative, and intellectual energy—illuminates the cottage manifesting in vibrant furnishings, light, and warmth. The cottage:

---

51 Deevy, 'Katie Roche', p. 61.
52 Butler, 'Performative Acts', p. 520; de Beauvoir, *The Second Sex*, loc. 2799; Foucault, *Discipline and Punish*, loc. 2745.
53 Foucault, *Discipline and Punish*, loc. 2515.
54 Iris Marion Young, *On Female Body Experience: 'Throwing Like a Girl' and Other Essays* (Oxford: Oxford University Press, 2005), p. 123.
55 See Chapter 11 in this volume.
56 Cathy Leeney, *Irish Women Playwrights 1900–1939: Gender and Violence on Stage* (New York: Peter Lang, 2010), p. 170.

now has an air of life and warmth. There are gaily coloured prints on the wall. Two or three cushions have vivid covers. The lamp on the table is lighted, the curtains are drawn and the fire is bright.[57]

However, the additions of colour, light, and warmth are surface dressing only. The stage directions read:

> STANISLAUS *and* KATIE *sit in front of the fire, side by side. They bend eagerly over some papers which* STANISLAUS *holds.* KATIE'S *arm is thrown about his shoulder. In her eagerness, bending forward, reading, she comes in the way of his view. He moves a little from her; she moves closer to him, drawing him down toward the papers.* STANISLAUS *quickly frees himself, sits back.*[58]

In sitting 'side by side' with Stanislaus, Katie physicalises her desire for equality with him. She is as eager as he to look over the documents, but it is Stanislaus who holds the power (represented by the documents) and, consequentially, the ability to control Katie's behaviour. She can only engage with the documents under his supervision and is allowed look at, but not hold, them. As Katie becomes more intellectually involved in the plans she obscures Stanislaus's view of them, putting her body in the place where his was. When she attempts to direct his body and attitude to align with hers he resists, creating more space for himself and removing the documents from her sight. Looking at the plans, Katie asks, 'Was it I made you do this? [...] Wasn't it because of our love?' [...] Were you thinking of me, and you working at it?'[59] Upon hearing that Stanislaus merely thinks of her 'very often', she replies: 'What good is "often" that should be "always"?'[60] Attempting to convince herself that the marriage to Stanislaus is indeed access, albeit vicariously, to passion and creativity, she 'looks at the plans again' saying, 'No matter—a prince' before showing them to Amelia and proclaiming her husband 'a genius'.[61] However, Katie is unable to sustain herself in her delusion as she then admits that Stanislaus's work is 'not so perfect' and that marriage to him offers neither intellectual nor physical passion, but a

---

57 Deevy, 'Katie Roche', pp. 72–73.
58 Ibid., p. 73.
59 Ibid.
60 Ibid.
61 Ibid., p. 73 and p. 74.

continuation of her former chaste and intellectually sterile seclusion.⁶² In this moment, the concertina music that has faintly sounded offstage previously during Act Two 'is heard again' and, as Michael passes the house, Katie invites him in, moving closer to the fire, attempting to spark the fire of Stanislaus's jealousy.⁶³

Katie succeeds in her attempt, but she does not anticipate Stanislaus's decision, to adopt Foucault's term, to discipline her for failing to embody his ideal, asexual, and 'docile' woman.⁶⁴ He leaves her in Ballycar while he returns to Dublin alone. During his absence—the passage of time between Acts Two and Three—Katie transforms the cottage into a prison house of religious pictures and texts in which the iconography of Catholic Ireland's devotional revolution is pressed into service. Deevy opens Act Three with the following stage directions:

> *The door at the right opens.* KATIE *comes in with a book in her hand. She has an air of exasperation; crosses the room swiftly, shuts the door, draws the curtains across the window, sits down at the table, and, elbows on table, fingers in ears, studies her books. A cheer from outside.* KATIE *jerks her chair closer to the table, bends over her book.*⁶⁵

In *Discipline and Punish*, Foucault discusses Jeremy Bentham's architectural design of the panopticon to exemplify how confinement, isolation, and the threat of surveillance can cause a person to curtail and shape their own behaviour.⁶⁶ Behind closed curtains and doors, with the gay furnishings gone and the architectural plans of Act Two substituted for religious tracts, Katie now studies saints' lives under the panoptic gaze of religious iconography. In a space materially and symbolically altered by her own hand, Katie now willingly undertakes the work that she once accused Stanislaus of attempting—taking herself to pieces so as to remake her heart, mind, and body into an assembly of parts that will be acceptable to her husband. Attempting to physically and mentally reject the outside world, Katie tells Amelia, 'I must be steady [...] I must

---

62 Stanislaus's sexual rejection of Katie is suggested in Katie's line 'Three months since we stood at the altar, and three times you drew from me', ibid., p. 75.
63 Ibid., p. 75.
64 Foucault, *Discipline and Punish*, loc. 2544.
65 Deevy, 'Katie Roche', pp. 87–88.
66 Foucault, *Discipline and Punish*.

read sensible books'.[67] This performance of behaving in a 'steady' way, holding firm in her performance of 'a good wife', is Katie's attempt to embody an idealised abstraction of womanhood and perform the role of domesticated Irish woman by secluding herself within the confines of the home where she will personify and embody ideals of piety, self-abnegation, and self-regulation.

Her performance falters when the confines of her world are penetrated. During what Eoin O'Sullivan and Ian O'Donnell might describe as Katie's non-institutional 'coercive confinement', Katie has attempted to reshape her mind, appearance, and behaviour.[68] However, music, dancing, and sexual expression intrude despite her attempts to physically barricade the house and her mind. The silences, repetitions, and bursts of laughter in Katie's dialogue, and the stage directions describing her body, reveal her attempts to reconstruct and discipline herself as strained and fragile. Realising that Stanislaus's return to the cottage will coincide with Michael and Jo coming to the house to borrow a bench for the post-regatta dance, Katie howls:

> KATIE: (*Gives a sudden laugh.*) What possessed him? Today of all days!... And the regatta on...and the boys...the boys will be coming up for the bench... Oh, Amelia...and he might— (*Cannot finish—with laughter.*)
>
> AMELIA: My dear! What's wrong?
>
> KATIE: Wrong? Is it? (*Controlled, defensive. Stands up.*) I must have his room ready—like a good wife. (*Goes to the door—laughs again, this time more happily.*) They'll be coming like...like last year. (*Goes.*)[69]

Early in Act One, Katie wanted to attend Riley's dance hall but was refused permission. In Act Three, Michael asks Katie, 'Will you come to the dance with me tonight?'[70] and this time Katie makes her own refusal. However, sensing a lapse in her resolve, Michael '*whirls her off the ladder*

---

67   Deevy, 'Katie Roche', p. 88.
68   Eoin O'Sullivan and Ian O'Donnell (eds), *Coercive Confinement in Ireland: Patients, Prisoners, and Penitents* (Manchester: Manchester University Press, 2012), p. xi.
69   Deevy, 'Katie Roche', pp. 88–89.
70   Ibid., p. 92.

and puts her down near the door. They laugh'.[71] The couple's brief dance anticipates the dance of the five Mundy sisters in Brian Friel's *Dancing at Lughnasa*, a dance that Kiberd argues 'expresses a longing for a world that passed [the sisters] by'.[72] In *Katie Roche*, the dance between Katie and Michael represents a world which has not yet passed but, as represented by the winning regatta team's journey by the Gregg cottage, is in the process of passing Katie and other Irish women by. The outside world—in the form of Michael, Jo, the regatta, dancing, and music—intrudes into the Gregg cottage, and Katie's performance of the domesticated Irish woman shatters, exploded by laughter that reveals the strain of that performance and her genuine joy in the memory of previous years' dancing. Murphy suggests that Katie 'vacillates between active rejection of, and active affiliation to, the prescribed role of wife in concordance with hegemonic gender ideology'.[73] In Act Three, this vacillation occurs with mercurial speed and, as a result, Katie's apparent transformation is highlighted for what it is—a performance. The momentary transformation of the Gregg living-room into a dance hall provokes more laughter, representing yet another slip in Katie's performance of the domesticated Irish woman. The impact of Katie's thoughts of, sights of, and proximity to the world outside the Gregg cottage impacts on her performance of the 'good wife'—the domesticated Irish woman—causing it to falter. The implication is that Katie's place within the home, and her confinement within it, is integral to the construction and performance of the domesticated Irish woman.[74] It also suggests that something more than physical constraints contains Katie tightly and inescapably within the idealised construct of the domesticated Irish woman.

As in Act Two, the curtains cannot hide the intrusions of the outside world. In Act Three, Katie attempts to conceal Michael behind them but Stanislaus, seeing him 'slipping' away, makes as though to return to Dublin as Katie cries defensively: 'The world doesn't stop still around any one man!'[75] He leaves without another word and *'terrified [...] Katie*

---

71 Ibid., p. 94.
72 Brian Friel, *Dancing at Lughnasa* (London: Faber and Faber, 1990); Declan Kiberd, 'Dancing at Lughnasa', *The Irish Review* 27 (2001), 18–39 (p. 24).
73 Murphy, *Hegemony and Fantasy*, p. 185.
74 Deevy, 'Katie Roche', p. 88.
75 Ibid., p. 95.

stands motionless', riveted by fear, telling Amelia 'Something terrible is going to happen'.⁷⁶ The terrible thing is that Stanislaus decides to take Katie away from Ballycar. At first, he refuses to tell her where, stating baldly, 'You're leaving here!'⁷⁷ Only after she asks for the second time does Stanislaus reveal: 'You're coming to Dublin…with me'.⁷⁸ After failed appeals against his decision, during which Katie mourns the loss of the trees, changing seasons, and the river of Ballycar and, in a brief interlude of silence, the stage directions read that '*In the house something falls.*'⁷⁹ In this Chekhovian moment, when a sound effect reverberates through the world of the play like a death knell, Deevy materialises the isolation and emptiness of Katie's future. Like the silent 'knell' in *The King of Spain's Daughter*, signalling Annie's profound realisation that all avenues of life but marriage to Jim Harris are closed to her—so, too, does Katie realise in this moment that she must leave a life of small, but precious freedoms, and submit herself entirely to a life in which Stanislaus will control her.⁸⁰ Sara Ahmed argues that 'power operates through directionality and orientation', and Stanislaus's power over Katie manifests in his ability to send, direct, and orient her towards a place of his choosing.⁸¹ When Katie realises her leaving is forever, she pleads to stay, pleas which Anthony Roche recognises as contributing to an ending that 'resists the romantic allure of "away"'.⁸² Stanislaus's ability to take Katie away from Ballycar illustrates that patriarchal control in 1930s Ireland extended beyond the physical space of the home and that freedom, for women living in the Free State, could not be achieved simply by walking out a doorway. As the play closes there are no less than five references to the permanency of Katie's leaving—each amplifying a sense of loss. Devastated by the knowledge of her fate Katie, guided by Amelia, experiences another epiphany:

---

76 Ibid.
77 Ibid., p. 96.
78 Ibid.
79 Ibid., p. 100.
80 Teresa Deevy, 'The King of Spain's Daughter', in *Teresa Deevy Reclaimed*, II, 16–26 (p. 24).
81 Sara Ahmed, *Living a Feminist Life* (Durham, NC: Duke University Press Kindle edition, 2017), loc. 442.
82 Anthony Roche, 'Woman on the Threshold: J. M. Synge's *The Shadow of the Glen*, Teresa Deevy's *Katie Roche* and Marina Carr's *The Mai*', *Irish University Review*, 25.1 (1995), 143–162 (p. 157).

KATIE: Brave is it? (*Bitter.*) There's no grandeur in this! Taken away...my own fault. (*Covers her face with her hands.*)

AMELIA: ...If you're brave, you can make it grand. My dear, you must!

KATIE: (*Gazes at her face for a moment, then:*) I think you're right!... (*Pause.*) I'm a great beauty...after all my talk—crying now... (*Grows exultant.*) I *will* be brave!

(*They catch hands.*)

AMELIA: We both will!

KATIE: (*Gentle now and suddenly perceptive.*) I think *you* were, always... 'Tis a promise between us—whatever'll come, good or bad.

AMELIA: A promise, my dear.

KATIE: I was always looking for something great to do—sure now I have it.[83]

'If you're brave, you can make it grand', Amelia says. Gazing at her, Katie realises that women, like Amelia, have been brave all along, silently and stoically accepting their fate as women in a world of compromise and self-sacrifice. Katie realises that her great deed, the 'something terrible' that she knew was coming, is a living death—a life with Stanislaus in which she must not simply *perform* the role of 'good wife', but a life in which she must actually relinquish her autonomy—her inward glow—and accept her transformation into a domesticated Irish woman.[84] Realising that she can only accept the subservient role assigned to her, Katie concedes to leave Ballycar.[85] That this is a metaphorical death is revealed in Katie's anguished cry: 'And I'll never be here in my life again! (*Covers her face with her hands and sobs*)'.[86] This anguish is not a moment of hysteria, or overstatement, but Katie's recognition that the

---

83 Deevy, 'Katie Roche', p. 102.
84 Ibid., p. 95, p. 88.
85 Ibid.
86 Ibid., p. 101.

very limited freedoms and possibilities open to her, as a young and unmarried woman, have now ended. Adding to the complexity of this moment, Deevy then asks the performer playing Katie to convey to the audience Katie's ability to imaginatively transform her surrender from one that suggests abjection and docility into 'something great'.[87] In the moment of her resolution that she *'will* be brave' she *'Grows exultant'*—a stage direction that recalls the disturbing joy Annie Kinsella expresses when she agrees to marry Jim Harris in *The King of Spain's Daughter*.[88]

Conclusion

In *Katie Roche*, Deevy exposes the domesticated Irish woman as a construct and highlights the disparity between that construct and the lives, experiences, behaviours, and appearances of her women characters and—by extension—of real Irish women. Deevy exposes how the physical and ideological containment of women in Ireland shaped women's behaviours, speech, bodies, and attitudes to fit with an impossible ideal of womanhood—the construct herein defined as the domesticated Irish woman. Employing space, physicality, and language, Deevy, in *Katie Roche*, dramatises the process whereby a young woman, full of life, vitality, and passion, is shaped as, and reduced to, a domesticated Irish woman. Throughout *Katie Roche*, Deevy shows that this shaping process is one that women sometimes resisted, sometimes performed, and to which many eventually submitted because of a lack of alternative options. Leeney asserts that in theatre, 'Woman has been the icon, and not the icon-maker. When she becomes the creator of representations, then the woman playwright must negotiate the representational inheritance in relation to which she inevitably works'.[89] We argue that, in *Katie Roche*, Deevy engages with such a negotiation of her representational inheritance creating a dramatic text that exposes and critiques that inheritance, as well as the ideologies and movements underpinning and propagating it. Through her curation of language, space and moments of self-conscious performances of gender roles, silence, physicality, and laughter, Deevy

---

87   Ibid.
88   Ibid., p. 102, emphasis in the original; for a reading of Annie Kinsella's decision to marry Jim Harris in *The King of Spain's Daughter* as self-sacrificial, see Úna Kealy, 'Resisting Power and Direction: *The King of Spain's Daughter* by Teresa Deevy as a Feminist Call to Action', *Estudios Irlandeses*, 15 (2020), 178–192.
89   Leeney, *Irish Women Playwrights*, p. 193.

subtly disrupts the realistic style of theatre that was also her inheritance as an Abbey playwright and exposes the deadening consequences of imposing idealised constructions of gender onto Irish women.

Bibliography

Adelman, Juliana, 'Food in Ireland Since 1740', in *The Cambridge Social History of Modern Ireland*, ed. by Eugenio F. Biagini and Mary E. Daly (Cambridge: Cambridge University Press, 2017), pp. 233–243, https://doi.org/10.1017/9781316155271.016

Ahmed, Sara, *Living a Feminist Life* (Durham, NC: Duke University Press Kindle edition, 2017), https://doi.org/10.1215/9780822373377

Beaumont, Caitriona, 'Women, Citizenship and Catholicism in the Irish Free State, 1922–1948', *Women's History Review*, 6.4 (1997), 563–585, https://doi.org/10.1080/09612029700200154

Beauvoir, Simone de, *The Second Sex*, trans. by Constance Borde and Sheila Malovany-Chevallier with an introduction by Sheila Robotham (London: Vintage Classics Kindle edition, 2015)

Bielenberg, Andy, and John O'Hagan, 'Consumption and Living Conditions, 1750–2016', in *The Cambridge Social History of Modern Ireland*, ed. by Eugenio F. Biagini and Mary E. Daly (Cambridge: Cambridge University Press, 2017), pp. 195–211, https://doi.org/10.1017/9781316155271.014

Butler, Judith, *Gender Trouble: Feminism and the Subversion of Identity*, 2nd edn (Abingdon: Routledge, 1990)

Butler, Judith, 'Performative Acts and Gender Constitution: An Essay in Phenomenology and Feminist Theory', *Theatre Journal*, 40.4 (1988), 519–531

Butler, Mary, 'Irishwomen and the Home Language (Continued)', *All Ireland Review*, 1.51 (1900), 4–5

Cannon-Harris, Susan, *Gender and Modern Irish Drama* (Indiana, IN: Indiana University Press, 2002)

Cooney, John, *John Charles McQuaid: Ruler of Catholic Ireland* (Dublin: Paperview in association with the *Irish Independent*, 2006)

Cox, Catherine, 'Health and Welfare, 1750–2000', in *The Cambridge Social History of Modern Ireland*, ed. by Eugenio F. Biagini and Mary E. Daly (Cambridge: Cambridge University Press, 2017), pp. 261–281, https://doi.org/10.1017/9781316155271.018

Daly, Mary E., 'The Irish Free State and the Great Depression of the 1930s: The Interaction of the Global and the Local', *Irish Economic and Social History*, 38 (2011), 19–36

Dean, Tanya, 'Staging Hibernia: Female Allegories of Ireland in *Cathleen Ni Houlihan* and *Dawn*', *Theatre History Studies*, 33.1 (2014), 71–82, https://doi.org/10.1353/ths.2014.0018

Deevy, Teresa, 'Katie Roche', in *Teresa Deevy Reclaimed*, I, ed. by Jonathan Bank, John P. Harrington, and Christopher Morash (New York: The Mint Theater, 2011), pp. 57–102

Delay, Cara, *Irish Women and the Creation of Modern Catholicism, 1850–1950* (Manchester: Manchester University Press, 2018)

Diamond, Elin, *Unmaking Mimesis: Essays on Feminism and Theatre* (Abingdon: Routledge, 1997)

Earner-Byrne, Lindsey, 'The Boat to England: An Analysis of the Offical Reactions to the Emigration of Single Expectant Irishwomen to Britain, 1922–1972', *Irish Economic and Social History*, 30 (2003), 52–70, https://doi.org/10.1177/033248930303000103

Friel, Brian, *Dancing at Lughnasa* (London: Faber and Faber, 1990)

Foucault, Michel, *Discipline and Punish: The Birth of the Prison* (London: Penguin Random House Kindle edition, 2020)

Government of Ireland, *Constitution of Ireland*, January 2020, https://www.irishstatutebook.ie/eli/cons/en/html

Hill, Shonagh, *Women and Embodied Mythmaking in Irish Theatre* (Cambridge: Cambridge University Press, 2019), https://doi.org/10.1017/9781108756327

Hoffman, Joan, '"She Loves with Love That Cannot Tire": The Image of the Angel in the House across Cultures and across Time', *Pacific Coast Philology*, 42.2 (2007), 264–271

Hogan, Gerard, *The Origins of the Irish Constitution: 1928–1941* (Dublin: Royal Irish Academy, 2012)

Hull, Eleanor, *The Cuchullin Saga in Irish Literature* (London: David Knutt, 1898), https://archive.org/details/cu31924026824940

Jagoe, Catherine, *Ambiguous Angels: Gender in the Novels of Galdós* (Los Angeles, CA: University of California Press, 1994)

Kealy, Úna, 'Resisting Power and Direction: *The King of Spain's Daughter* by Teresa Deevy as a Feminist Call to Action', *Estudios Irlandeses*, 15 (2020), 178–192, https://doi.org/10.24162/EI2020-9406

Kiberd, Declan, 'Dancing at Lughnasa', *The Irish Review*, 27 (2001), 18–39, https://doi.org/10.2307/29736015

Kiberd, Declan, *Inventing Ireland: The Literature of the Modern Nation* (London: Vintage Books, 1996)

Libreria Editrice Vaticana, 'Rerum Novarum: Encyclical of Pope Leo XIII on Capital and Labor' (1891), http://www.vatican.va/content/leo-xiii/en/encyclicals/documents/hf_l-xiii_enc_15051891_rerum-novarum.html

Lakoff, Robin, 'Language and Woman's Place', *Language in Society*, 2 (1973), 45–80

Leeney, Cathy, *Irish Women Playwrights 1900–1939: Gender and Violence on Stage* (New York: Peter Lang, 2010), https://doi.org/10.3726/978-1-4539-0373-5

Leeney, Cathy, 'Themes of Ritual and Myth in Three Plays by Teresa Deevy', *Irish University Review*, 25 (1995), 88–166

Luddy, Maria, *Hanna Sheehy Skeffington* (Dundalk: Dundalgan Press, 1995)

Luddy, Maria, 'Sex and the Single Girl in 1920s and 1930s Ireland', *The Irish Review*, 35 (2007), 79–91

Luddy, Maria, 'A "Sinister and Retrogressive" Proposal: Irish Women's Opposition to the 1937 Draft Constitution', *Transactions of the Royal Historical Society*, 15 (2005), 175–195, https://doi.org/10.1017/S0080440105000307

Molidor, Jennifer, 'Dying for Ireland: Violence, Silence, and Sacrifice in Dorothy Macardle's *Earth-Bound: Nine Stories of Ireland* (1924)', *New Hibernia Review*, 12.4 (2008) 43–61

Mulally, Siobhán, 'Presentation by Prof. Siobhan Mullally, UCC', in *Second Report of the Convention on the Constitution*, May 2013, pp. 14–18, https://citizensassembly.ie/wp-content/uploads/Role-of-Women-Woemn-in-Politics.pdf

Murphy, Paul, *Hegemony and Fantasy in Irish Drama, 1899–1949* (Houndsmills: Palgrave Macmillan, 2008), https://doi.org/10.1057/9780230583856

Murphy, Paul, '"That a Black Twisty Divil Could Be Hiding under Such Comeliness": Woman versus *woman* in Early Twentieth-Century Irish Theatre', *Theatre Journal*, 60.2 (2008), 201–216

O'Brien, Susan, 'The Blessed Virgin Mary', in *The Oxford History of British and Irish Catholicism, Volume IV: Building Identity, 1830–1913*, ed. by Carmen M. Mangion and Susan O'Brien (Oxford: Oxford University Press, 2023), pp. 154–172, https://doi.org/10.1093/oso/9780198848196.003.0009

O'Sullivan, Eoin, and Ian O'Donnell (eds), *Coercive Confinement in Ireland: Patients, Prisoners, and Penitents* (Manchester: Manchester University Press, 2012)

Owens, Rosemary Cullen, *A Social History of Women in Ireland 1870–1970* (Dublin: Gill and Macmillan, 2014)

Roche, Anthony, 'Woman on the Threshold: J.M. Synge's *The Shadow of the Glen*, Teresa Deevy's *Katie Roche*, and Marina Carr's *The Mai*', *Irish University Review*, 25.1 (1995), 143–162

Ryan, Louise, 'Nationalism and Feminism: The Complex Relationship between the Suffragist and Independence Movements in Ireland', in *Women and the Irish Revolution: Feminism, Activism, Violence*, ed. by Linda Connolly (Kildare: Irish Academic Press, 2020), pp. 36–55

Sihra, Melissa, 'Introduction: Figures at the Window', in *Women in Irish Drama: A Century of Authorship and Representation*, ed. by Melissa Sihra (Hampshire and New York: Palgrave, 2007), pp. 1–22, https://doi.org/10.1057/9780230801455

Valente, Joseph, 'Lost (and Found) in Translation: The Masculinity of O'Grady's Cuculain', in *Standish O'Grady's Cuculain: A Critical Edition*, ed. by Gregory Castle and Patrick Bixby (New York: Syracuse University, 2016), pp. 210–225

Valiulis, Maryann G., 'Virtuous Mothers and Dutiful Wives: The Politics of Sexuality in the Irish Free State', in *Gender and Power in Irish History*, ed. by Maryann G. Valiulis (Dublin: Irish Academic Press, 2008), pp. 100–114

Young, Iris Marion, *On Female Body Experience: 'Throwing Like a Girl' and Other Essays* (Oxford: Oxford University Press, 2005), https://doi.org/10.1093/0195161920.001.0001

10. The Liminal Space of Widowhood in Teresa Deevy's *Wife to James Whelan* (1937)

Christa de Brún

As long as there has been a distinct Irish literature, it has been closely bound to Irish society, culture, and family relationships. Indeed, as Anne Enright observes, the family '[...] is the fundamental (perhaps the only) unit of Irish culture, and one which functions beyond our choosing'.[1] In Ireland, the notion of family has been traditionally located within the institution of marriage, which has been devised as the ultimate and highest purpose of heteronormative love relationships. This dominant narrative of Irish nationhood thus not only places the welfare of the nation in its own definition of family, but it also specifies the roles that women must play within such institutions. As Christopher Morash notes, women in Irish society in the early twentieth century were typically confined to the domestic sphere, and in Irish culture defined in relation to the other; mother, wife, sister, and daughter, and widows occupied the interstices of this culture.[2] This chapter focuses on widowhood and the cultural history of widowhood in Ireland particularly as it is explored in Deevy's *Wife to James Whelan*.[3] Rejected by Ernest Blythe, managing director of the Abbey Theatre, in 1942, the play explores the strictures and confines of conventional society. Deevy excels in delineating the lives of women who have historically been confined to the domestic sphere and the private domain, and are thus largely hidden from public

---

1   Anne Enright, 'The Irish Short Story', *The Guardian*, 6 November 2010, p. 14.
2   Christopher Morash, 'Teresa Deevy: Between the Lines', in *Teresa Deevy Reclaimed*, 2 vols, ed. by Jonathan Bank, John P. Harrington, and Christopher Morash (New York: Mint Theater, 2011 and 2017), I, ix.
3   Teresa Deevy, 'Wife to James Whelan', in *Teresa Deevy Reclaimed*, I.

knowledge. This chapter claims a space for the narratives of widowhood in the public sphere as an integral part of the social fabric of Irish culture and creates a space for marginalised personal perspectives to inhabit and inform our cultural landscape.

In *Wife to James Whelan*, James Whelan, an ambitious, young man, leaves Nan Bowers and the town of Kilbeggan for a job in Dublin. James promises to return with better prospects, while Nan is left to contemplate their uncertain future. Act Two is set seven years later and James has returned to Kilbeggan as a successful businessman and 'sole proprietor' of The Silver Wings Motor Service.[4] Nan McClinsey is now a widow with a son and seeks work from James. At first obstinate, James eventually offers her a job performing administrative tasks but, after he finds her stealing money, he responds ruthlessly by having her sent to jail where she is sentenced to serve six weeks with hard labour. Set six months later, Act Three reveals unresolved tensions between James and Nan but, prompted by their mutual friend Kate, James re-employs Nan but this time 'to scrub the floor [...] to tend the fire and clean the grate'.[5] However, he reinstates her to her former administrative work when she reveals that Bill McGafferty had attempted to blackmail Nan by falsely accusing her of theft.[6] James's success contrasts with his conflicted emotional state, and his relationships with Nora Keane and Kate Moran add further complexity, highlighting the conflict between ambition and happiness. Deevy masterfully weaves complex characters and themes, creating a narrative that resonates with the struggles of individual and social aspirations in an atmosphere of stultifying conformity.

Although there has been significant scholarship on the portrayal of women in Deevy's plays, the marginal identity of widowhood has received little critical attention. Indeed, the cultural history of widowhood in Ireland has been largely hidden from public knowledge, as widowhood pushes women into a liminal space both physically and socially. Furthermore, widowhood has, historically, been perceived as a disruption of social order and a potential threat to moral order in what Caoilfhionn Ní Bheacháin calls 'stagnant rural communities that

---

4   Ibid., p. 125.
5   Ibid., p. 143.
6   Ibid.

stifle the vitality and potential of young Irish women'.⁷ A widow is, by definition, a liminal creature; she is not sexually intact, she is unattached to any male, her very unattachment a cause for anxiety, highlighting the danger inherent in existing in such a space. Deevy frequently explores the lives of women who exist in this liminal space, for example Nan Bowers in *Wife to James Whelan* and the eponymous Katie Roche. The situation of widowhood offers Deevy a unique opportunity to explore the social fabric into which such characters are woven, a society that defines and confines women and that struggles to contain the rupture to identity and ideology that widowhood presents.

Identities are created and performed in social and cultural contexts, characterised by historical and contemporary relations of power and control that can affect interpretations and psychological states. The dominant narrative, which upholds the centrality of the family unit and the role of women within that unit, may be ruptured by a transition which alters gendered expectations within a patriarchal society, and widowhood occupies such a space in Irish literature. Indeed, a review in the *Irish Times* noted 'All through the play, one seems to see an almost imperceptible change in the ordinary values of life'.⁸ This space may be defined as a liminal space, which Toni Morrisson refers to as a place 'where we are betwixt and between the familiar and the completely unknown'.⁹ Describing the grief of widowhood as such a space is to suggest that the boundaries that previously provided a secure understanding of the world and sense of self have, following bereavement, become more permeable. One's sense of being in the world is disorientated in the event of loss. The experience of grief has the potential to destabilise the world one lives in and shatter the meanings people use to hold up their world. Widowhood constitutes a liminal space necessitating the structuring of a new identity. As Harriet Shortt observes it can also be 'an anxious time where, for example, known norms, behaviours and identities are suspended thus giving way to uncertainty'.¹⁰ Spaces of

---

7   Caoilfhionn Ní Bheacháin, 'Sexuality, Marriage and Women's Life Narratives in Teresa Deevy's *A Disciple* (1931), *The King of Spain's Daughter* (1935) and *Katie Roche* (1936)', *Estudios Irlandeses*, 7 (2012), 79–91 (p. 80).
8   'Miss Deevy's New Play', *Irish Times*, 17 March 1936, p. 5.
9   Toni Morrisson, *Unspeakable Things Unspoken: The Afro-American Presence in American Literature* (Ann Arbor, MI: University of Michigan Press, 1988), p. 78.
10 Harriet Shortt, 'Liminality, Space and the Importance of Transitory Dwellings at

liminality may be perceived as a threat to conservative society because it can provide limitless opportunity to forge new identities and thus allow for creativity and subversive acts due to the eradication of the normal structures that tend to inhibit or obstruct behaviour. It is this sense of unstructure that destabilises and threatens the socially constructed narrative of widowhood.

A key aspect of widowhood, then, is the loss of a stable and fixed idea of the self. Once the protection of a husband no longer exists, a woman's positionality is one of submission or subversion. The positionality of a widow thus hinges on an inverted binary; either she is perceived as helpless, like the widow represented in the *Irish National Magazine*, described as 'timid in the consciousness of unprotected helplessness', or she is positioned as an unattached woman with sexual experience but without a male guardian, in which case she is perceived as a threat.[11] Widowhood thus operates as a space wherein dominant ideologies can be renegotiated in terms of emergent ideologies to create a new ideological space. However, as Jonathan Miller points out, such liminal spaces are contested spaces because the dominant cultural modes of identification never give easily to emergent ideas that threaten to unseat those historically granted power and control over the dissemination of identity.[12] Widowhood, thus, can be defined as a liminal space characterised by grief, loss, and unknowing.

Arnold van Gennep first outlined the term liminality in his seminal text *Rites of Passage* and claimed that all passages through the cycle of life shared a three-fold sequential structure: separation, liminality, and aggregation. Separation refers to leaving the familiar behind, liminality refers to a time of testing, learning, and growth, and aggregation to a reintegration.[13] Victor Turner consolidated van Gennep's work defining liminal as 'a state betwixt and between the positions assigned and arrayed by law, custom, convention, and ceremony', but introduced the concept of threshold people who 'elude or slip through the network of classifications that normally locate states and positions in cultural

---

    Work', *Human Relations*, 68.4 (2015), 633–658 (p. 637).
11   Thomas Le Messurier, 'The Widow', *The Irish National Magazine*, 1 (1846), p. 12.
12   Jonathan Miller, *Subsequent Performances* (London: Faber and Faber, 1986), p. 152.
13   Arnold van Gennep, *Rites of Passage* (London: Routledge, 1909), p. 26.

space'.¹⁴ This concept of threshold people illustrates the ambiguity of the unique situation of widows in Irish society. As a liminal figure, the widow is outside the confines of culture and outside the boundaries of the socially and politically dictated space of womanhood. Most significantly, the widow never reaches a post-liminal stage because she is a figure perpetually defined by her past—by what she once was but has ceased to be.

According to Turner, all liminality must eventually dissolve, for it is a state of great intensity that cannot exist very long without some sort of structure to stabilise it. However, *Wife to James Whelan* provides a sobering example of a widow trapped in a form of permanent liminality far beyond what was initially defined as a temporal state.¹⁵ Turner acknowledges that 'liminality becomes a permanent condition when any of the phases in this sequence becomes frozen, as if a film stopped at a particular frame' and the narrative of widowhood exists within a liminal phase that never actualises into a post-liminal state.¹⁶ Turner further refers to liminal situations as positive periods of renewal. However, liminal situations can also be periods of existential angst and despair. Van Gennep describes this experience as a boundless, marginalised one often accompanied by isolation and the suspension of social status.¹⁷ In such situations, people often live outside their normal environment where they come to feel nameless, spatio-temporally dislocated, and socially unstructured.¹⁸ A lengthy period in this stage can become dangerous resulting in widows remaining permanently marginalised within society at best and considered superfluous to society at worst.

Wife to James Whelan offers an interior view of the loss, grief, and crisis suffered by the widow, Nan Bowers. The loss of a husband signifies not only the loss of a spouse, but the woman's loss of her identity; she is a woman who was, but is now no longer, a wife. Colm Tóibín, reflecting on his reading of Mary Lavin's stories of widowhood, observes:

---

14 Richard Rohr, *Falling Upward: Spirituality for the Two Halves of Life* (San Francisco CA: Jossey-Bass, 2011), p. 34.
15 Victor Turner, *The Ritual Process: Structure and Anti-Structure* (Ithaca, NY: Cornell University Press, 1969), p. 51.
16 Arpad Szakolczai, *Permanent Liminality and Modernity: Analysing the Sacrificial Carnival through Novels* (New York: Routledge, 2017), p. 13.
17 van Gennep, *Rites of Passage*, p. 114.
18 *Breaking Boundaries: Varieties of Liminality*, ed. by Agnes Horvath, Bjørn Thomassen, and Harald Wydra (New York: Oxford Press, 2015), p. 128.

But the ones that dealt with the life of a widow were almost too close to the space between how we lived then in our house and what was unmentionable—the business of silence around grief, the life of a woman alone, the palpable absence of a man, a husband, a father, our father, my father, the idea of conversation as a way of concealing loss rather than revealing anything, least of all feeling.[19]

In *Wife to James Whelan*, Deevy similarly dramatises the silence surrounding these issues and how they were contained and restrained by stifling norms. Hers is, as Úna Kealy suggests, a 'theatre of subtext' rather than affirmation.[20] Deevy artfully sketches the story of Nan's emergent recognition of the liminal state she now occupies in the aftermath of her husband's death. The narrative conveys Nan's struggle to regain the identity 'she lost willingly in marriage, but lost doubly and unwillingly in widowhood'.[21]

Widowhood, essentially, constitutes a social death and Uma Chakravarti outlines two modes of representing the social death of the widow—ideological and material. The first is ideological—in the sense that what was once held as precious by the husband is now turned into a potential threat to society. The widow's social death stems from her alienation from reproduction and sexuality following the loss of her husband, and her exclusion from a functional family dynamic in the prevailing social context with her only hope of reintegration being remarriage.[22] According to Chakravarti, the second mode of representing the social death of the widow is material: the figure of Nan Bowers represents the economic vulnerability of women who exist outside the nuclear family unit of two parents and their children. The character of Nan Bowers also exposes the lack of material supports by the State for widowed women. Although widowhood is a time of potential autonomy for women this autonomy is curtailed by the omnipresent threat of poverty exacerbated by legal and economic

---

19 Colm Tóibín, 'Unmoored by Grief', *The Independent*, 3 November 2014.
20 Úna Kealy, 'Teresa Deevy: A Quiet Subversive', in *Abbey Theatre Research Pack: Teresa Deevy: Katie Roche*, researched and compiled by Marie Kelly, School of Music and Theatre, University College Cork (Dublin: The Abbey Theatre, 2017), pp. 8–13 (p. 9).
21 Mary Gordon, 'Mary Lavin and Writing Women', *American Journal of Irish Studies*, 10 (2013), 114–129 (p. 117).
22 Uma Chakravarti, 'Gender and Caste: Ideological and Material Structure of Widowhood', *Economic and Political Weekly*, 30 (1995), 95–113.

practice disadvantaging widows. [23]

Charkravarti refers to 'the widow's institutionalised marginality, a liminal state between being physically alive and socially dead'.[24] When Nan Bowers is first introduced, she is a carefree young woman whose independence is viewed with disapproval by her neighbours in Kilbeggan. In particular, her refusal to grieve for Whelan when he moves to Dublin incites hostility:

NAN: It won't break my heart to see him go.

BILL: I think she'll console herself,—won't you, Nan,— with someone else.[25]

After her husband's death, Nan is, at first, an object of pity. However, the compassion with which Nan is treated by her neighbours inspires suspicion, it designates what Kundera refers to as 'an inferior, second-rate sentiment' that connotes a certain condescension towards the sufferer.[26] Nan attempts to move on from the role of widow and redefine herself as a woman, but her refusal to consider marrying again in Act Two disrupts the conservative morality of Deevy's play: 'I'd be long sorry. Once married is enough for me'.[27] Nan's lack of participation in the circulation of power further marginalises her socially, creating what Cathy Leeney refers to as 'a dramaturgy of alienation, of occluded realities [...] dealing with issues that were effectively sidelined in the social history of the nation too'.[28] Nan's greatest sin, it seems, is her 'ungovernable longing for a more expansive sense of selfhood'.[29]

There is a poignancy to Nan's social and material transformation in the play from the vibrant woman with 'bright hair, clear face,

---

23 John Feeney, 'Poverty in Ireland—Widows', *Magill*, 1 November 1969, https://magill.ie/archive/poverty-ireland-widows
24 Chakravarti, 'Gender and Caste', p. 95.
25 Deevy, 'Wife to James Whelan', p. 110.
26 Milan Kundera, *The Unbearable Lightness of Being* (New York: Harper, 1984), p. 51.
27 Deevy, 'Wife to James Whelan', p. 129.
28 Cathy Leeney, 'Teresa Deevy (1894–1963): Exile and Silence', in *Irish Women Playwrights 1900–1939: Gender and Violence on Stage* (New York: Peter Lang, 2010), pp. 161–193 (p. 163).
29 *Selected Plays of Irish Playwright Teresa Deevy, 1894–1963*, ed. by Eibhear Walshe (Lewiston, NY: Edwin Mellen Press, 2003), p. 54.

carefree bearing' of Act One to the quiet woman of Act Two with 'a dark shawl covering her head and shoulders', the safeguard of female virtue, reflecting the narrow confinement of socially marginalised women's lives.[30] Nan is socially restricted by her widowed status, her lack of attachment is perceived as a threat and the only possibility of reintegration offered to her is remarriage. She is also materially restricted by her widowed status, forced into the humiliation of asking James Whelan, his attitude 'contemptuous', for any work available: 'I'd do anything, no matter what—sweeping or scrubbing'.[31] Nan, widowed only two years after she married, is still a young woman. Yet, the stage directions in Act Two note that she speaks 'quietly' to James and that '[h]er manner throughout is that of one past feeling very much—one whose life is over.'[32]

In *Wife to James Whelan*, Nan is obliged by circumstance to take up the mantle of widowhood and remake the rules for herself in light of her new identity. The inclusion of widowhood in *Wife to James Whelan* as part of Nan's narrative may be read as a concerted attempt by Deevy to dismantle theories of the family as they relate to specific Irish contexts. The historical moment that Deevy inhabited was a time when Article 41.2.1 of the Constitution (1937) clearly outlined women's place in the home:

> In particular, the State recognises that by her life within the home, woman gives to the State a support without which the common good cannot be achieved.[33]

As Morash notes, Deevy's critical stance is in sharp contrast to the official view of the role of women in the 1937 Constitution—a constitution that retains its original reductionist language and philosophy.[34] Article 41.2.2 further asserts that woman shall not be obliged to work outside the family home:

> The State shall, therefore, endeavour to ensure that mothers shall not be obliged by economic necessity to engage in labour to the neglect of their duties in the home.[35]

---

30 Deevy, 'Wife to James Whelan', p. 110 and p. 125.
31 Ibid., p. 128 and p. 129.
32 Ibid., p. 129.
33 Government of Ireland, *Constitution of Ireland*, January 2020, (Article 41.2.1).
34 Morash, 'Teresa Deevy: Between the Lines'.
35 Government of Ireland, *Constitution of Ireland* (Article 41.2.2).

Such a statement undermines the lived experience and social reality of widowed women with young children in early twentieth-century Ireland, women like Nan who worked out of economic necessity with little support from the State. In *Wife to James Whelan*, Deevy foregrounds the plight of a young widow whose circumstances 'revealed the emptiness of official rhetoric about mothers not being forced to work outside the home'.[36] John Feeney highlights the poverty of widows in the Irish state even after the introduction of the Widows' and Orphans' Pension Act in 1935:

> So it is then that young widows with children form a particularly salient example of hardship [...] the problem exists because of a political indifference that allows the machinery of assistance to clank past them [...]. The acute, if arbitrary and inconsistent standards used by officers to assess whether a person is justified in seeking assistance means that there are still considerable amounts of need still untouched by the distributive mechanics of welfare.[37]

Referring to some of the cases he encountered in his research, Feeney observed:

> The brutality of this system to old people and to mothers with young children is obvious. Because of its marginal political consequences however, this has not been electorally pursued with the vigour of more politically [sic] profitable issues. No clothes, no shoes, no recreation [...]. It is really a very pathetic account of a grimly opposed and officially supported poverty.[38]

It is little wonder, given the punitive economic situation of a widowed woman in early twentieth-century Ireland, that Nan steals from James Whelan, a character symbolic of power and privilege, to feed her child and clothe herself when, as Kate observes, 'Sometimes she hadn't enough to eat'.[39] James's response, and insistence on Nan's arrest and sentence with hard labour despite her desperate circumstances, represents the patriarchal social structures of a society that resents and resists female autonomy, punishing those who challenge the limiting parameters of state and its systemic inequalities with confinement:

---

36 Caoilfhionn Ni Bheacháin, 'Teresa Deevy and the Secrets of the Green Suitcase', *Irish Times*, 3 April 2021, p. 5.
37 John Feeney, 'Poverty in Ireland'.
38 Ibid.
39 Deevy, 'Wife to James Whelan', p. 136.

JAMES: What term did you serve?

NAN: Six weeks was the sentence.

JAMES: H'm...six weeks...with hard labour, I think.

NAN: Yes, with hard labour. It was you saw to it that I got so hard a term. (*Quietly.*)

JAMES: And I did right.[40]

It seems James Whelan is right about one thing—the difference it makes to have power and money. In discussing the political power of women, the historian Merry E. Wiesner-Hanks suggested that a distinction should be made between 'power—the ability to shape political events—and authority—power which is formally recognized and legitimated', and women rarely had the latter.[41] In *Wife to James Whelan*, Deevy develops her thematic interest, previously outlined in *Katie Roche* in the way men gain and wield economic and, as a consequence, emotional and sexual control over women and explores the implications of what Anthony Roche terms 'inherited patriarchal structures' in her work.[42] If we consider the reference to the widow in *The Irish National Magazine* it is clear that widowhood in twentieth-century Ireland placed women in not only a liminal state, but a disempowered state, too:

> She is a widow, a poor old widow, and, oh! what a miserable struggle has she had with the world since the death of her husband, which happened many years ago. He was in a respectable way but left nothing behind him. While he lived all was well. They were comfortable—something more, though not affluent. But his death, which was sudden, brought a miserable change. That event at once rendered her nearly destitute.[43]

The widow of the story is a pitiful and pitied creature and representative of the economic and social instability that followed the transition to the liminal space of widowhood. As Mary Cullen observes, during the

---

40 Ibid., p. 143.
41 Merry E. Weisner-Hanks, *Gender in History* (Oxford: Blackwell Press, 2001), p. 246.
42 Teresa Deevy, 'Katie Roche', in *Teresa Deevy Reclaimed*, I, 57–102; Anthony Roche, 'Woman on the Threshold: J. M. Synge's *The Shadow of the Glen*, Teresa Deevy's *Katie Roche* and Marina Carr's *The Mai*', *Irish University Review*, 25.1 (1995), 143–162 (p. 155).
43 Le Messurier, 'The Widow', p. 12.

period 1830–1970 most Irish women who lived to late middle age or old age became widows and were vulnerable to poverty.[44] The 1835–1836 Poor Law Inquiry identified widows with young children as highly likely to be destitute because the remuneration for women's work would never support a family. Cullen suggests that the cause of widow's poverty lay in the lower earning power of women compared to men and women's economic dependence on men.[45] Likewise, in *Wife to James Whelan*, Deevy highlights the vulnerability of widowhood:

JAMES: I was sorry the old man left you nothing.

NAN: He hadn't anything to leave. The pension died with him, you know.

JAMES: Three years a widow, and now you have nothing.[46]

Although Nan maintains her dignity and economic freedom throughout the play, the portrayal of her financial precarity bears pitiful testament to the official discourse surrounding the introduction of the limited Widows' and Orphans' Pensions Act of 1935, which described widows as 'deserving and helpless people' and precedes the political attention to the ideology of widowhood in the 1960's with the Succession Act of 1965.[47] It is interesting to observe how sharply the public discourse shifts from pity to judgement to derision. The play provides a critical and unremitting portrait of the refusal by society to allow Nan to move beyond the liminal space of widowhood and redefine and financially herself in her own right. Of all the liminal characters in Irish literature, it is widows who move closest to the possibility of transition to a post-liminal state, but in reality, there is no aggregation, just annihilation in what Edna O'Brien termed 'a land of strange, throttled, sacrificial

---

44 Mary Cullen, 'Widows in Ireland 1830–1970', in *The Field Day Anthology of Irish Writing Volume V*, ed. by Angela Bourke et al. (Cork: Cork University Press, 2022), pp. 609–618.
45 Ibid., p. 611.
46 Deevy, 'Wife to James Whelan', p. 128.
47 Mary Daly, *The Spirit of Earnest Inquiry* (Dublin: Institute of Public Administration, 1997), p. 37. When Charles Haughey, as Minister for Justice in 1965, introduced the Succession Act, he made provision to prevent spouses disinheriting their widowed partners or leaving them with only right of residence in the family house. The term 'Legal Right Share' was introduced within the 1965 Succession Act which was the first piece of Irish legislation to financially protect widowed people.

women', stifled by repressive Catholic values and idealised notions of womanhood in a public sphere that demanded domesticity and met independence with disdain.[48]

Michael Seidel observes that an exile is 'someone who inhabits one place and remembers or projects the reality of another' and this exilic mind is evident in the character of Nan who must reconcile herself to the loss of the life she had imagined and accept the social and psychological reality of the life imposed upon her, unwillingly, by her widowed status.[49] Nan reflects, as she sits in James's office: 'I am like a stranger in this place, although it is but six years since I was married'.[50] *Wife to James Whelan* is a play which conveys the ineffable pain of grief at the death of a husband, and the determinedly willed effort required to go on living and relating in a life beyond loss. In the play, Deevy offers an exploration of grief and the complicated structures that contain this traumatic transition. Cultural, political, and religious shifts have invariably shifted attitudes towards the concept of widowhood, and the ideological structure of widowhood embedded in Irish culture has been challenged and have changed. Deevy's texts explore and question the ideologies that placed Irish women in the 1930s in liminal spheres and scrutinise the values and axioms of the culture in which this occurred. From Annie Kinsella in *The King of Spain's Daughter* to Ellie Irwin in *A Disciple* (*In Search of Valour*), Deevy challenges prevailing contemporaneous social and cultural narratives relating to women who did not conform to the '[...] orthodoxies of respectable womanhood in 1930s Ireland'.[51] In *Wife to James Whelan*, Deevy explores a private world of unarticulated grief, a liminal world of becoming and unbecoming that is complicated for widows as a result of unavoidable social marginalisation and economic precarity. Theatre is a cultural construct and Deevy employs theatrical form to rewrite the narrative of widowhood, challenging the dominant ideology that misrepresented widowed women. *Wife to James Whelan*

---

48 Edna O'Brien, *A Scandalous Woman and Other Stories* (New York: Harcourt Brace, 1974), p. 35.
49 Michael Seidel, *Exile and the Narrative Imagination* (New Haven, CT: Yale University Press, 1986), p. 14.
50 Deevy, 'Wife to James Whelan', p. 126.
51 Teresa Deevy, 'The King of Spain's Daughter', in *Teresa Deevy Reclaimed*, II, 17–26; Teresa Deevy, 'In Search of Valour', *Teresa Deevy Reclaimed*, II, 3–13; Cullen, 'Widows in Ireland', p. 609; Ní Bheacháin, 'Sexuality, Marriage and Women', p. 79.

disrupts conservative patriarchal values and cultural narratives and, as such, functions as a disruptive force breaking fictions to reveal harsh realities but also new possibilities for Irish society. In sharing these narratives of widowhood, Deevy simultaneously dismantles the social construction of widowhood and weaves neglected narratives into the fabric of Irish culture, thus positioning theatrical space as a powerful instrument for social and political change.

Bibliography

Bank, Jonathan, John P. Harrington, and Christopher Morash (eds), *Teresa Deevy Reclaimed*, 2 vols (New York: Mint Theater, 2011 and 2017)

Chakravarti, Uma, 'Gender and Caste: Ideological and Material Structure of Widowhood', *Economic and Political Weekly*, 30 (1995), 95–113

Cullen, Mary, 'Widows in Ireland 1830–1970', in *The Field Day Anthology of Irish Writing Volume V*, ed. by Angela Bourke et al. (Cork: Cork University Press, 2022), pp. 609–618, https://doi.org/10.2307/j.ctv1fkgbfc.20

Enright, Anne, 'The Irish Short Story', *The Guardian*, 6 November 2010, p. 14, https://www.theguardian.com/books/2010/nov/06/anne-enright-irish-short-story

Daly, Mary, *The Spirit of Earnest Inquiry* (Dublin: Institute of Public Administration, 1997)

Deevy, Teresa, *Selected Plays of Irish Playwright Teresa Deevy, 1894–1963*, ed. by Eibhear Walshe (Lewiston, NY: Edwin Mellen Press, 2003)

Feeney, John, 'Poverty in Ireland—Widows', *Magill*, 1 November 1969, https://magill.ie/archive/poverty-ireland-widows

Gennep, Arnold van, *Rites of Passage* (London: Routledge, 1909)

Gordon, Mary, 'Mary Lavin and Writing Women', *American Journal of Irish Studies*, 10 (2013), 114–129

Government of Ireland, *Constitution of Ireland*, January 2020, https://www.irishstatutebook.ie/eli/cons/en/html

Horvath, Agnes, Bjørn Thomassen, and Harald Wydra (eds), *Breaking Boundaries: Varieties of Liminality* (New York: Oxford Press, 2015)

Kealy, Úna, 'Teresa Deevy: A Quiet Subversive', in *Abbey Theatre Research Pack: Teresa Deevy: Katie Roche*, researched and compiled by Marie Kelly, School of Music and Theatre, University College Cork (Dublin: The Abbey Theatre, 2017), pp. 8–13, https://www.abbeytheatre.ie/wp-content/uploads/2017/10/KATIE-ROCHE_RESEARCH-PACK-2017.pdf

Kundera, Milan, *The Unbearable Lightness of Being* (New York: Harper, 1984)

Le Messurier, Thomas, 'The Widow', *The Irish National Magazine*, 1 (1846), p. 12

Leeny, Cathy, *Irish Women Playwrights 1900–1939: Gender and Violence on Stage* (New York: Peter Lang, 2010), https://doi.org/10.3726/978-1-4539-0373-5

Miller, Jonathan, *Subsequent Performances* (London: Faber and Faber, 1986)

'Miss Deevy's New Play', *Irish Times*, 17 March 1936, p. 5, https://doi.org/10.7486/DRI.5999vb24x

Morrisson, Toni, *Unspeakable Things Unspoken: The Afro-American Presence in American Literature* (Ann Arbor, MI: University of Michigan Press, 1988)

Ní Bheacháin, Caoilfhionn, 'Sexuality, Marriage and Women's Life Narratives in Teresa Deevy's *A Disciple* (1931), *The King of Spain's Daughter* (1935) and *Katie Roche* (1936)', *Estudios Irlandeses*, 7 (2012), 79–91 (p. 80), https://doi.org/10.24162/EI2012-1903

Ni Bheacháin, Caoilfhionn, 'Teresa Deevy and the Secrets of the Green Suitcase', *Irish Times*, 3 April 2021, p. 5, https://www.irishtimes.com/culture/stage/teresa-deevy-and-the-secrets-of-the-green-suitcase-1.4522873

O'Brien, Edna, *A Scandalous Woman and Other Stories* (New York: Harcourt Brace, 1974)

Roche, Anthony, 'Woman on the Threshold: J. M. Synge's *The Shadow of the Glen*, Teresa Deevy's *Katie Roche* and Marina Carr's *The Mai*', *Irish University Review*, 25.1 (1995), 143–162

Rohr, Richard, *Falling Upward: Spirituality for the Two Halves of Life* (San Francisco CA: Jossey-Bass, 2011)

Seidel, Michael, *Exile and the Narrative Imagination* (New Haven, CT: Yale University Press, 1986)

Shortt, Harriet, 'Liminality, Space and the Importance of Transitory Dwellings at Work', *Human Relations*, 68.4 (2015), 633–658 (p. 637), https://doi.org/10.1177/0018726714536938

Szakolczai, Arpad, *Permanent Liminality and Modernity: Analysing the Sacrificial Carnival through Novels* (New York: Routledge, 2017), https://doi.org/10.4324/9781315600055

Tóibín, Colm, 'Unmoored by Grief', *The Independent*, 3 November 2014, https://www.theguardian.com/books/2014/oct/02/colm-toibin-literature-of-grief

Turner, Victor, *The Ritual Process: Structure and Anti-Structure* (Ithaca, NY: Cornell University Press, 1969)

Weisner-Hanks, Merry E., *Gender in History* (Oxford: Blackwell Press, 2001)

PRODUCTIONS AND PRACTITIONERS

11. Teresa Deevy's *Katie Roche*: Art, Culture, and Performance

Cathy Leeney

Fig. 11.1 Ros Kavanagh, production image from *Katie Roche* (2017), directed by Caroline Byrne for the Abbey Theatre, Amharclann na Mainistreach, featuring Caoilfhionn Dunne as Katie Roche. © Ros Kavanagh. All rights reserved.

Katie Roche is featured in *Modern Ireland in 100 Artworks* as the artwork for 1936, the year in which it was first performed at the Abbey Theatre (effectively the national theatre).[1] Fintan O'Toole, co-editor of the book, comments on the choice to affirm that Teresa Deevy's play

---

1 Teresa Deevy, 'Katie Roche', in *Teresa Deevy Reclaimed*, 2 vols, ed. by Jonathan Bank, John P. Harrington, and Christopher Morash (New York: Mint Theater, 2011), I, 57–102.

'raises startlingly blunt questions about the role of women in Eamon de Valera's Ireland'.[2] Placing the work in this historical cultural context is an acknowledgement of its social and theatrical significance. On the understanding that the past is a different country, seeing *Katie Roche* through the lens of the 1930s risks confining the play to a twenty-first-century interpretation of what it was and what it meant at the time, thereby limiting the cultural meaning we assign to it today. Positioned in *Modern Ireland in 100 Artworks* amidst a series of novels, paintings, sculptures, plays, and the works of poets and architects, the play's and Deevy's place in Irish culture and the national theatrical canon are recognised, but a question is implicitly posed—is *Katie Roche*, almost ninety years later, likely to be seen as museum theatre—albeit fascinating in that it reveals Ireland's 1930s' attitudes to those born outside of wedlock, and the socially endorsed limitations projected on them and on their expectations, their disadvantage, and alienation? While *Modern Ireland in 100 Artworks* raises questions about the historicity of artworks, their pasts and presences now, it also invites the reader actively to consider how all art lives in the moment of encounter with a spectator, listener, or reader, and perhaps that works of theatre art live most necessarily and intensely in performance before an audience. In costumes and hair styles that recall old films of the period, does *Katie Roche* reveal to audiences characteristic values and mores of the 1930s, and the period's social chasm between the uneducated and the professional, the divided expectations and lives of men and women, and the social dissonance of a young woman's ambition for self-development? All of these aspects of the play point towards *Katie Roche* as a valuable artefact, reminding new generations that conditions of life are changeful, containing over time possibilities of both human advancement and recession. The record of revivals of the piece at the Abbey Theatre problematises this historical view to suggest that the play continues to present difficult truths and confusions, requiring, over many decades, renewed examination.[3]

---

2   Fintan O'Toole, '1936: *Katie Roche*', in *Modern Ireland in 100 Artworks*, ed. by Fintan O'Toole, Catherine Marshall, and Eibhear Walshe (Dublin: Royal Irish Academy and *Irish Times*, 2017), pp. 61–63.

3   In Ireland, *Katie Roche* was produced in 1936 (and toured to Britain in 1937), in 1949 (this production was revived in 1953 when the Abbey had taken up residence at the Queen's Theatre), in 1975, in 1994 (on the smaller Peacock stage) and, most recently (and this time on the main stage), in 2017.

This chapter explores Deevy's 1936 play to argue for its status as a text that sustains contemporary revival. Elements that work in favour of this are the play's complex and layered structure that brings together a number of theatre genres (realism, expressionism, and comedy), and places at its centre a characterisation that contains multitudes. Beginning with *Katie Roche* as a valuable record of the conditions under which young women in Ireland in the 1930s lived, and the constraints they often experienced, this chapter looks at aspects of two revival productions at the Abbey Theatre to contrast the play's first reception with later stagings of the text.[4]

Deevy's spotlighting of girls or young women at formative points in their lives is one of her major contributions to the twentieth-century Irish theatrical canon. She recreates (but does not reproduce) such figures in *In Search of Valour* (Ellie), *The King of Spain's Daughter* (Annie), *Katie Roche*, and in *Wife to James Whelan* (Nan), exposing defining moments of aspiration, self-doubt, risk, desire, stubborn resistance, disillusion, and survival—comings of age. In this regard alone, these roles comprise a counter to the more common male-centred narrative of maturation. It is not unusual for Ellie, Annie, Katie, or Nan to be unfemininely self-absorbed, determined, ambitious, or impulsive. These qualities, controversial in women in the 1930s, remain easily relatable for current audiences even in a post-#MeToo context.[5]

As to Katie herself, her 'mind is a very opal';[6] she is by turn ecstatic,

---

4   Fintan O'Toole was one of the first critics to acknowledge *Katie Roche*'s theatrical genre/stylistic assemblage. See Fintan O'Toole, 'Second Opinion: What Katie Doesn't Do', *Irish Times*, 26 April 1994, p. 10.

5   In 2007, in Alabama, Tarana Burke first coined the phrase, Me Too, for an activist group she founded to work with survivors of sexual violence. On 15 October 2017, actor Alyssa Milano asked her Twitter followers to reply 'me too' if they had 'been sexually harassed or assaulted' (@Alyssa_Milano). Using the hashtag #MeToo, survivors of sexual violence, harassment, and coercion shared their testimony on various social media platforms in solidarity with other survivors and victims of sexual violence and called out the perpetrators. Legal proceedings against, and resignations of, high-profile people in media and entertainment followed. See Emma Brockes, '#MeToo Founder Tarana Burke: "You Have to Use Your Privilege to Serve Other People"', *The Guardian*, 15 January 2018, https://www.theguardian.com/world/2018/jan/15/me-too-founder-tarana-burke-women-sexual-assault; Ashwini Tambe, 'Reckoning with the Silences of #MeToo', *Feminist Studies*, 44.1 (2018), 197–203.

6   Feste in William Shakespeare, *Twelfth Night, or What You Will*, ed. by Jonathan Bate and Eric Rasmussen (Hampshire: Macmillan, 2008), III. 4. 82.

ambitious, powerless, abject, stubbornly a force of imbalance and unease. In 1936, Katie appeared to some as being beyond comprehension; Joseph Holloway, architect, inveterate theatre goer, and diarist wrote that she was 'the strangest character I ever saw on the stage'.[7] Several newspaper reviews express puzzlement at the character and the play too. The *Evening Herald* commented on Katie as 'the most complex creature, as near to insanity as makes no difference', and on the play as 'most evasive'.[8] Writing on the 1994 Peacock production, O'Toole renews the question of Katie's sanity: 'Katie's closeness to complete madness is embraced'.[9] Reading Katie as insane raises questions of judgement arising from socio-scientific changes in the way the discipline of psychology understands madness relative to social norms and constraints. Perhaps it is attitudes expressed towards Katie by other characters that are insane rather than the young woman herself? Playwright and perceptive critic, T.C. Murray, wrote in 1939 that the heroine, 'capricious and imaginative', allowed 'her romantic passions to rule her heart, while her social conditioning rules her head'[10]—at least recognising how Katie is torn between these opposing forces. Whilst the Abbey's 1936 premiere production was on tour to the Arts Theatre in Cambridge, *The Granta*'s very probably woman reviewer turned previous analysis on its head: the play 'is emphatically not [...] the story of an erring wife who takes on a job and fails to carry it out; rather it is the story of a crassly stupid husband'.[11] This critic found no mystery in *Katie Roche*, 'the spoken lines are so good that we can without any effort fill in the blanks'.[12] This critic's relaxed identification with the title role is, for whatever reason, refreshingly out of harmony with recorded views inside Ireland in 1936, and opens a field of possibility around the nature of the lead character and her world.

---

7   Joseph Holloway, *Joseph Holloway's Irish Theatre*, ed. by Robert Hogan and Michael J. O'Neill, 3 vols (Dixon, CA: Proscenium Press, 1969), II (1932–1937), 52.
8   Digital Repository of Ireland (DRI), The Teresa Deevy Archive, M.B., '"Katie Roche": Miss Deevy's New Play at Abbey', *Evening Herald*, 17 March 1936, PP/6/178(14), https://doi.org/10.7486/DRI.5999vb24x
9   O'Toole, 'Second Opinion', p. 10.
10 T.C. Murray, 'Two Irish Playwrights' [Unattributed newspaper cutting].
11 DRI, The Teresa Deevy Archive, *The Granta*, 24 February 1937, https://doi.org/10.7486/DRI.5999vb26g
12 Ibid.

Katie Roche places a captivating character in the midst of a social environment that will almost certainly overwhelm her, humble her, and re-shape her into some kind of acceptability. It is not so much the physical setting in which she lives that confines her—a small, rural cottage surrounded by countryside and a beautiful river landscape. For Katie, this is a life-saving source of pleasure and beauty, but the demands of marriage mean that she will be taken away from it. It is the social environment that traps Katie, and she must rely almost entirely on her inner self to deal with that. Pictured as she is defined by Deevy's stage directions, we meet Katie in a domestic space that is not her own, that is at odds with her aspirations, and that she tries but fails to transform. It is the stage that tells us of Katie's inner life, of her thoughts and desires as she gazes offstage into forbidden freedoms and pleasures. The drama is, in part, a meta-drama of ownership of the stage as she tries hopelessly to control it.

Early twentieth-century Irish theatre is marked by several influential plays that, with careful discretion, explore the social and sexual issues involved in the power play of heterosexual relationships between young women and older men. Examples include any of the play versions of the story of mythical Deirdre, Synge's *The Shadow of the Glen* (1903), Gregory's *Grania* (1912) and, later, T.C. Murray's *Autumn Fire* (1924).[13] Alongside Gregory, who never achieved an Abbey production of *Grania*, Deevy's choice to explore the older man/younger woman plotline foregrounds the young woman's emotional journey and the imbalances of social power that it reveals. Synge's precedent *The Shadow of the Glen* shares with *Katie Roche* key aspects of staging, such as silences, uneasy dialogue, bodies repressed or desiring, and the creation of environments and spaces that seem to shape how the power dynamic operates. Synge reshaped the folk tale that inspired his play, turning it away from tragedy and towards imaginative poetic romance that overlays earlier images of Peggy Cavanagh's abject existence, stravaging the roads—Nora escapes into a utopian adventure in the beauty of the

---

13 J.M. Synge, *The Shadow of the Glen*, 1903; Augusta Gregory, 'Grania', in *Irish Folk-History Plays* (New York: G.P. Putnam's and Sons, 1912), pp. 1–67; T.C. Murray, *Autumn Fire* (n.p., 1924). Plays based on the mythic Deirdre include George Russell's in 1902, W.B. Yeats's in 1906, and Synge's in 1909. See A.E., *Deirdre: A Drama in Three Acts* (Dublin: Maunsel and Co., Ltd., 1907), pp. 8–53; J.M. Synge, *Deirdre of the Sorrows*, 1909; W.B. Yeats, *Deirdre* (Dublin: Maunsel and Co., Ltd., 1907), pp. 1–45.

natural world, seductively expressed by the Tramp.[14] Deevy returns to the trope, but dares to unsettle either/or actions, potentially allowing a space of theatrical uncertainty, a gap between what may be said and what may be done, so that both are present uncomfortably together. The textual ending of *Katie Roche* refuses defined closure; it is persistently unstable and open to interpretation.

Katie is the figure that haunted Irish society in the 1930s and that haunts Irish society again now—marked out through no fault of her own, betrayed by the Catholic Church and by Mrs Roche who brought her up but did not educate her, the nuns who exploited her for profit, and her community, which tolerates her but will not accept her into it. She is the embodiment of everything that Irish society did not wish to acknowledge and respect. Yet, Katie's personality powers the play. She is the most interesting person onstage. She is loved by Amelia and Michael. Whether because he once loved Katie's mother, or to advance his career, Stanislaus wants to marry her and thinks he loves her. And she has the nerve to take herself seriously, to have high ambitions to find 'something great to do'.[15] *Katie Roche* stands out in the centrality of Katie herself, chief protagonist, the spark, the charge that connects with spectators.

> KATIE: Why I said now I wouldn't marry you—I was thinking in my mind—if I were to lose my soul and my body—that would be a bad thing. [...] And how do I know would I have the grace to withstand you?[16]

She hesitates to marry and recognises the operations of power for a young woman in a relationship with a much older man. Her insights into the risk to her self grow out of her belief in her own potential as a person. Deevy creates Katie as a lone individual, without the advantages of education, independence, or social opportunity, who holds to her conviction that she has 'something great to do' in life. The audience watches her

---

14 For insightful analysis of Katie's love for the natural world's open spaces, outside the confinements of Stanislaus's house, see Anthony Roche, 'Woman on the Threshold: J.M. Synge's *The Shadow of the Glen*, Teresa Deevy's *Katie Roche* and Marina Carr's *The Mai*', *Irish University Review*, 25.1 (1995), 143–162.
15 Deevy, 'Katie Roche', p. 102.
16 Ibid., p. 61.

struggle towards this ambition and judges whether she achieves her goal, or not. Deevy's plays are remarkable in many respects, but most remarkable perhaps is her choice to write about girls and young women whose circumstances of birth, and/or whose lively imaginations and ambitions, were anathema to the patriarchal attitudes that were closing in and closing down such initiatives in Irish women's lives, for example in de Valera's Constitution of 1937. Girls and young women who gave birth when unmarried, and their children, were victimised and deemed socially intolerable. The first two decades of the twentieth century had fostered a rebellious energy towards ideals of gender equality that inspired so much of women's political activism in that period. The 1930s, however, saw gradual reversals in social mores and legislation concerning women's roles in society that damaged and delayed access to their rights, status, and social participation as citizens.[17] But the figure of Katie Roche confronts spectators, challenging them to recognise and care about her, when, in that decade and for long afterwards, Church and State were intent on disappearing her from society, wiping her out of the record and, literally in some cases, obliterating her identity.[18] Not only in *Katie Roche*, but in her earlier short play *In Search of Valour*, or *A Disciple*, too, Deevy's action in making the choice to place Katie and Ellie centre stage amounts to a provocation.[19] In response to Judy Friel's 1994 production and Derbhle Crotty's vividly complex performance, O'Toole was perhaps the first critic to recognise how the play delivered a deeply unstable and destabilising emotional charge, careering between absurd laughter, fury, desire, and despair.

Aside from the powerful attraction of Katie as the pulsing centre

---

17 See Rosemary Cullen Owens, *A Social History of Women in Ireland 1870–1970* (Dublin: Gill and Macmillan, 2005), pp. 190–214; Mary E. Daly, *Women and Work in Ireland* (Dundalk: Irish Economic and Social History Society of Ireland/Dundalgan Press, 1997); Diarmaid Ferriter, 'A Fascist and Slave Conception of Woman', in *Judging Dev: A Reassessment of the Life and Legacy of Eamon De Valera,* ed. by Diarmaid Ferriter (Dublin: Royal Irish Academy, 2007), pp. 235–275.

18 See *Ireland and the Magdalene Laundries: A Campaign for Justice,* ed. by Claire McGettrick, Katherine O'Donnell, Maeve O'Rourke, James M. Smith, and Mari Steed (London: I.B. Tauris/Bloomsbury, 2021).

19 The play's first title in performance and publication was *A Disciple*. It was retitled as *The Enthusiast* and published under that title in 1938, see Teresa Deevy, 'The Enthusiast', *One Act Play Magazine*, 1.9 (1938), n.p. Finally, it was republished in 1947 as *In Search of Valour* (in a collection of one act plays), a title that better flags its central idea.

of *Katie Roche* and her appeal to Abbey audiences over the past almost ninety years, *Katie Roche* the play is, theatrically speaking, kaleidoscopic, presenting many production possibilities of emphasis and genre, and thus of casting, scenographic presentation, and interpretation in performance. As such, with other works whose authors play with or break the rules of genre (Ibsen and Synge come to mind), the play shares the power to upset expectation and to shock audiences into attention, sending them away unsettled and stimulated into doubt. While learning to lip-read in London, Deevy has cited how, in her frequent theatre visits, the works by Chekhov and Bernard Shaw (she saw *Heartbreak House*) influenced her especially; earlier, at school, she had read symbolist playwright Maeterlinck's *The Blue Bird* (1908) which, translated into English, had premiered in London at the Theatre Royal Haymarket in 1910.[20] From these experiences it is reasonable to conclude that her understanding of theatrical form drew from a relatively wide platform that included Chekhov's wild mix of pathos, comedy, and the absurd; Shaw's theatre of ideas and polemic; and, from her reading, Maeterlinck's symbolic dream spaces, stillness, and internalised static drama and 'school of silence' in *The Blue Bird*.[21] When T.C. Murray observes *Katie Roche*'s 'strange tantalizing quality', it is easy to see a connection with Maeterlinck's style.[22] Chiefly though, expressionist techniques seem to have offered Deevy ways of exposing inner states of mind, thus making, in T.S. Eliot's famous words, 'a raid on the inarticulate'.[23] Most thoroughly in her early one-act *In Search of Valour* (1931), the playwright recruits an army of modernist/expressionist

---

[20] Eileen Kearney, Charlotte Headrick, and Kathleen Quinn, 'Introduction', in *Irish Women Dramatists 1908–2001*, ed. by Eileen Kearney and Charlotte Headrick (Syracuse, NY: Syracuse University Press, 2014), pp. 1–27; George Bernard Shaw, *Heartbreak House: A Fantasia in the Russian Manner on English Themes* (London: Constable, 1919), https://www.gutenberg.org/files/3543/3543-h/3543-h.htm; Maurice Maeterlinck, *The Blue Bird: A Fairy Play in Six Acts*, trans. by Alexander Teixeira De Mattos (London: Methuen, 1910).

[21] See Katharine Worth, *The Irish Drama of Europe from Yeats to Beckett* (London: Athlone Press, 1986), pp. 72–87. See also Eileen Kearney and Charlotte Headrick, 'Teresa Deevy (1894–1963)', in *Irish Women Dramatists 1908–2001*, pp. 41–43, p. 42.

[22] Murray, 'Two Irish Playwrights'. See also moments of stillness, dream, and fantasy in *The King of Spain's Daughter* (1935) and *Wife to James Whelan* (1942): Teresa Deevy, 'The King of Spain's Daughter', in *Teresa Deevy Reclaimed*, II, 17–26, and Teresa Deevy, 'Wife to James Whelan', II, 109–158.

[23] T.S. Eliot, 'East Coker', in *Four Quartets* (London: Faber, 1944), p. 31.

devices—archetypal characters, bizarre setting, vocal incantation and repetition, abrupt changes of action, 'harsh audio effects [and] confusion of inner and outer reality'.[24]

This is not to suggest that *Katie Roche* is purely an expressionist drama, but to acknowledge its potential for expressionist stagings in its sometimes oneiric and constantly interrupted actions, its comedic character types (Margaret Drybone and Frank Lawler) and rhetoric-spouting archetypes such as Reuben, its silences and repetitive dialogue, all of which work in tension with what is most immediately visible in the play: a psychological, emotional narrative and the realist social drama of Katie's disadvantage.[25] The 2017 Abbey staging of *Katie Roche* materialises some of this potential in both scenography and in performance, while the 1994 production makes visible Deevy's deliberately fractured dramaturgy.

Katie Roche in 1994 at the Peacock Theatre[26]

Director Judy Friel took Deevy's written text in all of its aesthetic complexity and opposing energies, staging *Katie Roche* as written, paying attention to the many and detailed stage directions which signal the author's wish, perhaps, for her textual meaning to be fully performed, intensely seen as well as heard. Friel judged that 'the ending [of *Katie Roche* ...] is a whitewash'.[27] In rehearsal, she found no way around the tenuously 'happy' ending and chose resolution over ambiguity.[28] The convention of definitive closure is evoked in this decision and, perhaps, militated against the disturbance that the production had effectively created through what had gone before: the abrasive fractured styles of

---

24 Judith E. Barlow, 'Introduction', in Sophie Treadwell, *Machinal* (London: Nick Hern Books, 1993), pp. vii–ix (p. viii). *Machinal*, an expressionist masterpiece, was first produced in New York in 1928 and revived in London by the Royal National Theatre in 1993 with Fiona Shaw in the role of Woman.

25 The potential of Deevy's work to inspire innovative production is evidenced by Amanda Coogan's adaptation of *The King of Spain's Daughter* in *Talk Real Fine, Just Like a Lady* at the Peacock Theatre in 2017, which was created by Dublin Theatre of the Deaf in collaboration with Coogan and produced by Live Collision.

26 *Katie Roche*, dir. by Judy Friel, Peacock Theatre, Dublin, 13 April–21 May 1994.

27 Judy Friel, 'Rehearsing *Katie Roche*', *Irish University Review*, 25.1 (1995), 117–125 (p. 123).

28 Ibid., p. 123.

performance and Crotty's powerful playing of Katie.

The setting indicated in the play text of Deevy's *Katie Roche* is that all action takes place within one room, and reading the semiotics of that room is a significant part of the production's dramaturgy. It is 1936 on an August afternoon in the living room of Stanislaus's cottage in Lower Ballycar, a generic small Irish country town. There are flowers in a bowl and the sun streams through the window, 'throwing shadows of chairs and table'. 'It is a pleasant little room', the stage direction continues, 'time-worn now and scantily furnished'.[29] The poster image for the production was of Derbhle Crotty, wearing a gingham, cotton dress and white apron, and smiling into the sun. Her beauty and promise were, it was hinted, at stake in the drama. The front entrance to the house opens directly into this room, so that the natural world surrounding it, although offstage, is immediately within reach. Overall, Paul McCauley's set supported Deevy's description of the setting, as seen from the audience space, and flagged a realist reading of the play. It is worth noting that the play text opens on an empty living room. Stanislaus is the first to enter. Indeed, although Katie and Amelia are the long-term residents, neither of them is very much truly 'at home'. This is emphasised when it is revealed later that Stanislaus, and not Amelia, owns the house. Amelia was absent for much of the performance and, when she was present, fell into reliance on her obsessive concerns for the ritual of tea and scones to give at least some impression of domesticity. The Peacock stage signalled modest, cosy warmth, but the space was repeatedly a place of passage; Act Two did convey some sense of homeliness that quickly fell apart in the dislocated conversation between Katie and Stanislaus.

Friel cast the play brilliantly with Derbhle Crotty as a captivating, emotional changeling Katie, weirdly sharing the same stage with an odd mix of characters played by performers who had huge experience of the Abbey Company style, with Clive Geraghty as Stanislaus, Fedelma Cullen as Amelia, Maire O'Neill as Margaret Drybone, and Niall O'Brien as a hilarious Frank Lawlor. In the role of Reuben, an archetypal figure out of medieval drama, Roy Hanlon (who was repeatedly cast at the Abbey as authoritative, patriarchal figures) turned the question of style topsy turvy. Out of this entertaining whirligig, Crotty in the character of Katie

---

29   Deevy, 'Katie Roche', p. 57.

held our look. Her vitality, vulnerability, wilfulness, determination, and her glaring out-of-placeness amidst restrictive social surroundings, may be read as a character-based and fascinating exposé of Deevy's impossible task—to dramatise the forces surrounding Katie and her contest with them in their external and internalised forms, without also thoroughly devaluing and defeating Katie herself. Character held prominence over full confrontation with the shocking roughness with which Katie is treated by her biological father and, at times, by Stanislaus; the unspoken pressures found only oblique expression within the production's realist conventions of setting and gesture. The kaleidoscopic instability of Deevy's play, its mix of genres—realist drama, social comedy, expressionist coming of age, Abbey farce—was revealed. So within the dominant realist style and setting, Reuben's announcement that he is Katie's father was unconvincing. Back in the 1975 production at the Abbey (under the direction of Joe Dowling), Jeananne Crowley, playing Katie, pointed to this moment as a performance impossibility—Katie is given no time to absorb this momentous information. Dramatically, in terms of realist style, it was like an explosion that the play does not deal with.[30] How to manage this scene in a way that blends with events before and after and resonates with the moral absolutism of English medieval drama is a key challenge to directors of the play. In the 1994 production, it was the most unbalancing of a series of shifting theatrical styles across the performance's discordant genre complexity, tested against the realist cottage setting in the confines of the Peacock stage. The 2017 Abbey production, in contrast, presented a spatially dystopian image of Katie's existence, and one that moves the play totally out of realist representation, and into expressionism and ritualised action.

In his critique of the 1994 Peacock production, O'Toole renewed the question of the heroine's sanity. More recently, O'Toole has put aside the issue of madness and moves to issues of unstable identity, assessing Katie as having 'fantasy versions of herself [...] a saint, a lover or the child of "great people". But she has no fixed self'; he continues, 'such a thing is a luxury her society will not allow her. [... The play's] central character has no character'.[31] In Ireland, in light of the Ryan Report"

---

30 Jeananne Crowley interview with Cathy Leeney, 31 January 2000, Dublin. See Cathy Leeney, *Irish Women Playwrights, 1900–1939* (New York: Peter Lang, 2010), p. 180.
31 O'Toole, '1936: *Katie Roche*', p. 63.

(the Report of the Commission to Inquire into Child Abuse) and Justice Quirke's Magdalen Commission Scheme (2013) for redress for those held illegally in Magdalene Laundries, one may appreciate this emphasis on the power of society to define the individual as a literal nobody, to exile them from social definition, identity, and rights by hiding, falsifying, or refusing to release their true history.[32] Considering *Katie Roche* in Ireland in 2022 invites recollection of the first hundred years since the formation of the Irish State—work for another day— but with odd irony, 2022 was also chosen by many to celebrate the centenary year of modernism and its notion of the empty character, a vacuum filled by cultural fragments and discourses but owning no essence. Katie recognises how some others view her in this way when she replies to Stanislaus's qualified admission of love for her, 'My heart and my mind! A queer way to love!... Taking a body to pieces!'[33] Deevy's control of character exposition certainly supports this view; nobody will talk to Katie about her life and origins, and when, for example, Reuben abruptly reveals his identity as her father, the bare facts are offered with insulting brevity, refusal of responsibility, and inherent disdain.[34]

Katie Roche in 2017 at the Abbey Theatre[35]

Katie Roche at the Abbey Theatre in 2017 loosened the play from its 1936 context, which was visually present through costume and prop design. As a radically contrasting approach to Deevy's text, this production raises fascinating issues of textual integrity, the hermeneutic impact of stage space and design, casting, and of the power of visuality in theatre for a twenty-first century audience. Addressing all of these points is beyond the scope of this chapter and the body in space is the focus of attention here. What the spectator sees often shapes their engagement and responses definitively. In Roland Barthes's terms images are polysemic, unstable, and exceed explanation, and, in this sense, the

---

32   The Commission to Inquire into Child Abuse, *Commission to Inquire into Child Abuse Report*, 6 vols (Dublin: Stationery Office, 2009).
33   Deevy, 'Katie Roche', p. 71.
34   Ibid., see p. 60, p. 63, p. 79, respectively.
35   *Katie Roche*, dir by Caroline Byrne, Abbey Theatre, Dublin, 26 August–23 September 2017.

spectator becomes the maker of meaning.[36] In the process of making performance, visual and textual meanings create the embryo for the fully-grown staging that goes on to live in the mind of the spectator. Visual information in performance focusses on the body in space and flows powerfully, beyond language, to make meaning in the audience. The embodiment of character or role is a defining decision, and is disarmingly malleable and subjective, as the power to create meaning resides as much, if not more, in body and space than in narrative and speech.

Aspects of Caroline Byrne's staging that relate to her key choice to make the stage Katie's— choices made to externalise Katie's inner state spatially and visually—are foregrounded here. Gone is the cottage living room, its modest domesticity and crushing atmosphere of stasis. This led to the fulfilment of Byrne's wish to free the play from its historical theatrical context of Abbey realism.[37] In collaboration with designer Joanna Scotcher, the scenography would externalise Katie's inner world in terms of spatial proportions, imposing angular shapes, textures, and materials such as faux marble, glass, and dark earth in contrast with hard white surfaces.[38] With dramaturg Morna Regan, Byrne set out to 'explore the play as a psychological drama and an expressionistic drama' and '[t]o create a very sealed experience'.[39] From this premise, daring decisions were taken by Byrne and Regan to find the through line of the drama that expresses this internal world, so that Katie's thoughts, dreams and fears, and identity would be made visible materially and viscerally, in classic expressionist style. Some images of Scotcher's stage and costume designs show the kind of decisions made to accommodate this reading of *Katie Roche* as 'a personal/psychological space'—an externalised expression of Katie's internal world.[40] The, relatively, much larger Abbey Theatre stage allows for an imposing architectural

---

36 Roland Barthes, 'Rhetoric of the Image', in *Image Music Text*, trans. by Stephen Heath (London: Fontana Press, 1977), pp. 32–51. Barthes lays out the conditions applying to 'open' texts.

37 Caroline Byrne and Marie Kelly, 'Interview with the Director', in *Abbey Theatre Research Pack: Teresa Deevy: Katie Roche*, researched and compiled by Marie Kelly, School of Music and Theatre, University College Cork (Dublin: The Abbey Theatre, 2017), pp. 36–40 (p. 36).

38 Ibid., p. 36.

39 Ibid., p. 36 and p. 37, respectively.

40 Ibid., p. 38.

structure making a marble-effect, pillared framework for the white stage floor. Above the centre, a glass guillotine hangs ominously over the action. At the centre stands an oblong table, shaped like an altar (which it later becomes), all white. The floor is covered with dark earth, obscuring the white beneath except where a pathway has been made. Severe angles and squared-off shapes contrast with the softness of the human bodies, and the soft brown earth, at one moment, offers a sense of rootedness and the natural, and, at another, is an image of stained humiliation when Katie lies or crouches on the floor, soiling her clothes and marking her out as unsocialised and animalistic. Caoilfhionn Dunne as Katie is seen downstage, seated. Only the costumes and chairs reflect the period of the action. The height of the setting extends an image of the height of Katie's aspirations, their grandeur relative to the self-image that has been imposed upon her, down in the dirt. Katie's ownership of the space is emphasised in expressionist fashion through her starkly lit and isolated actions of reflection and imagining, such as watching water flowing from a cup into a saucer—an onstage reference to her pleasure in the flow of the offstage river in the place she calls home. Other parodic images, such as the enormous platter of scones offered by Amelia in the midst of an emotional crisis, reference the ridiculous comedy of social conventions.

There are scenes throughout the play text when Katie is alone and re-organising the space for her own purposes—hanging images of saints whose glory she wishes to emulate, or inviting Michael for drinks. Dunne's flirtatious behaviour with Michael (played by Kevin Creedon) was counter-pointed by an innocent posy of snowdrops, their heads bowed, sprouting from a tiny mound of earth. This delicate object was repeatedly near her, or in Katie's hands. The ritual of her marriage to Stanislaus was performed more as a sacrifice at the altar of pure white. Meanwhile, in the background, the ghostly hands of black-clad stage technicians tidied away any domestic disorder. Dunne's embodiment of Katie Roche in 2017 contrasts significantly with Crotty's. While both embodied a dizzy-making series of emotional states, Crotty's Katie often had significant authority on the stage, when she challenged Reuben's physical attack on her, for example, and also through her articulate insights into Stanislaus's and Amelia's personalities. Dunne's performance veered through bewilderment, frustration, ecstasy, flirtation, physical androgyny, to threatened pride; there were times when her anger and powerlessness were physically acted out in flashes of harshness that seemed to be turned inwards against herself.

Very substantial editing of Deevy's text was required to clear away the stylistic theatrical mix in the full text and to invite audiences to understand a reading of Katie in new terms, making available, but not defining, a sustained subtext to Deevy's dialogue. This mode of deconstruction of the dramatic text challenges the spectator to be alert to visual messages without being offered a single way of interpreting their meanings. The un-decidability of meaning, the labile potential of scenography, opens an opportunity for the audience to connect with the scene in relation to their own world view and their sense of the social context of the time of performance—the world outside the theatre building. The spectator is uprooted from familiar conventions of character and action and invited to experience the play cut loose from its theatrical origins. This production, I would argue, enabled a full dramatisation, not of individual characters and situations in 1930s Ireland, but of the forces surrounding Katie and fighting for her attention. Audiences saw her contest with those forces in their external forms (personal history, social/economic environment, and gender), while crucially the entire stage space expressed the pressures in her internal soul and mind. In this way, the audience could connect with, and find some understanding of, Katie's internalised fears, doubts, and aspirations. In common with the 1994 production, but in different terms, I would argue that this was achieved without diminishing or devaluing the young woman's lost promise and her vulnerable, fascinating self. The forces operating around and within Katie are not, in twenty-first-century Ireland or elsewhere, by any means erased from contemporary realities of hierarchies, social class, and gendered power.

Comparing *Katie Roche* in 2017 and in 1994 (the only performances I have seen live) involves a valuable balance of losses and gains where Deevy's text is concerned. Struggle, humour, charm, waste, and absurdity were disrupting and welcome aspects in 1994, and the Peacock production celebrated not only the nuanced complexity of the play, but the skill of Abbey Theatre performers in handling the variety of playing styles demanded and showcasing a highly professional and accomplished style of performance. In 2017, the play was tested before a twenty-first-century audience and proved its power to resonate with contemporary realities, while confronting the painful histories of young women such as Katie. Byrne's production was an illustration of the rich potential of this text to accommodate interpretation and re-interpretation for contemporary audiences. It was a test of the play as an open text, one that accommodates multiple points of entry with extraordinary, layered spaciousness; *Katie Roche* allowed for processes of careful deconstruction and coherent and deliberate re-emphasis to explore what Katie means to spectators now in 2017 and, putatively, in the future.

Arguably, many plays unseen for decades or even centuries, deserve our re-consideration, not as remnants of the past, but as sites of contemporary theatrical adventure. The feminist project of retrieving lost work by women, and initiatives to recover work by authors from other cultural or racial minorities, have proved that brilliant texts, unvalued or dismissed by prejudiced critics or academics, are now recognised as a vital part of the canon and crucial to the social impact of theatre performance.[41] The theatrical potential of play texts to live outside of their time of writing, to engage present-day audiences, questions assumptions of 'museum' theatre.[42] Their renewal demands the activation of the full vocabulary of performance, scenography, and stage technology to bring old texts to life in the always present moment of performance, to reveal connections and dissonances between the contemporary and the historical; thus, cycles of progress and recession may be exposed, leading to a deconstruction of the myth of absolute progress and a sense of change as something to be made rather than undergone. The liveliness, flexibility, and renewal of the Irish theatrical canon is enhanced and deepened by such projects. Further explorations of Deevy's work, in general, such as those created by Amanda Coogan, lie waiting in the wings as part of a palimpsest for production involving cultural and theatrical processes of re-evaluation and re-invention.[43]

---

41   Outstanding English language examples internationally are Aphra Behn's *The Rover* (1677), Susan Glaspell's *Trifles* (1916), Sophie Treadwell's *Machinal* (1928), and Lorraine Hansberry's *A Raisin in the Sun* (1959). In Ireland, the growth of interest in Teresa Deevy's work in the 2010s and 2020s outstrips what might have been thought possible thirty years ago.
42   Byrne and Kelly, 'Interview with the Director', p. 36.
43   Teresa Deevy's *Possession* was created and directed by Amanda Coogan in collaboration with Lianne Quigley, Alvean Jones, Linda Buckley, Dublin Theatre of the Deaf and Cork Deaf Community Choir. Creative producer Lynette Moran

Bibliography

A.E., *Deirdre: A Drama in Three Acts* (Dublin: Maunsel and Co., Ltd., 1907), https://archive.org/details/deirdredramainth00ae18/page/n9/mode/2up

Bank, Jonathan, John P. Harrington, and Christopher Morash (eds), *Teresa Deevy Reclaimed*, 2 vols (New York: Mint Theater, 2011 and 2017)

Barlow, Judith E., 'Introduction', in Sophie Treadwell, *Machinal* (London: Nick Hern Books, 1993), pp. vii–ix

Barthes, Roland, 'Rhetoric of the Image', in *Image Music Text*, trans. by Stephen Heath (London: Fontana Press, 1977), pp. 32–51

Brockes, Emma, '#MeToo Founder Tarana Burke: "You Have to Use Your Privilege to Serve Other People"', *The Guardian*, 15 January 2018, https://www.theguardian.com/world/2018/jan/15/me-too-founder-tarana-burke-women-sexual-assault

Byrne, Caroline, and Marie Kelly, 'Interview with the Director', in *Abbey Theatre Research Pack: Teresa Deevy: Katie Roche*, researched and compiled by Marie Kelly, School of Music and Theatre, University College Cork (Dublin: The Abbey Theatre, 2017), pp. 36–40, https://www.abbeytheatre.ie/wp-content/uploads/2017/10/KATIE-ROCHE_RESEARCH-PACK-2017.pdf

Commission to Inquire into Child Abuse, *Commission to Inquire into Child Abuse Report*, 6 vols (Dublin: Stationery Office, 2009), https://childabusecommission.ie/?page_id=241

Daly, Mary E., *Women and Work in Ireland* (Dundalk: Irish Economic and Social History Society of Ireland/Dundalgan Press, 1997)

Deevy, Teresa, 'The Enthusiast', *One Act Play Magazine*, 1.9 (1938), n.p.

Eliot, T.S., 'East Coker', in *Four Quartets* (London: Faber, 1944), p. 31

Ferriter, Diarmaid, 'A Fascist and Slave Conception of Woman', in *Judging Dev: A Reassessment of the Life and Legacy of Eamon De Valera*, ed. by Diarmaid Ferriter (Dublin: Royal Irish Academy, 2007), pp. 235–275

Friel, Judy, 'Rehearsing *Katie Roche*', *Irish University Review*, 25.1 (1995), 117–125

Gregory, Augusta, 'Grania', in *Irish Folk-History Plays* (New York: G.P. Putnam's and Sons, 1912), pp. 1–67, https://archive.org/details/irishfolkhistory00greg/page/66/mode/2up

---

produced *Possession* at the Project Arts Centre 21–24 February 2024, while Susan Holland produced it at the Granary Theatre for the Cork Midsummer Festival, 21–23 June, 2024. *Possession* was funded as part of ART:2023: A Decade of Centenaries Collaboration (the Arts Council and the Department of Tourism, Culture, Arts, Gaeltacht, Sport, and Media).

Holloway, Joseph, *Joseph Holloway's Irish Theatre*, ed. by Robert Hogan and Michael J. O'Neill, 3 vols (Dixon, CA: Proscenium Press, 1969)

Kearney, Eileen, and Charlotte Headrick, 'Teresa Deevy (1894–1963)', in *Irish Women Dramatists 1908–2001*, ed. by Eileen Kearney and Charlotte Headrick (Syracuse, NY: Syracuse University Press, 2014), pp. 41–43

Kearney, Eileen, Charlotte Headrick, and Kathleen Quinn, 'Introduction', in *Irish Women Dramatists 1908–2001*, ed. by Eileen Kearney and Charlotte Headrick (Syracuse, NY: Syracuse University Press, 2014), pp. 1–27

Leeney, Cathy, *Irish Women Playwrights, 1900–1939* (New York: Peter Lang, 2010), https://doi.org/10.3726/978-1-4539-0373-5

Maeterlinck, Maurice, *The Blue Bird: A Fairy Play in Six Acts*, trans. by Alexander Teixeira De Mattos (London: Methuen, 1910), https://www.gutenberg.org/files/8606/8606-h/8606-h.htm

McGettrick, Claire, Katherine O'Donnell, Maeve O'Rourke, James M. Smith, and Mari Steed (eds), *Ireland and the Magdalene Laundries: A Campaign for Justice* (London: I.B. Tauris/Bloomsbury, 2021), https://doi.org/10.5040/9780755617524

Murray, T.C., *Autumn Fire* (n.p., 1924)

Murray, T.C., 'Two Irish Playwrights' [Unattributed newspaper cutting]

O'Toole, Fintan, '1936: *Katie Roche*', in *Modern Ireland in 100 Artworks*, ed. by Fintan O'Toole, Catherine Marshall, and Eibhear Walshe (Dublin: Royal Irish Academy and *Irish Times*, 2017), pp. 61–63

O'Toole, Fintan, 'Second Opinion: What Katie Doesn't Do', *Irish Times*, 26 April 1994, p. 10

Owens, Rosemary Cullen, *A Social History of Women in Ireland 1870–1970* (Dublin: Gill and Macmillan, 2005)

Roche, Anthony, 'Woman on the Threshold: J.M. Synge's *The Shadow of the Glen*, Teresa Deevy's *Katie Roche* and Marina Carr's *The Mai*', *Irish University Review*, 25.1 (1995), 143–162

Shakespeare, William, *Twelfth Night, or What You Will*, ed. by Jonathan Bate and Eric Rasmussen (Hampshire: Macmillan, 2008)

Shaw, George Bernard, *Heartbreak House: A Fantasia in the Russian Manner on English Themes* (London: Constable, 1919), https://www.gutenberg.org/files/3543/3543-h/3543-h.htm

Synge, J.M., *Deirdre of the Sorrows*, 1909, https://www.gutenberg.org/files/1922/1922-h/1922-h.htm

Synge, J.M., *The Shadow of the Glen*, 1903, https://www.gutenberg.org/files/1618/1618-h/1618-h.htm

Tambe, Ashwini, 'Reckoning with the Silences of #MeToo', *Feminist Studies*, 44.1 (2018) 197–203, https://doi.org/10.15767/feministstudies.44.1.0197

Worth, Katharine, *The Irish Drama of Europe from Yeats to Beckett* (London: Athlone Press, 1986)

Yeats, W.B., *Deirdre* (Dublin: Maunsel and Co., Ltd., 1907), https://archive.org/details/deirdre00yeatgoog/page/n54/mode/2up

12. Teresa Deevy and Contemporary Performance Practice: Edited Transcript of Teresa Deevy Practitioner Panel Discussion

Jonathan Bank, Caroline Byrne, Amanda Coogan, and Lianne Quigley[1]

In their discussion, Jonathan Bank, Caroline Byrne, Amanda Coogan, and Lianne Quigley, share insights into their performance-making processes and their experiences of working with Deevy's texts.

Úna Kealy (ÚK): *Jonathan, how did Deevy come into your life? Tell us a little bit about your work with the texts that you've produced.*

Jonathan Bank (JB): Deevy came into my life in 2009. I couldn't think of the names of any Irish women playwrights from the first half of the last century after Lady Gregory—and that puzzled me, that felt wrong

---

[1] Hosted by Úna Kealy and Kate McCarthy as part of the Active Speech: Sharing Scholarship on Teresa Deevy conference, the Practitioners' Panel took place on 10 December 2020. The panel was facilitated online and comprised Jonathan Bank, Amanda Coogan, Alvean Jones, and Lianne Quigley with Irish Sign Language translation from Isabella Walsh and Amanda Coogan, and technical support from Ken McCarthy (South East Technological University Waterford). The panel was funded by Maynooth University, SETU, and Waterford Libraries. A captioned and Irish Sign Language (ISL) translated recording of this panel discussion is available (see *Practitioners' Panel*, online video recording, YouTube, 10 December 2020, https://youtu.be/fSX7FqOVFXk). In recasting a live, online conversation as prose, some parts of the discussion herein are edited and adapted from the original conversation.

to me, that felt unlikely to me. At the Mint Theater, I'm in the business of finding neglected plays and, usually, a play comes to me just through serendipity, where I'll run across a reference to a title, or an author, and that reference is not because I'm looking for it. I'm reading about one play, and a critic mentions another, and I think, that sounds interesting. But in this case: I set out looking.

Fig. 12.1 Richard Termine, production image from Teresa Deevy's *Temporal Powers* (2011), directed by Jonathan Bank, Mint Theater, featuring Rosie Benton as Min Donovan. © Richard Termine. All rights reserved.

I sat down with the production history of the Abbey Theatre. It was Lennox Robinson's 1951 volume, which has great indexes—there's a list of every play, author, and dates—and I started looking for women's names.² I decided right from the start that I was going to ignore the fact that a woman might be masking her identity with initials, or with a pseudonym, and that I would look for the Marys and the Katherines, and see what I could find. I made a list, not of every name, but of every name that had multiple occurrences. And I was only looking at the Abbey production history and not anything broader than that.

To the best of my recollection, I think I had eight names—it might have been six names—but it was not two, and it was not twelve. But Deevy's name occurred six times over the course of about five years. Once I started Googling these names—I mean, it's tricky! I don't have that list anymore and I don't remember everybody who was on it, but there are some names that are just so common that they [the playwright I was looking for] might have been on page twelve of the search results as an author. But basically, Deevy was the one author who returned any pages, and she was the one author who returned pages [and] who had work published. And, in fact, more than published—she had her volume of three plays published by Macmillan, and it was on the shelf at the New York Public Library.³

And I was able to just go from reading a sentence of description about this playwright to get on the subway, grab a copy of the book, take it home, and within three or four pages of the first play I looked at, which was *Katie Roche*—one of three plays in that volume—I knew that I was in the presence of a writer, of a compelling voice, a surprising voice. And, as is my wont as a play picker and as a producer and as, I guess, a historian, I knew I wanted to produce Deevy, but I wanted to read everything before I decided on what I would work [on first].⁴ I set about looking for the rest of her work and I found a copy of *Temporal Powers*, which had been published in the 70s or 80s.⁵ I think there were five hundred copies of that published, but I managed to find a used one and have it shipped, and I used the *Irish University Review* edition—the

---

2   Lennox Robinson, *Ireland's Abbey Theatre: A History 1899–1955* (London: Sidgwick and Jackson, 1951).
3   Teresa Deevy, *Three Plays by Teresa Deevy: Katie Roche, The King of Spain's Daughter, The Wild Goose* (London: Macmillan, 1939).
4   For more on the Mint Theater's productions of Teresa Deevy's work, see the Mint Theater, *Production Archives*, https://minttheater.org/production-archives/
5   Seán Dunne (ed.), 'Teresa Deevy Special Number', *Journal of Irish Literature*, 14.2 (May 1985).

Deevy jubilee edition—to read *Wife to James Whelan*.[6] That was the play that I was most eager to read because I knew that was a great story—the story of the play not being done—the Abbey rejected this play. And I read both of those plays and I loved them both and, truthfully, I loved them both more than I loved *Katie Roche*. I think that's kind of a purely personal, artistic perspective, but it may be informed by my kind of warped view of the dramatic canon. *Katie Roche* was the famous play, even though it was not famous! It was published in *Famous Plays of 1935–36*—the Victor Gollancz series of plays—and the publisher felt the necessity of adding a note in that edition to say we're including it because we think it's really good, even though we know we can't call it famous because it hasn't been produced outside of Dublin.[7]

Fig. 12.2 Carol Rosegg, production image from Teresa Deevy's *Wife to James Whelan* (2010), directed by Jonathan Bank, Mint Theater, featuring Aidan Redmond as Tom Carey and Janie Brookshire as Nan Bowers. © Carol Rosegg Photography. All rights reserved.

ÚK: *So what you're saying is that the importance of publishing, the importance of the records, the importance of availability of scripts—that was what brought*

---

6   Teresa Deevy, 'Wife to James Whelan', *Irish University Review*, 25.1 (1995), 29–87.

7   *Famous Plays 1935–6* (London: Victor Gollancz, 1936).

Deevy to you. You talk about getting on the subway in New York, of being able to go to the library to get a copy of the play, and that immediate sense of access. Lianne, maybe you'd talk about your entry point.

Lianne Quigley (LQ): I heard about Teresa Deevy in 2014, so relatively recently after you, Jonathan. I was really, really interested in theatre—being a theatremaker [myself]—and [in] what was going on in the Dublin theatre scene. And there was a series of lectures in Trinity about theatre and disability, theatremakers and disability, and that's when I first heard of Teresa Deevy.[8] And to be honest, I nearly fell out of my standing—a woman writer who was deafened! As a Deaf theatremaker, this is astonishing.[9] And so, I came across *The King of Spain's Daughter*, which was the play that I couldn't get out of my mind.[10] Now, in 2014, this was pre #WakingTheFeminists, and there was very little when I was Googling, and having a look around for her; but I got my hands on a script.[11] At the time, I was working with Amanda on another project

---

8   Lecture Series 2014–15: Disability & Literature, Trinity Long Room Hub Arts & Humanities Research Institute.

9   Fiona Murphy explains that: 'Identity is a fluid concept and a personal choice. Lowercase deaf refers to deafness as a medical condition. It does not indicate the degree of hearing loss an individual may have. Some people with hearing loss may prefer to use the term "hard of hearing". Uppercase Deaf refers to people who identify as culturally Deaf and may use sign language. Given the ongoing suppression of sign-language education, not all Deaf people are fluent signers or even have access to the Deaf community. Again, this word does not indicate the degree of hearing loss an individual may have'. See Fiona Murphy, *The Shape of Sound* (Melbourne: Text Publishing Company, 2021), n.p. Thus, our capitalising of the word 'Deaf' here recognises Deafness as a social category and Deaf people as a group who share a particular history and culture. In line with Dublin Theatre of the Deaf, the Irish Deaf Society, the Irish Deaf Youth Association, the Centre for Deaf Studies, Trinity College Dublin, and researchers in the field, we capitalise the letter D in the word Deaf, when appropriate, to signal accord with the positive values within the Deaf community and Deaf culture. We use a lowercase d when referring to audiological status. When we determine that the reference is to both audiological status and Deaf culture we use the term d/Deaf. For more on d/Deaf, see the entry on 'Deaf, deaf', in the Centre for Integration and Improvement of Journalism, *The Diversity Style Guide* (2024), https://www.diversitystyleguide.com/glossary/deaf-deaf/ and the entry for 'Deaf' in The National Centre for Disability and Journalism, Arizona State University, *Disability Language Guide* (2021).

10 Teresa Deevy, 'The King of Spain's Daughter', in *Irish Women Dramatists 1908–2021*, ed. by Eileen Kearney and Charlotte Headrick (New York: Syracuse University, 2014), pp. 44–58.

11 From November 2015 to November 2016 #WakingTheFeminists functioned as a grassroots movement and campaign that called for equality for women in the Irish Theatre sector. #WakingTheFeminists commissioned a study entitled *Gender*

that we were doing in the Project Arts Centre, and we said that our next one is possibly this [*The King of Spain's Daughter*]. And we just couldn't get over that it was a deafened person who was a writer, who had this history in the Abbey, who was forgotten, neglected, and we wanted to reclaim her. I began working with Amanda because the aim of our collaboration was to tell the story of Deaf people and to tell the story of the Deaf community in Ireland on a mainstream stage.

Amanda is a CODA, which means her mum and dad are Deaf, and sign language is her first language—this is her heritage, her culture as well.[12] We wanted to talk about—to speak to what we call the mainstream, to hearing people—about the richness of our [Deaf] culture and our language. And we started breaking down *The King of Spain's Daughter,* which was written in the 30s. And we started looking at the history of Deaf women in the 30s and tried to draw a kind of a parallel. This is when the Constitution—Bunreacht na hÉireann—came into our lives.[13] And we really believe that Deevy was one of the women who suffered under that constitution.

So, we paralleled a reading of the play with what was happening in Irish Deaf women's lives and picked up on the themes of oppression. We really looked at the character of Mrs Marks in the play. I'm signing her like this [three loops around the head]. This is the sign we gave Mrs Marks because we had these funky costumes on her. We put her as the symbol of oppression—so not specifying the oppression, not just as a

---

Counts: An Analysis of Gender in Irish Theatre 2006–2015, ed. by Brenda Donohue, Ciara O'Dowd, Tanya Dean, Ciara Murphy, Kathleen Cawley, and Kate Harris (Belfast: Ulster University, 2017). The study demonstrated the underrepresentation in key roles (e.g., director and costume designer) of people who identified as women and men and analysed the relationship between public funding and representation in ten organisations funded by The Arts Council of Ireland (An Chomhairle Ealaíon). For more on #WakingTheFeminists, see Patricia O'Beirne, 'A Gendered Absence: Feminist Theatre, Glasshouse Productions and the #WTF movement', in *Perspectives on Contemporary Irish Theatre: Populating the Stage*, ed. by Anne Etienne and Thierry Dubost (Cham: Palgrave Macmillan/Springer Nature, 2017), pp. 269–290; Claire Keogh, *#WakingTheFeminists and the Data-Driven Revolution in Irish Theatre* (Cambridge: Cambridge University Press, 2025), https://doi.org/10.1017/9781009523066

12   Georgina Heffernan and Elizabeth Nixon define CODAs as hearing children of one or two Deaf parents in 'Experiences of Hearing Children of Deaf Parents in Ireland', *The Journal of Deaf Studies and Deaf Education*, 28.4 (2023), 399–407.

13   Bunreacht na hÉireann (Constitution of Ireland) was ratified on 29 December 1937. Government of Ireland, *Constitution of Ireland*, January 2020.

patriarchal moment—and we took the oppression to be the oppression of [exercised also against] our language, Irish Sign Language (ISL), but there's even more detail than that. I will talk about women's signs and the gendered vocabulary in Ireland that we have in our sign language [ISL], which is also awesome.

There were two deaf schools [in Ireland at the start of the twentieth century]: St Joseph's for Boys and St Mary's for Girls—[which were] completely segregated.[14] In St Mary's, they used a vocabulary that we now call women's sign, but it kind of died out, was left by the wayside, because St Joseph's signs are what we call normal ISL.[15] That is the vocabulary that we use now. So, in parts of our production, we were remembering [women's sign] this very specific, gendered language of sign language that we have in this country that is dying out. These women who still know it and used it in school are in their 70s and 80s at this stage. Let me give you an example [of women's sign]: this is the sign for black [draw first finger down the left forearm], and the women's sign for black is this [first two fingers curved and brought down over the eyes]. So, we littered our translations of the play, or any vocabulary that we used, with women's signs only.

And you might wonder why we called it [our production] *Talk Real*

---

14   St Mary's School for Deaf Girls opened in August 1846, 'St Mary's School for Deaf Girls, Cabra, Commission to Inquire into Child Abuse Report, 2.15', in *Commission to Inquire into Child Abuse Report*, 6 vols (Dublin: Stationery Office, 2009), II, 551–556. St Joseph's School for Deaf Boys was founded in 1856 and the school opened in 1857, 'St Joseph's School for Deaf Boys, Cabra ('Cabra'), 1857–1999', in ibid., I, 555–580. The Mary Immaculate School for Deaf Boys (later renamed as Mary Immaculate School for Deaf Children) was located in Stillorgan, County Dublin. Recognised on 10 April 1956, the school prepared children aged three to ten for St Joseph's. The school closed in 1998, 'Mary Immaculate School for Deaf Children', in ibid., II, Child Abuse Report, 557–560.

15   Women's sign is also referred to as 'female sign'. For more on the gendered nature of Irish Sign Language see Barbara LeMaster, 'Language Contraction, Revitalization, and Irish Women', *Journal of Linguistic Anthropology*, 16.2 (2006), 211–228; Barbara LeMaster, 'School Language and Shifts in Irish Identity', in *Many Ways to Be Deaf: International Variation in Deaf Communities*, ed. by Leila Monaghan, Constanze Schmaling, Karen Nakamura, and Graham H. Turner (Washington, DC: Gallaudet University Press, 2003), pp. 153–172; Úna Kealy and Kate McCarthy, 'Shape Shifting the Silence: An Analysis of *Talk Real Fine, Just Like a Lady* (2017) by Amanda Coogan in Collaboration with Dublin Theatre of the Deaf, an Appropriation of Teresa Deevy's *The King of Spain's Daughter* (1935)', in *The Golden Thread: Irish Women Playwrights, 1716–2016*, 2 vols, ed. by David Clare, Fiona McDonagh, and Justine Nakase (Liverpool: Liverpool University Press, 2021), I, 197–210.

Fine, Just Like a Lady?[16] So we removed it from *The King of Spain's Daughter*, and we called it *Talk Real Fine, Just Like a Lady* because we went to the Nina Simone 'Mississippi Goddam' song, this blistering anthem of civil rights.[17] It was really a beautiful pop culture link with our production, which aimed to strive for justice and social equality. So, our production fronted ISL and our sign language users completely.

We played in the Peacock which is underneath—the smaller theatre in the Abbey. What we wanted to do is immerse [the audience] completely into a Deaf, sign-language-using world. Jimmy is a character from the play *The King of Spain's Daughter* and we had multiple Jimmys, and we called them the comrades. And they were walking around in these brown overalls, very much taken from the script, walking around the audience, and they brought the audience into the auditorium. We had a character who was dressed up as Teresa Deevy, just walking around chatting—in sign language obviously, [to the] Deaf [audience members]. And now, in terms of our exploration of oppression, we folded this into the experience, too. This is the sign in ISL for oppression [clenched fist in one hand—outstretched palm in the opposite hand pressing down on the fist].

So, when you came into the auditorium, we had this massive piece of fabric that was propped up by these three Mrs Marks characters who had a sign for authority, authoritarianism, and oppression. And we had five Annies, dotted within the seats of the auditorium. And this big piece of fabric was over everybody. So, you walked in, and you were settled down under the fabric and then at an alarm bell cue, which flashed lights, the fabric came down and the audience member popped their head through it.

So, in terms of the parallel with Irish d/Deaf history and why we really forefronted the oppression of Mrs Marks on Annie—in our examination of the experience of Deaf women in Ireland, we [Deaf people] were forced really to learn how to speak [verbally]. And, as you can imagine, as Deaf women, this is the disability we cannot overcome.

---

16   *Talk Real Fine, Just Like a Lady* created by Dublin Theatre of the Deaf in collaboration with Amanda Coogan, produced by Live Collision, Peacock Theatre, Amharclann na Mainistreach, 19–23 September 2017.

17   Nina Simone, *Nina Simone: Mississippi Goddam*, online video recording, YouTube (recorded 24–25 July 1965, uploaded 26 February 2013), www.youtube.com/watch?v=LJ25-U3jNWM

And so, it was recognised in the Ryan Report on institutional abuse that this was an abusive experience within the deaf schools in Ireland.[18]

Fig. 12.3 Patrick Redmond, 'Talk real fine', production image from *Talk Real Fine, Just Like a Lady* (2017), created by Dublin Theatre of the Deaf in collaboration with Amanda Coogan, produced by Live Collision, Peacock Theatre, Amharclann na Mainistreach, featuring Ann O'Neill as Mrs Marks. © Patrick Redmond. All rights reserved.

We [Deaf women] used to be told to 'talk real fine'—so this is the sign for talk real fine [outstretched palm tapped under the chin]—this is what the teachers and nuns in St Mary's would say to us at all times: 'talk', 'speak up', 'hold out your chin', 'try and articulate with your voice'. And we really included the processes of religion as we experienced them in the deaf school when we signed a translation of the Hail Mary at one stage, which we subverted then in the middle of the lines.[19] Mrs Marks

---

18   Published on 20 May 2009, the *Final Report of the Commission to Inquire into Child Abuse* (the Ryan Report) includes two chapters relating to St Joseph's and St Mary's Schools: Commission to Inquire into Child Abuse, 'St Joseph's School for Deaf Boys, Cabra ('Cabra'), 1857–1999', in *Commission to Inquire into Child Abuse Report*, I, 555–580; and 'St Mary's School for Deaf Girls, Cabra', in ibid., II, 551–556.

19   The 'Hail Mary' is a devotional prayer to Mary, mother of Jesus, traditionally prayed by Roman Catholics as a standalone prayer or as part of the Rosary. For details of the Rosary and the full text of the Hail Mary, see 'The Mysteries of the Rosary', vatican.va, https://www.vatican.va/special/rosary/documents/misteri_en.html. For more

was delighted with it. She gestured to us—us, the Annies—her delight in it. Then once we inflected the Hail Mary, when we hit [the word] 'womb', we woke up in our play and realised we were embodied people with ideas, fantasies, sexual fantasies, ideas beyond the structure that was imposed on us; then she, Mrs Marks, came down hard on us.

And we opened the play with the sign for looking [outstretched palm held over the eyebrow], which is [taken] directly from the script, where Jimmy is looking around the field. And this sign beautifully inflects [through a slight but distinct physical movement] to become Ireland. Looking at Ireland, I suppose, is how we completely opened our production, marking it from the first utterances.

Fig. 12.4 Patrick Redmond, 'The men shade their eyes and look left and right', production image from *Talk Real Fine, Just Like a Lady* (2017), created by Dublin Theatre of the Deaf in collaboration with Amanda Coogan, produced by Live Collision, Peacock Theatre, Amharclann na Mainistreach. © Patrick Redmond. All rights reserved.

ÚK: *Caroline, while Amanda and Lianne were working in the Peacock, you*

---

on the rise of the figure of the Blessed Virgin Mary in Ireland in the early twentieth century see Susan O'Brien, 'The Blessed Virgin Mary', in *The Oxford History of British and Irish Catholicism, vol. IV: Building Identity, 1830–1913*, ed. by Carmen M. Mangion and Susan O'Brien (Oxford: Oxford University Press, 2023), pp. 154–172.

were working upstairs in the Abbey, so maybe talk to us a little bit about that.

Caroline Byrne (CB): I had just directed a play at Shakespeare's Globe called *The Taming of the Shrew* and that coincided with the #WakingTheFeminists movement was taking off in Dublin. Our production was very much in conversation with that movement and with the promises made to Irish women in 1916 that were unfulfilled one hundred years later as we celebrated the centenary [of the 1916 Rising].

Fig. 12.5 Patrick Redmond, 'The sign for Ireland', production image from *Talk Real Fine, Just Like a Lady* (2017), created by Dublin Theatre of the Deaf in collaboration with Amanda Coogan, produced by Live Collision, Peacock Theatre, Amharclann na Mainistreach. © Patrick Redmond. All rights reserved.

Neil [Murray] and Graham [McLaren] saw the show and asked if I was interested in reviving a significant canonical play, which piqued my interest, and when they said it's *Katie Roche*, I confessed I'd never heard of it.[20] They presumed, as an Irish theatre director, that I would know this play and I felt like I should, too, but it had never crossed my path. I guess that when they saw my work on *The Taming of the Shrew* at

---

20 Murray and McLaren occupied the roles of co-directors of the Abbey Theatre from 2016 to 2021.

the Globe—a woman being tamed—and *Katie Roche* could very well be considered another shrew and I seemed like a good fit for the play.

Graham spoke so enthusiastically about *Katie Roche*, comparing it to *Hedda Gabler* and *A Doll's House*.[21] I do, however, recall my response to it as not so enthused as his. I found it really challenging to grasp the syntax, the style, the characters, and what message it was delivering. It felt sometimes overwritten and underwritten; poised somewhere between the three-act modern play and an expressionistic drama. It confused more than compelled me. But I was intrigued by it, by Katie, and also by Deevy.

Fig. 12.6 Ros Kavanagh, production image from *Katie Roche* (2017), directed by Caroline Byrne for the Abbey Theatre, Amharclann na Mainistreach, featuring Caoilfhionn Dunne as Katie Roche. © Ros Kavanagh. All rights reserved.

I sought permission from the Abbey to reimagine it for 2017, and draw out the expressionism that I felt Deevy was exploring. There were some negotiations around whether I could make some cuts and changes and

---

21 Henrik Ibsen, *Hedda Gabler*, in *The Norton Anthology of Drama*, shorter edition, ed. by J. Ellen Gainor, Stanton B. Garner Jr., and Martin Puchner (New York: W.W. Norton and Company, 2010), pp. 716–771; Henrik Ibsen, *A Doll's House*, in *The Harcourt Brace Anthology of Drama*, 3rd ed., ed. by William B. Worthen (Florida: Harcourt, 1993), pp. 601–624.

employ a dramaturg (Morna Regan) to do so.²² I didn't want it to be a museum piece, nor did I want it to be programmed as a reaction to #WakingTheFeminists. I wanted the play to stand alone and be its own thing rather than redressing something. That permission was granted by the Abbey and the Deevy estate, and Morna and I made some small changes to distill it and draw out its expressionism.²³

Fig. 12.7 Ros Kavanagh, production image from *Katie Roche* (2017), directed by Caroline Byrne for the Abbey Theatre, Amharclann na Mainistreach, featuring Siobhán McSweeney as Amelia. © Ros Kavanagh. All rights reserved.

I talked to as many experts as possible about [Deevy's] work. I visited the archives in Maynooth.²⁴ I consulted with Professor Christopher

---

22 For more on Morna Regan's dramaturgical approach to *Katie Roche*, see 'Interview with the Dramaturg: Interview with Morna Regan by Maire Kelly (August 2017)', in *Abbey Theatre Research Pack: Katie Roche*, researched and compiled by Marie Kelly, School of Music and Theatre, University College Cork (Dublin: Abbey Theatre, 2017), pp. 41–43.

23 *Katie Roche* by Teresa Deevy, directed by Caroline Byrne, and produced by the Abbey Theatre, Dublin, 28 August–23 September 2017. Amongst the dramaturgical decisions made by Regan and Byrne were the decisions to cut the characters of Margaret Drybone and Frank Lawlor from the theatrical text.

24 The Russell Library in Maynooth University, National University of Ireland, Maynooth houses the physical archive of Teresa Deevy. Some documents held by the Russell Library, Maynooth can be accessed online via a Digital Repository of Ireland website page entitled 'The Teresa Deevy Archive'. Digital Repository of Ireland (DRI), The Teresa Deevy Archive, https://doi.org/10.7486/DRI.95944b38t

Morash. These conversations were instrumental to my understanding and appreciation of Deevy. The result was I could then see the play, its importance, its originality, and I loved working on it. Morna and I began working on the text, workshopping it many times before we went into rehearsals with it.[25]

ÚK: *Amanda, would you take on that point that Caroline made around getting into the syntax, the underwritten, the overwritten.*

Amanda Coogan (AC): Lianne was the great discoverer of this little, gold nugget and, in terms of our practice together, it was manna from heaven, in terms of a deafened writer, a woman writer. I, gloriously, come from the visual arts. I'm a performance artist, but I come from the visual arts, so I don't care about literature. I have a fabulous disregard for words—syntax. I am almost really bold about it as well—how I throw this [syntax] against the wall and smash it. So, it was never, with me as the artist—and I'm loath to say director because I think Lianne and Alvean [Jones] are more of the actual theatre directors. I am more of the, 'oh let's try this', 'let's try that', kind of person. I always call myself the artist within our collaborations, but with something that was going to come through my practice—it [my interpretation of Deevy's text] was never going to be a straightforward reading.

And so, I cannot tell you the zeal of the Dublin Theatre of the Deaf—the zeal of that lady there, Lianne Quigley, they're bursting to tell their stories—it [our discovery of Deevy's work] was a brilliant opportunity for somebody [like me] who doesn't care about literary theatre. I think the Irish theatre canon is castrated by the word (but that's a whole other conversation). I was just so excited to start drawing the parallels [between d/Deaf experience and the experience of women in Deevy's dramatic text]. In the first instance we sat down, and we translated the play into ISL because the company are all ISL users. So, myself and Alvean Jones did a reading of it, we translated an equivalent in ISL—you know, Jimmy said this, and Annie said that, and Mrs Marks. And then a match was lit in terms of 'that sounds like what happened in St Mary's', 'that sounds like the way that this happened here, or there'. Like a great example is in *The King of Spain's Daughter*, I think the

---

25   For more on Byrne's directorial approach to *Katie Roche*, see 'Interview with the Director: Interview with Caroline Byrne by Maire Kelly (August 2017)', in *Abbey Theatre Research Pack: Katie Roche*, researched and compiled by Marie Kelly, School of Music and Theatre, University College Cork (Dublin: Abbey Theatre, 2017), pp. 36–40.

original script talked about the flame red dress…

ÚK: *The 'flamin' red' and the 'shimmerin' green' and the 'pale, pale gold'.*[26]

AC: Dreaming of these great, glorious dresses that she wants to wear, and I read it as this kind of fantasy moment. And I wanted to inflect it [our interpretation] with a sexual fantasy as well because we are an embodied company: everything comes back to the body. I wanted to read everything with the body, and a female body, an oppressed female body—I wanted to inflect it with the sexual reading. And so, what we did was, we projected a film in the background. We took the performance off the stage—of course, so oppositional—I took it off the stage and so the play happened within the seats of the auditorium, so the audience [were immersed within our interpretation]. And the Annies are in blue, but we had a screen and so, as part of our show, we took one of the Annie characters, and behind her on the screen is an image of a naked woman swimming underwater.

Fig. 12.8 Patrick Redmond, production image from *Talk Real Fine, Just Like a Lady* (2017), created by Dublin Theatre of the Deaf in collaboration with Amanda Coogan, produced by Live Collision, Peacock Theatre, Amharclann na Mainistreach, featuring Paula Clarke as Annie. © Patrick Redmond. All rights reserved.

---

26 Teresa Deevy, 'Temporal Powers', in *Teresa Deevy Reclaimed*, I, p. 19 and 21.

AC: It's this great, glorious, female sexual dream, orgasmic dream. And she, this girl is, or this Annie, this version of our Annie, is trying to sing like an opera singer. So, with us, we saw the oppression not as Annie having to choose between getting married or going over to the mainland to work in a factory, it was all about the experience of learning to speak, or [of] being a really good girl [simply] because you could articulate something [with your voice], or being a really bad girl because your vocal cords couldn't articulate these sounds that you can't literally hear as a Deaf person, and also [about] being punished for signing, which was the experience of all of our company members. So, this girl just falls into a reverie.

We had a piece of opera beautifully sung by Michelle O'Rourke and I, up at the top of the auditorium, did a [reference to Samuel Beckett's play] *Not I*—I'm also a magpie in terms of my references—where I put a torch on my mouth so that Paula, a Deaf actor, could read my lips at the start.[27] It was an Italian opera piece, a Monteverdi, and she could follow my lips. Then I closed the light off and our Annie just fell into this beautiful reverie about what the equivalent for us was—the flaming red dress, the green, emerald dress.[28] Deevy's Annie has a couple of terms for her great fantasy of expressing herself and being free and being liberated—so this was where we made that happen within our production, I suppose.

Kate McCarthy (KMcC): *Jonathan, we've heard a lot of examples of the many opportunities Deevy's work presents, and some of the challenges. From your experience, what were some of those opportunities that you saw in that work and bringing it to audiences in America?*

JB: For me, I don't find a distinction between opportunities and challenges—I think they're synonymous. I think most theatremakers feel that way. You have to consider your challenges to be opportunities, and an interesting opportunity is probably a challenging opportunity. But for me, the key thing with Deevy goes, maybe, to that question of

---

27 Samuel Beckett, 'Not I', in *Collected Shorter Plays of Samuel* (London: Faber and Faber, 1984), pp. 213–223.
28 Áine Fay's score incorporated pre-recorded excerpts from Beethoven's final unfinished symphony and included a version of Monteverdi's Si dolce è'l tormento. See Kealy and McCarthy, 'Shape Shifting the Silence'.

overwritten versus underwritten. I guess where I land is that it's neither—it's perfectly written—in the sense that what I think Deevy does that has, I think, very little to do with being Irish, or female, or d/Deaf, but has more to do with her genius as a writer—or maybe has everything to do with all those things—but I understand it as her genius as a writer, is her ability to create real humans who hold contradictory desires and feelings in every moment. So, the challenge of the work is really—for an actor—to be able to live that contradiction; and the opportunity is to create a real human being, or to live up to the psychological complexity of the writing.

Fig. 12.9 Richard Termine, production photo from *Strange Birth* as part of *The Suitcase under the Bed* (2017), directed by Jonathan Bank, Mint Theater, featuring Aidan Redmond as Bill and Ellen Adair as Sara Meade. © Richard Termine. All rights reserved.

I never thought about, I mean, there was no place for me to think about how am I going to translate this work for an American audience? I'm an American—I consider a director to be kind of straddling, standing in for the audience and representing the author, or not representing the author, but attempting to *understand* the author, but from the perspective of the audience. I mean, what I really feel is that my job as a director is to deliver to the audience the experience I have in reading the play, so that my first exposure to the play becomes the touchstone of what I'm trying to make sure happens for an audience. And so, my first exposure to Deevy's work was kind of wonderment and not clarity, but confusion. And I didn't think that…I never felt that my job was to choose between multiple interpretations, [but rather] that my job was to allow, or to enable, or to hope that the living contradictions in every moment breathed and that an audience had the experience of being in the room with humans who were struggling.

AC: This is an interesting point, Jonathan. Lianne, maybe you can help here because we desperately wanted to make a feminist piece of work. Of course, we were literally in the wave of #WakingTheFeminists, but we found our experience, the company's experience [was similar], and also in the play was this great idea of the young woman who wanted to be liberated and the older generation of women stopping her doing that. So, this Mrs Marks/Annie dichotomy was not a nice, tidy narrative of all women working together—we know this is the fantasy [of feminism], but that complexity was really interesting as it allowed us to speak to the actuality of real life and real-life experiences in some way—that it's [life is] not all beautifully tidied up and with neat hems.

LQ: I think that we really looked at how women oppressed other women—whether it's hearing women oppressing Deaf women—but we really reflected on our experiences as d/Deaf children being brought up in the way that we were forced into oralism.[29] I think at the end of our production we did a scene with hair brushes where Annie, as Amanda just described, [exposed] this fantasy. She is bashed by the other Annies with hairbrushes—the symbolic female prop or object. She is literally bashed in those terms—in a parallel way—to the way that Mrs Marks tells Annie to get over herself and marry. But we then inflected it again; we turned the hairbrushes around as they were white hair brushes with the rectangular back and we made them into these placards for protest, which is the glorious thing that we did.

At the time when we made the production, we really wanted to promote awareness of ISL to the mainstream audience as ISL was not

---

29 Oralism is a teaching methodology that focuses on lip-reading and speech rather than sign language. St Mary's School introduced oralism in 1946 (*Commission to Inquire into Child Abuse Report*, II, 551).

legally recognised at the time: actually, we got legal recognition literally three months after.[30] We do say that the arts community's acceptance of our language was certainly an amazing way of giving us confidence in our language, giving a kind of recognition and, certainly, in the National Theatre of Ireland, recognising our language and putting it on stage was really significant in those terms as well.

KMcC: *Caroline, you mentioned that you were trying to find a way of responding to the expressionistic elements, and you mentioned that you worked with a dramaturg, and the more you got into the text of* Katie Roche, *the more you found your way, so what were some of the crucial decisions for you in responding to that text, and particularly around the style since you mentioned that?*

CB: When I first read the play, Reuben (Katie's father) was the key character for me that was signalling the expressionism of the play because he's kind of magical—a conjured strange and mythic creature that fulfils a psychic rather than naturalistic function for Katie. He is borne out of her need, out of her mind. So, I started with him. I asked myself: 'what visual world would he fit in?' That was the beginning of building a psychic space for the play—that the world we see expresses Katie's mind, not her reality. Once I began with this, everything came alive to me. The domestic (the cottage) could be housed inside of the expressionistic world very comfortably, but not the other way round.

I started with the design elements of it and how the materials that Katie is surrounded by are an expression of her inner life. I used soil to represent her relationship with the earth and the outside. I coupled that with marble to explore her greatness, her expansiveness. How marble forms were so apposite of her journey; it's formed from fossils. I also loved how great architects used marble as a statement of grandeur and beauty and, to me, Katie has this potential in her—to be an architect, and to be grand. I was interested in glass because when I spoke to Chris Morash, he talked about Deevy's lived experience as a deafened woman. He shared that when Deevy moved into radio dramas, she would sit

---

30 The Irish Sign Language Act was enacted on 24 December 2017 and recognises 'the right of Irish Sign Language users to use Irish Sign Language as their native language'. See Irish Statute Book, *Irish Sign Language Act 2017*, (Article 3.1). The Irish Sign Language Bill commenced on 23 December 2020.

behind a glass booth, lip-reading the actors. This image of her, behind a layer of glass, really struck me and felt like Katie too. So, glass, soil, and marble were the materials that I used to express Katie's dilemmas and aspirations.

Fig. 12.10 Ros Kavanagh, production image from *Katie Roche* (2017), directed by Caroline Byrne for the Abbey Theatre, Amharclann na Mainistreach, featuring Caoilfhionn Dunne as Katie Roche, set and costume design by Joanna Scotcher, and lighting design by Paul Keogan. © Ros Kavanagh. All rights reserved.

Both with the dramaturg and the set designer [Joanna Scotcher], we created a world where the ideogrammatic language of the play would be really strong. Like Amanda was saying—there is a visual language that expresses the characters' desires that often bypasses the [spoken] language. The work I make uses the semiotics of the stage to comment on the character's dilemma. It's not just the language that's working the audience, but the non-verbal world. I also found the character's use of language untrustworthy at times, and so I wanted Katie to have a life beyond the verbal, which seemed to capture something of Deevy herself, too.

When I started work on the play, I put together all the stage directions in one document. From an eighty-page script there were twenty pages of stage directions, which was very revealing of the non-verbal world of the play. I workshopped the stage directions at the Young Vic [in London] to reveal the choreography of Deevy's characters and world. It revealed a silent and rebellious world of movement and dance. I also noticed that there were fifty-three silences written into the stage directions. I used these clues to detect what Deevy wanted in terms of the action of the play. So, that's where I began: Reuben, the stage directions, and the silences. From there, I could create a visual world that would be like a playground for Katie to be able to express herself as an artist. Over the course of the play, she created with the set [using the soil on the stage] like an artist. Katie is without a platform because she is illegitimate and a woman so I tried to give her a canvas.

KMcC: *One of the themes that has also come out of this discussion is the importance of the relationship with your creative team in bringing these plays to life, so that it moves beyond language into the visual. Jonathan, would you like to give us a little bit of an insight into how you worked with your creative team, staging Deevy's many works at the Mint.*

Jonathan: Well, I've staged four complete productions, the fourth production was four short plays including *The King of Spain's Daughter*, so that's a lot of different creative teams having a lot of different conversations, although my set designer [Vicki R. Davis] has been consistent throughout, and she and I are long-time collaborators.[31]

And just to focus in on *Katie Roche*—we did have a cottage—we had a ground plan and knew we weren't done and it's kind of the most assertive I am, contrary to my colleagues here. For us, the question was how to help the audience see the end of the play the way we did—and when I say the way we did—the way we felt Deevy intended, and not with a concern for the year in which we were producing it, nor with a concern for the year in which she wrote it, but just with a concern for the text. And so, we made some very specific decisions about how to help tell the story. I would say it was something that I felt was really bold and, I think, it went completely unnoticed as a bold directorial move—which I think is, for me, a sign of its success and that it just felt like it

---

31 Directed by Jonathan Bank at the Mint Theater (New York), Deevy's texts included: *Wife to James Whelan* (2010), *Temporal Powers* (2011), and *Katie Roche* (2013). *Strange Birth, In the Cellar of My Friend, Holiday House,* and *The King of Spain's Daughter* followed in 2017, comprising *The Suitcase under the Bed* production.

was intended. Basically, we just wanted to see a moment past the final moment of the play.

The directors who feel that the first thing they want to do is black out stage directions are interesting to me as there's so much information that Deevy wants us to have there. Having edited two volumes of her work, which means proofreading plays time and time and time again, her stage directions are critical. She doesn't tell an actor how to say a line; she writes the line and then gives the direction after the fact that you should understand—just in case you're confused about what was intended by that line, here's a little more information—but it's not really an instruction, it's additional information, by and large.

LQ: For our creative team, the big thing was that we were completely invested in promoting ISL awareness and we played, during ISL Awareness Week, an embodied piece of work, an immersive piece of theatre.[32] Audiences came into our world in both physical and visual ways. The sign language that was used in Ireland [in the] last century is very different to what we use today, so we mixed between women's gendered signs of the 1930s to young women/girls' signs now.

AC: The gendered nature of Irish Sign Language is anthropologically, sociologically unique in the world. ISL is the first language for the company [Dublin Theatre of the Deaf] and so, I think what we call women's signs was really a major conversation with the creative team. And a really major conversation because all of our creative team were

---

32 Taking place annually, Irish Sign Language (ISL) awareness week aims to break down the barriers of communication between d/Deaf, hard of hearing, and hearing communities. ISL Awareness Week (16–24 September, 2017) ran in tandem with the third International Conference of the World Federation of the Deaf under the theme of 'Full Inclusion with Sign Language', making the case that full social inclusion of d/Deaf people was only possible when Irish Sign Language was recognised and used widely used within society. The ISL campaign argued that the failure by the Irish State, at that time, to officially recognise ISL as a language and to fully implement the United Nations Convention on the Rights of Persons with Disabilities (UNCRPD) had a detrimental impact on d/Deaf people's lives and prevented them from achieving their goals. For an overview of the themes of the campaign, see Irish Deaf Society, *Irish Sign Language (ISL) Awareness Week, 16th–24th September 2017*. Heath Rose and John Bosco Conama's analysis of ISL as the subject of linguistic imperialism in Ireland usefully contextualises the 2017 ISL campaign. See Heath Rose and John Bosco Conama, 'Linguistic Imperialism: Still a Valid Construct in Relation to Language Policy for Irish Sign Language', *Language Policy*, 17 (2018), 385–404.

women, all of us were sign language users, and most of us, except me, were Deaf. So, we had the resources within our company to do this first-hand research on how d/Deaf women said the Hail Mary, which is one of those ritual things that you just speak without considering the individual words. How did they do this? How did they say black? How did they say white? Why did they say white? We made the sign for white [index finger touching the middle of the opposite hand's outstretched palm] into a whole poetic gesture and, actually, very beautifully. This [women's sign for white came into being] because they used to wear white gloves—[we used] all of that lovely detail. We could really read [the historical context of] the 1920s and 1930s [within the lives of] the women in the deaf school [i.e. St Mary's]. Teresa Deevy didn't go to the deaf school, but her contemporaries [women of the 1920s and 1930s who did attend St Mary's and] who were deaf, wore white gloves when they went for their walks and that's why they designated the sign [described above] for white as in 'like my gloves'. We used the sign for water as we were translating the poem, 'A Drover', within the play.[33] Women's sign for water is this [both hands and fingers outstretched, shaking in quick succession]. This is the sign for water we use every day [middle finger bounced off the chin twice], which is the St Joseph's Boys' sign, in comparison to the women's sign for water, which is this shimmering, glittering, beautiful thing, so these decisions also helped to create and bring out the poetic gestures.

We were coming from our perspective as culturally Deaf people who are using sign language. It was really interesting that both Jonathan and Caroline talked about the stage directions, and I would say from a Deaf perspective that that's completely understandable—you contextualise everything in the visual, in the vision that you're seeing. In our research, we found that her sister [Deevy's sister, Nell] interpreted for her quite a lot. Her sister was very much a bridge to the world. There were some comments that when her sister died before her, she (Deevy) was very isolated. So, [as a d/Deaf person] there's a lot of those interrelationships with the world if you're facing into the world—like speaking from an embodied perspective—you're facing into the world and the visual is your most important sense.

---

33   Padraic Colum, 'A Drover', in *Wild Earth and Other Poems* (New York: Henry Holt and Company, 1916), pp. 5–6.

Fig. 12.11 Patrick Redmond, 'The women's sign for white', production image from *Talk Real Fine, Just Like a Lady* (2017), created by Dublin Theatre of the Deaf in collaboration with Amanda Coogan, produced by Live Collision, Peacock Theatre, Amharclann na Mainistreach. © Patrick Redmond. All rights reserved.

JB: I think it's important to just clarify that her sister interpreted, but her sister didn't sign—they had a communication.

AC: It's not the formal way that we have sign language interpreters, but certainly, what we'd talk about is home signs. I think, Lianne, you came across some evidence of home signs—so, small, intimate gestures that two people would have the understanding for, and certainly her sister was a communicator—in whatever way that was—whether she spoke more clearly that Teresa could understand her, or whatever way it happened, she had a conduit within her sister to the hearing world, or the mainstream world.

Bibliography

Bank, Jonathan, John P. Harrington, and Christopher Morash (eds), *Teresa Deevy Reclaimed*, 2 vols (New York: Mint Theater, 2011 and 2017)

Beckett, Samuel, *Collected Shorter Plays of Samuel* (London: Faber and Faber, 1984)

Byrne, Caroline, 'Interview with the Director: Interview with Caroline Byrne by Maire Kelly (August 2017)', in *Abbey Theatre Research Pack: Katie Roche*, researched and compiled by Marie Kelly, School of Music and Theatre, University College Cork (Dublin: Abbey Theatre, 2017), pp. 36–40, https://www.abbeytheatre.ie/wp-content/uploads/2017/10/KATIE-ROCHE_RESEARCH-PACK-2017.pdf

Centre for Integration and Improvement of Journalism, *The Diversity Style Guide* (2024), https://www.diversitystyleguide.com/glossary/deaf-deaf/

Colum, Padraic, *Wild Earth and Other Poems* (New York: Henry Holt and Company, 1916), https://archive.org/details/wildearthotherpo00colu/page/n3/mode/2up

Commission to Inquire into Child Abuse, *Commission to Inquire into Child Abuse Report*, 6 vols (Dublin: Stationery Office, 2009), II, https://childabusecommission.ie/?page_id=241

Deevy, Teresa, *Three Plays by Teresa Deevy: Katie Roche, The King of Spain's Daughter, The Wild Goose* (London: Macmillan, 1939)

Deevy, Teresa, 'Wife to James Whelan', *Irish University Review*, 25.1 (1995), 29–87

Donohue, Brenda, Ciara O'Dowd, Tanya Dean, Ciara Murphy, Kathleen Cawley, and Kate Harris (eds), *Gender Counts: An Analysis of Gender in Irish Theatre 2006–2015* (Belfast: Ulster University, 2017), https://pure.ulster.ac.uk/ws/portalfiles/portal/11631340/Gender_Counts_WakingTheFeminists_2017.pdf

Famous Plays 1935–6 (London: Victor Gollancz, 1936)

Dunne, Seán (ed.), 'Teresa Deevy Special Number', *Journal of Irish Literature*, 14.2 (May 1985)

Government of Ireland, *Constitution of Ireland*, January 2020, https://www.irishstatutebook.ie/eli/cons/en/html

Hefferman, Georgina, and Elizabeth Nixon, 'Experiences of Hearing Children of Deaf Parents in Ireland', *The Journal of Deaf Studies and Deaf Education*, 28.4 (2023), 399–407, https://doi.org/10.1093/deafed/enad018

Ibsen, Henrik, 'A Doll's House', in *The Harcourt Brace Anthology of Drama*, 3rd ed., ed. by William B. Worthen (Florida: Harcourt, 1993), pp. 601–624

Ibsen, Henrik, 'Hedda Gabler', in *The Norton Anthology of Drama*, shorter edition, ed. by J. Ellen Gainor, Stanton B. Garner Jr., and Martin Puchner (New York: W.W. Norton and Company, 2010), pp. 716–771

Irish Deaf Society, *Irish Sign Language (ISL) Awareness Week, 16th–24th September 2017*, http://dublindiocese.ie/wp-content/uploads/2017/09/ISL-Awareness-Week-2017-Campaign-Messages.pdf

Irish Statute Book, *Irish Sign Language Act 2017*, https://www.irishstatutebook.ie/eli/2017/act/40/enacted/en/print#sec3

Kealy, Úna, and Kate McCarthy, 'Shape Shifting the Silence: An Analysis of *Talk Real Fine, Just Like a Lady* (2017) by Amanda Coogan in Collaboration with Dublin Theatre of the Deaf, an Appropriation of Teresa Deevy's *The King of Spain's Daughter* (1935)', in *The Golden Thread: Irish Women Playwrights, 1716–2016*, 2 vols, ed. by David Clare, Fiona McDonagh, and Justine Nakase (Liverpool: Liverpool University Press, 2021), I, 197–210 https://doi.org/10.3828/liverpool/9781800859463.003.0015

Kearney, Eileen, and Charlotte Headrick (eds), *Irish Women Dramatists 1908–2021* (New York: Syracuse University, 2014)

Keogh, Claire, *#WakingTheFeminists and the Data-Driven Revolution in Irish Theatre* (Cambridge: Cambridge University Press, 2025), https://doi.org/10.1017/9781009523066

LeMaster, Barbara, 'Language Contraction, Revitalization, and Irish Women', *Journal of Linguistic Anthropology*, 16.2 (2006), 211–228

LeMaster, Barbara, 'School Language and Shifts in Irish Identity', in *Many Ways to Be Deaf: International Variation in Deaf Communities*, ed. by Leila Monaghan, Constanze Schmaling, Karen Nakamura, and Graham H. Turner (Washington, DC: Gallaudet University Press, 2003), pp. 153–172

Mint Theater, *Production Archives*, https://minttheater.org/production-archives/

Murphy, Fiona, *The Shape of Sound* (Melbourne: Text Publishing Company, 2021)

National Centre for Disability and Journalism, Arizona State University, *Disability Language Guide* (2021), https://ncdj.org/wp-content/uploads/2021/08/NCDJ-STYLE-GUIDE-EDIT-2021-SILVERMAN.pdf

O'Beirne, Patricia, 'A Gendered Absence: Feminist Theatre, Glasshouse Productions and the #WTF movement', in *Perspectives on Contemporary Irish Theatre: Populating the Stage*, ed. by Anne Etienne and Thierry Dubost (Cham: Palgrave Macmillan/Springer Nature, 2017), pp. 269–290, https://doi.org/10.1007/978-3-319-59710-2_19

O'Brien, Susan, 'The Blessed Virgin Mary', in *The Oxford History of British and Irish Catholicism, vol. IV: Building Identity, 1830–1913*, ed. by Carmen M. Mangion and Susan O'Brien (Oxford: Oxford University Press, 2023), pp. 154–172, https://doi.org/10.1093/oso/9780198848196.003.0009

Regan, Morna, 'Interview with the Dramaturg: Interview with Morna Regan by Maire Kelly (August 2017)', in *Abbey Theatre Research Pack: Katie Roche*, researched and compiled by Marie Kelly, School of Music and Theatre, University College Cork (Dublin: Abbey Theatre, 2017), pp. 41–43, https://www.abbeytheatre.ie/wp-content/uploads/2017/10/KATIE-ROCHE_RESEARCH-PACK-2017.pdf

Robinson, Lennox, *Ireland's Abbey Theatre: A History 1899–1955* (London: Sidgwick and Jackson, 1951)

Rose, Heath, and John Bosco Conama, 'Linguistic Imperialism: Still a Valid Construct in Relation to Language Policy for Irish Sign Language', *Language Policy*, 17 (2018), 385–404, https://doi.org/10.1007/s10993-017-9446-2

13. 'You Can Feel the Change in the Air': Reflecting on *Talk Real Fine, Just Like a Lady*, a Shapeshifting of Teresa Deevy's *The King of Spain's Daughter*

Amanda Coogan, Alvean Jones, and Lianne Quigley

This panel formed part of the Active Speech: Sharing Scholarship on Teresa Deevy conference and was recorded in December 2020.[1] All three participants are members of the Deaf community with Amanda being a hearing CODA (Child of Deaf Adult(s)) whose first language is Irish Sign Language (ISL).[2] A captioned and ISL translated recording of this

---

1   Funded by South East Technological University (then WIT), Maynooth University, and Waterford Libraries, the conference took place online from 12–19 February 2021.
2   Georgina Heffernan and Elizabeth Nixon define CODAs as hearing children of one or two Deaf parents in 'Experiences of Hearing Children of Deaf Parents in Ireland', *The Journal of Deaf Studies and Deaf Education*, 28.4 (2023), 399–407. Fiona Murphy explains that: 'Identity is a fluid concept and a personal choice. Lowercase deaf refers to deafness as a medical condition. It does not indicate the degree of hearing loss an individual may have. Some people with hearing loss may prefer to use the term "hard of hearing". Uppercase Deaf refers to people who identify as culturally Deaf and may use sign language. Given the ongoing suppression of sign-language education, not all Deaf people are fluent signers or even have access to the Deaf community. Again, this word does not indicate the degree of hearing loss an individual may have'. See Fiona Murphy, *The Shape of Sound* (Melbourne: Text Publishing Company, 2021), n.p. Thus, our capitalising of the word 'Deaf' here recognises Deafness as a social category and Deaf people as a group who share a particular history and culture. In line with Dublin Theatre of the Deaf, the Irish Deaf Society, the Irish Deaf Youth Association, the Centre for Deaf Studies, Trinity

panel discussion is available.³ In this conversation, Amanda Coogan, Lianne Quigley, and Alvean Jones discuss their ongoing collaboration and, in particular, their experiences engaging with Teresa Deevy's life and work. As well as discussing their collaboration on *Talk Real Fine, Just Like a Lady*, they also explore their connections with Deevy's life experiences.

Amanda Coogan (AC): My name is Amanda Coogan; I'm an artist specifically working in performance art. I have a long-standing relationship with the Dublin Theatre of the Deaf (DTD), working closely with Alvean Jones and Lianne Quigley.

Alvean Jones (AJ): As Amanda mentioned, she and I have a long-standing relationship, collaborating on many projects in performance art and various other theatre work. I've also been involved in many different theatres for a long time—in many aspects of theatre—working with Amanda and others.

Lianne Quigley (LQ): I'm an artist: I write plays, direct, and act. I'm involved in many areas of the theatre world, and I have worked with Amanda on various projects. My vision and ambition is to play in mainstream theatres to show that Deaf people are capable of being involved in all aspects of the arts.

AC: Lianne, can you explain when you first heard about Teresa Deevy?

LQ: It was at an evening workshop for theatremakers in Trinity College Dublin, during Disability Awareness Week.⁴ I went and heard of Teresa Deevy and

---

College Dublin, and researchers in the field, we capitalise the letter D in the word Deaf, when appropriate, to signal accord with the positive values within the Deaf community and Deaf culture. We use a lowercase d when referring to audiological status. When we determine that the reference is to both audiological status and Deaf culture, we use the term d/Deaf. For more on d/Deaf, see the entry on 'Deaf, deaf', in the Centre for Integration and Improvement of Journalism, *The Diversity Style Guide* (2024), and the entry for 'Deaf' in The National Centre for Disability and Journalism, Arizona State University, Disability Language Guide (2021)

3   *Practitioners' Panel: Talk Real Fine, Just Like a Lady*, online video recording, YouTube, 12 February 2021, https://www.youtube.com/watch?v=EIRLkX_95R8&t=35s. In reshaping a live, online conversation as prose, some parts of the discussion herein were edited and adapted from this original conversation.

4   Lecture Series 2014–15: Disability & Literature, Trinity Long Room Hub Arts & Humanities Research Institute.

that she was deaf; I couldn't believe that I had never heard of her before then, and my interest was piqued. A few days later, brainstorming ideas for a new project with Amanda, I mentioned Teresa Deevy and we decided to ask DTD to help us research—to show everyone within the Deaf community that we do have d/Deaf artists. We didn't know much about Teresa's background, whether she was an ISL [Irish Sign Language] user, if she was profoundly deaf, or how she communicated with her family, but we wanted to celebrate this famous, deaf person who was recognised within the mainstream art world.

AC: Alvean, when did you first hear about Teresa Deevy?

AJ: I first heard about Deevy at the same time; it could have been the same event. It was a great match to my personal interests in Irish history. I then discovered the Teresa Deevy Archive in Maynooth University whilst there at a history conference.[5]

As we know, not all d/Deaf people are the same: we are all individuals and have an array of experiences, as do the hearing community. However, the one commonality we have is our experience of deafness: that's the common ground. It doesn't matter if you went to a school for the d/Deaf or to a mainstream school, if you were born d/Deaf or were deafened later in life; that unique ingredient, that lived experience, brings an awareness and understanding that hearing people just don't have. Teresa Deevy had that lived experience of deafness and carried on regardless; that's why I had such an interest in her work.

AC: So, Teresa Deevy was not a sign language user and lost her hearing? Is that correct?

AJ: Yes, that's right, she was deafened.

AC: Did we read somewhere that her sister, Nell, acted as her interpreter? Would it be fair to say there was some translation going on from some kind of signed utterances, or what we would refer to as a home sign, or a way of communicating particular to Deevy and Nell?[6]

---

5 The Russell Library in Maynooth University, National University of Ireland, Maynooth houses the physical archive of Teresa Deevy. Some documents held by the Russell Library, Maynooth can be accessed online via a Digital Repository of Ireland website page entitled 'The Teresa Deevy Archive'. Digital Repository of Ireland (DRI), The Teresa Deevy Archive, https://doi.org/10.7486/DRI.95944b38t

6 Seán Dunne notes that 'with Nell acting as her ears, she [Deevy] kept up an interest

Fig. 13.1 Photographer unknown. (L-R) Nell and Teresa Deevy. © Courtesy of Jacqui Deevy. All rights reserved.

AJ: It could it have been that Nell was interpreting via lipspeaking, not necessarily sign language per se: there is a distinct difference.

LQ: Also, it's important to remember that Deevy's family would be familiar with her voice and understand her well enough to relay the messages—in the way that our families are familiar with our voice. Most d/Deaf people, as you say, have a similar experience in their own homes in that the family don't have sign language, but the d/Deaf family member has a way of communicating, be that lipspeaking, gesture, or whatever way the family develop a system to communicate.[7]

---

in every detail of theatrical and cultural life in Dublin. When people spoke in ways that were too difficult for her to lip-read, Nell interpreted for her'. See Seán Dunne, 'Rediscovering Teresa Deevy', *Cork Examiner*, 20 March 1984, p. 10.

7   Dunne records that, as Deevy explained to Kyle Deevy, her nephew, she and Nell 'had perfected their ability to talk under all conditions' (ibid.). Deevy was deafened in early adulthood. In relation to her ability to verbally converse with hearing people, her friend James Cheasty, recalling a car journey he took with her and Nell, describes how his replies to Deevy's spoken conversation 'were transmitted to her by Nell whom she was able to lip-read. Nell was really Teresa's ears' (James

AC: So a 'family communication system' rather than a 'home sign system'. Rounding back to your points on Deevy the artist. You mention she has a beautiful interpretation [of the d/Deaf experience] expressed through her work. And could you read that, as a Deaf person, that her work captured her experiences, her life, her work, through the deaf experience or 'deaf eyes' if you will?

AJ: A d/Deaf lens.

AC: A d/Deaf lens. Yes. Was there a reason you picked the play *The King of Spain's Daughter* to focus on?[8]

LQ: That was the first script that we had. We searched high and low and came across *The King of Spain's Daughter*.

AC: You first heard about Teresa Deevy in 2014. Is that correct? Before the #WakingTheFeminists movement. So, as we began to consider our next project, we were specifically interested in Deevy as a deaf artist. Then the #WakingTheFeminists movement added an extra layer of interest. We were reclaiming a deaf artist and a woman playwright who had been sidelined within the story of Irish theatre.[9]

If I remember rightly, we three began researching using our own different strengths. Alvean, your interest is d/Deaf history, you're a Deaf historian and a Deaf artist and, Lianne, as you have a strong interest in how things are mainstreamed, will you explain your roles?

LQ: I'm very interested in bringing d/Deaf people into mainstream life

---

Cheasty, 'The Curtain Rises', *Irish Farmers' Journal*, 6 June 1964, p. 28).

8   Teresa Deevy, 'The King of Spain's Daughter', in *Irish Women Dramatists 1908–2021*, ed. by Eileen Kearney and Charlotte Headrick (New York: Syracuse University, 2014), pp. 44–58.

9   From November 2015 to November 2016 #WakingTheFeminists functioned as a grassroots movement and campaign that called for equality for women in the Irish Theatre sector. #WakingTheFeminists commissioned a study entitled *Gender Counts: An Analysis of Gender in Irish Theatre 2006–2015*, ed. by Brenda Donohue, Ciara O'Dowd, Tanya Dean, Ciara Murphy, Kathleen Cawley, and Kate Harris (Belfast: Ulster University, 2017). The study demonstrated the underrepresentation of people who identified as women and men in key roles across the sector. The report also analysed the relationship between public funding and representation in ten organisations funded by The Arts Council of Ireland (An Chomhairle Ealaíon); Claire Keogh, *#WakingTheFeminists and the Data-Driven Revolution in Irish Theatre* (Cambridge: Cambridge University Press, 2025), http://doi.org/10.1017/9781009523066

and culture, but I want to take you back maybe ten years, or so, when I couldn't find any d/Deaf artists. It became my mission almost [to find d/Deaf artist role models] and it was the shared mission of DTD and Alvean. We have the same philosophy in that we want to show the mainstream world that there is a variety of talent within the d/Deaf community. We decided to develop the work of d/Deaf artists and to make our productions completely ISL based, from the beginning to the end, and design them as accessible to d/Deaf and hearing audiences.

From the moment that audiences entered the Peacock Theatre [for *Talk Real Fine, Just Like a Lady*], the audience was guided to their seats by Deaf performers. The housekeeping and safety announcements were relayed as ISL videos in the cafe. Although Deevy may not have used sign language, we invited d/Deaf and hearing people to experience Deevy's work brought to life via sign language. We demonstrated that, like us, she too had to face barriers in her lifetime. d/Deaf people can relate to this as they face barriers daily. We wanted to explore the challenges that Deevy faced as a deaf artist and how, despite this, she made significant work, and that we, as contemporary Deaf artists, were taking inspiration from her to make new work.

AJ: Yes, Teresa Deevy was an experienced and an accomplished playwright and she was deaf, but no one made much of this. We thought, 'Hang on, this is a big deal!' In the Deaf community, we think it's a big deal that Deevy was deaf, and we wanted to recognise her as a deaf artist, a deaf playwright. Doing so is very important because such recognition has implications for contemporary society and politics.

AC: To return to our production. We believed that the 1937 Constitution's inclusion of the phrase 'The woman's place is in the home' had grave ramifications for Deevy.[10] That was the starting point for us. So, at the beginning of the project, we sat down and went through the play, line by line, taking notes. Then we worked with DTD, forming a company with them to make a verbatim read-through of the play—translating it, line by line, into ISL. Then we began to look at the parallels between the lived experiences of those within our company and the sign language used by d/Deaf women in the 1930s, the time the play was written. Most

---

10   Bunreacht na hÉireann (Constitution of Ireland) was ratified on 29 December 1937. Government of Ireland, *Constitution of Ireland*, January 2020.

d/Deaf women in Ireland were sent to St Mary's School for Deaf Girls as boarders from a young age. Can you contextualise St Mary's School and what happened there in the 1930s?

AJ: Prior to the main schools for the d/Deaf being set up in Ireland, there were schools for deaf people in Ireland. These schools were either Protestant or non-Catholic in ethos. The new institution, established in 1845, had ties to a deaf school, Le Bon Sauveur in Caen, northern France, as the Irish nuns received their training in the instruction of deaf children there. Upon their return to Ireland in August 1846, they opened their first school, St. Mary's for Deaf Girls.[11] For example this 'V' we use in ISL is the sign for Friday [finger spelt letter for V held upright brought across the chin bouncing from one side to the next]. This is directly influenced from French Sign Language and the French word for Friday.[12] Hence, ISL has some similarities with old French Sign Language.

By the turn of the century, the 1901 census and 1911 census reveals that most deaf women in Ireland were single and institutionalised. At that time, before Ireland was partitioned, there were four educational institutions for deaf children, one in the North, the Claremont School,

---

11   The first public school for deaf children in Ireland, the Claremont School for the Deaf and Dumb, was established in Glasnevin in 1816 by Charles Orpen and was Church of Ireland in ethos. The Catholic Institution for the Deaf and Dumb (later renamed The Catholic Institution for the Deaf, then the Catholic Institute for Deaf People, and now known as Reach Deaf Services) was founded in 1845. In January 1846, the Catholic Institution for the Deaf and Dumb sent two girls and a group of nuns over to Le Bon Sauveur for eight months so that the Irish nuns could learn how to teach deaf children when they returned to Ireland. While the two girls were in France, they picked up old LSF, (French Sign Language). Upon the group's return to Ireland St Mary's School for Deaf Girls was established and opened in August 1846 (Commission to Inquire into Child Abuse, 'St Mary's School for Deaf Girls, Cabra, Commission to Inquire into Child Abuse Report, 2.15', in *Commission to Inquire into Child Abuse Report*, 6 vols (Dublin: Stationery Office, 2009), II, 551–556). St Joseph's for Deaf Boys opened in 1856 and the school was relocated and given over to be managed by the Christian Brothers in 1857. ('St Joseph's School for Deaf Boys, Cabra ('Cabra'), 1857–1999', in ibid., I, 555–580). The Mary Immaculate School for Deaf Boys (later renamed as Mary Immaculate School for Deaf Children) was located in Stillorgan, County Dublin. Recognised on 10 April 1956, the school prepared children aged three to ten for St Joseph's. ('Mary Immaculate School for Deaf Children', in ibid., II, Child Abuse Report, 557–560).Other schools for deaf children were established elsewhere in Ireland at roughly the same time, and these were non-Catholic in ethos. The editors are grateful to Alvean Jones for her help in creating this footnote.
12   In French, 'Friday' is 'vendredi'.

and two schools under the auspices of the Catholic Institution for the Deaf and Dumb in which the Dominican nuns looked after the education of deaf Catholic girls and the Christian Brothers looked after the education of deaf Catholic boys in Dublin.

By the 1930s, the situation hadn't changed much but, a fact that many people don't know, and which may come as a shock, is that different sign languages were used in the two Dublin schools and different sign language variations, male and female variations, developed in those two schools. Variation in signs remains in ISL, although there is more of an overlap now, but it's important to know that Irish Catholic schools [for deaf people] were segregated. Men's and women's signs were separate and used among segregated communities. The signs developed were very distinct, for example, when you sign the days of the week the signs used today are mostly men's signs, but women's signs are different: there are sign variations.[13]

Another thing to consider is, because in Ireland there were two separated schools under the auspices of the one institution and two different languages: when deaf people became adults, the expectation was that women would change their signs and learn the male variations, which were regarded as superior. But, funnily enough, the sign for Friday is one example where women had a small victory: their variation for 'Friday' became more predominantly used in current ISL use. That's one instance of women's sign becoming dominant.

In Ireland in the 1930s, deaf men were not expected to learn their wives' sign and when deaf people married, or got together in groups, they would use their own signs and so the men, sometimes, would not know what women were saying because they were using women's signs. We realised that attitudes in the 1930s towards women [deaf and hearing] overlapped and we wanted to show that in our production.

AC: To put this in context, Barbara LeMaster, an American linguistic researcher visited Ireland in the 1980s to research women and men's sign language in Ireland (she stayed with my family). She researched and recorded the different signs used between men and women at that time and made a stunning discovery. She described ISL as the starkest example of gendered language differences in the world.[14] For us, as a company, that was *very* interesting as was the fact that

---

13 The men's ISL sign variation for 'Friday' also uses a V sign, but it is turned horizontally and moved under the chin, slid from right to left.

14 For research into the gendered nature of Irish Sign Language, see Barbara LeMaster, 'Language Contraction, Revitalization, and Irish Women', *Journal of Linguistic Anthropology*, 16.2 (2006), 211–228; Barbara LeMaster, 'School Language and Shifts

women's sign is dying out in ISL. Those signs were something we wanted to remember and so our production was full of women's signs, isn't that right?

AJ: Yes, that's exactly it.

LQ: Yes, and religious signs, also. The linguistic research [into women's signs] was carried out by you two and a number of others within the company. Also, just to let people know, our company was all women with the exception of one man who played the role of a comrade. Also, everyone in the company, with the exception of Amanda, myself, and Lorraine, were past pupils of St Mary's School for Deaf Girls, right?

AC: Yes, almost everyone involved in the company had deep roots and connections with St Mary's School for Deaf Girls, and part of what we wanted the production to do was to highlight the school's hidden, but significant, position in Irish d/Deaf history and culture.

AJ: Just to fold back on the idea of hidden stories and to go back to social history again. There were different sign languages for men and women and also, at the same time, separate, deaf social clubs for men and women existed, and men and women were forbidden by the religious orders in charge to integrate in these clubs. There were, however, many other ways for men and women to meet up.

AC: So keeping the clubs separate was motivated by a type of eugenics so that deaf people would not marry and would not have more deaf children?

LQ: Something to note around women signs is that research also shows religious signs were influenced by women's signs. Take the prayer, the Hail Mary, for example.[15] 'Hail Mary, full of grace'—these signs are women's sign

---

in Irish Identity', in *Many Ways to Be Deaf: International Variation in Deaf Communities*, ed. by Leila Monaghan, Constanze Schmaling, Karen Nakamura, and Graham H. Turner (Washington, DC: Gallaudet University Press, 2003), pp. 153–172; Úna Kealy and Kate McCarthy, 'Shape Shifting the Silence: An Analysis of *Talk Real Fine, Just Like a Lady* (2017) by Amanda Coogan in Collaboration with Dublin Theatre of the Deaf, an Appropriation of Teresa Deevy's *The King of Spain's Daughter* (1935)', in *The Golden Thread: Irish Women Playwrights, 1716–2016*, 2 vols, ed. by David Clare, Fiona McDonagh, and Justine Nakase (Liverpool: Liverpool University Press, 2021), I, 197–210.

15 The 'Hail Mary' is a devotional prayer to Mary, mother of Jesus, traditionally prayed by Roman Catholics as a standalone prayer or as part of the Rosary. For details of the Rosary and the full text of the Hail Mary, see 'The Mysteries of the Rosary', vatican. va, https://www.vatican.va/special/rosary/documents/misteri_en.html. For more on the rise of the figure of the Blessed Virgin Mary in Ireland in the early twentieth century see Susan O'Brien, 'The Blessed Virgin Mary', in *The Oxford History of British and Irish Catholicism, vol. IV: Building Identity, 1830–1913*, ed. by Carmen M. Mangion

variations, not men's. This influence is from the early 1900s, 20s, and 30s. In Deevy's work we can see religious influence too; the religious [institutions] were the authority. You can see this in the deaf school, as well as the fact that deaf women's lives had [a] strong religious influence.

AC: I think it would be interesting to talk about the theatre process and what it was. Firstly, we translated the play into ISL with our company [DTD]. Then we tried to find a way in, a way to claim the Deaf artist in the first place. Secondly, we wanted to show the similarities with our Deaf lived experience and to talk about feminism or the oppression of women. We wanted to talk about the 1937 [Irish] Constitution and how it oppressed women. To talk about how that oppression was paralleled with the oppression experienced by deaf women of that time. So we looked back at old, deaf, women's sign language as a first place to investigate. As an exercise, we translated the poem—*The Drover* by Padraic Colum—which is where the title of the play *The King of Spain's Daughter* comes from.[16] We translated the poem into pure women's signs and then we took it from there.

Fig. 13.2 Patrick Redmond, production image from *Talk Real Fine, Just Like a Lady* (2017), created by Dublin Theatre of the Deaf in collaboration with Amanda Coogan, produced by Live Collision, Peacock Theatre, Amharclann na Mainistreach. © Patrick Redmond. All rights reserved.

---

and Susan O'Brien (Oxford: Oxford University Press, 2023), pp. 154–172.

16   Padraic Colum, 'The Drover', in *Wild Earth and Other Poems* (New York: Henry Holt, 1916), pp. 5–6.

AC: We projected images of our translation of *The Drover* and, during the production, the video projection [which was projected onto a cyclorama situated upstage] was un-writing and re-writing Deevy's text. We were re-writing or appropriating the text. This scene was the first way we got into the play. It was perfect for us to make the leaps we needed with the text. And, as Lianne mentioned, Deevy's play begins with two men on a country road, looking around with their hands over their eyes, remember?

LQ: Yes.

AC: Then it became the sign for Ireland.

LQ: Yes—our sign for searching morphed into the sign for Ireland. [17]

AC: Then we began with the 'Hail Mary', uttered using women's signs. We carried on the prayer until the word 'womb' comes in. Then we had an awakening—an abrupt realisation—a realisation of our bodies, women's bodies, and of the place of women, and [we] moved our story from there. Right?

LQ and AJ: Yes, that's right.

AC: It was like this sign we used for the poem, a splash or a small explosion, a series of splashes.

AJ: Like mud pulling you down, like your feet getting sucked down, stuck in mud.

LQ: The squelching sound of the poem we were looking to portray.

AC: Squelching...

AJ: Yes, yes. This represented the drudgery of daily life. Repeating itself, over and over.

AC: Before we get into that, maybe we should go back and explain why we decided this production should be an immersive experience. Why, for example, we had three Mrs Marks, five Annies and, outside the auditorium, we had all the comrades.

---

17 The ISL sign for 'looking' is easily inflected to become the ISL sign for 'Ireland'. See Figures 12.4 and 12.5 in Chapter 12 in this volume.

Fig. 13.3 Patrick Redmond, production image from *Talk Real Fine, Just Like a Lady* (2017), created by Dublin Theatre of the Deaf in collaboration with Amanda Coogan, produced by Live Collision, Peacock Theatre, Amharclann na Mainistreach. © Patrick Redmond. All rights reserved.

AC: As you came down the stairs of the Peacock Theatre, firstly, you encountered the health and safety announcement delivered in ISL on video. It was a performative video—with the content of the safety announcement there—but in the background, an exuberant march for ISL recognition was [also] going on. To enter the auditorium then, the audience were guided by 'comrades' who helped them to physically navigate getting in under the cover—Mrs Marks' skirt—before putting [their] heads through the fabric. This [immersive quality and the fact that the audience was under the skirts of the Mrs Marks characters] was really important to us because it symbolised Mrs Marks' dress spreading outwards in pervasive oppression. The sign for oppression in ISL [clenched fist in one hand—outstretched palm in the opposite hand pressing down on the fist] is beautiful and perfect: it shows that oppression.

AJ: People expect the play to start when you enter the auditorium, but really that wasn't the case. It had already started when you arrived at the bottom of the stairs into the Peacock. That's really where the experience started. The comrades were placed around the lobby, just signing between each other and the [hearing members of the] audience were a bit taken aback by the experience. They had that disjointed feeling. They experienced the comrades signing to them, without voices, as they ushered them into the auditorium. Like that, the [hearing members of the] audience were the outsiders in this environment. d/Deaf people were the majority, and the minority were non-d/Deaf. Mrs Marks was there in the auditorium, towering above us, and the impact of that could be seen as the audience put their heads though the fabric. Only the audience's heads were allowed above Mrs Marks' skirt: that gave it [the auditorium] a really stark feeling.

Fig. 13.4 Patrick Redmond, production image from *Talk Real Fine, Just Like a Lady* (2017), created by Dublin Theatre of the Deaf in collaboration with Amanda Coogan, produced by Live Collision, Peacock Theatre, Amharclann na Mainistreach, featuring Amanda Coogan as Annie. © Patrick Redmond. All rights reserved.

AC: And they were all beside each other—it was a close encounter for audience and performers.

LQ: We have to remember the political impact was also what we wanted to achieve. Remember the time; the campaign for ISL recognition was in full swing. We wanted to show that ISL is part of the Deaf World and is the centrality of Deaf Communication. We wanted to show the subtlety of it, to have that quiet impact on the audience. Not a wild show, but quietly directing the audience in and having them taken aback with that up-close and personal experience. The fact that they went in under the cover and had to poke their heads through holes to access the play—to look around over this fabric at the Mrs Marks characters towering above—and with the comrades greeting everyone from the get-go, the audience were immersed in a signing world. We directed the comrades not to attempt to speak or use their voice with the audience—only to use sign language. That silence had impact; we wanted ISL recognition—now![18]

Fig. 13.5 Michael O'Meara, front cover of programme for *Talk Real Fine, Just Like a Lady*, created by Dublin Theatre of the Deaf in collaboration with Amanda Coogan, produced by Live Collision, Peacock Theatre, Amharclann na Mainistreach, 2017. © Michael O'Meara. All rights reserved.

18　The Irish Sign Language Act was enacted on 24 December 2017 and recognises 'the right of Irish Sign Language users to use Irish Sign Language as their native language'. See Irish Statute Book, *Irish Sign Language Act 2017*.

AC: To explain: firstly, we had Mrs Marks as the authority figure we looked up at. She represented 'the oppressor'. We were very much looking at oppression. Throughout the development of the piece, we talked about double oppression, even triple oppression. Lianne, you were involved in the campaign for the recognition of ISL. Could you explain how you were one of the leaders in the campaign and how our play was on in the theatre throughout National ISL Awareness Week of September 2017 while the [ISL] campaign was at its height?[19]

Fig. 13.6 Patrick Redmond, production image from *Talk Real Fine, Just Like a Lady* (2017), created by Dublin Theatre of the Deaf in collaboration with Amanda Coogan, produced by Live Collision, Peacock Theatre, Amharclann na Mainistreach. © Patrick Redmond. All rights reserved.

---

19   ISL Awareness Week (16–24 September 2017) ran in tandem with the third International Conference of the World Federation of the Deaf under the theme of 'Full Inclusion with Sign Language', making the case that full social inclusion of Deaf people was only possible when Irish Sign Language was recognised and used widely used within society. The ISL campaign argued that the failure by the Irish State, at that time, to officially recognise ISL as a language and to fully implement the United Nations Convention on the Rights of Persons with Disabilities (UNCRPD) had a detrimental impact on Deaf people's lives and prevented them from achieving their goals. For an overview of the themes of the campaign, see Irish Deaf Society, *Irish Sign Language (ISL) Awareness Week, 16th–24th September 2017*. Heath Rose and John Bosco Conama's analysis of ISL as the subject of linguistic imperialism in Ireland usefully contextualises the 2017 ISL campaign. See Heath Rose and John Bosco Conama, 'Linguistic Imperialism: Still a Valid Construct in Relation to Language Policy for Irish Sign Language', *Language Policy*, 17 (2018), 385–404.

LQ: Yes, our production took place just shy of when—a few months before—ISL was legally recognised, about three months prior [to the legal recognition], in fact. The campaign was really a very important thing for me. It definitely influenced our take on the play and how we aimed to embed ISL within it. We wanted to show that ISL was a living, thriving language and what it [ISL] means to the Deaf community—to show what was hidden to everyone, to show how ISL is a national language. And to be on stage at the Peacock, the National Theatre, was very important. The Abbey has shown great leadership in recognising ISL and providing access to their work [i.e. Abbey productions] for so long—more than twenty years. It [the Abbey] has been very inclusive of the Deaf community. It [that inclusive relationship] started slowly and Deaf access built up—we were even invited to be involved in the #WakingTheFeminists movement as well.

AC: Also the Abbey's acceptance of ISL was really a cultural acceptance of ISL—the cultural and social aspects of ISL, not a medical or paternalism view of the language. It was quite a powerful acceptance that our beautiful language—ISL—is part of Irish culture. That's what it meant for our National Theatre to accept ISL.

LQ and AJ: Yes, Yes.

AC: It was very powerful to present our work in the Peacock. Alvean, could you explain about the double or triple oppression?

AJ: Well, we need to talk about different levels of oppression: [and how] people, not just d/Deaf people, not just women, not just LGBT, not just Travellers, everyone can experience it. Firstly, we can talk about Irish people being oppressed: women have experienced oppression—Irish women have that double oppression. So, Irish d/Deaf women have another layer of oppression added to that.

AC: This is the triple oppression you are talking about?

AJ: It's a triple oppression.

AC: We read in Deevy's script, instances of women's oppression of other women. The young Annie, for example, by Mrs Marks. She was authoritative and oppressive. We really looked at that symbolically and paralleled this [experience of oppression] with with our company members' own experience as young, d/Deaf children whose schooling focused on [vocalised] speech acquisition. Our production, *Talk Real Fine, Just Like a Lady*, is exactly about that damaging, or abusive experience, [that members of] the company had: of being taught how to speak, how to use their voices, [of teachers of oralism] dismissing sign language; [of] being told to 'talk fine', to 'speak up', to 'use their voice'.

Fig. 13.7 Patrick Redmond, 'Talk real fine', production image from *Talk Real Fine, Just Like a Lady* (2017), created by Dublin Theatre of the Deaf in collaboration with Amanda Coogan, produced by Live Collision, Peacock Theatre, Amharclann na Mainistreach, featuring Ann O'Neill as Mrs Marks. © Patrick Redmond. All rights reserved.

AJ: 'Use your voice'. That's why people look and talk about 'the deaf voice'. There is no getting away from that. d/Deaf people usually have a d/Deaf tone, a d/Deaf voice—that's there. So in classes where teaching speech happened, to make it work, one student was brought out of the class for one-to-one sessions, most of the time. This was at primary level where a lot of time was spent focusing on [vocalising] speech and how to pronounce words correctly. Lianne, do you agree?

LQ: Yes.

AJ: This didn't happen at second level; it was only primary. The teachers would say, 'use your voice, you have a lovely voice use it'. That gave people a false hope and the false idea that they could speak well, that they had a lovely voice and should use it to speak up—that repetitive [phrase]—'use your voice: use it' [—was common]. Then when you left school and met people and started speaking…of course, most [hearing] people are not used to the d/Deaf voice, that d/Deaf tone, and they were taken aback. They asked us to repeat ourselves, not understanding [our d/Deaf voices]. Very few people could understand what we were saying; that knocks the confidence of a d/Deaf speaker—that realisation, realising it's not such a beautiful voice.

LQ: Yeah, talking about this 'lovely speech' mantra in deaf education, it was like a competition amongst us—a student competition. To see who could really speak, judging our speech, judging whether it was 'okay', or 'rubbish'. It was like a show. The teacher would dismiss some students and applaud others. Those with 'lovely speech' were applauded and those without—their confidence was knocked. It was like, as we mentioned, [an] oppression. This time deaf [people] oppressing other deaf [people]. It was the system applauding lovely speech and dismissing those without it. This system produced double, or even triple, oppression.

AJ: Just to add to what Lianne said about the school system. Maybe people are not aware of this, but deaf children were separated in school into different groups. They [educators within deaf educational establishments] assessed the children on their ability to speak—if they could speak, or not. Depending on how they sounded [speaking orally], they were then separated into one of three groups. The first group for 'hard of hearing', or those that could speak well. Profoundly deaf children were in this group, so it was not about hearing ability—it was only based on speech articulation. The second group was for the 'profoundly deaf' students; these students were all taught through this oral method.[20] The third group were known as 'oral failures'—those

---

20 In primary school, these groups occupied completely separate spaces but post-primary they occupied the same space within the school building leading to the divisions as described above. The term 'hard of hearing' was the classification used by the school authorities for the first group—those who were assessed as having clearer speech, regardless of their actual hearing level. However, the pupils themselves did not use this term, as hard of hearing had a different meaning within the Deaf community. Instead, they referred to this group as partially deaf. The

who simply could not succeed through oral/spoken English, or had additional needs.[21] These three groups were kept completely separate at primary school level. Then, in my time at secondary school, two groups were at war! The labels and stigma of 'you're partially deaf', or 'you're profoundly deaf', were the taunts of our war. These labels were thrown about. But then, with the third group—the signers—we never saw them in school. They were completely separated from us. We had different social times [break times].[22] That is oppression, oppression, oppression!

Fig. 13.8 Patrick Redmond, production image from *Talk Real Fine, Just Like a Lady* (2017), created by Dublin Theatre of the Deaf in collaboration with Amanda Coogan, produced by Live Collision, Peacock Theatre, Amharclann na Mainistreach. © Patrick Redmond. All rights reserved.

---

wording reflects the terminology used by the pupils rather than the official school categorisation. The editors are grateful to Alvean Jones for her help in creating this footnote.

21 For a definition of 'oral failures' (created in 1908 and within an American context) reflecting the seemingly well-intentioned, but actually oppressive, discriminatory, and paternalistic thinking and language from which such terminology emanates, see Edward S. Tillinghurst, 'What is Failure in Oral Instruction?', *American Annals of the Deaf*, 53.4 (1908), 308-22 (p. 311).

22 Chapters two and three of Helena Saunders' M. Phil dissertation entitled 'Growing up deaf in Ireland' usefully contextualises the changing practices of deaf education in Ireland in the late nineteenth and early twentieth centuries. See Helena Saunders, 'Growing Up deaf in Ireland' (unpublished M. Phil thesis, Trinity College Dublin, 1997).

AC: It was a very, very poisonous system—shockingly damaging for the community. Can you remember in Deevy's script where Annie dreamed about the red dress and her fantasies—wanting to become the King of Spain's daughter? We, in parallel, had one of our Annies wanting to speak, to sing even, that great scene [in *Talk Real Fine, Just Like a Lady*] where she uses her deaf voice alongside some opera singing and, after the song is finished, she continues in an ecstatic, fantastical reverie. That was our moment. We had one of our Annies do the dreaming of having a beautiful voice—as she was being taught and schooled to believe was the best thing [for her] to have. We also gave a sexual frisson to her reverie: on the screen behind her, we had a naked swimmer floating through the screen—a symbol of freedom—sexual freedom—freedom to express herself. When we made this scene in the rehearsal room it was very strong, very potent, and very difficult for the company, extremely difficult. We had a lot of tears. It really touched the company emotionally. We hit on a heart-wrenching memory for many of the Dublin Theatre of the Deaf company [members] when we bashed our Annie and dragged her out of her reverie. We bashed her with a particularly female symbol—a hairbrush—waking her out of her dream. The oppression of student against student—that war between the two classes of deaf students in St Mary's School for Deaf Girls—they were very upsetting memories and very real, and affected us all deeply. It really touched the taboo or difficult emotions; it was pulling at heartstrings—especially when we were lifting her [Annie] up and then bashing her down with the hairbrushes.

AC: Showing that oppression and how it was—that sense of being at war for the children of St Mary's, for Deaf girls. I remember [that scene] well, it was a visceral feeling of emotions; upsetting emotions that were very real and affected us deeply.

LQ: Talking about that emotion: I remember the feelings around the brush scene and how at school we were made to feel that competitiveness against each other—to talk well and use our voices. Then to have those [hopes of success] dashed and taken away from us. When we were using the brushes in the play—smacking down with the hairbrush—it just brought me back to those difficult memories. That pushing down of us, of our Deafness, of our community members. Pulling them down. And yes, you are right, it was very emotional. We had to rehearse and repeat that scene quite a bit to help us get through it—to desensitise ourselves to the raw emotions of those difficult memories—all of us, actors and the comrades, as well. It was very powerful. At the same time, it is the truth that had to be shown. It is part of our hidden history.

AC: So, when as d/Deaf children you were attempting to speak, these authoritative figures were the oppressors and, within your school experience, you felt a negative competitiveness between classes. It was quite brave to allow our production to speak about that and show it. And I think hearing people were affected emotionally by it, too.

AJ: It was like our oppression was accepted and projected onto the audience—that was the thing.

AC: That is an experience [that] many oppressed minority communities have had. But then, we made a conscious decision to come together—that community togetherness—to make a positive impact. Hence the hairbrush, and the choice of white-coloured hairbrushes was carefully chosen because we could inflect it. We turned these weaponised hairbrushes around to show a blank rectangle. In that turning, they become something different—a blank protest placard, maybe. We can't speak to how this will be read in the future, but now, we are seeing the ISL campaign as a coming together of the community. Really it was showing how the recognition of ISL was, in that moment, a coming together of a community, in some way? Right? Am I wrong, or right?

AJ: You're right.

AC: Before there was the division: that was the oral system, a division between those that could talk, and those that could not; those who could belong in the hearing world, and those that couldn't. Sign language, you see, is for everyone and is accessible for everyone. Everyone is on the same side.

AJ: We see something similar in Deevy's work. Annie and Mrs Marks have that same antagonism. Mrs Marks always wanted that societal approval. Annie herself wasn't bothered—she wanted independence. That's where the antagonism was embedded. You can see it in all walks of life, these differences, these variations. So that brought us to the end of the production and the showing of the recognition of ISL. The [ISL] campaign was joyous, celebratory, a joy in the struggle, a joy in that collective voice, standing together, and being recognised.

LQ: The ISL celebrations brought together different people: it didn't matter if you read lips, or you used ISL, in all our diversity it still brought everyone together. We are all different, but united in one thing that we all wanted to achieve: one aim for every d/Deaf person. ISL is one thing, but the coming together of the Deaf community was our focus. When we stood in the Peacock and turned those hairbrushes around—from weapon of oppression to campaigning object—this represented the [Deaf] community coming together in the campaign of ISL recognition. We showed the joy and the emotions, the highs and lows of the campaign. We came together as one—it was very moving.

LQ: Our production began with the three of us here, researching and developing this piece. But, that final scene, of all of us just standing still, showing the back of our hairbrushes as campaigning placards, which we had just used to bash our friend—that was very powerful. Just standing, holding up our hairbrush/placards and standing there, in witness. It felt like we had come through a journey. Through oppression and continuous struggle, we stood still and held that symbol of resistance high. For me, I felt like a statue that had a dream [of equality] and that dream was moving closer. Remember, this production was a few months before the legal recognition of ISL—the realisation of that dream. I remember the video behind us in the Peacock, of us all frolicking around joyously making our ISL recognition march, and seeing the audience stunned and with tears in their eyes watching that final scene. We stood there for—I don't know—ten minutes, holding up our symbols of resistance and smiling. It was a very emotional end. We stood there with pride.

AC: I remember we decided in rehearsals how we would stop the aggression with the brushes—that Alvean would stand out from the crowd, hold up her hand and say, 'STOP—NO MORE'. She stopped us and then we turned around and turned this weapon into something positive. Then we just stood still, as Lianne mentioned, full of pride and full of passion. Letting all the fun and joy happen in the projection behind us. We just stood there like witnesses. It was emotional.

AJ: It was like this was a perfect example of that idea of pleasing society and accepting the social norms. But like Lianne described, society is just a construct. Who changes society? That is for the individuals within it. Remember our five Annies? One of our Annies was a singer. The others ganged up on her, attacking her, until another Annie stood up and said, 'STOP'. That's where change happens. When we all agree, mutual consensus. Together, we agree to change society, that's what it is, that's it.

AC: It's the power of standing together for what's right.

LQ: And when we produced this work, we were reading the oppression of women. Deevy wanted to shine a light on women, on their lives, and how they were being oppressed. And the fact that Deevy's works famously fell out of favour in the new, conservative Ireland post-Constitution. Her work was put aside, forgotten. I found out about her in 2014, and it has been amazing to watch the re-discovery of her work.

AJ: Definitely, Lianne. People are now recognising her work. Even ten years ago, I had no idea who she was and now, there is much more awareness. When you look back at the 30s, when there were few women writers, she was there telling the stories of women's oppression, religious oppression. She was against censorship. She was very outspoken. If you look at the 1916 Proclamation and the words it uses.[23] It says men and women are equal. Then in the 1937 Constitution: oh, my God! Each line had to be passed by the Pope in the Vatican!

AC: It [the 1937 Constitution] says: 'In particular, the State recognises that by her life within the home, woman gives to the State a support without which the common good cannot be achieved'.[24]

AJ: Now, talking about the 1937 Constitution, in my opinion, Teresa Deevy was both a woman of her time and a woman ahead of her time.[25]

LQ and AJ: Yes, yes, yes.

---

23 The full text of the '1916 Proclamation of Independence' can be accessed here: https://www.gov.ie/en/publication/bfa965-proclamation-of-independence/.
24 Government of Ireland, *Constitution of Ireland*, January 2020 (Article 41.2.1).
25 Bunreacht na hÉireann (Constitution of Ireland) was ratified on 29 December 1937. Ibid.

AJ: She had those two things in one person—that's my view of her.

LQ: To refer back to what Alvean mentioned about the 1916 Proclamation, I have a passion for Irish history. Post-1916, we had the War of Independence, which I read as a war for equality. Things changed. Then, with independence, there was more religious control in the country and those conservative changes were relatively rapid and widespread. That alone was difficult for those women who were active in the war; they had to obey the new structures and new governments. And then, the Constitution in 1937. I imagine those women involved in 1916 were not happy at all about that. And again, you have to remember the religious control here.

AC: And we must remember d/Deaf and any 'othered' people were thrown into institutions. We know about the institutions and the stories about the institutional lives now. It's important to keep remembering and telling those stories.[26]

AC: Lianne, would you tell us more about the importance of the lived experience?

LQ: Yes, for the last few years people have been researching Teresa Deevy's work, and I think it's very important to recognise her lived experience. She's a deaf or deafened person, so, for example, as she was losing her hearing, she was traveling around London, the UK, London in particular—she attended various theatres. She became fascinated with the theatre and writing plays. She used to try to access the theatre through lip-reading. Imagine the barriers that she faced? We have to imagine her lived experience as a deaf person. She missed out on so much because she couldn't hear. That was my first point. My second point is how did her life experience influence her writing? I passionately believe the barriers she faced on a daily basis must have influenced her work.

AJ: I would love to do more research. I'd like to add that there is another

---

26 *Ireland and the Magdalene Laundries: A Campaign for Justice*, ed. by Claire McGettrick, Katherine O'Donnell, Maeve O'Rourke, James M. Smith, and Mari Steed (London: I.B. Tauris, 2021); James M. Smith, *Ireland's Magdalen Laundries and the Nation's Architecture of Containment* (Notre Dame, IN: University of Notre Dame Press, 2007).

example of a deaf writer who had a similar experience: a deaf man, in this case; his deafness strongly influenced his writing. His name was Jonathan Swift and, whenever I tell people that he was deafened, there's always an element of shocked reaction. And he, like Deevy, was deafened, so maybe there are some parallels there between the two. I think, for him, he was deafened by Ménière's [disease], that is what caused his hearing loss.[27] His work is heavily influenced by his time spent people watching, which helped influence his satires. Similar to Deevy, I suppose—we can see some comparisons there. I know it would need a lot more research on the subject, but I think there may be some parallels between Swift's writing as a deafened author and Deevy as a deafened author. She wrote about society and the role of women in society. We don't exactly know what her interests were at the time. Maybe she observed what was happening in society from her perspective. Sometimes, being d/Deaf or deafened, the writer can bring a completely different perspective to a hearing writer's perspective on the world and, hence, that may influence their writings. I mean there are other famous d/Deaf people, but for the moment we're just focusing on these two.

LQ: I read something about Deevy and how she was very close with her sister. Apparently, she went everywhere with her—to meetings, the theatre, etc. Her sister was always there and maybe acted like an interpreter for her. Whether she was lipspeaking, or they had their own signing system, I'm not sure. But apparently, later on, people used to say she became very quiet after her sister had passed. They said she was lost without her sister.[28]

AJ: She began to isolate herself more from the world, that's exactly the kind of experience d/Deaf people have that others can't relate to. Yes, especially if you're d/Deaf or deafened, it isn't relevant in general society. People can look at a Deaf person and say that they are very quiet but then, when they see the same person in the company of Deaf people,

---

27   Jonathan Swift (1667–1745) contracted the disease in his early twenties and it seems he became deafened shortly, thereafter, in 1690. For more on Swift's contraction and experience of Ménière's disease, see H. Dominic W. Stiles, '"Brandy for giddiness, 2s"—Jonathan Swift's Meniere's Disease [sic]', UCL Ear Institute & Action on Hearing Loss Libraries, *University College London*, 13 April 2018. Deevy was also deafened as a result of Ménière's disease.

28   See footnote six of this chapter.

they're shocked to see a different personality. While speaking their first language, they are more outgoing because it is more inclusive for them, and they know what is being said. Maybe they seemed quiet from an outsider's perspective; maybe Deevy was lost and preferred to be by herself because she didn't know what people were saying around her. Maybe she just preferred to be alone on a bicycle—you know, she was a famous figure going around on her bicycle in the town.[29]

AJ: Lianne, do you want to talk more about the emotional aspect of the process of making *Talk Real Fine, Just Like a Lady*?

LQ: The emotional aspects of our play in the Abbey Theatre, do you mean? Yeah, it was interesting. Prior to our discussions and the brainstorming, we were really proud of this project. We were talking about how it was so emotional and powerful, the research process—the whole journey in fact. You have to remember at the time, back in 2017, we were tirelessly campaigning for ISL recognition. I think the emotion you see throughout the play, especially the triumph at the end, is both partly acting, but also an innate connection with Teresa Deevy and her life experience. There's such a strong connection that just couldn't be denied. Ten years prior to this, I had never even heard of Teresa Deevy, but there was just an innate kinship that gave me the hunger and the drive to continue the research and uncover as much as possible about her life experience as a deafened woman.

AC: Can we just put this in context? So, ISL has just been enacted, literally days prior to this recording here today.[30] So, at the moment, we are sitting in a completely different world to that of years gone by, before the legislation arrived. Everything now is in a different context. Now, I know it's not perfect and nothing is going to change overnight, but this was huge for us, especially for me. From my personal experience, it is my home language. I was always told by my mother, when I was younger, 'Don't use sign language on the street. It's our secret, it's not for on the street, we only use sign language at home'. The difference is that, now, ISL is recognised in the law of this country. I think by the end of our production of *Talk Real Fine*, when we stood up there, proud, even

---

29   Dunne, 'Rediscovering Teresa Deevy'.
30   The Irish Sign Language Bill commenced on 23 December 2020.

though the Act still had not been passed, we were still in the middle of the campaign, we knew in our hearts that there was a lot at stake.

LQ: Absolutely, you're right, and when you describe your experience growing up and being told not to use ISL in public, that's completely different from my experience. I grew up in a family as the only d/Deaf person. My family were all hearing, my family never signed, they never signed with me because they took their advice from the so-called 'experts' who told them that sign language was bad. I think, when we stood there proud, we were thinking of the younger generation: campaigning for their future, so they will have it better than we had, and the girls of my time. I was lucky, in a sense: my parents accepted and encouraged my language choice. While my father never really learned full sign language, some of the family members would use a mixture of a few signs they learned and gesture. I learned to sign very early, but the difference between then and now is, if a child is born deaf into a hearing family, or the parents are Deaf, the opportunities they have now are amazing! The recognition of ISL as a language will make a huge difference in comparison to my time; back then, it was taboo. So, I suppose, I never really comprehended the enormity of it, through the years of the campaign, until it became a reality. This was no mean feat! Like you said, it won't be perfect, and will evolve over time, but you can feel the change in the air. I don't know if you saw, just there on the 23rd of December—the day the law was enacted—on that morning, the Minister for Children, Equality, Disability, and Integration and Youth stood up and addressed the public using ISL, along with Senator Mark Daly.[31] That was quite something to see. I know it took effort and, five years ago, I probably would have criticised their efforts, but they have to be commended. No one asked, or forced them, to learn sign language. They did it out of their own interest. This really gives me hope for a better, more inclusive future. I know there is a lot of interest in sign language, at the moment, and I do hope more and more people will learn sign language and people will see the bigger picture that there is a future with less blurred lines.

---

31 In 2020, Mr Roderic O'Gorman, TD, was elected to this ministerial position and Senator Mark Daly was appointed as the Cathaoirleach of Seanad Éireann (Chairperson of the Irish Senate).

Bibliography

Bank, Jonathan, John P. Harrington, and Christopher Morash (eds), *Teresa Deevy Reclaimed*, 2 vols (New York: Mint Theater, 2011 and 2017)

Centre for Integration and Improvement of Journalism, *The Diversity Style Guide* (2024), https://www.diversityguide.com/glossary/deaf-deaf/

Colum, Padraic, *Wild Earth and Other* Poems (New York: Henry Holt, 1916), https://archive.org/details/wildearthotherpo00colu/page/n3/mode/2up

Commission to Inquire into Child Abuse, *Commission to Inquire into Child Abuse Report*, 6 vols (Dublin: Stationery Office, 2009), https://childabusecommission.ie/?page_id=241

Cheasty, James, 'The Curtain Rises', *Irish Farmers' Journal*, 6 June 1964, p. 28

Deevy, Teresa, 'The King of Spain's Daughter', in *Irish Women Dramatists 1908–2021*, ed. by Eileen Kearney and Charlotte Headrick (New York: Syracuse University, 2014), pp. 44–58

Donohue, Brenda, Ciara O'Dowd, Tanya Dean, Ciara Murphy, Kathleen Cawley, and Kate Harris (eds), *Gender Counts: An Analysis of Gender in Irish Theatre 2006–2015* (Belfast: Ulster University, 2017), https://pure.ulster.ac.uk/ws/portalfiles/portal/11631340/Gender_Counts_WakingTheFeminists_2017.pdf

Dunne, Seán, 'Rediscovering Teresa Deevy', *Cork Examiner*, 20 March 1984, p. 10

Heffernan, Georgina, and Elizabeth Nixon, 'Experiences of Hearing Children of Deaf Parents in Ireland', *The Journal of Deaf Studies and Deaf Education*, 28.4 (2023), 399–407, https://doi.org/10.1093/deafed/enad018

Irish Deaf Society, *Irish Sign Language (ISL) Awareness Week, 16th–24th September 2017*, http://dublindiocese.ie/wp-content/uploads/2017/09/ISL-Awareness-Week-2017-Campaign-Messages.pdf

Irish Statute Book, *Irish Sign Language Act 2017*, https://www.irishstatutebook.ie/eli/2017/act/40/enacted/en/print#sec3

Kealy, Úna, and Kate McCarthy, 'Shape Shifting the Silence: An Analysis of *Talk Real Fine, Just Like a Lady* (2017) by Amanda Coogan in Collaboration with Dublin Theatre of the Deaf, an Appropriation of Teresa Deevy's *The King of Spain's Daughter* (1935)', in *The Golden Thread: Irish Women Playwrights, 1716–2016*, 2 vols, ed. by David Clare, Fiona McDonagh, and Justine Nakase (Liverpool: Liverpool University Press, 2021), I, 197–210, https://doi.org/10.3828/liverpool/9781800859463.003.0015, https://www.liverpooluniversitypress.co.uk/pb-assets/OA%20chapters/Una%20Kealy%20and%20Kate%20McCarthy%20chapter-1710157142.pdf

Keogh, Claire, *#WakingTheFeminists and the Data-Driven Revolution in Irish Theatre* (Cambridge: Cambridge University Press, 2025), https://doi.org/10.1017/9781009523066

LeMaster, Barbara, 'Language Contraction, Revitalization, and Irish Women', *Journal of Linguistic Anthropology*, 16.2 (2006), 211–228, https://doi.org/10.1525/jlin.2006.16.2.211

LeMaster, Barbara, 'School Language and Shifts in Irish Identity', in *Many Ways to Be Deaf: International Variation in Deaf Communities*, ed. by Leila Monaghan, Constanze Schmaling, Karen Nakamura, and Graham H. Turner (Washington, DC: Gallaudet University Press, 2003), pp. 153–172

McGettrick, Claire, Katherine O'Donnell, Maeve O'Rourke, James M. Smith, and Mari Steed (eds), *Ireland and the Magdalene Laundries: A Campaign for Justice* (London: I.B. Tauris/Bloomsbury, 2021), https://doi.org/10.5040/9780755617524

Murphy, Fiona, *The Shape of Sound* (Melbourne: Text Publishing Company, 2021)

National Centre for Disability and Journalism, Arizona State University, Disability Language Guide (2021), https://ncdj.org/wp-content/uploads/2021/08/NCDJ-STYLE-GUIDE-EDIT-2021-SILVERMAN.pdf

O'Brien, Susan, 'The Blessed Virgin Mary', in *The Oxford History of British and Irish Catholicism, vol. IV: Building Identity, 1830–1913*, ed. by Carmen M. Mangion and Susan O'Brien (Oxford: Oxford University Press, 2023), pp. 154–172, https://doi.org/10.1093/oso/9780198848196.003.0009

Rose, Heath, and John Bosco Conama, 'Linguistic Imperialism: Still a Valid Construct in Relation to Language Policy for Irish Sign Language', *Language Policy*, 17 (2018), 385–404, https://doi.org/10.1007/s10993-017-9446-2

Saunders, Helen, 'Growing Up Deaf in Ireland' (unpublished M. Phil thesis, Trinity College Dublin, 1997)

Smith, James M., *Ireland's Magdalen Laundries and the Nation's Architecture of Containment* (Notre Dame, IN: University of Notre Dame Press, 2007)

Stiles, H. Dominic W., '"Brandy for giddiness, 2s"—Jonathan Swift's Meniere's Disease [sic]', UCL Ear Institute & Action on Hearing Loss Libraries, *University College London*, 13 April 2018, https://blogs.ucl.ac.uk/library-rnid/2018/04/13/brandy-for-giddiness-2s-jonathan-swifts-menieres-disease/

Tillingshurst, Edward S., 'What is Failure in Oral Instruction?', *American Annals of the Deaf*, 53.4 (1908), 308–322

Index

'37' Theatre Club 144, 146–147
#MeToo 245
#WakingTheFeminists 267, 273, 275, 280, 293, 304

Abbey Experimental Theatre 136–137, 144
Abbey School of Acting 146
Abbey Theatre 5–6, 12, 15, 20, 24, 26, 29–30, 42–51, 65–66, 77–79, 81, 83, 85–86, 94, 99, 106, 112, 124, 131, 133–135, 137–139, 141–147, 149–150, 176, 178, 181, 195, 197, 222, 227, 243–247, 250–255, 257, 264, 266, 268, 270, 274, 304, 314
Albericci, Josephine 6, 146
All on a Sunny Day 145
amateur drama 22, 135, 149
angel in the house 203, 208
Anglo-Irish Treaty 81
Anomalies 135
archives 23–25, 58–60, 62–64, 67–69, 71–73, 77, 92–93, 96, 108–109, 111, 113, 275
Aronson, Jack 146
Arts Theatre, Cambridge 246
Arts Theatre, Dublin 144
atmosphere 25, 70, 105, 118, 123, 139, 141, 228, 255
Austen, Jane 82–83

BBC 7, 49, 98, 106, 141, 145
Beckett, Samuel 278
Behan, Brendan 147
Bernadette Players 145
big house 80, 82–83, 103

Blackheath 96–98, 105, 110
Blessed Virgin Mary 205, 209
Blythe, Ernest 51, 66, 79, 136, 143, 227
bodies 19, 27–28, 129, 139, 177, 179, 181–182, 185–187, 189, 191, 193–196, 198, 202, 208, 221, 247, 256, 299
Brady, Erina 144
Brecht, Bertolt 180, 197
Brennan, Denis 146
Broadway 42
Bunreacht na hÉireann 206–208, 249, 268, 294, 298, 311–312
  Article 41 65, 206, 208, 234, 311
Butler, Judith 28, 202, 214

canon 20–23, 25, 29, 92, 183, 244–245, 258, 266, 276
Carroll, Paul Vincent 99
Cassin, Barry 146–148
Cathleen Ni Houlihan. See Kathleen Ni Houlihan
Catholic x, 26, 42, 45, 48, 51, 53, 57, 65, 81, 83, 99, 101, 123, 125–129, 205–206, 208, 216, 238, 295–296
censorship 25, 61, 79, 311
Cheasty, James 9, 11, 16, 19, 26, 45, 71, 133, 147–148
Chekhov, Anton 4, 50, 52, 83–84, 129, 178, 219, 250
children 5, 30, 45, 48–49, 101, 158, 163, 177, 182–183, 197, 209, 232, 235, 237, 249, 280, 295, 297, 305–306, 308–309, 315
Christ 123, 125–126, 195
Churchill, Caryl 197
Clarke, Austin 144

class xi, 1, 30, 80, 82, 88, 100, 158–159, 211, 257, 305, 308
Clyde Road 10–11, 147
Cogley, Désirée Bannard 50, 135–136, 144, 148
collections management 24, 59–60, 63, 72
Colum, Padraic 164, 298
comedy 84, 127, 130, 245, 250, 253, 256
Connolly, James xxi
control 85, 93, 208, 215, 219, 229–230, 236, 247, 254, 312
Cork Deaf Community Choir 18
Cork Examiner ix, xi, 44, 91
costume 2, 82, 94, 163, 179, 244, 254–256, 268
Crotty, Derbhle 249, 252, 256
Cumman na mBan x, 4
Cumman na nGaedheal 207
Cusack, Cyril 144

D'Alton, Louis 146
dance/dancing 185, 194–195, 197, 209, 217, 283
d/Deaf 23, 30, 270, 276, 279–280, 285, 291–294, 297, 301, 304, 306, 308–310, 312–313, 315
deaf 168, 276, 281, 285, 291, 293–298, 306–307, 312. *See also* d/Deaf
Deaf 16, 30, 168, 267–268, 270, 280, 285, 289–290, 293–294, 298, 301, 304. *See also* d/Deaf
deafened x, xii, 6, 23, 26, 30, 48, 65, 128, 168, 177, 197, 291–292, 312–314
de Beauvoir, Simone 28, 158, 202, 205, 210
de Valera, Eamon 244, 249
de Valois, Ninette 137
Deevy Clarke, Miriam 45, 47–48
Deevy, Edward 1, 94, 106, 110, 112
Deevy, Jack 44, 47, 53, 91, 96, 124
Deevy, Jacqui 96, 98, 106
Deevy, Josie 8, 48, 97–98, 109
Deevy, Mary Bridget 1, 3, 5
Deevy, Nell x, 6–9, 47–48, 94, 97, 106, 108–109, 124, 140, 142, 147, 285, 291

Deevy, Noleen 96
Devoy, Chris. 108
dialogue 8, 22, 28, 31–32, 50–51, 71, 83, 103, 106, 126–127, 176, 202, 213, 217, 247, 251, 257
Dignity 18, 184, 188
disability 22, 94, 128, 267, 270, 315
Disability Awareness Week 290
Disciple, A 5–6, 15, 146, 238, 249
diversity 22–23, 58, 63, 72, 166, 310
divorce 50, 102
domestic service 27, 158–159, 208, 214
domestic space 28, 65, 182–183, 185, 201, 206–207, 214, 247
domesticated Irish woman 27, 201–202, 208, 211, 213–214, 217–218, 220–221
Donaghy, Lyle 135
dramaturgy 23, 26–27, 29, 31–32, 71, 84, 133, 176–177, 179, 183, 187–190, 195–197, 202, 213, 233, 251–252
Dublin Dance Theatre Club 144
Dublin Drama League 135, 137
Dublin Globe Theatre 144, 146
Dublin Jewish Dramatic Society 135
Dublin Little Theatre Guild 136
Dublin Magazine 79, 84, 139, 144
Dublin Marionette Group 144
Dublin Opinion 82
Dublin School of Acting 6, 146
Dublin Theatre of the Deaf xii, 15, 17–19, 30, 69, 276, 284, 290, 308
Dublin University Modern Language Society 144
Dublin University Players 144
Dublin Verse Speaking Society 145
Dunne, Caoilfhionn 256
Dunne, Seán 12, 24, 44, 46–47, 51–52, 91, 96

Earlsfort Players 144
Edwards, Hilton 94, 136
ellipsis/ellipses 103, 106, 119–120, 124
emigration 27, 157, 160, 165
empathy 63, 67, 69

epiphany 27, 120, 127, 214, 219
equality 58, 72, 179, 204, 215, 249, 270, 310, 312, 315
Ervine, St John 7, 31
Evening Herald 81, 246
exclusion 20, 53, 62, 79, 93, 232
expressionism/expressionist 27, 30, 103, 147, 178, 197, 245, 250–251, 253, 255–256, 274, 281
exultant 120–121, 124, 221

Faul, Denis 60
feminist 18, 176–177, 180, 182, 187, 197, 204, 258, 280
Finding of the Ball, The 103
Firstborn, The 25, 92, 97–98, 100, 103, 105, 107, 110
Fitzsimons, Patrick 136
Fornés, Maria Irene 197
Forristal, Desmond 60
Fortune Society 144
Foucault, Michel 28, 202, 213, 216
Fox, R.M. 80, 82, 84
French Sign Language 295
Friel, Brian 218
Friel, Judy 12, 29, 176, 178, 181, 249, 251–252
Funge, Josephine 147
Funge, Patrick 147

Gaiety School of Acting xx
Gaiety Theatre 146
Garter Lane Arts Centre 12, 14
Gate Theatre 136, 140
gender 158–159, 182, 202, 204, 211, 213–214, 218, 221, 249, 257
gesture 31–32, 138, 167, 213, 253, 272, 285–286, 292, 315
Gifford, Sidney 203
Going Beyond Alma's Glory 18, 105, 188
Goode, D.V. 91, 96, 98, 100, 103–105, 107–113
Granta, The 246
Gregory, Augusta x, 20, 43, 52, 81, 247, 263

Hackett, Florence 6–8, 26, 50, 94–95, 97, 106, 118, 121, 133, 135, 137–142, 145
Hail Mary 271, 285, 297, 299
hard-of-hearing 23, 30
Higgins, Fredrick R. 143
Hogan, Robert 44
Holiday House 5, 14, 142
Holloway, Joseph 246
hooks, bell 156, 168, 180
Horniman, Annie 134
Hull, Eleanor 203–204
Hunt, Hugh 8, 140, 149
Hutchinson, Pearse 24, 63

Ibsen, Henrik 178, 180, 182–183, 250
  A Doll's House 274
  Hedda Gabler 180, 183, 274
identity 26, 28, 94, 111–112, 128, 203, 214, 228–232, 234, 249, 253–255, 265
Ilsley-McCabe Productions 146
Imagine Arts Festival 16
immersive performance 17, 30
In Search of Valour 6, 146, 245, 249–250
In the Cellar of My Friend 11, 15, 25–26, 117–120, 122–123, 125, 127, 129, 148, 184, 186
Inghinidhe na hÉireann 134, 203
Irish Academy of Letters 9, 49
Irish Civil War 65, 81, 87, 179
Irish Constitution. *See Bunreacht na hÉireann*
Irish Independent 82, 88
Irish Language Theatre of Ireland 134
Irish Monthly 58
Irish National Magazine 230, 236
Irish National Theatre Society 134
Irish PEN 7
Irish Players 138
Irish Press 145
Irish Republican Army 81, 87
Irish Sign Language 16, 18, 29–30, 72, 269, 276, 280, 284, 289, 291
  women's sign 30, 269, 285, 296, 298

Irish Times xv, 65, 82–83, 229
Irish Women's Writing Network 19
Irish Writing 49

Jacob, Rosamond 94, 107
Ja-rim, Kim 18
Johnston, Denis 8, 137, 149
Jordan, John 10, 43–45, 49, 78, 80, 82, 186, 188
Journal of Irish Literature 12, 91
Joyce, James 26, 133
   Dubliners 157
   'Eveline' 27, 159–160, 163–164
   Ulysses 157

Kathleen Ni Houlihan 81, 86, 135
Katie Roche 5, 12, 14, 16, 25, 82, 122, 128, 158, 176, 181, 183–187, 201, 206–209, 211, 218, 221, 229, 236, 243–245, 247–251, 254–258, 265–266, 273–274, 281, 283
Kavanagh, Patrick 49
King of Spain's Daughter, The 5, 12, 14–16, 26–27, 30, 43, 82, 94, 101, 117–118, 120, 122, 127, 137–139, 160, 163, 165–166, 179, 183–185, 187, 219, 221, 238, 245, 267–268, 270, 276, 283, 293, 298
Kirkwood Hackett, Eveline 135

La Hija del Rey de España 15
Landscape (house) 1, 6–7, 11, 44, 46–48, 71, 96, 106, 117
language 7, 28, 30–32, 46, 51, 68–69, 104–105, 111, 119, 124, 127–129, 167, 184, 202, 206, 208, 210–211, 213, 221, 234, 255, 268–270, 281–282, 284
Lantern Theatre 147
Laverty, Maura 18
Le Fanu, Sheridan 2
Let Us Live 25, 92, 97, 99–101, 104, 107
Leventhal, A. J. 83, 144
Lever, Nora 146, 148
Light Falling xxii, 5–6, 16, 26, 50, 118, 123, 128, 137, 145, 177, 183–184, 186, 188, 192

liminality 24, 179, 184, 230–231, 233, 236–237
lip-reading x, 4, 9, 48, 84, 124, 250, 282, 312
Lodwick, John 135
Longford, Christine 6
Longford, Edward 146
Longford Productions 140, 144–146
Lorde, Audre 197
Lynch, Patricia 49, 124
Lyric Theatre Company 144

Mac Anna, Tomás 45, 148
MacCarthy, B.G. 145
mac Liammóir, Micheál 94, 136
Maeterlinck, Maurice
   The Blue Bird 3, 250
Magdalen Commission Scheme 254
Manning, Mary 135
Marcus, David 48, 107
marginalisation xii, 16, 60–61, 93, 238
marriage 99, 101–102, 120, 161–162, 165–166, 169, 178, 184, 192, 195, 208–209, 211–215, 219, 227, 232, 234, 247, 256
material 19, 21, 25–28, 44, 46, 59–60, 64, 66, 69–70, 72–73, 77–78, 82, 85, 92, 109, 111, 118, 133, 135, 142, 168, 176–178, 181, 185–198, 205, 232–233, 281–282
Maynooth University 96, 109, 112, 133, 291
Maynooth University Library 24, 57, 92
McEvoy, Frank xi, 45, 95–96
McLaren, Graham 273
Meldon, Maurice 147
Mellone, Dora 203
Ménière's disease 4, 11, 46, 48, 68, 168, 313
meta-audience 27, 177, 194–196
meta-theatre 194
Miller, Liam 147
Milligan, Alice 135
Mint Theater 13–14, 19, 30, 96, 117, 188

modernisation 100, 103
Moiseiwitsch, Tanya 140
Molière 145
Molloy, M.J. 45, 48
Mooney, Ria 6, 48, 136, 145
Moylan, Jo 148
Murray, Neil 273
Murray, T.C. 246–247, 250
museum theatre 244
mysticism 26, 123–125, 128–129

na gCopaleen, Myles 49
National Library of Ireland 45, 92, 117
National Theatre Society 134
naturalism 18, 27
New York Theatre Guild 138
Nic Shiubhlaigh, Máire 134

O'Casey, Seán x, xx, 51, 137, 155, 178, 181
O'Connor, Frank 43, 49–50, 94, 141, 149
O'Connor, P.J. 6
Ó'Faoláin, Seán 49
O'Flaherty, Liam 49
O'Gorman, W. 6
Ó hAodha, Micheál 42, 44, 46
O'Herlihy, Michael 146
Ok-joo, Jean 18
O'Leary, Liam 136
Ó Lochlainn, Gearóid 136
O'Meadhra, Seán 136
One Look and What It Led To 18, 26, 125–128, 184, 195
open access xiv, 23–24, 58, 60
oppression 28, 30, 63, 183, 268–270, 278, 298, 300, 303–304, 306–311
oralism 280, 305
Orion Productions 146
Ormond Dramatic Society 134
O'Sullivan, Seamus 94
O'Toole, T.D. 109
Outsider, The 62, 69, 73

Padre Pio 51, 124
paratextual elements 100, 102, 109
Parks, Suzan-Lori 197
Patmore, Coventry 203
patriarchal 16, 18, 26, 28, 141, 164, 208, 210, 219, 229, 235–236, 239, 249, 252, 269
Peacock Theatre 15, 50, 294, 300
physicality 28, 181, 193–194, 202, 211–213, 221
Pike Theatre Club 144, 146–147
Pilgrim Productions 144, 146
Port of Refuge 25, 121
Possession xii, 5, 17, 20, 86
power 21, 24, 31, 60–61, 68–69, 85, 93, 99, 104, 155, 167–168, 177, 182, 187, 197, 209, 211, 215, 219, 229–230, 233, 235–237, 247–248, 250, 254–255, 257–258, 311
Practice and Precept 25, 92, 97, 100, 102, 104
Project Arts Centre 268

Quigley, Godfrey 146, 148

radio x, 6–7, 21–22, 26, 49–50, 64, 66, 92, 98–100, 103, 105–106, 108, 110, 113, 124, 131–133, 140–142, 145–146, 149, 177, 188, 191–192, 194–198, 281
radio drama 132, 140–141
Radio Éireann 145
Raidió Teilifís Éireann 86
realism 18, 27, 104, 106, 122, 178–180, 183, 197, 245, 255
Reapers 5, 24, 77–88, 95, 101, 105, 112, 137, 178
Red Kettle Theatre Company xviii
Regan, Morna 255, 275
Report of the Commission to Inquire into Child Abuse 254
representation 24, 27–28, 64, 68, 73, 81, 167, 201–204, 207–211, 213, 221, 253
revelation 25, 126–127
Richards, Shelah 8, 144, 148

Richards-Walsh Productions 144
Robinson, Dolly 142
Robinson, Lennox 8, 20, 43, 45, 48, 50, 78, 85, 88, 94, 103, 135, 178, 264
Ryan, Mary 47
Ryan, Phyllis 9, 146–147
Ryan Report. *See* Report of the Commission to Inquire into Child Abuse

Saorstát Éireann 81–82, 88
Saro-Wiwa, Ken 24, 63, 72
scenography 32, 179, 251, 255, 257–258
Scotcher, Joanna 255, 282
Shakespeare, William
  As You Like It 2
  The Taming of the Shrew 273
Shange, Ntozake 197
Shaw, G. B. 4, 84, 87, 178
  Heartbreak House 176, 250
  In Good King Charles' Golden Days 145
  Saint Joan 147
Sheehy-Skeffington, Hanna 203
Shields, Arthur 85
sign language 285–286, 291–292, 294, 296–297, 302, 305, 309, 314–315
silence 25, 51, 53, 103, 119–120, 128, 156, 162, 167, 169, 217, 219, 221, 232, 247, 250–251, 283, 302
Simone, Nina 270
Simpson, Alan 146
Sinn Féin 5
Smith School of Acting 148
Smith, Terence 48
social justice 24, 58, 60, 63
Solomons, Estella 94
space 134–135, 164, 175, 177, 180, 182–185, 187, 189, 197, 202, 207, 213–216, 219, 221, 228–232, 237, 247–248, 250, 252, 254–257, 281
spectators 129, 248–249, 258
St John of the Cross 126–127, 129
St Mary's School for Deaf Girls 295, 297, 308

St Teresa of Ávila 126
St Thérèse of Lisieux 126
stage directions 28, 120–121, 138–139, 176, 178–179, 189, 191, 202, 212, 215–217, 219, 234, 247, 251, 282–285
stage properties 27, 92, 179, 191
Staunton, Helen 49
Stephens, James 49
Strange Birth 14, 117, 177, 182, 186, 188, 191–193
'Strange People' 49
Studio Theatre Club 10, 50, 135, 144, 147–148
studio theatre practice 26, 132, 134, 136, 144, 149
subtext 32, 52, 138, 213, 232, 257
Suitcase under the Bed, The 14, 117
Supreme Dominion 11, 26, 46, 124–125, 128, 148
Swift, Carolyn 146
Swift, Jonathan 313
Synge, J. M. 166, 250
  The Playboy of the Western World 164
  The Shadow of the Glen 247
syntax 25, 119, 127–128, 185, 274, 276

Talk Real Fine, Just Like a Lady 15–16, 30, 270, 290, 294, 308
Temporal Powers xi, 5, 13, 15, 91, 99, 104, 137, 178–179, 181, 183–187, 192, 195, 197, 265
Teresa Deevy Archive 24–25, 52, 64, 66, 69, 72–73, 77, 91, 108, 112, 291
Toksvig, Signe 94, 159, 162
Travellers 304
Tribute: The Teresa Deevy Story 17, 86
Troy, Una 107

University College Dublin Dramatic Society 144
Unseen Plays 16

violence 18, 26, 166, 182, 211

Wadding, Luke 11, 124, 148

Walsh, Michael 144
War of Independence 65, 81, 87, 312
Waterford Drama Circle 148
Waterford Dramatic Society 140
Waterloo Road 10, 48, 71, 108, 142, 147
Watermans Arts Centre 12
Weekly Examiner 109
Wertenbaker, Timberlake 197
Westby, Gerard 107
widowhood 28, 227–228, 230–232, 234, 236–239
Wife to James Whelan ix, 6, 10, 12, 25–26, 28, 49, 104, 118, 121–122, 131, 143, 145–147, 227–229, 231–232, 234–238, 245, 266
Wild Goose, The 5, 16, 137, 141
Wilton, Ernest 138
Within a Marble City 16, 18, 188
women playwrights 22, 42, 52, 169, 201, 263
Women Writers' Club 8
Women's Personality Parade 80
working women 100–101
World War I 48, 65, 87, 97
World War II 98

Yeats, Jack B. 8, 48
Yeats, William B. x, xx, 24, 43, 50–51, 77–79, 81, 85, 135, 141

About the Team

Alessandra Tosi was the managing editor for this book.

Adèle Kreager proof-read the final version; Úna Kealy compiled the index; Laura Rodriguez created the Alt-text.

Jeevanjot Kaur Nagpal designed the cover. The cover was produced in InDesign using the Fontin font.

Jeremy Bowman typeset the book in InDesign and produced the paperback, hardback and EPUB editions. The main text font is Tex Gyre Pagella and the heading font is Californian FB.

Cameron Craig produced the PDF and HTML editions. The conversion was performed with open-source software and other tools freely available on our GitHub page at https://github.com/OpenBookPublishers.

Raegan Allen was in charge of marketing.

This book was peer-reviewed by Prof. Elizabeth Redwine and an anonymous referee. Experts in their field, our readers give their time freely to help ensure the academic rigour of our books. We are grateful for their generous and invaluable contributions.

This book need not end here...

Share

All our books — including the one you have just read — are free to access online so that students, researchers and members of the public who can't afford a printed edition will have access to the same ideas. This title will be accessed online by hundreds of readers each month across the globe: why not share the link so that someone you know is one of them?

This book and additional content is available at
https://doi.org/10.11647/OBP.0432

Donate

Open Book Publishers is an award-winning, scholar-led, not-for-profit press making knowledge freely available one book at a time. We don't charge authors to publish with us: instead, our work is supported by our library members and by donations from people who believe that research shouldn't be locked behind paywalls.

Join the effort to free knowledge by supporting us at
https://www.openbookpublishers.com/support-us

We invite you to connect with us on our socials!

BLUESKY
@openbookpublish
.bsky.social

MASTODON
@OpenBookPublish
@hcommons.social

LINKEDIN
open-book-publishers

Read more at the Open Book Publishers Blog
https://blogs.openbookpublishers.com

You may also be interested in:

Trix
The Other Kipling
Barbara Fisher

https://doi.org/10.11647/OBP.0377

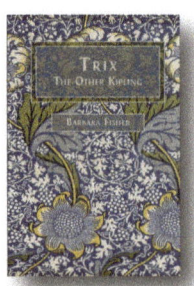

Breaking Conventions
Five Couples in Search of Marriage-Career Balance at the Turn of the Nineteenth Century
Patricia Auspos

https://doi.org/10.11647/OBP.0318

Yeats's Legacies
Yeats Annual No. 21
Warwick Gould (editor)

https://doi.org/10.11647/OBP.0135

Making the Void Fruitful
Yeats as Spiritual Seeker and Petrarchan Lover
Patrick J. Keane

https://doi.org/10.11647/OBP.0275

www.ingramcontent.com/pod-product-compliance
Lightning Source LLC
Chambersburg PA
CBHW040319300426
44111CB00023B/2955